Complete Catering Science

Complete Hairdressing Science
                    (with Marguerite McGarry)
An Introduction to the Physical Aspects of Nursing Science
An Introduction to the Chemical Aspects of Nursing Science
An Introduction to the Biological Aspects of Nursing Science
Shopping Science
Multiple-choice Questions in Biology and Human Biology
Multiple-choice Questions in Food and Nutrition
*Multiple-choice Questions in Hairdressing and Beauty Therapy
    Science*
Multiple-choice Questions in the House and its Services
At Home with Science
Experimental Science for Catering and Homecraft Students
                    (with Aileen L'Amie)
Mastering Biology (The Macmillan Press Ltd)
Mastering Nutrition (The Macmillan Press Ltd)
Work Out Biology GCSE (Macmillan Education Ltd)

Complete Catering Science

O. F. G. KILGOUR

BSc, CBiol, Chartered Biologist, MIBiol, MSCS

HEINEMANN : LONDON

Heinemann Professional Publishing Ltd
22 Bedford Square, London WC1 3HH

LONDON MELBOURNE
AUCKLAND JOHANNESBURG

First published 1968
Second edition 1970
Revised edition 1972
Third edition 1976
Revised edition 1980
Fourth edition 1986
Reprinted 1987

British Library Cataloguing in Publication Data
Kilgour, O.F.G.
  Complete catering science—4th ed.
  I. Science 2. Home economics
  I. Title II. Kilgour, O.F.G. Introduction to
  science for catering and homecraft students
  502′.464 TX149

ISBN 0 434 91051 1

Typeset by Wilmaset, Birkenhead, Wirral
Printed in Great Britain by Redwood Burn Ltd,
Trowbridge, Wiltshire

To
David and Richard

Contents

Preface to the fourth edition

This book was designed for catering, institutional management and domestic science students in schools and colleges. As a former lecturer in daily touch with students in the applied science laboratories and researching with them in the catering kitchens, home economics flat and laundry, I became aware of the difficulties involved in teaching science in these situations. The result was a book embodying a direct and simple approach aimed at the non-academic student with no previous knowledge of science.

This fourth edition, with its new section on human nutrition in addition to the existing and updated introductory treatment of science applied to food, textiles, materials, hygiene, cleaning, services and accommodation studies, now provides *a complete* introduction from first principles to the scientific aspects of catering, cookery and home economics for all newcomers working in catering, the home, and residential institutions.

The revised edition includes many minor additions and new material concerning modified starches and gel formation. In its new form the book should prove eminently suitable for students taking such courses as:

Business and Technician Education Council
City and Guilds catering, domestic science and cookery
GCE 'O' and 'A' level Home Economics and domestic subjects
National Council for Home Economics science supplementary to homecraft

ONC and OND in Catering and Institutional Management
HCIMA Membership (Intermediate)
College of Education courses in Home Economics and Institutional Housekeeping
Certificates in Food Hygiene, Royal Institute of Public Health and Hygiene

The examination student will find the following companion title helpful: *Experimental Science for Catering and Homecraft Students*, O. F. G. Kilgour and Aileen L'Amie (Heinemann). References to relevant sections of the title is given at the end of each chapter.

I wish to thank Mrs V. C. Stirling for her efficient preparation of the typescript. I also acknowledge the permission granted by the Food and Agriculture Organization of the United Nations, and the Ciba-Geigy organization, to use reference material and to quote from the *Geigy Scientific Tables*, the latter a generous example of an industrial organization contributing to education.

I thank most sincerely the staff of William Heinemann, for all their help during the last seventeen years of publication, and Barbara my wife for her continuous forbearance. I wish to record my sincere gratitude to Meinwen Parry for reading the work and suggesting improvements; and the Purdie family for the use of their home.

O.F.G.K.
Waikanae, New Zealand and
Hen Golwyn, Wales-Cymru

PART I

Physical Aspects

INTRODUCTION – PHYSICAL ASPECTS

In this part the *properties of materials* used in catering, cookery and the home are considered, together with *physical changes* which may affect the materials due mainly to heat or pressure changes.

The *energy needs* of a dwelling *space* in the form of heat, light, electricity and other services such as water are considered together with fossil fuels and foods as *energy sources*.

1 Measurement

Recent developments in such fields as food processing, preserving, textiles, and detergents make an intelligent understanding of science more than ever essential. Without a knowledge of science the professional caterer, hotelier, chef, houseworker, and home economist will be little different from the amateur who practises cookery as a pastime.

Science is a word which simply means *knowledge*. It is a study requiring careful observation and the methodical collection of all information concerning the earth and its animal, vegetable, and mineral products. It also deals with the effect of light, heat, and electricity.

BRANCHES OF SCIENCE

Physics, *chemistry*, and *biology* are the branches of science of special importance in catering and housecraft.

Physics, the study of electricity, heat, light and mechanics, finds particular application in connection with refrigerators, electrical appliances and wiring, room heating, and the testing of dough and syrup.

Chemistry is the study of the composition of matter. Food colouring, soaps and soapless detergents, paints, plastics, textiles, and dyeing are its applications.

Biology, the science or knowledge of life and living things, informs us of food sources, the structure and function of the human body, food infection, pests, and diseases.

CLASSIFICATION OF MATTER

All matter exists in one of three physical states: *solid*, *liquid*, or *gas*. They differ because the *molecules* – the tiny particles of which they are made – are arranged in different ways.

Solid molecules are packed together in an orderly manner, as in common salt crystals. Liquid molecules are less closely packed together, as in water. Gas molecules are far apart, as in air.

MEASUREMENT OF MATTER

Physics is a science of measurement, dealing with such quantities as length, volume, and weight. The SI or international system of measurement is used universally in science. The international system, SI, of measurement involves the use of *prefixes* such as deci, centi, and milli; and of *units* such as litre, gram, metre and derived units the joule and pascal.

Prefixes represent numbers or numerical quantities which are given individual symbols by means of letters.

kilo = k = 1 000 = one thousand
mega = M = 1 000 000 = one million
deci = d = 1/10 = one tenth
centi = c = 1/100 = one hundredth
milli = m = 1/1 000 = one thousandth
micro = μ (a Greek letter) = 1/1 000 000 = one millionth

These are some of the prefixes that will be encountered in this book.

MEASUREMENT OF LENGTH

The *metre* (m) is the unit for measuring length.

One thousand metres, 1 000 m = one kilometre (km)

A metre is divided into a hundred smaller parts called *centimetres* (cm), or one metre (m) = 1 000 centimetres (cm).

Each centimetre is made up of ten smaller parts called *millimetres* (mm), or one centimetre (cm) = 10 millimetres (mm).

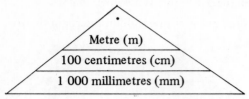

The simplest instrument for measuring length is a wooden metre rule.

MEASUREMENT OF VOLUME

The *litre* (1) is used for measuring volume and capacity, it is made up of ten parts called *decilitres* (dl)

One litre (1) = ten decilitres (dl)

Each decilitre is made up of ten parts called *centilitres* (cl)

One decilitre (dl) = ten centilitres (cl)

Alternatively a litre is made of one thousand smaller parts called *millilitres* (ml)

One litre (1) = one thousand millilitres (ml)

Most laboratory volume measuring instruments are marked in millilitres (ml), whilst certain domestic measures are marked in decilitres (dl).

Note: the millilitre (ml) for most general purposes is equal to a cubic centimetre (cm^3),

one millilitre (ml) = one cubic centimetre (cm^3)

Apparatus for measuring volume

The more important instruments for measuring the volumes of liquids and solids are:

Measuring cylinders (sizes range from 10 cm^3 to 21). They are fairly accurate instruments used for most general purposes.

Pipettes (10 to 50 cm^3). They measure small amounts of liquid accurately. The liquid is sucked into the pipette and retained by placing the index finger over the open end (Figure 1.1).

Graduated or measuring flasks (10 cm^3 to 31). They are accurate instruments used for making solutions of known strength such as the red dyes used to retain the colour of the cherry when it is preserved in syrup. Small quantities of Erythrosine B.S. dye are weighed carefully and dissolved in either water or syrup contained in a graduated flask;

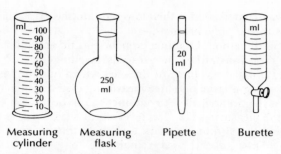

Figure 1.1. Apparatus for measuring volume

normally a 0·02 per cent solution of red dye is required.

Burettes are measuring instruments used for delivering small amounts of liquid accurately. From 0·1 to 99·8 cm^3 of liquid is delivered through the glass tap or pinch-cock. The instrument is frequently used in determining the hardness of water (Figure 1.1).

When reading the level of liquid in any measuring vessel, hold the instrument at eye level and read the lower line of the *meniscus*, or liquid surface (Figure 1.2).

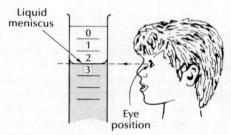

Figure 1.2. Reading the level of liquid in a measuring instrument

Determination of the volumes of solids

1. Solids such as lumps of suet, potatoes, rice, peas and carrots, which are not greatly affected by water, can be lowered into the displacement can (Figure 1.3) and the amount of water displaced, collected in a measuring cylinder. The volume of water displaced is equal to the volume of the solid.

2. Cakes, biscuits, and bread which absorb water readily, are dipped in low-melting-point paraffin wax to provide a coat of wax, which prevents water absorption.

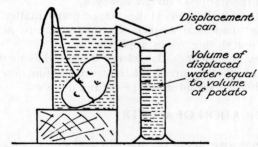

Figure 1.3. Measurement of volume using the displacement can

The wax-coated solid is then lowered into the displacement can as in the previous method.

3. Seed method. Obtain a large biscuit tin and fill it with either rape, mustard or linseed seeds, levelling them off with a ruler. Find the volume of the seed which fills the biscuit tin by using a large one-litre measuring cylinder. Place the cake in the tin and fill the container to the brim with seeds from the measuring cylinder; level off the seeds with a ruler, catching the surplus seeds in a shallow tray (Figure 1.4). The volume of the seed remaining, together with the volume of surplus seed levelled off, will be a measure of the volume of the cake. Using a smaller container, the same method can be used for flour dough dusted with dry flour to prevent the seeds sticking to the dough.

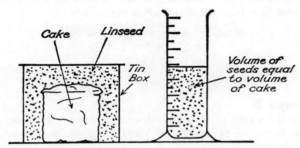

Figure 1.4. Using seeds to find the volume of a cake

Measuring cups and spoons

The British Standards Institution (B.S.I.) serves to establish uniform standards for such measures as 'cup', 'teaspoon', and 'tablespoon'.

The B.S.I. measure for a cup is 300 cm³; the tablespoon measure is 15 cm³; a teaspoon is 5 cm³. The B.S.I. measures can be purchased as plastic or metal containers.

Metric measuring spoons are available as follows: 1·25, 2·5, 5, 10, 15, and 20 cm³. Recipe instructions should be written: use a 10 cm³ spoon of milk, not a dessertspoon. Metric measuring jugs are marked in decilitres (dl) or in tenths of a litre, one decilitre being 100 cm³.

MEASUREMENT OF WEIGHT OR MASS

Weight is the pull of the earth's force of gravity on the body. Since this force varies over the earth's surface a body may weigh differently in different parts of the world. *Mass* is the amount of matter contained in a known volume of substance; it never varies.

For our purposes we may assume that weight and mass are equal to each other. When we place a body on a balance or a pair of scales, we are finding its weight.

The *kilogram* (kg) is the unit for measuring weight, and is divided into one thousand smaller weights called *grams* (g), also spelt *gramme*

One kilogram (kg) = one thousand grams (g)

Each gram can be divided into one thousand smaller parts called *milligrams* (mg)

One gram (g) = one thousand milligrams (mg)

A further division of the gram into one million parts called micrograms (μg) is also possible

One gram = one million micrograms (μg)

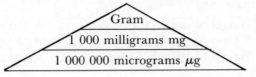

DENSITY

Density is the relationship between weight and volume;

$$\frac{\text{Weight}}{\text{Volume}} = \text{Density}$$

It indicates the weight of matter in a certain volume, and is expressed in kilograms per cubic metre (kg/m³). Density is a method of comparing 'heaviness' or 'lightness' of different materials by finding the weights of equal volumes of them.

The weights of a sponge cake and a fruit cake can be measured and then their volumes determined by the methods previously described. A calculation of their densities will show the fruit cake to have a greater density than the sponge cake.

UNIT AND BULK DENSITY

If the density of a potato is determined it will be found to have a density value of 1 125 kg/m³, this is called its *unit* density. If a plastic bag full of potatoes has its density determined by measuring the volume of the bag and its contents, its density is found to be 750 kg/m³, this is the *bulk* density, and is a measure of the density of the potatoes *plus* the air forming the spaces between each potato in the bag.

Bulk density applies to most solid catering items purchased in bulk, such as flour, peas, beans, rice bought in large bags or sacks.

UNIT AND BULK DENSITY OF FOODS (kg/m³)

Food	Unit density	Bulk density
Apples	800	575
Oranges	950	760
Potato	1 125	770
Rice	1 360	575
Wheat	1 420	800
Wheat flour	1 450	500

Experiments

1. To measure the *unit* density of solids, cheese, bread, and potatoes:

Cut a cube of cheese with sides 4 cm in each direction. Carefully weigh the cube and calculate the density as follows:

Unit density of food =

$$\frac{\text{weight of cube}}{\text{volume (i.e. length} \times \text{breadth} \times \text{height)}}$$

2. To measure the *unit* density of liquids:

Obtain a clean dry measuring cylinder and find its weight using a direct-reading balance. Fill the measuring cylinder with water to the 100 cm³ mark and obtain the weight of the water and cylinder:

Results:

Weight of water plus cylinder	= 150 g
Weight of empty cylinder	= 50 g
Weight of 100 ml of water	= 100 g

$$\text{Density of water} = \frac{100\ \text{g}}{100\ \text{cm}^3} = 1.00\ \text{g/cm}^3$$

The density of other liquids such as milk, vinegar, cooking oils, and olive oil can be determined in the same way.

3. To measure the *bulk* density of powdered materials, flour, dried milk, and sugar:

Obtain a container such as a 50 cm³ beaker or small mustard tin and weigh it empty. Then fill it to the brim with the powdered material, tap the container gently to allow the material to settle, and restore the level to the brim by adding further material. Now weigh the container and its contents. Find the volume of the container by filling it with water, and measuring the water in a measuring cylinder.

Results:

Weight of container and flour	= 65 g
Weight of empty container	= 35 g
Weight of flour	= 30 g

Volume of container is 50 cm³

$$\text{Density of flour} = \frac{30\ \text{g}}{50\ \text{cm}^3} = 0.6\ \text{g/cm}^3$$

A small 50 cm³ graduated flask can be used to give more accurate results.

4. To measure the *unit* density of substances which absorb water: bread and cakes:

The substances are carefully weighed and dipped into low-melting-point paraffin wax and their volumes measured using the displacement can described earlier. The method can also be used for rice, peas, beans, and barley without wax immersion.

The table below shows the *unit* densities of some common substances from which it can be seen that: (*a*) butter is less dense than water, which partly explains the cream line on milk; (*b*) ice cubes will float on iced drinks because solid ice is less dense than liquid water.

UNIT DENSITIES OF SOME COMMON SUBSTANCES

Substance	kg/m³	Substance	kg/m³
Mercury	13 600	Butter	930
Iron	7 900	Ice	920
Aluminium	2 600	Peanut oil	920
Sea water	1 050	Lard	910
Milk	1 030	Olive oil	900
Vinegar	1 020	Ethanol, methy-	
Water	1 000	lated spirits	830

Calculations involving density

The main type of calculation encountered requires the determination of the capacity of bins and other containers, using the following formulae:

Since
$$\text{Density} = \frac{\text{mass or weight}}{\text{volume}}$$

therefore   Mass or weight = density × volume

and
$$\text{Volume} = \frac{\text{mass or weight}}{\text{density}}$$

Example 1

The bulk density of flour is 592 kg/m³. Calculate the weight of flour in a bin 1 m × 1 m × 2 m.

$$\begin{aligned}
\text{Mass or weight} &= \text{density} \times \text{volume} \\
&= 592 \times 1 \times 1 \times 2 \\
&= 1\ 184\ \text{kg}
\end{aligned}$$

Example 2

Find the capacity of a container that holds three bags of flour (one bag of flour = 54·5 kg); the bulk density of the flour is 592 kg/m³.

$$\begin{aligned}
\text{Volume} &= \frac{\text{mass or weight}}{\text{density}} \\
&= \frac{3 \times 54.5}{592} \\
&= 0.27\ \text{m}^3
\end{aligned}$$

RELATIVE DENSITY (formerly specific gravity)

Relative density (R.D.) is the mass of a known volume of a substance divided by the mass of the *same volume* of water.

$$\text{Relative density} = \frac{\text{mass or weight of substance}}{\text{weight of equal volume of water}}$$

Relative density means the *number of times* a substance is heavier or lighter than an equal volume of water. If the R.D. of lead is 11, it means that it is eleven times as heavy as a volume of water equal to the volume of the lead.

Experiment

To find the relative density of different liquids:

Use a clean dry glass bottle, fitted with a glass or rubber stopper, or a special-purpose relative density bottle. Weigh the bottle, together with its stopper, empty. Fill the bottle to the brim with water and insert the stopper, making sure no air bubbles are beneath the stopper, and reweigh. Use the same bottle (i.e. the volume of the bottle is the same), fill it with milk, insert the stopper carefully as before, and reweigh. The experiment can be repeated using vinegar, evaporated milk, condensed milk, and syrup.

Results:

Mass of bottle and			Mass of bottle and		
water	=	70 g	milk	=	71·5 g
Mass of bottle empty	=	20 g	Mass of bottle empty	=	20·0 g
Mass of water	=	50 g	Mass of milk	=	51·5 g

$$\text{Relative density of milk} = \frac{\text{mass of milk}}{\text{mass of equal volume of water}}$$

$$= \frac{51 \cdot 5}{50 \cdot 0} = 1 \cdot 03$$

Milk is 1·03 times as heavy as an equal volume of water.

Hydrometers

The hydrometer is the instrument (Figure 1.5) used to find the relative density of different liquids by direct measurement. The hydrometer has a weighted bulb and a graduated stem marked with the relative density scale. It is allowed to float in the liquid and the depth to which it sinks is indicated directly on the stem R.D. scale, thus dispensing with the lengthy method of R.D. determination described previously.

Figure 1.5. A hydrometer

All liquids are subject to changes in volume as the temperature rises and falls (*see* Chapter 6), and consequently their R.D. will be different at different temperatures. It is therefore essential to measure relative densities of liquids at a definite temperature and 20°C is the standard used, which is usually marked on the hydrometer. For general purposes it is sufficient for the liquid to be tested at *room* temperature.

Hydrometers are used in a variety of trades, including catering, chocolate and confectionary manufacture, milk processing, brewing, and in laundry work. They are used to measure relative densities over a wide range between 0·5 and 2·0. A single hydrometer could not cover this range as such an instrument would require a very long stem and would not provide the accurate readings which are necessary in all hydrometry work; a number of special-purpose hydrometers are therefore available of which the following are the more important for catering and household purposes.

Saccharometers

Saccharometers are hydrometers used to determine the strength of sugar solutions. The Brix saccharometer has a stem marked with the percentage of sugar by weight up to 85 per cent, the depth to which the saccharometer sinks in the sugar solution being shown directly.

Baumé and Twaddell hydrometers are also used for sugar solutions, but they do not give direct readings of the solution's percentage strength: their stem readings are converted into relative density by the use of special tables or by simple calculation. The Twaddell hydrometer covers a very wide relative density range and is available as a set of six hydrometers in a case; it has the advantage of being used to test all kinds of different liquids, while the Brix and Baumé are used mainly for sugar as saccharometers.

Experiment

To prepare a sugar solution of definite relative density, or how to make water ices:

A sugar solution of 31 per cent or 31 degrees Brix, or 17 degrees Baumé, is required, this solution being of relative density 1.13. It can be made by dissolving 30 g of sugar in 70 cm^3 of warm water. When the sugar has dissolved and the solution has *cooled* to room temperature, the hydrometer is made to float in it. More sugar is added a little at a time until the hydrometer has sunk to the correct stem reading: if too much sugar is added, a little water is added to restore to the correct value. Fruit flavouring and colouring are added and the solution is cooled in a refrigerator with frequent stirring. The table below shows the saccharometer table for making various sugar preparations.

SACCHAROMETER TABLE FOR SUGAR PREPARATIONS

Preparation	Baumé scale	Brix or % sugar	R.D.	Sugar to 1 litre of water
Water ices	17	31	1·13	450 g
Stewed fruit compote	20	38	1·17	610 g
Stock sugar syrup	28	51	1·24	960 g
Sweets	33·5	63	1·30	1 702 g
Crystallized fruits	40	75	1·38	3 000 g
Glazed fruits	42·5	80	1·41	4 000 g

Lactometers

The lactometer is the hydrometer for the preliminary testing of milk; it has stem graduations from 1·00 to 1·04, the relative densities encountered in the milk industry. The letter *W* on the stem scale is for the R.D. of water, *M* is for pure milk of R.D. 1·03, while *S* is for skim milk. The relative density of fresh cow's milk is between 1·029 and 1·033. If water is added to milk its relative density will be lowered.

Alcoholometers

Alcoholometers, or Sikes hydrometers, are used by the customs and excise authorities to test the relative density of alcoholic beverages, wines, beers, and spirits. The amount of ethanol in the beverage is recorded as the number of degrees proof. The alcoholometer will determine whether a beer or spirit has been diluted, and also show the sugar content of a wine. R.D. dry wine = 1·0; sweet wine = 1·02; medium dry wine = 1·01.

Salinometers

Salinometers are hydrometers used for determining the R.D. of the brine or sodium chloride solutions used for curing or pickling bacon or ham. Brine has an R.D. between 1·14 and 1·19 for general purposes. So-called sweet-cured bacon is preserved in a sugar and sodium chloride mixture.

APPLICATIONS OF RELATIVE DENSITY

1. Egg testing
The freshness of an egg can be found by making an egg float in salt water, made by dissolving 100 g of sodium chloride in 1 000 cm^3 (or 1 litre) of water. If the egg is fresh it will *sink* while the bad egg will float. Staling is due to loss of water through the porous shell and the formation of a large air-space causing buoyancy.

2. Lightness of cakes
The low density of cakes is achieved by leavening agents which increase the volume of the dough or mix by blending in air or carbon dioxide.

3. Mineral additives in flour
Flour may purposely contain added mineral substances of a chalky nature, which give it important nutritive value; the additive may also be a raising agent. If a portion of the flour is shaken up in a test tube with trichloromethane (chloroform) (*poisonous material and flammable*), the less dense flour will float on the surface, whereas the denser mineral matter will sink to the bottom. The amount of sediment is a rough indication of the mineral matter present in the flour.

4. Potatoes
Potatoes suitable for baking or frying will *sink* in a solution of 120 g of sodium chloride in a litre of water, whilst potatoes for boiling will float.

SUGGESTIONS FOR PRACTICAL WORK

1. Determine the capacity of small kitchen utensils used as domestic cookery measures: teaspoon, dessertspoon, tablespoon, tea cup, breakfast cup, tumbler, and small pudding bowl. Fill the utensil to the brim with water and pour into a measuring cylinder. Tabulate your results.

2. Determine the densities of lard, butter, margarine, and cooking fat.

3. Determine the weight of one level breakfast cup full of each of the following materials: sifted flour, sugar, lard, dried fruit, and cornflour.

4. See *Experimental Science for Catering and Homecraft Students*, Practical work 19.2, 26.1 and 26.2.

QUESTIONS ON CHAPTER 1

1. Draw and describe the instruments you would use to measure: (*a*) 25 cm^3 of water accurately; (*b*) 25·5 cm^3 of water; and (*c*) 250 cm^3 of 45 Brix syrup approximately.

2. Explain the following terms, giving definitions wherever possible: (*a*) bulk density; (*b*) relative density; (*c*) unit density; (*d*) litre; (*e*) millilitre.

3. Describe with diagrams the construction and mode of action of a lactometer. Give an account of its main uses.

4. What are hydrometers? Give a full account of their uses in the food trades.

5. Write short notes on: (*a*) hydrometers; (*b*) cake lightness; (*c*) egg-testing; and (*d*) British Standards Institution.

6. Describe the method you would use to determine the density of a small sponge cake.

7. Write a short account on the use of domestic utensils as cookery measures.

8. Describe methods which could be used to test: (*a*) flour contaminated with chalk; (*b*) watered milk; (*c*) eggs suspected to be bad; (*d*) vegetable cooking oil adulterated with liquid paraffin; and (*e*) the accuracy of a cheap plastic kitchen measure.

9. Describe a method of finding the density of fresh milk. What is the relative density of milk? Calculate the weight in grams of a litre of milk.

MULTIPLE CHOICE QUESTIONS ON CHAPTER I

1. The molecules are closer together in:
   - (*a*) fluids
   - (*b*) solids
   - (*c*) liquids
   - (*d*) gases

2. Which of the following is more suitable for measuring 3.5 cm^3 of liquid food colouring?
   - (*a*) pipette
   - (*b*) burette
   - (*c*) measuring cylinder
   - (*d*) graduated flask

3. A tablespoon has an approximate capacity of:
   - (*a*) 5 cm^3
   - (*b*) 10 cm^3
   - (*c*) 15 cm^3
   - (*d*) 20 cm^3

4. The number of milligrams in one gram is:
   - (*a*) one
   - (*b*) ten
   - (*c*) thousand
   - (*d*) million

5. If one litre measures of the following are weighed, which will have the least weight compared to the others?
   - (*a*) peanut oil
   - (*b*) ethanol
   - (*c*) milk
   - (*d*) olive oil

6. The relative density of milk is determined by means of the:
   - (*a*) lactometer
   - (*b*) saccharometer
   - (*c*) hydrometer
   - (*d*) alcoholometer

7. The component which increases the density value of a

sweet wine is:

(*a*) sugar   (*c*) water

(*b*) ethanol   (*d*) yeasts

8. Which of the following correctly describes the term 'lightness' of baked confectionery?

(*a*) low unit weight   (*c*) low unit density

(*b*) high relative density   (*d*) high unit weight

9. A pint of milk has the equivalent metric measure:

(*a*) 284 cm^3 (*c*) 852 cm^3

(*b*) 568 cm^3 (*d*) 1 136 cm^3

10. A pound of butter has the following equivalent metric weight:

(*a*) 0·226 kg   (*c*) 0·678 kg

(*b*) 0·453 kg   (*d*) 0·907 kg

2 Pressure in fluids

Fluids – for example, water and air – are substances that can *flow*. The term fluid is used to describe liquids and gases.

Pressure is something we have all experienced. For example:

(a) we notice water pressure when we try to hold back the water from an open tap;

(b) solid pressure is experienced when we stand in wet sand or when we press a suit or dress;

(c) gas pressure is felt when we try to prevent the gas escaping from a lemonade bottle or soda siphon.

PRESSURE EXERTED BY SOLIDS

Figure 2.1 illustrates the effect of pressure exerted by solids, namely, shoe impressions in soft wet sand. *A* sinks deeply into the sand because the body weight is supported on a very small area with pointed heel shoes. *B* sinks into the soft sand to a lesser extent because the surface area is greater, whereas *C* sinks very little because of the large surface area of the boards tied to the shoes. Thus, the pressure exerted by the body on the feet depends on the weight of the body and the area of the feet. The greater the surface area of the feet, the less will be the pressure upon them.

UNIT OF MEASUREMENT OF PRESSURE

Force is measured in units called *newtons* (abbreviation N). Pressure is force divided by area and is thus measured in newtons per square metre (N/m^2), the unit is called the *pascal* (abbreviation Pa).

$$\text{Pressure (in pascals)} = \frac{\text{force (in newtons)}}{\text{area (in square metres)}}$$

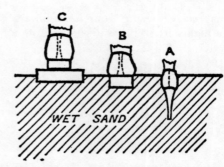

Figure 2.1. Shoe impressions in wet sand to show the relation between weight and surface area of shoes

Note that 1 meganewton (MN) = 1 000 000 N; 1 kilonewton (kN) = 1 000 N. The force of gravity on a 1-kg mass is about 10 N.

APPLICATIONS OF THE PRESSURE OF SOLIDS

1. Pointed heels can cause damage to floor surfaces by the body weight acting on the small area of the heel. The pressure exerted is of a very high value.

2. Large ball castors are preferable for furniture rather than small wheel castors, which result in considerable pressure on the floor surface and consequent damage to carpets and floor coverings.

WATER OR LIQUID PRESSURE

The important property of water pressure is illustrated in Figure 2.2. The pressure of water increases with depth or height, spout *A* having the least water pressure, while spout *C* has the greatest pressure.

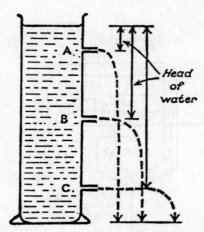

Figure 2.2. Pressure in liquids increases with depth or height

The vertical distance between the level of the water in the tank and the level at the open end or spout is called the *head* of water; it is a term used by water engineers for describing water pressure.

APPLICATION OF WATER PRESSURE

1. The domestic water supply

Many towns receive water from a mountain reservoir, situated at a higher level; the water flows from a high level to a low level.

The reservoir dam wall is thicker at the bottom, to meet the increasing water pressure there. A thick-walled pipe brings the water to the consumer in the low-lying towns and villages, the water flow being controlled by a hydrant. If there is a burst in the main water pipe, a great fountain will be produced, due to the great head of water pressure.

The water enters the residence by the service pipe, which can be controlled by a Water Board *stop tap*; this is situated immediately outside the residence or near the cold-water tap in the kitchen. The service pipe supplies the cold drinking-water tap in the kitchen, the remaining cold-water taps in the bathrooms and toilets, and finally fills the cistern storage tank in the attic. This method of supplying all cold-water taps from the rising main is called the *intermittent* system. If the stop tap is turned off no cold water will be available to the taps or cistern tank. It is usual to turn off the stop tap in the event of a burst pipe, if a tap needs repairing, or when a residence is to be left unattended (Figure 2.3).

In London and some other areas all cold-water taps are supplied from the cistern storage tanks: this is indicated if the water pressure from the cold-water tap is lower than that from the drinking-water tap in the kitchen. The difference in the tap pressure or rate of water flow is due to the smaller head of water from the attic cistern tank, compared to the main water pressure in the *drinking*-water tap. It is therefore important to draw drinking water from the main water supply taps and not from taps supplied by the cistern tank; the tank is liable to be contaminated with dust and the water is only suitable for toilet purposes.

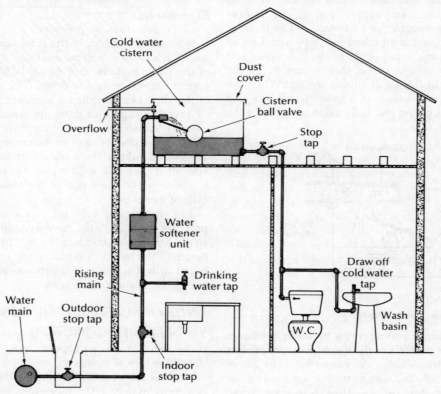

Figure 2.3. Domestic water supply

2. Water tap

Before examining any tap see that the water is turned off at the main tap. The movable part of a bib tap (Figure 2.4) is called the '*jumper*'. This controls the water flow and is supported by the '*washer*'. In a cold-water tap the washer is made of leather, but in a hot-water tap the washer is of composition fibre and is red or black in colour.

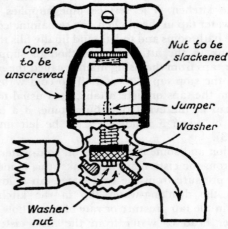

Figure 2.4. Water tap showing the 'jumper' and 'washer'

3. Ball-valve

A ball-valve is used to control water-closet flush cisterns, water storage cisterns, and other tanks which have an automatic control to the water supply, e.g. café set boilers and steam provers for doughs (*see* Figure 2.5). The floating ball is made of plastic and is attached to a long arm hinged by a split pin. If the tank is full of water the ball floats and the arm presses on a sliding valve; this in turn stops the water flow by means of the small rubber *washer*. When the tank is partly empty, the ball is at a lower level, bringing with it the arm which moves the slide valve and allows the water to flow into the tank.

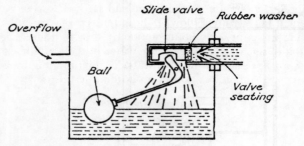

Figure 2.5. Ball-valve

4. Instantaneous gas water heater

This water heater (Figure 2.6) operates by water pressure. When the water tap is turned on, the water pressure presses on a soft *diaphragm* which causes the gas to flow; the gas in turn is lit by a continually burning *pilot light*. Turning off the water tap closes the gas supply, thus providing small amounts of hot water with economy of gas.

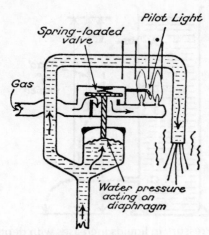

Figure 2.6. Instantaneous gas water heater

GAS AND AIR PRESSURE

The earth is surrounded by a layer of air or *atmosphere*. This layer of air has weight and is continually pressing on the earth's surface, causing air or atmospheric pressure.

Experiments

1. To illustrate air pressure:

Fill a glass tumbler to the brim with water and cover the top with a sheet of stiff paper. Press the paper with the palm of the hand making sure no air bubbles remain. Carefully turn the tumbler upside down. The water does not fall out of the glass because the air pressure is acting on the paper; its pressure is greater than the water pressure.

2. To construct a simple mercury barometer:

The instruments used to measure air pressure are called *barometers*. Take a thick-walled glass tube about 1 m long and fill it carefully with liquid mercury. Placing the index finger over the open end of the tube, invert the tube in a dish of mercury.

The mercury is kept up to a certain height by the air pressure acting on the mercury surface in the dish. The space above the mercury in the tube is a *vacuum*. If the height of the mercury is measured from the mercury surface in the dish it is found to be about 760 mm or 76 cm; this is called the barometric height.

UNITS OF MEASURING AIR PRESSURE

The method of measuring the length of a mercury column is convenient for many purposes, gas pressure being recorded in millimetres of mercury.

Normal air pressure is equal to 760 mm of mercury; this is approximately 100 kilonewtons per square metre or 100 kilopascals.

APPLICATIONS OF GAS PRESSURE

1. Gas supply to premises (Figure 2.7)

Town gas is held in a large gasholder over a water seal. The main pipe carries gas to the residence, the flow being controlled by a gas cock situated next to the meter.

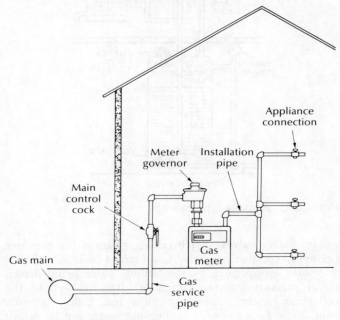

Figure 2.7. Domestic gas supply

2. Pressure of the gas supply

If a U-shaped tube is half full of water the water levels will be equal, as the same air pressure is acting on the water in each half of the tube. When one end of the tube is connected to a gas tap and the gas turned on, the gas and air pressure will force the water level down in one arm and up in the other (Figure 2.8). The difference in levels in millimetres is an indication of the town gas pressure, which is about 200 mm of water or 2 kilopascals. The true pressure of the town gas supply is equal to the water pressure plus the atmospheric pressure:

True town gas pressure = air pressure + water height in millimetres.

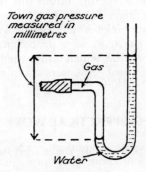

Figure 2.8. Pressure of the gas supply

3. Gas governors

Governors are always fitted to gas appliances to provide a steady flow of gas into the appliance and to prevent fluctuations in the size of the flame due to changing pressure of the gas supply (Figure 2.9). The gas governor contains a flexible diaphragm which moves under the influence of changing gas pressure, thus providing a steady flow independent of fluctuations in the main gas pressure.

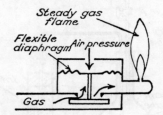

Figure 2.9. Gas-pressure governors

4. Pressure gauges

Pressure gauges are fitted to most boilers and pressure cookers. Inside the gauge is a thin flexible copper tube which extends like a party blower-toy when the gas pressure is increased. The movement of the flexible tube is magnified by a series of cogs and levers which move the pointer over the pressure scale.

5. Altitude

As an aeroplane ascends, the air pressure becomes less. This *decrease* in air pressure with altitude has a number of effects. Cooking at high altitude is affected; for example, cakes will rise quicker and less raising agent must be used.

THE SIPHON

The *siphon* is a useful device for drawing liquids from large containers, from a higher to a lower level. A long rubber tube full of the liquid has one end placed in the container of liquid to be siphoned; the other end is then lowered and opened. A continual flow of liquid takes place until the tubing is empty. Siphonic action is due to the *combined* action of the air pressure on the water in the container and the water pressure or head of water in the tube. Figure 2.10 shows the siphonic action in an automatic flush cistern.

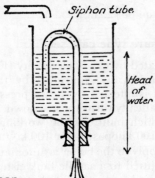

Figure 2.10. Siphon

STEAM PRESSURE

When water is boiled in the flask, the steam escapes through outlet *A* (Figure 2.11). When *A* is closed, the steam pressure will collect and drive the boiling water from the flask into the *infuser* tube, which can contain tea leaves or coffee grains and provide a rapid infusion of tea or coffee.

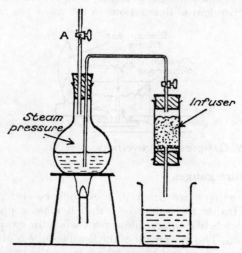

Figure 2.11. Pressure-type café set: laboratory apparatus

APPLICATIONS

1. Coffee percolators

The coffee grains are contained in the infuser; hot boiling water is made to percolate through the infuser by steam pressure (Figure 2.12).

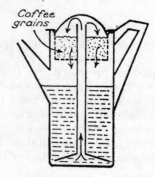

Figure 2.12. Coffee percolator

2. Steam-pressure type café set

The boiler is heated by gas or electricity (Figure 2.13). Gas heating is automatically controlled by the *pressurestat*, a diaphragm that is affected by steam pressure; high steam pressure automatically turns the gas down. The boiler has a *pressure gauge* which indicates the working pressure to be approximately 100 kilopascals or 100 kN/m^2.

The water supply to the boiler is automatically controlled by a ball-valve fitted to a saddle tank cistern. The amount of water in the boiler is indicated by the glass water-level

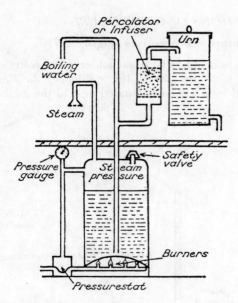

Figure 2.13. Pressure-type café set

gauge. Safety valves, which release steam if the pressure becomes excessive, are fitted to all steam boilers.

A café set operates by the boiling water being driven under pressure into the infuser or filter, followed by the collection of the infusion in glass tea, coffee, or milk containers. Live steam or boiling-hot water can be drawn from the café set for warming tea or milk.

'Espresso' machines produce coffee by steam-pressure boilers working at 140 to 275 kilopascals or 140 to 275 kN/m^2 and use special coffee grains. The high-pressure also produces the attractive foam associated with 'Espresso' coffee.

AEROSOL SPRAYS (FIGURE 2.14)

Aerosol sprays are popular forms for dispensing a variety of products ranging from fly killers to whipped cream. The aerosol contains a propellent liquid which is a *liquefied gas* that evaporates or changes into a gas simply by releasing some of the gas pressure or by the heat of the hand. (Therefore store aerosol sprays in a cool place.)

When the nozzle is depressed, the propellent gas pressure forces a fine mist of volatile liquid out of the dispenser. Immediately the finger is released from the nozzle, the aerosol gas pressure closes the escape valve. The commonest liquefied gas used as a propellent is 'Arcton', or dichlorotetrafluorethane, which is also used in refrigerators. Whipped cream aerosol dispensers contain *nitrous oxide*.

SUGGESTIONS FOR PRACTICAL WORK

1. Locate the position of the main stop tap in your kitchen.

2. Find out whether the cold-water taps and water-closet

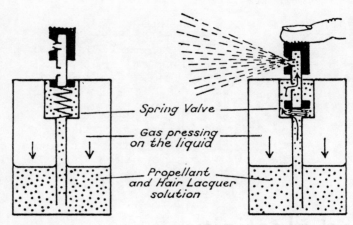

Figure 2.14.

cisterns are supplied from the rising main or from the attic storage cistern tank.

3. Locate the position of your water storage cistern and note (*a*) whether it has a dust cover, (*b*) if it is fitted with a stop tap.

4. Investigate the origin of your town's water supply and arrange to visit your local waterworks.

QUESTIONS ON CHAPTER 2

1. Describe a simple experiment to show water pressure. Briefly outline how the water supply is brought to a residence from a mountain reservoir.

2. Give a simple account of the construction and method of operation of either a tap or a cistern ball-valve.

3. Explain the meaning of the term atmospheric pressure and describe one household fitting controlled by air pressure.

4. Explain how one of the following works: (*a*) coffee percolator; (*b*) pressure-type café set; (*c*) aerosol spray; (*d*) pressure gauge; and (*e*) soda water siphon.

5. What is the siphon? Describe one household fitting which incorporates the principle of the siphon.

6. Write short notes on: (*a*) head of water; (*b*) town gas pressure; (*c*) gas governors.

MULTIPLE CHOICE QUESTIONS ON CHAPTER 2

1. The amount of fresh water on the earth is approximately the following amount of the total water on earth:
   (*a*) 5%   (*c*) 50%
   (*b*) 25%   (*d*) 75%

2. Pressure is the relationship shown as follows:
   (*a*) $\dfrac{\text{weight}}{\text{height}}$ (*c*) $\dfrac{\text{weight}}{\text{area}}$
   (*b*) $\dfrac{\text{area}}{\text{length}}$ (*d*) $\dfrac{\text{volume}}{\text{weight}}$

3. The unit for measuring water and gas pressure is called the:
   (*a*) pound per square foot   (*c*) watt
   (*b*) pascal   (*d*) therm

4. Which of the following pipes found in a house is controlled by a stop tap?
   (*a*) rising main tap   (*c*) flush pipe
   (*b*) cistern overflow pipe   (*d*) sink waste pipe

5. The part of a sink tap which wears out and is most likely to need replacing is the:
   (*a*) jumper   (*c*) seating
   (*b*) spindle   (*d*) washer

6. The supply of water to a water closet, or water storage cistern is controlled internally by a:
   (*a*) governor   (*c*) spring valve
   (*b*) ball valve   (*d*) pressure gauge

7. The main water supply is usually sterilized by:
   (*a*) fluoridation   (*c*) sedimentation
   (*b*) chlorination   (*d*) precipitation

8. Air pressure can be measured by means of the:
   (*a*) barometer   (*c*) hydrometer
   (*b*) thermometer   (*d*) hygrometer

9. Steam pressure gauges fitted to steam pressure boilers operate within a pressure range measured in kilopascals of:
   (*a*) 1 to 3   (*c*) 140 to 275
   (*b*) 14 to 30   (*d*) 1 500 to 3 000

10. A typical washbasin will hold the following approximate amount of water:
   (*a*) 0.5 litre   (*c*) 20 to 25 litres
   (*b*) 5 to 10 litres   (*d*) 50 to 55 litres

3   Surface behaviour and elasticity

SURFACE TENSION

Surface tension is the force of attraction that exists between solid and liquid surfaces, or a force within the surface of a liquid whereby the surface tends to contract in area.

Examples of the effects of surface tension

1. Water drops will cling to a greasy window-pane.
2. The surface of the liquid in a glass beaker resembles a skin; this is made more evident if powdered sulphur or dust is sprinkled on to the water. The margins of the liquid surface creep up the sides of the container; this is called the *meniscus* of the liquid. (See Figure 1.2.)

APPLICATIONS OF SURFACE TENSION

1.   Detergent action

The washing of clothes and dishes is aimed at the removal of soiling materials. These consist mainly of grease, solid particles of soot, food, etc., clinging to the grease layer, and water-soluble salts.

Textile fibres, such as wool, are covered with a natural greasy coating of *lanolin*, which serves primarily to waterproof the fleece. When woollen garments are washed in a detergent the film of natural grease together with its solid soil particles, are removed from the fibre by the surface action of the detergent, which reduces the surface attraction that exists between the fibre and its greasy coating, the latter floating away into the washing water.

Hot water and agitation both contribute to reducing the surface tension between the fibre or dish surface and the soiling material.

2.   Waterproofing

Waterproofing of textile materials involves the use of either oily materials, linseed oil now displaced by the *silicones*. Silicones are chemical compounds of silicon and have remarkable powers of repelling water from fibres and other surfaces.

Drip-dry materials and garments are made from textiles impregnated with water-repelling silicones or from man-made fibres, e.g. polyamides and polyesters, with reduced water-absorbing properties.

3.   Release agents

Release agents are now employed in the baking industry to prevent baked bread from sticking to the baking tins. By impregnating paper cups and lining paper for cake tins with release agents, baked cakes are allowed to slip away from the paper without part of the cake sticking to the paper or tin. The release agent contains silicone compounds.

4.   Polishes

Furniture and car polishes contain small amounts of silicones which, because of their low surface tension, allow the polish to spread easily and are resistant to moisture, heat, and smearing by finger marks.

5.   Waterproofing of buildings

Waterproofing of outside walls can be achieved by painting with water-repelling silicone wall paints.

6.   Silicones

Silicones find a variety of uses ranging from hand barrier-creams and silicone pressing cloths to prevention of foaming in deep-fat frying, washing of sliced potatoes, blanching of vegetables, and fermentation of food manufacture.

7. Non-stick utensils

Non-stick frypans and other cooking utensils are coated with poly tetrafluoroethene P.T.F.E. plastic or treated with silicones.

CAPILLARITY

Capillarity is the phenomenon of liquids rising in narrow tubes of hair-like dimensions.

Take two sheets of glass of approximate size 10 × 10 cm, place a matchstick between the plates at one end, and bind the plates together with strong elastic bands. Insert the plates in a shallow dish of water coloured with a few drops of ink. Notice how the water rises most where the plates are closest together, and least where the plates are separated by the matchstick.

1. Rising damp

Rising damp in brick walls is due to water rising through the tiny capillary tubes present in the porous bricks. By inserting a *damp-proof course* (D.P.C.) in the first layer of bricks, near to the foundations, the rising damp is prevented. (See Figure 3.1.) The damp-proof course can be either sheet lead or waterproofed felt. As the rising dampness evaporates, it leaves behind a deposit of salt which encourages further dampness by absorbing water from the air.

2. Window frames

Window frames with close-fitting surfaces encourage capillarity or the creeping of water between the frames. To overcome this, grooves are made in the frame and on the window ledge, and this halts the capillary rise (Figure 3.1). Grooves on the ledges are called *throats*.

3. Sweating of concrete floors

Sweating is caused by the absence of the porous layer of hardcore or broken bricks, which prevents capillary rise of damp from the subsoil below the concrete. Concrete contains tiny pores which encourage capillary rise (Figure 3.1).

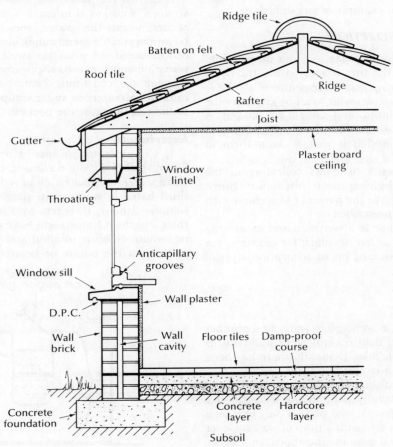

Figure 3.1. Structure of a building

4. Migration of colour in coloured fabrics

The tiny spaces between fibres, in, for example, wet woollen fabrics, allow water-soluble dye colours, which are not fast, to travel by capillarity into the surrounding fibres and cause the *running* or spreading of the colour. This is seen in well-washed multi-coloured knitted woollens when the migration of the colours is due to one-sided drying. Slow drying, for example between towels, prevents colour migration.

DIFFUSION

Liquids and gases are made up of tiny *molecules* that are continually moving. This movement can be illustrated by placing crystals of blue copper (II) sulphate in a beaker and covering them with water: the crystals dissolve slowly, forming a deep blue liquid. If the beaker is set aside in a quiet place for a few weeks, the blue colour will spread uniformly through the liquid, showing that the spread of the colour is due to the movement of the copper (II) sulphate molecules.

Diffusion involves the movement of molecules from a region of *high* concentration to a region of *low* concentration in fluids, until a fluid of *uniform* concentration is formed.

The spreading of cooking and perfume odours through the air of a residence is an example of gas diffusion.

ABSORPTION AND ADSORPTION

If some dried peas are placed to soak in water they rapidly take in water which fills the tiny spaces within the peas. This taking in of water or fluids into the centre of a solid is called *absorption*. Other examples which can be given are the effects seen when dry gelatine and dough are soaked in water. Stored foodstuffs can readily absorb the odours of paint, disinfectants, etc., and it is wise to keep them in separate stores.

Indigestion can be caused by gases collecting in the stomach and intestine and giving rise to discomfort. Burnt toast or charcoal biscuits have the power of absorbing such gases and these are often prescribed.

Adsorption is closely similar to absorption and means the collection of fluids on the *surface* of solids; for example, tea cups and egg spoons are stained by an adsorption layer of stain on the solid surface.

OSMOSIS

If a dried prune is placed in some plain water and another in water containing sugar, the prune in plain water swells and that in sugar syrup shrinks. Evidently there has been some movement of water into and out of the prune.

Living things, whether animal or plant, are made up of millions of tiny cells. Carefully peel off the silky cellular lining seen inside an onion scale and place a part of it on a glass microscope slide together with a drop of water. Cover it with a glass cover slip and examine the appearance of the cell under the microscope. The cells of plants have walls which enclose a nucleus; this is surrounded by the cell sap and has a cover or cell lining. If the cover slip is removed, and a little salt water is added, viewing the onion cells under the microscope will show the cell lining to have shrunk away from the cell wall (Figure 3.2).

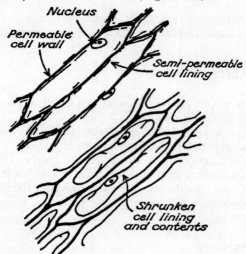

Figure 3.2. Osmosis in cells of onion

Osmosis is the passage of *water* from a weak solution to a stronger solution through a *semi-permeable membrane*. This occurs when the water goes through the cell lining (semi-permeable membrane) into the cell sap, causing the cell or the dried prune to swell. When the cell is in salt water or sugar syrup, the water in the cell sap goes out through the cell lining (semi-permeable membrane) and into the salt water or sugar syrup; this causes the shrinkage of the cell lining or the prune.

Experiments

1. Cut a potato into small strips exactly 50 mm long and 5 mm thick, i.e. potato *allumete*. Place some potato chips in clean water, another batch in sodium chloride water, and a third batch in water containing sugar. Leave the chips to soak for 1 hour, then remove them and carefully measure their lengths. Osmosis will have caused the chips to shrink in sodium chloride solution and sugar syrup.

2. Trim the potato or beetroot to the shape shown in

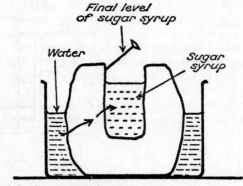

Figure 3.3. Osmosis in beetroot

Figure 3.3 and partly fill the centre with syrup or strong sugar solution. Mark its level with a pin and insert the potato in a dish of plain water. Leave for a while and note how the syrup level rises.

3. Tie a portion of *Visking* tubing over the end of a thistle funnel or similar tube. Partly fill the tube with sugar syrup and immerse it in clean water. Repeat the experiment by filling the tube with clear water and immersing in sugar syrup. The change in liquid levels in the tubes will be due to osmosis.

APPLICATIONS OF OSMOSIS

1. Osmosis explains how water in food is absorbed from the intestine into the blood.

2. Cut grapefruit sprinkled with sugar and allowed to stand overnight produces a juicy extract on the flesh by osmosis and diffusion.

3. The freshness of fruits and vegetables depends on osmotic pressure keeping the cells *turgid*. Loss of water leads to flaccid cells and staleness. Sugar should be sprinkled on strawberries at the latest opportunity otherwise the fruits lose their attractive firmness and become soft and limp. Lettuce can be revived or crisped by immersing the leaves in fresh water, which enters by osmosis.

4. Meat boiled in plain water retains most of its natural juices, whereas meat boiled in salted water loses a certain amount of natural juice (many proteins are more soluble in weak salt water, therefore useful for stocks). The part boiling of meat in plain water *followed by* the addition of salt, after the heat has destroyed the semi-permeable membranes of the meat cells, is a good example of science applied to cookery.

5. Salting of fish, particularly herrings and cod, causes the cell water to pass out of the fish flesh by osmosis into the solid sodium chloride, which becomes a solution. Salting of the fish causes the flesh to shrink and become solid in the case of salt cod. The reverse process of osmosis is performed by immersing the salt fish in plain water before cooking.

6. Radishes, onions, carrots, and celery can be made into decorative shapes by splitting the vegetables lengthwise and immersing them in fresh water; they then curl up into attractive decorative forms by osmosis of the cell sap into the water.

7. Fruits which have been preserved in sugar syrups tend to shrink if too much sugar is present; therefore it is essential to can fruits in the right strength of sugar syrup. If the syrup is too weak the fruit skins will burst.

8. Soaking chipped potatoes in salted water before frying removes some water by osmosis: this will help to crisp them during frying.

9. *Slow freezing* causes cell fluids to become more concentrated as ice freezes out, this results in osmosis and damage to cells of frozen food (see page 42).

ELASTICITY

Elasticity is the property which enables a substance to change its shape when a force is applied to it and to recover its shape when the stretching force is removed, provided the elastic limit has not been exceeded.

Wool, nylon, cotton, and hair are textile fibres with elastic properties of considerable importance. Flour dough and meat also have important elastic properties which can be demonstrated.

Experiment
To show the elastic nature of flour dough:

Fix a large cup hook into a piece of wood, and support firmly in the jaws of a clamp fixed to a stout iron retort stand. Screw another large cup hook into the narrow end of a cork and fix a light pan (tin lid) or empty plastic carton to the cork with three strong thread supports. A similar apparatus, suitable for baked bread and dough, is shown in Figure 3.4.

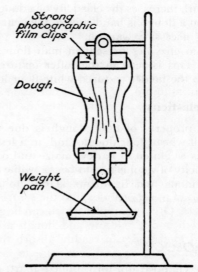

Figure 3.4. Tensile strength of bread and dough

Obtain 50 g of kneaded white flour dough and shape into a ball. Insert the cup hooks into the centre of the dough ball and allow the weight pan to hang down.

(a) Either carefully add weights to the pan or run lead shot into the ice-cream tub until the dough is about to break after extension.

(b) Record the weight required to extend the dough to breaking point.

(c) Repeat the experiment at least three times, making sure to re-form the dough into a ball with the minimum amount of kneading.

(d) Repeat the experiment using wholemeal flour.

This simple apparatus can be described as a dough *extensometer* to measure the stretching power of the dough. A more accurate instrument is available called the *extensograph* which records the behaviour of the stretching dough on a chart.

The Brabender farinograph determines the strength of a

flour dough by measuring the force required to turn paddles through the dough.

The *alveograph* measures the strength of dough by finding the pressure required to blow a sheet of dough into a bubble.

Factors affecting the elasticity of flour dough

(*a*) The elasticity of dough increases with kneading, to a certain point, but if the dough is over-kneaded, the elasticity *decreases*. This can be confirmed using the simple dough extensometer described above.

(*b*) Added chemical substances or *improvers* can strengthen the elasticity of the flour dough. Storage or ageing with oxygen-rich chemicals makes the dough more resilient. Other chemicals can make the dough over-elastic or soft and sticky: this is seen in wholemeal flours which contain dough softening substances from the wheat germ.

(*c*) Warmth increases the elasticity of a dough and this is evident when a dough is hand-mixed; the heat of the hands provides the necessary warmth.

(*d*) Certain enzymes present in malt flour can make a dough soft. This is seen in the softer textured malt loaf, compared to the bolder textured white-flour loaf.

Causes of elasticity

The elastic property of flour dough is due to the *gluten* formed in all wheat flour doughs and, to a lesser extent in rye. There is *no* gluten in barley, maize and oats.

The elasticity of wool is due to *keratin*, while the elasticity of meat tendons and ligaments is due to *actin*, *myosin*, *reticulin*, *collagen* and *elastin*.

FOOD RHEOLOGY

Food can be chopped up, torn, pulled apart, ground, and sliced during the eating or mastication process, and in this way its *texture* is determined in the mouth as being, tough, sticky, crisp, creamy, rubbery, greasy and much more.

Food rheology is the science of measurement concerned with measuring those forces needed to *deform* food materials, or to study the *fluidity* of liquid foods.

Foods show properties of *elasticity*, already described, and show *viscosity* or the property of the liquid to resist relative motion within itself seen in batters, sauces, syrups, and can be measured using instruments called *viscometers*.

Adhesion or stickiness of foods is related to surface properties of such foods as toffees, or other foods which when chewed, stick to the teeth. The force of adhesion can be measured using instruments called *hesion balances*.

Compression is that pressure needed to squash foam or spongy foods such as bread, or cakes, to determine their tenderness or staleness. Various devices are used for this measurement under the title of *compressimeters*, or *tenderometers*.

Breaking strengths of dry foods such as biscuits, potato crisps, egg shells, and spaghetti, are found by various instruments which apply an increasing load until the sample breaks.

Shearing is the force needed to cut, or slice through the food, such as meat, fish, fruits and vegetables and give an indication of their toughness.

Penetrometers are instruments used to measure the force needed to push an object or penetrate through a food sample such as jelly, cooking fat, margarine, canned and fresh peas, and fruits.

Universal testing machines are available which can perform all the following tests on foods; shearing, compression, extrusion, extension, juice extraction, and penetration.

SUGGESTIONS FOR PRACTICAL WORK

In addition to the experiments described above, the following can be performed:

1. The tensile or breaking strength of baked bread and cakes can be found using the apparatus in Figure 3.4. Slices of bread measuring 50 × 100 mm are supported in strong clips and the weight required to tear the bread determined. Differences in tensile strength will be evident for fresh and stale bread. This method can also be used for dough.

2. Investigate the use of silicone release agents for baking tins and paper cake cups.

3. Stretch a piece of washed cotton material over a circular embroidery frame, treat one half with a silicone waterproofing agent, and allow to dry. Sprinkle droplets of water on the material and note the water-repelling properties of the treated portion.

4. Obtain a dry building brick and find its weight. Soak the brick in a bucket of water for a few days. Remove, dry off the excess water, and determine the weight of water absorbed by the porous brick.

5. See *Experimental Science for Catering and Homecraft Students*, Practical work 11.1, 11.3, 13.1, 18.2, 21.1, 26.3, 26.4, 41.1 to 41.5.

QUESTIONS ON CHAPTER 3

1. What is meant by surface tension? Give at least two examples of its effects.

2. Explain the term capillarity. Describe how capillarity damp in houses can be prevented.

3. Flour dough has elastic properties. Describe a simple experiment to show the elastic property of dough. What conditions affect the elastic nature of flour dough?

4. Define osmosis. Describe how the process occurs in a living plant cell. Give two applications of osmosis in cookery practice.

5. What are silicones? Give a brief survey of important uses of these compounds.

6. Write short notes on: (*a*) drip-dry garments; (*b*) absorption; (*c*) adsorption; and (*d*) window-ledge throats.

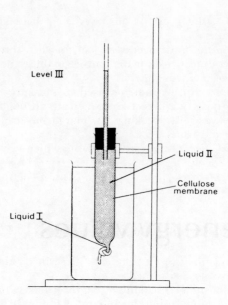

Level III

Liquid II

Cellulose membrane

Liquid I

Figure 3.5

MULTIPLE CHOICE QUESTIONS ON CHAPTER 3

1. Dried peas and powdered gelatine swell up and absorb water by the process of:
   (a) capillarity   (c) imbibition
   (b) syneresis   (d) dehydration

2. Jellies and bread if stored for long periods appear to 'sweat' out droplets of water. This process of water loss is called:
   (a) sublimation   (c) evaporation
   (b) syneresis   (d) hydrolysis

3. In the presence of water one of the following test reagents changes from a pink to a blue colour:
   (a) litmus paper
   (b) cobalt (II) chloride paper
   (c) anhydrous copper (II) sulphate
   (d) lead ethanoate (acetate) paper

4. A piece of rich fruit cake in a container is found to gain weight when exposed to air, whilst a piece of fresh bread in the same sealed container loses weight. The reason for this increase in weight of the cake is:
   (a) the eggs in the cake imbibe water
   (b) capillary rise between the cake crumbs
   (c) sugars in the cake are hygroscopic
   (d) the surface of the cake condenses water

5. Propanetriol (glycerine) is added to piping jelly and glazed cherries for the purpose of being a:
   (a) colouring   (c) humectant
   (b) emulsifier   (d) desiccant

Questions 6 to 9 refer to Figure 3.5 which shows a laboratory apparatus.

Liquid I does not give positive results with tests for any food nutrient.

Liquid II gives a white cloudy precipitate with silver (I) nitrate solution.

Liquid II is seen to rise up the capillary tube to level III, after the bag of liquid II is immersed in the beaker of liquid I.

6. What is the solution liquid II inside the cellulose material bag?
   (a) egg white   (c) aqueous sodium chloride
   (b) sucrose syrup   (d) distilled water

7. The special cellulose membrane of the bag which allows the passage of some substances but not others is said to be:
   (a) permeable   (c) porous
   (b) semi-permeable   (d) impermeable

8. Liquid I in the beaker is:
   (a) water   (c) egg white
   (b) sucrose syrup   (d) seawater

9. The movement of liquid I through the cellulose membrane into liquid II is a process called:
   (a) capillarity   (c) dehydration
   (b) osmosis   (d) transfusion

10. If lettuce leaves are limp they can be crisped by immersion in cold fresh water, the water enters the lettuce mainly by:
   (a) imbibition   (c) osmosis
   (b) hydration   (d) hygroscopic action

4 Heat, temperature, and energy values

Heat is the basic agent for all cooking processes. Scientists define heat as a form of *energy*, i.e. heat can be made to do *work*. For example, petrol burns in an engine which turns the wheels of the motor-car; so much heat is made by the motor-car engine that cold water is needed to cool it.

Energy is the capacity for doing work. This definition applies equally to the energy required by the human body.

Energy is of two kinds:

(a) *Potential energy* or stored energy, e.g. the energy which is stored in food or fuel.

(b) *Kinetic energy* or active energy in motion, e.g. the energy which is released from food during exercise and muscle movement.

Heat is only *one* form of energy. The main forms of energy are summarized in the following table:

FORMS OF ENERGY

Forms of energy	Uses
The sun is the primary source of energy for the earth	Gives energy to all living green plants; these are sources of energy for animals. Plant and animal remains give coal and petroleum
Heat energy	From fuels; drives engines. Food energy gives bodily warmth
Electrical energy	Gives heat, light, and power
Atomic energy	A source of heat
Light energy	Used by all green plants to make food
Chemical energy	From burning coal, petrol, matches; used to provide electrical mechanical, and light energy

EXPANSION

EXPANSION OF SOLIDS

1. Solids *expand* on heating and *contract* on cooling. This can be shown by the bar and gauge experiment. Before heating, the bar fits the gauge; after heating, the bar increases in size and no longer fits the gauge. A hot saucepan lid will not fit into a cold saucepan.

2. Invar metal hardly expands on heating. If a bimetal strip, made of strips of brass and Invar joined together, is heated, it curves owing to unequal expansion of the two metals; the brass expands more than the Invar (Figure 4.1).

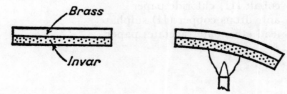

Figure 4.1. The bimetal strip

APPLICATIONS OF EXPANSION OF SOLIDS

1. Tight-fitting caps or stoppers on jars and bottles can be eased off by alternate heating under a stream of hot water to expand the cap followed by contraction under a stream of cold water. This method is not suitable for containers with volatile contents such as ethanol spirit.

2. When molten chocolate is poured into a mould, it contracts on cooling, and so is easily detached from the mould.

3. Bread which has been allowed to cool in the baking tin

is difficult to detach. If the tin is heated slightly it will expand more than the baked bread, thus allowing the bread to be removed from the warm tin; alternatively, silicone release agents can be used. (See page 16.)

4. After being placed aside to cool, bottling jars should have their screw-caps tightened to take up any slackness caused by the differing contraction of metal and glass on cooling.

5. The door and other metal parts on ovens usually have slight gaps between adjoining surfaces to allow for the expansion of the metal parts on the heating of the oven.

6. Fire alarms, fitted into the cabins and apartments of large ships and hotels, operate on the principle of a bimetal strip; the outbreak of fire causes the strip to bend and make electrical contact. This will either ring a warning bell or cause a light to appear on a central control board. Figure 4.2 shows this automatic fire alarm.

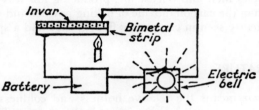

Figure 4.2 The automatic fire alarm

Thermostats

A *thermostat* is a device used to keep temperature steady; its main part is the bimetal strip (brass/Invar).

Experiment

To demonstrate the action of a thermostat (Figure 4.3):

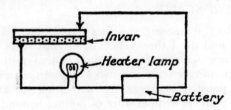

Figure 4.3. Thermostat experiment

A 12-volt lamp is connected to a suitable battery, and the bimetal strip made to touch the contact point. (Note the reverse arrangement of the strip to that of the fire alarm.) The heat produced by the lamp causes the bimetal strip to bend *away* from the contact and the lamp is switched off. The cooling of the strip causes the lamp to switch on again.

Some uses of thermostats are shown in the following table:

USES OF THERMOSTATS

Thermostat	Use
Room thermostat (Figure 4.4)	Controls room temperature and prevents wastage of gas or electricity
Oven thermostat (Figure 4.5)	Keeps the oven at a steady temperature, an essential for good cooking. The gas-oven thermostat consists of an Invar rod inside a brass tube; electric ovens have similar devices
Water heater thermostat	Fitted to gas and electric water heaters. It turns off the heating power when the water reaches the correct temperature
Automatic thermostatic mixing valve	Fitted to shower sprays to provide water at steady temperature, thus preventing sudden surges of scalding hot water
Simmerstat	On cookers it allows pans of cooking foods to simmer by means of the bimetal control
Appliance thermostats, fitted to kettles, pop-up toasters, electric irons, electric blankets, and numerous gas appliances	Fitted thermostats prevent overheating and subsequent burning-out of the heating unit
Central heating system thermostat	Fitted *outside* the building; as temperature outside falls the interior heating system is automatically turned on. Also fitted individually to radiators.

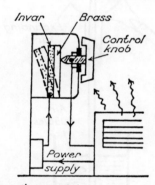

Figure 4.4. Room thermostat

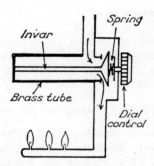

Figure 4.5. A gas-oven thermostat

EXPANSION OF FLUIDS

The expansion of liquids can be demonstrated using the apparatus in Figure 4.6. When the water bath is heated, the levels of the different liquids in the tubes are seen to rise. Different liquids expand by different amounts for the same rise in temperature.

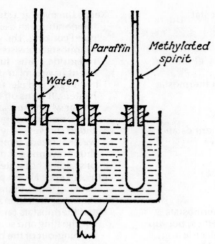

Figure 4.6. Expansion of liquids

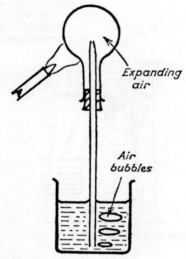

Figure 4.7. Expansion of air

The expansion of air can be demonstrated with the apparatus shown in Figure 4.7. When the flask is cooled, the contracting air draws in water to replace the air expelled by expansion.

APPLICATIONS OF EXPANSION OF FLUIDS

1. When gases or liquids expand, their volumes *increase*; their densities will therefore *decrease*, or, they can be said to become lighter. This explains why hot water can float on cold water, causing *stratification* in a hot-water storage tank. Similarly hot air will rise above cold air and this explains the movement of air currents.

2. Water contracts on cooling down to 4°C, then *expands* greatly down to 0°C, freezing to cause bursts in pipes, which are not evident until the ice thaws. This expansion can also be seen if ice trays or ice-lollipop moulds are filled to the brim with liquid and frozen, when the ice will be seen to project or hump up above the rim. Milk frozen in bottles

pushes out the foil cap, another good example of water expanding on freezing.

3. When fruits or vegetables are preserved, the hot liquids evaporate and the vapour drives out *air* from the container. Screw-caps or lids are placed firmly on the container, which is allowed to cool. The cooling causes contraction and the formation of an airless space or *vacuum* above the contents, hence the necessity of piercing the lid before removing to allow air to enter and relieve the vacuum.

4. *Leavening* agents are either air, steam, fat, or the gas carbon dioxide, all of which function on the principle of expansion on heating. Air can be beaten or blended into a mixture; gaseous carbon dioxide can be released from the mixture by chemical or yeast action; or particles of fat can be mixed into a pastry. Each ingredient expands on heating, causing the mixture to rise to varying extents. The fat particles melt and release air, producing less leavening action than the carbon dioxide of baking powder and yeast; this is clearly seen in comparing flaky pastry and a sponge cake.

TEMPERATURE

Temperature means the relative hotness and coldness of a body compared with melting ice or boiling water. *Thermometers* are used to record temperature.

The ordinary laboratory mercury-in-glass thermometer consists of a glass capillary tube with a bulb and graduated stem. The stem is divided into a number of degrees according to the thermometer scale. The principle on which a thermometer operates is that of the expansion of liquids as demonstrated in Figure 4.6.

TEMPERATURE SCALES

The two chief temperature scales are the Celsius (or Centigrade) and the Fahrenheit. The Celsius scale is now used to conform with the international system of units.

Each thermometer scale has two *fixed points*, namely the lower fixed point or temperature of melting ice and the upper fixed point or temperature of boiling water (Figure 4.8).

The *Celsius* or Centigrade scale is divided into 100 degrees, between 0°C, the lower fixed point, and 100°C, the upper fixed point. This temperature scale is the international scale.

The *Fahrenheit* scale is divided into 180 degrees, between 32°F, the temperature of melting ice, and 212°F, the temperature of boiling water. The Fahrenheit scale has now been displaced by the international Celsius scale.

Types of thermometer

1. *Laboratory thermometer*. This is an accurate mercury-in-glass thermometer available with Celsius or Fahrenheit scales; it is used by chemists, physicists, and other scientists.

2. *Room thermometer*. This is a thermometer mounted on a

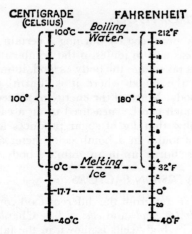

Figure 4.8. Temperature scales

wooden scale containing either mercury or red-coloured ethanol. Rooms should be kept at 18°–21°C for comfortable warmth. This temperature can be maintained by the room thermostat.

3. *Bimetal thermometers* are fitted with a bimetal coil (brass/Invar) whose movements are indicated by a pointer travelling over a thermometer scale. Oven and desk thermometers are usually of this type.

4. *Bath thermometers* are important for determining the correct temperature of bath water for children and elderly people (38°–43°C).

5. *The maximum and minimum thermometer* is used for recording the highest (maximum) and lowest (minimum) temperatures experienced during a certain period, for example in conservatories.

6. *Refrigeration thermometers.* Because of the low temperatures they record, they are filled with red-coloured ethanol. The thermometers are used in a variety of places, including ice-cream and cold stores, the range of temperature being −30° to −100°C.

7. *Confectionery or sugar-boiling thermometers* are mercury-in-glass thermometers with a range of 10° to 230°C.

8. *Dough-testing thermometers* are mercury-in-glass thermometers with a range of 10° to 43°C.

9. *Meat thermometers* are mercury-in-glass thermometers enclosed within a protective iron case with a sharp spiked point. Well-cooked meat has an internal temperature of 80°C, rare cooked meat reaches 65°C.

10. *Oven thermometers* are of the mercury-in-glass type and have a range of 10° to 370°C; suitable temperatures for baking meat, bread, etc., are marked on the brass scale.

MEASUREMENT OF HEAT ENERGY

Heat energy is measured in units called *joules* (J), using an instrument called a *calorimeter*.

Heat and temperature are *not* the same thing. This can be demonstrated by placing a beaker containing 100 cm³ of water over a Bunsen burner and placing another beaker containing twice the amount of water, i.e. 200 cm³, over

another Bunsen burner. The heating of water is started at the same time and the temperatures taken every 2 minutes. At the end of 5 minutes the temperature of the beaker containing 100 cm³ of water will be seen to be higher than that containing 200 cm³. Although both beakers have had the *same* amount of heat they are at *different* temperatures.

Calorimeters

If a small amount of sugar is placed in a porcelain dish and heated strongly, it will first melt, then catch fire. The experiment can be repeated using paraffin oil, cooking fat, etc.

The *bomb calorimeter* is an instrument used to measure the amount of heat energy produced by burning a substance. Similar instruments are available for measuring the heat produced by small animals or even human beings.

UNITS OF HEAT MEASUREMENT

(*a*) The *joule* (J) is the international unit for measuring the quantity of *heat energy*. One thousand joules are equal to one *kilojoule* (kJ), this is used for measurement of food energy values.

1 000 joules = one kilojoule (kJ)

A million joules are equal to one *megajoule* (MJ), this is used for daily energy need measurement, and for measuring the energy value of fuels

1 000 000 joules = one megajoule (MJ)

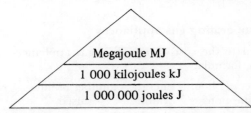

(*b*) The *therm* is a non-SI unit used mainly in gas energy value measurements and is mentioned on the gas bill. It is equal to 105·5 megajoules.

One therm = 105·5 megajoules (MJ)

How to read a gas meter

Read the four lower dials from left to right (Figures 8.3 and 8.13). Each dial hand should always be read as indicating the figure it has *last passed*, and not the one it is nearest to. If the hand is between two figures, write down the lower figure, with the exception of 0 and 9, when you should write down 9.

If the reading is 2525 add two noughts and the correct meter reading will now be 252 500 hundreds of cubic feet. Always read the meter from left to right and add the two noughts.

To determine the number of cubic feet of gas used subtract the first-meter reading, for say, 13 May from the second on 17 May:

Second reading, 17 May = 252 300
First reading, 13 May   = 242 000
Cubic feet consumed = 10 300

Calculation of gas bills

There are various *tariffs* used in charging for town gas and your local Gas Board will give details.

The cost of gas is partly dependent on the heating value or *energy value* of the gas for each cubic foot. The average energy value is 510 kilojoules per cubic foot; the correct figure is on the gas bill.

Cost of gas used =

$$\frac{\text{Number of cubic feet used} \times \text{energy value of gas} \times \text{cost per therm}}{100\ 000}$$

SI units in the gas industry

The energy value of gas will be in megajoules per cubic metre (MJ/m^3). The energy value of coal gas was $18\ MJ/m^3$ whilst the present North Sea or Natural gas has an energy value of $34\ MJ/m^3$, so town gas appliances have to be converted. Gas meters will probably record gas in cubic metres (m^3) or cubic decimetres (dm^3) instead of cubic feet.

$$1 \text{ cubic foot} = 0 \cdot 028 \text{ m}^3 = 28 \text{ dm}^3 = 28 \text{ litres}$$

Appliance ratings for input and output of heat will be in megajoules per hour, with the equivalent kilowatt value in brackets: MJ/h (kW).

Cost of operating gas appliances

To calculate the cost of operating gas appliances use the following formula:

$$\frac{\frac{\text{Cubic feet per hour}}{\text{consumption}} \times \frac{\text{energy}}{\text{value}} \times \frac{\text{number of hours}}{\text{used}} \times \frac{\text{rate per}}{\text{therm}}}{100\ 000}$$

Examples

1. A hall heater, consuming 15 ft^3/hr, is in continuous use for 24 hours. Calculate the cost of gas consumed at the rate of 15p per therm. (Energy value of the gas = 500 kJ/ft^3.)

$$\text{Cost} = \frac{15 \times 500 \times 24 \times 15}{100\ 000}$$

$$= \frac{2\ 700\ 000}{100\ 000} = 27\text{p} = \text{£0·27}$$

2. A small hotel kitchen has three cookers in continuous operation for 6 hours. Calculate the gas cost at 15p per therm if each cooker is rated at 80 ft^3/hr. (C.V. of the gas = 500 kJ/ft^3.)

$$\text{Cost} = \frac{3 \times 80 \times 500 \times 6 \times 15}{100\ 000}$$

$$= \frac{10\ 800\ 000}{100\ 000} = 108\text{p} = \text{£1·08}$$

ENERGY VALUE OF FOODS

The heat energy produced by burning a certain weight of sugar can be measured in joules in the bomb calorimeter.

When sugar is taken into the body as food, it finds its way ultimately into the blood where it is 'burnt' to supply energy for the body. Much of the energy produced is in the form of heat, which can be measured using a calorimeter. Experiments show that 1 g of sugar produces almost the same number of joules in a bomb calorimeter as when a gram of sugar is 'burnt' up in an animal's body.

ENERGY CONVERSION FACTORS

The amount of energy from the different food components, *proteins, carbohydrates, lipids* and *ethanol* (see Chapters 16, 17 and 18) for use by body cells is shown in the table below. The amount of energy obtainable from each food component is called an *energy conversion factor*.

ENERGY CONVERSION FACTORS

Food component	kJ/g
Protein	17
Carbohydrate	17
Lipid	37
Ethanol	29

Thus a lipid fat will have an energy conversion factor almost *twice* that of the energy available from an *equal weight* of pure carbohydrate or protein (see also Chapter 28).

Calculation of energy value of foods (see pages 186 and 221)

Dieticians, caterers, and school-meal organizers have to determine the energy value of a meal and this can be done by considering the energy values of each food item. These values are obtained from published tables, e.g. *The Composition of Foods* by A. A. Paul and D. A. T. Southgate, Medical Research Council Special Report (London, H.M.S.O.). The tables list the nutrient composition and energy values per 100 grams or per ounce of the food items. See also Appendix B.

From percentage composition or composition per 100 g

This is the usual method for finding the energy value of a food. The calculation of energy value when the percentage composition is known is as follows:

(*a*) Multiply the percentage protein and carbohydrate by 17, and multiply the percentage lipid by 37.

(*b*) Add the products, which will give kilojoules per 100 g. Then multiply the answer by 0·3 (i.e. $^{30}/_{100}$) to convert to kilojoules per 30 g portion.

For example, fresh eggs contain: protein 12·8 per cent, fat 11·5 per cent, carbohydrate 0·7 per cent, by weight.

Protein	12·8% × 17 = 210 kJ
Lipid fat	11·5% × 37 = 420 kJ
Carbohydrate	0·7% × 17 = 12 kJ
Total energy value per 30 g portion =	642 × 0·3 = 192 kJ

From gram composition per ounce

If the gram composition is known, calculate the energy value as follows:

(*a*) Multiply the protein and carbohydrate gram compositions by 17 and the lipid gram composition by 37 for kilojoule values.

(*b*) Add each individual energy value to obtain the total energy value of the food per ounce (kJ/oz).

Example

The composition of cheese per ounce is: protein 7 g, fat 9 g, carbohydrate 0·6 g.

Protein	7 g × 17 =	119 kJ
Lipid fat	9 g × 37 =	333 kJ
Carbohydrate	0·6 g × 17 =	10 kJ
Total energy value per 30 g or ounce		= 452 kJ

Energy value of a meal

By knowing the weight of food portions served and by reference to food-value tables, it is now possible to calculate the total energy or nutritive value of a meal. As an example, the popular meal of fried cod in batter (180 g), chipped potatoes (180 g), and bread and butter (45 g) has the following nutritive value:

Fried cod in batter

Protein	5·3 g × 17 =	90 kJ
Lipid fat	3·4 g × 37 =	126 kJ
Carbohydrate	1·4 g × 17 =	24 kJ
Total energy value per 30 g portion		= 240 kJ

A 180 g portion of fish = 240 kJ × 6 = 1 440 kJ

Chipped potatoes

Protein	1 g × 17 =	17 kJ
Lipid fat	7 g × 37 =	260 kJ
Carbohydrate	10 g × 17 =	170 kJ
Total energy value per 30 g portion		= 447 kJ

A 180 g portion of chips = 447 kJ × 6 = 2 682 kJ

Bread

Protein	2·3 g × 17 =	39 kJ
Lipid fat	0·2 × 37 =	7 kJ
Carbohydrate	15·6 g × 17 =	265 kJ
Total energy value per 30 g portion		= 311 kJ

A 30 g portion of bread = 311 × 1 = 311 kJ

Butter

Protein	0·1 g × 17 =	2 kJ
Lipid fat	23·4 g × 37 =	865 kJ
Total energy value per 30 g portion		= 867 kJ

A 15 g portion of butter = 867 × 0·5 = 433 kJ

Total energy value of the meal

180 g fried cod in batter	= 1 440 kJ
180 g chipped potatoes	= 2 682 kJ
30 g bread	= 311 kJ
15 g butter	= 433 kJ
Total energy value	= 4 866 kJ
	or 4·866 MJ

Later we shall see that the average daily energy requirement of a sedentary adult is 11·0 MJ (*see* Chapter 28); a meal of fried fish and chipped potatoes therefore goes a long way to providing this.

Specific heat capacity

If the *same weights* of different liquids, e.g. water, ethanol and a cooking oil, are heated in separate beakers in a warm bath at the same time and their temperatures measured every 2 minutes, it will be seen that the different liquids heat up or take in heat at *different* rates – yet they are all being heated by the same heat source. This difference is called the *specific heat capacity* and is the heat required to raise the temperature of a kilogram of the substance by one degree Celsius. The units of measurement are joules per kilogram per degree Celsius.

Differing specific heat capacity explains why copper utensils heat up quicker than aluminium and why milk boils quicker than water.

Foods with a high water content, such as vegetables, will have specific heat values almost the same as the water in which they are most often cooked. Foods with a low water content such as sugar, butter, margarine, and cooking oils, have much lower specific heat capacities and require less heat energy to heat them up compared to equal weights of water.

SPECIFIC HEAT CAPACITIES IN
JOULES PER KILOGRAM PER DEGREE
CENTIGRADE (J/kg/°C)

Brass	380
Copper	400
Iron	460
Aluminium	900
Sugar	1 130
Flour	2 100
Butter and cooking oils	2 100
Ethanol	2 400
Milk	3 780
Potato	3 800
Sodium chloride or sea water	3 900
Water	4 200

Since most foods are complex mixtures of different components, the rate at which they heat up during cooking will depend on their composition and water content.

SUGGESTIONS FOR PRACTICAL WORK

1. Using both a Celsius and a Fahrenheit thermometer, determine the temperatures of: a room; a cup of hot tea; cold water from a tap; the hottest water from a tap; the oven temperature at different heat settings. Make checks on the temperature of water used for dishwashing and in the cold room.

2. Obtain specimen gas bills and details of your local Gas Board's tariff charges. Find out what is meant by (a) flat-rate, (b) two-part, and (c) variable block tariffs.

3. Make a list of all the gas-operated appliances in your home, hotel, or college. Find out the hourly gas consumption rate for each appliance: this may be shown on the manufacturer's label attached to the appliance or details may be obtainable from your local Gas Board showrooms.

4. See *Experimental Science for Catering and Homecraft Students*, Experiments 35·2 and 35·3.

QUESTIONS ON CHAPTER 4

1. Give a brief account of the main sources of heat and the effect of heat during the cooking of food.

2. Explain the structure and function of a thermostat. Give examples of the use of thermostats in the catering trade.

3. Draw and describe how a gas-oven thermostat operates.

4. Give a brief account of the effect of heat on fluids, together with examples in cookery practice.

5. Describe a sugar-boiling or confectionary thermometer, an oven thermometer, and a meat thermometer. Give the approximate temperature ranges which are associated with these thermometers.

6. Explain the following: (a) kilojoule; (b) megajoule; and (c) therm. What instruments are used to measure heat?

7. A home has two gas convector heaters (35 ft^3/hr each) and a hall heater (15 ft^3/hr). Calculate the cost of gas used of energy value 55 kJ ft^3 if the heaters are in continuous use for 7 days. One therm of gas costs 15p.

8. A small hotel kitchen has the following gas appliances: storage water heater (20 ft^3/hr); oven (20 ft^3/hr); grill (30 ft^3/hr); fish fryer (100ft^3/hr). Calculate the gas costs if the appliances are used for 6 hr daily for a week. The calorific value of gas is 520 kJ/ft^3 and a therm of gas costs 12p.

9. Lobster has the following composition per ounce: protein 5·7 g; fat 1·1 g; carbohydrate 0·3 g. Lettuce has composition: protein 0·3 g; carbohydrate 0·5 g; and tomatoes: protein 0·3 g; carbohydrate 0·7 g. The portions served are lobster 170 g, lettuce 57 g, and tomato 57 g. Calculate the energy value of this salad dish in kilojoules.

10. Cow's milk has the following composition per ounce: 0·9 g protein; 1·0 g fat; 1·2 g carbohydrate. Calculate how many grams of cow's milk are required by a one-year old child to obtain a daily dietary allowance of 5·5 MJ.

11. Ice-cream has the following percentage composition: protein 2·9 per cent; fat 20 per cent; carbohydrate 4 per cent. Calculate the energy value of a 120-g portion in kilojoules.

MULTIPLE CHOICE QUESTIONS ON CHAPTER 4

1. One of the following is unable to provide energy for use by the body:
   (a) proteins   (c) minerals
   (b) carbohydrates   (d) lipids
2. One megajoule is a measure equal to:
   (a) 100 joule   (c) 100 000 joule
   (b) 1000 joule   (d) 1 000 000 joule
3. One gram of pure carbohydrate or protein provides the following amount of energy:
   (a) 4 kJ   (c) 17 kJ
   (b) 29 kJ   (d) 37 kJ
4. One hundred gram of lipid provides the following amount of energy:
   (a) 9 kJ   (c) 3·7 MJ
   (b) 37 kJ   (d) 1·7 MJ
5. The solid fuel used in a cooking stove with the highest energy content is:
   (a) wood   (c) coke
   (b) bituminous coal   (d) anthracite
6. A special canned evaporated milk has the following composition; protein 10 g, carbohydrate 10 g, lipid 10 g. Its total energy content will be:
   (a) 10 × 17 kJ   (c) 10 × 17 kJ
       10 × 17 kJ   10 × 38 kJ
       10 × 29 kJ   10 × 38 kJ
   (b) 10 × 17 kJ   (d) 10 × 17 kJ
       10 × 17 kJ   10 × 17 kJ
       10 × 38 kJ   10 × 17 kJ

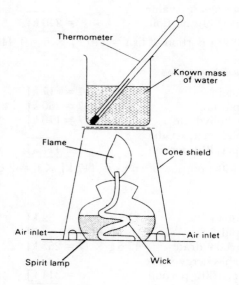

Thermometer

Known mass of water

Flame

Cone shield

Air inlet

Air inlet

Spirit lamp

Wick

Figure 4.9

7. The simple apparatus shown in Figure 4.9 is a calorimeter and can be used to find the energy value of one of the following:

(*a*) instant coffee   (*c*) whole eggs
(*b*) cooking oil   (*d*) golden syrup

8. One gram of pure food is burnt in air and the temperature of 200 g of water rises 20°C. The energy value of the food will be calculated as follows:

(*a*) $200 \times 20 \times 4 \cdot 2 = 16.8$ kJ/g
(*b*) $100 \times 20 \times 4 \cdot 2 = 8.4$ kJ/g
(*c*) $200 \times 10 \times 4 \cdot 2 = 8.4$ kJ/g
(*d*) $200 \times 40 \times 4 \cdot 2 = 33.6$ kJ/g

9. A one gram sample of a liquid was burnt in air and the temperature of 100 g of water rose by 7°C. The energy value

9. A one gram sample of a liquid was burnt in air and the temperature of 100 g of water rose by 7°C. The energy value of the liquid is calculated as follows:

(*a*) $100 \times 7 \times 4 \cdot 2 = 30$ kJ/g
(*b*) $200 \times 7 \times 4 \cdot 2 = 60$ kJ/g
(*c*) $\;\;50 \times 7 \times 4 \cdot 2 = 15$ kJ/g
(*d*) $150 \times 7 \times 4 \cdot 2 = 40$ kJ/g

10. The liquid burnt in Question 9 is possibly:

(*a*) egg white   (*c*) treacle
(*b*) peanut oil   (*d*) ethanol

5 Heat on the move

Heat may travel from one point to another by three methods (Figure 5.1): (*a*) conduction; (*b*) convection; and (*c*) radiation.

Conduction is the method by which heat travels from the heat source through the solid base of the pan to the handle of the saucepan.

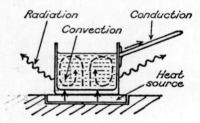

Figure 5.1. How heat travels

Convection is the method by which heat rises from the heat source and moves through the liquid in the pan.

Radiation is heat travelling as invisible rays straight out from the hot saucepan.

CONDUCTION

Conduction is the process of heat passing from molecule to molecule in solids and fluids without the molecules moving bodily.

When a frying pan is heated, the heat travels through the metal from molecule to molecule, until it reaches the inner surface and causes the fat to melt.

CONDUCTION IN SOLIDS

A simple experiment demonstrating conduction in solids uses a wooden disc with four different metals arranged on the radii. Small ball-bearings are attached to the outward ends of the metal strips with grease and the innermost ends of the metal are slowly heated with a Bunsen-burner flame. Heat is conducted along each metal strip and melts the grease, causing the ball-bearings to fall off. The order of falling is noted; this indicates the relative *conductivities* of the various materials.

The following table shows the order of conductivity of various substances, poor conductors of heat being called heat *insulators*;

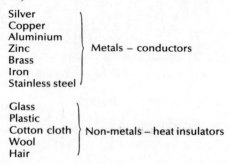

Silver
Copper
Aluminium
Zinc   Metals – conductors
Brass
Iron
Stainless steel

Glass
Plastic
Cotton cloth   Non-metals – heat insulators
Wool
Hair

CONDUCTION IN LIQUIDS

Conduction in liquids can be illustrated by filling a large boiling tube with cold water and inserting an ice-cube weighted with wire gauze. The top of the boiling tube is heated and the water is made to boil but the ice remains unaffected. This shows that water is a poor conductor of heat (Figure 5.2).

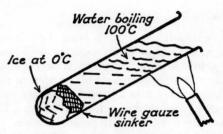

Figure 5.2. Experiment to show that water is a poor conductor

CONDUCTION IN GASES

Conduction in air or gases is difficult to demonstrate by simple methods. Air is a very bad conductor of heat, as is shown by the fact that although the temperature of a Bunsen-burner flame is 600°C, the air temperature 15 cm away from the flame is only 25°C. The heating of rooms and ovens does not depend on conduction for heat transfer but relies also on convection and radiation.

Experiment

To compare the heat insulation powers of different materials (Figure 5.3):

Fill a number of metal containers with different insulating materials, e.g. glass wool, hair, cotton wool, expanded mica, and commercial samples of insulating materials. Fit each container with a thermometer and stopper. Place the containers in the hot-water bath and record their temperatures after 30 minutes. The best insulator will show the least rise in temperature; the insulating powers of the other materials will be indicated by their rise in temperature.

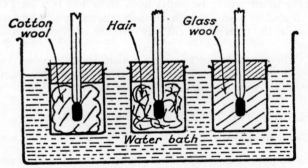

Figure 5.3. Experiment to compare insulation properties

APPLICATIONS OF CONDUCTION

1. Food preparation

(*a*) Cooking utensils, tea and coffee pots have handles made of poor conducting materials such as wood and plastics. The metals copper and aluminium are used in the construction of cooking utensils; copper has a greater heat capacity than aluminium, although the latter has the advantage of being less dense and easier to handle. The bottoms of pans used with electric boiling plates should have perfectly flat surfaces to make the most efficient contact with the plate.

(*b*) Cooking ovens and refrigerators have a basically similar construction: they are boxes which are insulated with fibre glass or metal foil, the insulation serving to *keep in* heat (ovens) or to *keep out* heat (refrigerators).

(*c*) Hay-box cooking, a means of energy saving, depends on heating a food preparation, e.g. stew, in the normal manner, and placing the heated food in a box packed with hay, straw or wood shavings; the packing causes the heat to be retained and allows the food to cook slowly over a period of hours.

(*d*) Oven ranges with solid-top boiling tables depend on conduction for pans on the hot metal top. Waffle irons and contact grills provide hot metal surfaces which heat the batter by conduction; food frying and sauteing are similarly processes of heating by conduction.

Certain foods, e.g. meat, are very poor conductors of heat and it is therefore necessary to give ample cooking time to allow the heat to penetrate the centre of the meat. A meat thermometer is of considerable value in indicating cooking progress, the internal temperature of cooked meat being between 60° and 85°C.

Bones in meat have a greater specific heat capacity than the flesh, so that the meat next to the bone is often better cooked; for this reason the bulb of the meat thermometer should not be touching the bone in a meat joint but should be inserted in the centre of the flesh. Cooking with water or steam is a quicker process than dry heat methods such as baking, since water and steam are better conductors than air.

2. Clothing and bedding

Clothing keeps the body warm by means of the heat-insulating *air* pockets between the clothing material threads and fibres. For this reason, loose-fitting string and cellular garments are warmer than tight-fitting clothing.

Bedding depends similarly for its warmth on the non-conducting layers of air trapped between the bedding materials. Eiderdowns filled with eider feathers, polyesters or kapok, together with honeycomb-weave woollen blankets, are warmer than the heavier, tightly woven wool blankets.

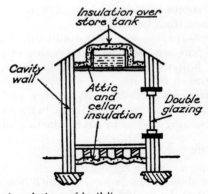

Figure 5.4. Insulation of buildings

3. Insulation of buildings

As will be seen from Figure 5.4:

(*a*) The outer walls of modern buildings are composed of a double layer of brickwork separated by an air-space, forming *cavity walls*. The air-space, being a good insulator, diminishes heat loss through the walls of the building. (See Figure 5.5 showing methods of heat loss.)

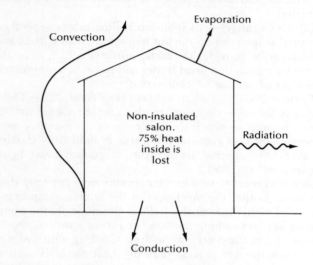

Figure 5.5. Heat losses

(*b*) Windows are often double glazed, having an air-space between two sheets of glass; the air-space provides an insulation layer in the same manner as the cavity wall. Double glazing is also a useful means of sound insulation to prevent entry of noise into hotel rooms from busy streets.

(*c*) Attic, loft, and cellar spaces can be insulated with material laid across ceiling and floor joists. This prevents heat loss through ceilings and floors. Insulation material should not be placed beneath the attic storage tank but over it.

(*d*) Hot- and cold-water tanks and pipes are usually insulated or *lagged* to prevent heat loss and to prevent the pipes and tanks freezing in winter-time.

4. Cooking

(*a*) Double-bottom cake tins have air-spaces to prevent the cake bottom from burning.

(*b*) Earthenware is a poor heat conductor, consequently earthenware pots are used for *slow* cooking of pot roasts, daubes, and hotpots. Metalware containers are used for *rapid* cooking as in roasting.

(*c*) Food coatings such as pastry, sauces, and batters of various thickness act as *insulators* of heat, in the same way as the air-filled meringue does in baked alaska pudding.

CONVECTION

Convection in fluids is the process in which heat travels by the movement of the heated molecules.

CONVECTION IN LIQUIDS

Convection currents in liquids can be demonstrated visually by mixing aluminium powder with water in a beaker and gently heating the contents over a small flame: the aluminium powder particles will be seen to move. The apparatus which resembles a model hot-water system, can be used to demonstrate convection in liquids. The upper container or cistern is filled with coloured water; the boiler flask and connecting tubes contain cold water. When the boiler flask is heated, the coloured cold water descends to the boiler flask while the hot water rises to the upper container.

CONVECTION IN GASES

Convection currents in air can be shown by the chimney apparatus (Figure 5.6).

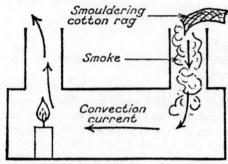

Figure 5.6. Convection in air

If the tissue wrapping paper from an orange is placed on a plate and lit with a match, the ash remaining will be seen to rise in the convection current produced by the burning paper.

Candle-lit table decorations which include revolving tinsel angels, stars, wheels, etc., depend on the rising convection currents from the burning candles.

APPLICATIONS OF CONVECTION CURRENTS

1. Food preparation

(*a*) Cooker ovens are heated by natural convection currents rising from the heater elements, the top part of the oven being hotter than the lower part. Similarly, refrigerators have convection currents of warm air rising towards the freezer unit and cold air descending (Figure 5.7). *Forced convection* is heat circulated by an electric fan.

(*b*) The following cooking methods all depend on convection for heat transfer: boiling, baking, roasting, steaming, and deep-fat frying. The dry-heat methods of roasting and baking depend on the circulation of heat by convection and to a lesser extent on conduction of heat from the pan into the food.

Boiling, steaming, and deep-fat frying depend entirely on convection; they are quicker methods of cooking owing to the greater heat capacity and conducting powers of the water, fat, and steam compared to air.

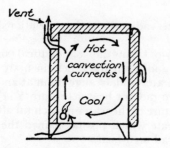

Figure 5.7. Natural convection in an oven

2. Hot-water systems

The *low-pressure* hot-water system (Figure 5.8) is typical of the type fitted in many residences and often includes an electric immersion heater built into the hot-water cylinder. Water from the attic storage tank supplies the hot-water cylinder. This tank is at a higher level in order to provide the necessary head of water pressure to supply the system. The immersion heater is fitted into the base of the cylinder, so that the heated water rises to the top of the cylinder, allowing cold water to be drawn in for heating.

The expansion or safety pipe is a safety outlet to allow steam to escape from the system either into the attic storage tank or directly through the roof into the air.

Heat radiators are often fitted as part of many hot-water systems.

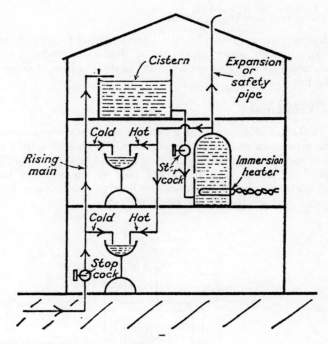

Figure 5.8. Hot-water system

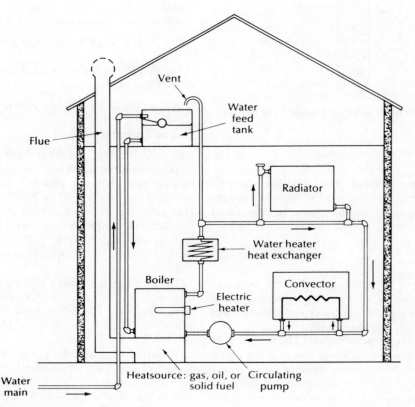

Figure 5.9. Central heating system

3. Central heating systems

Heated *water* or *air* can be circulated by water pumps or air fans, through water pipes or air ducts, to reach room heaters. Figure 5.9 shows a central heating system circulating hot *water*.

4. Ventilation

Ventilation of rooms using a heating appliance depends on the formation of convection currents. The warm stale air rises and flows out through the top part, while the cool fresh air flows in through the lower part of the window or ventilator. Figure 5.10 shows the balanced flue convector heater with its special exterior flue.

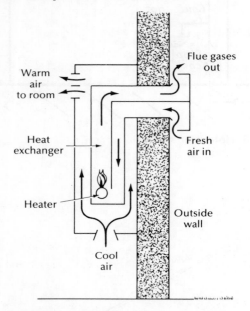

Figure 5.10. A balanced flue convector heater

5. Gas-burner flames

Gas-burner flames lose a good deal of heat through convection round the edges of the pan. If the gas burners are turned down just to touch the base pan, heat loss and fuel wastage will be reduced.

RADIATION

Radiation is the process by which heat travels from one point to another by means of waves or rays that can travel without the aid of molecules and therefore can pass through empty space or a vacuum (see page 74).

The sun gives out heat rays which travel 150 megametres (million kilometres) across empty space towards the earth. Heat rays are also given the scientific name of *infra-red rays*; any hot body which gives out heat also produces infra-red rays. A coal fire gives out heat or infra-red rays, and similarly the heater elements of a grill.

Experiments

To demonstrate radiation and its relationship to surface texture:

1. Obtain two clean tins of identical size, polish the surface of one and paint the other tin matt black. Fill the tins with cold water and arrange them at an equal distance from an electric radiant heater (Figure 5.11). Observe the rise in temperature of the water in each tin after 45 minutes. This will indicate which tin has gained the more heat by absorption of radiated heat.

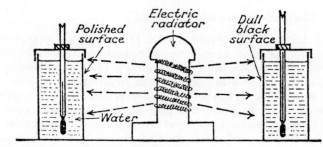

Figure 5.11. Radiation experiment

2. Fill a polished and a matt black tin with boiling water and fit each tin with a lid and thermometer. Take frequent temperature readings of each tin and allow them to cool for 1 hour. Determine which tin loses the more heat by radiation.

These two experiments show that:

(*a*) A dull black surface is a good radiator and absorber of heat.

(*b*) A polished surface is a poor absorber but a good reflector of heat.

APPLICATIONS OF RADIATION

1. Food preparation

Grilling, broiling, salamandering, and toasting are all cooking processes relying on radiant heat. Grill cookers consist of a heating element (either gas or electrically powered) supported by a highly-polished reflector plate. Gas grills have *radiants*, which are either of an incombustible fireclay composition or metal fret which becomes white hot on heating. Electric grills consist of heater elements backed by fireclay composition radiants or polished metal reflectors.

Infra-red cookers have electrically-heated wire elements enclosed in a tube of glass-like silica; the tube protects the wire elements. The silica itself cannot melt. The 'quartz-plate' cooker and ceramic top plate are further modifications.

Roasting spits may be gas or electrically heated. The gas flame impinges on incombustible radiants; the heat is also partly reflected from a polished metal surface on to the slowly rotating meat, which is turned by a small electric motor (Figure 5.12).

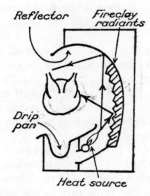

Figure 5.12. Roasting spit

2. Radiant heating

Radiant or reflector heaters operate by gas, oil, or electricity (Figure 5.13). The radiant heat is reflected from a polished reflector, whose clean smooth surface will determine the efficiency.

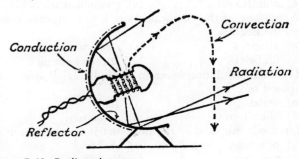

Figure 5.13. Radiant heater

Radiators and radiant panels give out 80 per cent of their heat by natural convection and are incorrectly called radiators. Their surfaces should have a rough, matt black finish to provide maximum radiant heat.

3. Polished metal surfaces

Highly-polished silver and plated tea pots, coffee pots, and hot-water jugs will keep their contents hotter for a longer time than unpolished containers. Dull, rough bases to saucepans and frying pans encourage the absorption of heat whereas their furbishing would lead to heat losses by reflection. Cooking utensils and kettles used over open coal fires were always allowed to remain black, on the outside, to improve their heat-absorbing property.

4. Vacuum containers

Vacuum containers are useful for keeping foods warm or cold, as the case may be. The container (Figure 5.14) is a double-walled glass vessel, the inner surfaces of which are silvered and from between which all air has been removed, leaving a vacuum space. The silvered surfaces reflect any radiant heat which attempts to enter or leave the container,

while the vacuum space prevents heat losses by conduction and convection. Plastic stoppers, being non-conductors, prevent heat loss from the mouth of the container.

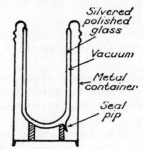

Figure 5.14. Vacuum flask

5. Solar heating

The sun's infra-red radiation can be absorbed by copper pipes carrying water, which are fixed against a dark black background, usually located on the rooftop. In this manner solar heat can help to heat the domestic hot-water system.

HEAT TRANSFER IN COOKING

Cooking method	Heat transfer process
Boiling and simmering	
Poaching	Convection
Steaming	
Stewing, braising and pot roasting	Conduction and convection
Shallow frying	Conduction
Deep frying	Convection
Grilling, toasting	Radiation
Roasting and baking	Convection – natural and forced

SUGGESTIONS FOR PRACTICAL WORK

1. An alternative method for comparing insulating powers of different materials is: Fill a large tin with insulating material. Embed a smaller tin in the insulating material and fill it with boiling water. Insert the thermometer and stopper immediately and allow the apparatus to cool. Take the temperature reading after 30 minutes, when the fall in temperature will indicate the heat loss through the insulating system.

2. Investigate the hot-water system of your home. Find out if the system is adequately insulated.

3. Set up a Bunsen burner between a strong source of light (e.g. a filmstrip projector) and a screen. The convection currents will be seen clearly projected on the screen when the burner is lit.

4. Determine the temperature of the following cooking processes: boiling; simmering; deep-fat frying; pressure cooking; steaming; and meat toasting (using a meat thermometer for the last).

5. Determine the temperatures in the upper and lower parts of a warm oven. Find the coldest and warmest parts of the refrigerator.

QUESTIONS ON CHAPTER 5

1. Draw a labelled diagram of a domestic hot-water system. Describe one other way in which convection currents are useful in the home.

2. Name the three methods of heat transfer and give one example in each case of their application to cooking or the home.

3. Describe how you would demonstrate the thermal conductivities of two different metals. Give a brief account of the use of non-conducting materials in establishment maintenance.

4. Describe a simple experiment to show the insulating properties of a non-conducting material. Give examples of the use of asbestos, glass wool, and expanded mica in a residence.

5. Name four different methods of cooking meat; describe how the heat is transferred to the meat from the heat source in each case.

6. Describe the structure of and the method of heat transfer in: an oven; radiant reflector fire; convector heater; infra-red heater; and refrigerator cabinet.

7. 'Space heating and building ventilation are complementary processes.' Discuss this statement and illustrate your answer with suitable diagrams.

8. Write short notes on: cavity walls; double glazing; loft and cellar-space insulation; and lagging.

9. Describe how scientific principles would guide you in your selection of bedding and curtaining materials.

MULTIPLE CHOICE QUESTIONS ON CHAPTER 5

1. Radiant heat transferred to food in grilling and toasting consists mainly of:
   (*a*) ultra violet rays   (*c*) infra-red rays
   (*b*) gamma rays   (*d*) radio waves

2. When a potato is cooked the heat passes from its skin into the interior by:
   (*a*) radiation   (*c*) forced convection
   (*b*) conduction   (*d*) natural convection

3. Hot water circulates within the piping of pumped central heating system by:
   (*a*) radiation   (*c*) forced convection
   (*b*) conduction   (*d*) natural convection

4. Which of the following cooking methods can produce the highest temperatures?
   (*a*) boiling   (*c*) stewing
   (*b*) roasting   (*d*) poaching

5. One hundred gram portions of the following foods are all heated together at the same rate in the same heating bath from 20°C. Which will be the last to reach a temperature of 60°C? Specific heat capacities are indicated.
   (*a*) sugar 1 130 J-Kg-°C   (*c*) butter 2 100 J-kg-°C
   (*b*) egg 3 200 J-kg-°C   (*d*) potato 3 800 J-kg-°C

6. Which cooking pan with a bottom made of one of the following metals heats more rapidly than the others:
   (*a*) copper   (*c*) tinned steel
   (*b*) aluminium   (*d*) enamelled iron

7. Which one of the components of a heat storage cooker stores the heat:
   (*a*) asbestos   (*c*) steel castings
   (*b*) firebricks   (*d*) vitreous enamel

8. The heat insulating layer in double glazed windows is composed of:
   (*a*) wood   (*c*) air
   (*b*) aluminium   (*d*) a vacuum

9. Lipid oils are used as the heat distributing medium in:
   (*a*) poaching   (*c*) sautéing
   (*b*) toasting   (*d*) braising

10. Which of the following devices maintains a steady temperature at a specific oven setting in a gas heated oven:
   (*a*) thermostat   (*c*) governor
   (*b*) pressure gauge (*d*) thermometer

6 Boiling, freezing, and damp

Substances can be classified into one of three physical states: solids, liquids, and gases.

Most substances can change their physical state by (*a*) adding heat to them or *heating*; (*b*) withdrawing heat from them or *cooling*. For example, water can exist as solid ice, liquid water or gaseous steam by heating or cooling.

The following diagram indicates the main changes of physical state and gives the names of the types of change:

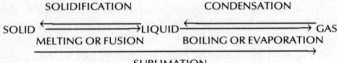

MELTING

Melting or *fusion* is the change from a solid to a liquid; it takes place at a definite temperature called the *melting point*.

The melting point of pure substances is always a constant value: it is lowered by adding other substances. For example, if two parts of crushed ice and one part sodium chloride are mixed, the ice melts and freezes again at 18° *below* the melting point of ice of 0°C. This lowering of the melting point of ice by means of sodium chloride is used in removing ice from roads and in making an ice-cream freezing mixture.

Experiment

To determine the melting point of lard, cooking fat, or butter:

Take a small beaker (100 cm³) and three-quarters fill it with lard; insert a thermometer supported by a clamp. Heat the lard over a small Bunsen-burner flame until it has completely melted. Note how the temperature rises and then remains steady for a period until all the lard has melted, after which the temperature begins to rise again. Turn off the Bunsen burner and allow the melted lard to cool. Take thermometer readings of the melted lard every minute until it has solidified.

The melting point of the lard can be obtained from your results by noting the temperature readings that remain stationary over a period of about 10 minutes.

APPLICATIONS OF MELTING

1. Pure food materials such as pure lard and sugar have sharp melting points: lard 36°–39°C and sugar 160°C. Certain unrefined fats, dripping, and butter have less distinct melting points, as the unrefined material consists of mixtures of different substances; similarly, toffee and other sugar confectionery have indistinct melting points, better described as *softening points*.

2. *Rendering* is the process of removing oil from lipid tissues; it involves heating fatty animal tissue by using dry heat, boiling water, or steam. The oil is liberated from the fat cells or *adipose* tissue, by the cells bursting under the influence of heat (Figure 6.1).

3. Automatic-sprinkler systems fitted in the ceilings of large hotels and buildings consist of water nozzles whose open ends are plugged with a low-melting-point metal alloy. If a fire breaks out, the rising heat causes the plugs to melt and so release water to extinguish the fire (Figure 6.2).

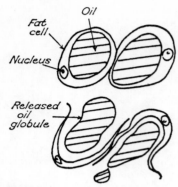

Figure 6.1. Fat cells bursting under influence of heat

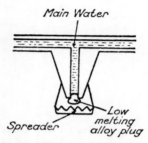

Figure 6.2. Sprinkler fire-extinguisher

LATENT HEAT OF MELTING

The first experiment in this chapter showed that when lard was heated its temperature rose, a visual indication that heat was entering the solid lard. At the melting point the temperature remained steady and no visual indication was given that heat was needed to bring about the change of state from solid to liquid. This invisible heat is described as *latent heat* of the heat required to change the state of a substance without raising its temperature.

If a lump of cooking fat is melted in a pan, the temperature of the fat will not rise until the last trace of solid fat has disappeared.

BOILING

Boiling is the change from a liquid to a gas. The change takes place throughout the *body* of the liquid at a definite temperature: the *boiling point*.

When a thermometer is inserted into a beaker of cold water and the water is heated, the temperature is seen to rise steadily until the water boils. Then the temperature remains steady, at the boiling point. The heat which is being used to change water into steam is the *latent heat*.

The boiling point of pure substances is always a constant value, but it can be altered by two factors:
(a) The presence of dissolved substances or impurities.
(b) The effect of air pressure.

BOILING POINT AND DISSOLVED SUBSTANCES

Prepare solutions of sodium chloride in water of the following percentages: 10, 20, and 30 per cent. Determine their boiling points using a laboratory thermometer. If calcium(II) chloride is used instead of sodium chloride much higher boiling points can be obtained.

The experiment shows that the boiling point of a pure liquid is increased by the presence of dissolved solids.

APPLICATIONS OF BOILING POINTS

1. Adding salt to foods which are being boiled will make the water boil above 100°C.
2. Calcium(II) chloride dissolved in water can raise the boiling point to 115°C, i.e. 15° above the normal boiling point of water. This high temperature is useful for sterilizing bottles and crockery.
3. The boiling points of sugar solutions are of importance in sugar cookery, where temperatures between 110° and 170°C are encountered in making fudge and toffee (see page 111).

BOILING POINT AND PRESSURE

The effect of pressure on the boiling point can be demonstrated as follows:

Lowering the pressure. Boil water in a round-bottomed flask, insert the rubber stopper and thermometer, then cool the flask under a cold-water spray. The cooling causes some steam to condense and the air pressure inside the flask becomes less. The water now boils again although the temperature is only 70°C.

Conclusion: When the air pressure is lowered, the boiling point of water is lowered.

To achieve a low air pressure above a boiling liquid, the air above can be removed by a suction or vacuum pump.

APPLICATIONS OF AIR PRESSURE AND BOILING POINTS

1. Air pressure is considerably less on a mountain summit, and consequently water will boil at a lower temperature; cooking in Alpine hotels therefore takes slightly longer than in the valley hotels.
2. Milk, when boiled in open pans, undergoes changes in its composition due to the high boiling point of milk. If milk is boiled in low-pressure vacuum evaporating pans, the boiling point will be lowered and there will be little change in its chemical composition. Condensed and evaporated milk are made in this way (see page 196).
3. Vacuum evaporation or low-pressure boiling is also used for concentrating meat extracts and fruit juices, and in sugar refining and jam making. An extension of the method is used for drying foods: dried potato, peas, and fruits are prepared by vacuum drying, for example. Powdered soluble coffee extract and dried milk powder are produced by methods which involve vacuum evaporation followed by spray drying (see page 135).

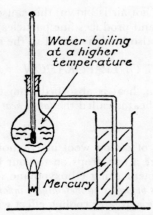

Figure 6.3. Water boiling under high pressure

Increasing the pressure. Water is boiled in a round-bottomed flask and the steam is led into the mercury container (Figure 6.3). The mercury imposes a high pressure on the boiling water and the water now boils at a temperature above 100°C.

Conclusion: Increased air pressure raises the boiling point of water.

APPLICATIONS OF BOILING UNDER PRESSURE

1. *Pressure cookers*, sterilizers, and autoclaves are all very similar instruments which can make water boil at a higher temperature than normal.

(*a*) Pressure cookers will cook foods much quicker. Pressure cooking can be completed in from one-fifth to one-third of the usual time for ordinary cooking; it therefore finds an application in industrial catering and the home.

(*b*) Sterilizers and autoclaves are used for destroying microbes present on dressings, instruments, and the dishes used for micro-biological work (*see* Chapter 26). A sterile material is completely free of all microbes. The structure of the pressure cooker or autoclave is shown in Figure 6.4.

(*c*) Lard-rendering from pork fat is performed on a large scale using large autoclaves at a temperature of 110°C.

Figure 6.4. Sterilizer or autoclave

2. Hot-water or steam boilers are of importance in large hotels and buildings: the hot water is used for central heating and toilet purposes and the steam for heating kitchen cooking-pans or for laundry.

The simplest boiler is the *vertical* type, exemplified by the kitchen low-pressure café set, which was described on page 14. Large buildings and hotels use *horizontal* boilers, the hot gas heating the water which is either carried through tubes or waterways. The water boils under high pressure at a temperature above 100°C.

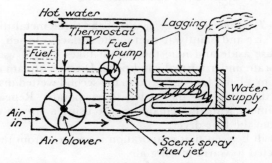

Figure 6.5. Thermostatically controlled boilers

Modern boilers are automatically stoked with gas, oil, electricity, or coal, and are controlled by a thermostat situated inside or outside the building (Figure 6.5). If the room thermostat gets too hot, the boiler radiator supply is turned down, whereas if the outside air temperature goes down, the radiator supply from the boiler will automatically be turned up. Similarly, the thermostat can control both the supply of heat to the boiler fire box and the fan which supplies the draught of air to feed the fossil fuel flames.

EVAPORATION

Evaporation is the change from a liquid to a gas; it takes place from the surface of the liquid at *any* temperature.

Volatile liquids evaporate readily, e.g. perfume, petrol, and dry-cleaning solvent. Non-volatile, fixed oils, evaporate with difficulty, e.g. cooking oil and liquid paraffin.

The following conditions are important in assisting evaporation: (*a*) a large surface area; (*b*) wind or moving air currents; (*c*) dry air or low humidity; and (*d*) high temperature.

Experiments

To illustrate the rate of evaporation under various conditions:

(*a*) *Surface area:* Take three beakers (250 cm³) and measure 100 cm³ of water into each. Cut two pieces of blotting paper of different sizes and place them in beakers as in Figure 6.6. Put the beakers aside for one week and note the water loss. The greatest water loss will be from the beaker having the piece of blotting paper of large surface area.

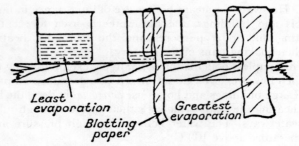

Figure 6.6. Evaporation and surface area

(*b*) *Temperature and moving air:* Take three metal discs of equal size and paint water on to the surfaces of each. Place one disc aside and note the time it takes for the water to evaporate under normal conditions. Direct a stream of *cold* air from a hand hair-dryer on to the second wetted disc and note the time for the water to evaporate. Repeat the experiment with the remaining disc using a stream of hot air from the hair-dryer.

It will be seen that evaporation is greatest from the disc subjected to warm moving air.

(*c*) *Air humidity:* Obtain two beakers containing the same amount of water and insert into them blotting paper strips of equal size. Place one beaker under a bell-jar and the other on the bench outside the bell-jar. After one week it is observed that the water loss is less under the bell-jar, as the moist humid air reduces the rate of evaporation.

APPLICATIONS OF EVAPORATION

1. Bread and cakes, if allowed to remain uncovered, will dry out, a process which contributes to *staling*; bread and confectionery should therefore be kept in covered tins or bins.

2. Saucepans are fitted with lids to prevent excessive evaporation of the liquid. Narrow, deep pans will lose less liquid by evaporation than broad, shallow frying-pans, which present a large surface area.

3. Clothes drying is a process that will proceed rapidly on a warm, breezy, dry day, provided the clothes are hung out to offer their maximum surface area.

4. Many household materials cleanse better by including volatile solvents. Window-cleaning preparations contain ethanol, metal polishes contain ammonium hydroxide, shoes and furniture waxes contain turpentine, or white spirit, and all of these evaporate easily, allowing furbishing with a dry cloth.

5. *Dehydration* of foods is a modern preservation process applied to milk, potatoes, eggs, vegetables, and dried fruits. The foods to be dehydrated travel down a long tunnel through which hot air circulates, so removing the moisture from the damp fruit or vegetables. (See page 135.)

Sun-dried fruits, raisins, currants, prunes, etc., are prepared using the more economical process of nature, and this is also applied to the drying of cereal grains, wheat, etc.

6. *Spray drying* is a method which involves spraying, for example, milk, down a large cone-shaped chamber up

which a current of hot air is blown; this causes the milk to evaporate rapidly and produces fine particles of dried milk powder. Eggs can also be dehydrated in the same way.

COOLING EFFECT OF EVAPORATION

During evaporation, heat is absorbed from the surroundings; this invisible heat is called the *latent heat of evaporation*.

Experiments

1. Soak a piece of cotton wool in ethanol (methylated spirits) and squeeze a few drops on to your bare forearm. Repeat the experiment using ethoxyethane (ether). *Extinguish all naked flames before using these highly inflammable liquids.* You will experience a greater cooling effect with ether than with the ethanol (methylated spirits).

2. Wrap pieces of cotton wool round the bulbs of three thermometers and soak each piece separately in water, ethanol, or ethoxyethane (ether). Support the thermometers near an open window and note the rapid fall in temperature due to evaporation of the different liquids. Observe also the formation of snow on the cotton wool which is soaked in ethoxyethane (ether); this substance is *highly flammable* and the vapour is *toxic*.

APPLICATIONS OF COOLING EFFECT

1. Sweating is the process in which the sweat glands of the skin produce a clear fluid; this evaporates and cools the skin surface. The body is thus cooled when over-heated by fever or strenuous activity.

2. Butter and milk can be kept cool in summer-time by wrapping a damp cloth round the bottle or food container: the cooling effect due to water evaporation keeps the food cool (Figure 6.7). Porous pot covers and containers are alternative methods for food cooling and for keeping ice-cubes.

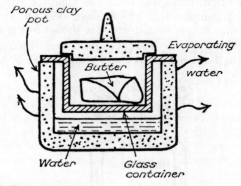

Figure 6.7. Butter cooler

REFRIGERATION

Refrigerators operate on the principle that when a liquid evaporates, it draws heat from its surroundings and produces the cooling effect previously described.

The liquids used in refrigerators are called *refrigerants*; they are mainly liquefied gases, i.e. gases which have been changed into a liquid state. Ammonia is normally a gas but it can be liquefied to form liquid ammonia; this must not be confused with ammonium hydroxide in water used for household purposes. The main refrigerants in current use are liquid ammonia, chloromethane (methyl chloride), Freon 12, and Arcton 6. (The last two are proprietary names for liquefied gases – or chloro-fluoro-ethanes.)

There are two main types of refrigerator: (*a*) the compressor type and (*b*) the absorption type.

Compressor refrigerator

1. Compressors (see Figure 6.8) are small electrically-driven pumps which compress or squeeze the Freon, Arcton, or dichlorotetrafluorethane into a liquid state. This change gives out heat, which is radiated and convected into the air outside the refrigerator cabinet.

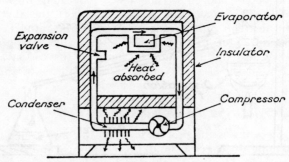

Figure 6.8. Compression refrigerator

2. The liquefied refrigerant is driven into an evaporator inside the refrigerator cabinet; the liquid now evaporates, drawing heat from inside the cabinet and producing the cold which causes the water in the ice trays to freeze to ice. Cabinet temperatures are 0° to 5°C.

3. The gaseous refrigerant now returns to the compressor pump to continue the refrigeration cycle.

Thermostats are fitted to refrigerators to turn the compressor motor on and off depending on the temperature within the refrigerator cabinet.

Absorption refrigerator

The refrigerant is liquid ammonia (see Figure 6.9).

1. A small boiler containing the ammonia dissolved in water is heated by a small gas flame or by an electric heating element. The *absorbed* heat causes the ammonia to pass as a gas to the condenser under high pressure.

2. In the condenser, the ammonia gas under pressure is cooled and changed into liquid ammonia; heat is given out into the air outside the cabinet.

3. Driven by the gas pressure, the liquid ammonia evaporates in the evaporator or freezer and in so doing draws heat from the contents of the refrigerator cabinet and freezes the water in the ice trays.

4. Finally, the ammonia gas is redissolved in the water and then passes to the boiler to continue the refrigeration cycle.

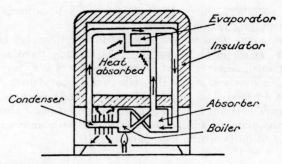

Figure 6.9. Absorption refrigerator

A thermostat is fitted in absorption refrigerators to control the boiler heater.

Domestic refrigerator frozen-food compartments

One-star rating stores food for one week at 6°C, two-star rating stores food up to one month at −12°C, whilst three-star rating stores up to three months at −18°C. Deep-freeze cabinets store at −18° to −20°C.

Other methods of refrigeration

(*a*) *Solid carbon dioxide* (proprietary name 'Cardice') is carbon dioxide gas which has been solidified. It is a white solid used for cold storage in small boxes or refrigerated vans.

It *sublimes* to produce a gas, *sublimation* being a physical change from a solid to a gas without melting, or the formation of a liquid taking place. No liquid therefore remains as a residue that would encourage microbe growth. Carbon dioxide also slows down the ripening process of fruits in store and also prevents multiplication of certain bacteria.

(*b*) *Liquids* such as 'Freons', the liquid used in refrigerators, will produce temperatures as low as −30°C, whilst liquid nitrogen produces much lower freezing temperatures of −196°C at its boiling point. Foods can be deep frozen by immersing them in the liquid 'Freons' or spraying them with liquid nitrogen.

(*c*) *Blast freezing* is a method of rapid deep freezing of either packed cooked or uncooked foods, which travels through a tunnel to meet a current of cold air at temperatures as low as −40°C. Many precooked foods can be deep frozen in this way and stored for use until required.

Food in the form of small particles, peas, and diced vegetables are frozen by the *fluidized bed* process a method which involves blowing very cold air through the perforated bottom of a trough, this causes the food particles to be supported by the air and prevents the particles of food coming together and freezing into a solid mass.

A *turbulent* bed freezer is a similar method to fluidized bed where a current of cold air passes through the food on a vibrating conveyer belt.

(*d*) *Contact freezing* is the method of placing packaged food such as fish between refrigerated plates, and stacking them together under pressure in special cabinets to complete the freezing process.

During the process of slow, ordinary freezing, large crystals of ice form *between* the cells causing them to be compressed, whereas quick freezing produces very tiny ice crystals *within* and *around* the cells that do not damage the cells of the food. Thawing of slow-frozen food will cause the cell juices to drain out of the food, making it lose valuable nutrients, flavour, and attractive colour; these are retained in thawed quick-frozen food (Figure 6.10).

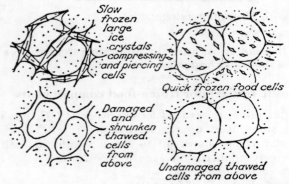

Figure 6.10. Formation of ice crystals in quick-frozen and slow-frozen food tissues

As ice crystals form outside the cells in slow freezing, the remaining liquid becomes concentrated in salts which draws water *out* of the cells by *osmosis* leaving waterless spaces *inside* the cells.

When certain starch thickened gravies, sauces, and puddings are frozen then thawed, they show 'weeping' and 'curdling', with a generally unattractive appearance. This is due partly to water being squeezed out of the gel, and the starch gel undergoing a change called *retrogradation*.

If certain modified or waxy starches are used, they do not show weeping or curdling and are said to have a greater *freeze–thaw stability* (see pages 110 and 134).

CONDENSATION

Condensation is the change from a gas or vapour to a liquid.

APPLICATIONS OF CONDENSATION

1. The appearance of damp patches on the cold outer walls of a building is caused by the condensation of the water vapour present in the air. Condensation damp is seen in kitchens, bathrooms, and laundry rooms.

2. Window condensation is caused by the condensation of atmospheric moisture on cold glass surfaces, causing 'steaming'. It can be overcome by double glazing or by fitting small tubular heaters along the window sill.

3. Over six times the amount of heat is needed to change water into vapour or steam, than is needed to raise the temperature of water at 0° to 100°C. This considerable amount of *latent heat of vaporization* of steam is returned to food in moist heat cookery methods such as steaming,

pressure cooking, or the steam oven baking method used for bread. When the steam vapour *condenses* on the food surface it gives up its heat of vaporization. Steam is liable to cause more serious scalds compared to hot water.

DISTILLATION

Distillation is a process of heating or boiling a liquid and condensing the vapour in a water-cooled condenser, the condensed liquid or *distillate* being collected in a receiver. Figure 6.11 shows the apparatus for simple distillation of water which can also be used as an example of the apparatus for distilling fermented liquids to produce gin, brandy, and whisky.

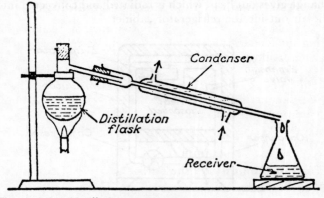

Figure 6.11. Distillation apparatus

Steam distillation is used for distilling perfumes and essences from flowers and herbs (see Figure 6.12).

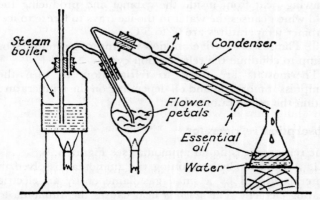

Figure 6.12. Steam distillation

Vacuum distillation is an important method of distilling liquids which decompose at their normal boiling points. Milk is evaporated or condensed by a method similar to vacuum distillation.

APPLICATIONS OF DISTILLATION

1. Whisky, brandy, and gin are produced by distillation under a Customs and Excise licence: it is illegal to distil ethanol or alcoholic liquors without this permit.

2. Coal heated in closed containers is dry-distilled to produce coal gas, coal tar, and *smokeless* fuels.

3. Petroleum is distilled to produce petrol and different grades of lubricating oils.

HUMIDITY

Humidity means the presence of water vapour in the air; it has entered the air from the following main sources:

1. Evaporation of water from rivers, lakes and seas.

2. Water produced by the respiration of plants and animals.

3. Water vapour produced by burning fossil fuels.

Sources of humidity in kitchens and buildings

1. Cooking processes, releasing water by evaporation from the food during baking; water is also released during frying, boiling, and steaming.

2. Frequent use of hot water for dishwashing and laundering.

3. Laundering processes, particularly during boiling, steam pressing, and ironing.

4. Respiration and perspiration of many people in a confined area.

Effect of humidity on the body

Excess humidity reduces the amount of oxygen in the air and prevents efficient evaporation of sweat from the skin. The total effect is to cause tiredness, headache, and bodily discomfort.

Hygroscopic properties of food materials

A *hygroscopic* substance is one that can draw water vapour into itself from the air. Chemical substances are hygroscopic, as can be demonstrated by placing a few pellets of sodium hydroxide (caustic soda) in a watch-glass and putting the specimen aside for a few days.

The hygroscopic nature of biscuits can be shown by weighing some dry biscuits, exposing them to the damp air for a period of days, and reweighing to determine the increase in weight due to absorbed water.

Sodium chloride is a hygroscopic substance, but if certain additives are used, it loses the hygroscopic property and becomes free-running; this is important when using in salt cellars.

Treacle toffee contains hygroscopic ingredients, which cause the toffee to turn to a sticky liquid on long exposure to air.

Anhydrous silica gel and calcium chloride are hygroscopic substances used as drying agents.

MEASUREMENT OF HUMIDITY

The humidity of the air is measured with a *hygrometer*. The hygrometer indicates the *relative humidity* of the air expressed as a percentage; the term means the ratio between the amount of water vapour that the air *could* hold and what it actually does hold at the same temperature:

Relative humidity

$$= \frac{\text{actual amount of water in the air}}{\text{maximum amount the air could hold at the same temperature}}$$

The hygrometer incorporates a strand of fifty degreased human hairs. When the air is humid, the hairs absorb water and increase in length. When the air is less humid or dry, the hairs lose water and become shorter. Wool and cotton fibres react in the same way. The movement of the hairs is transmitted to the pointer through the system of pulleys and the atmospheric humidity is directly indicated on a scale (Figure 6.13).

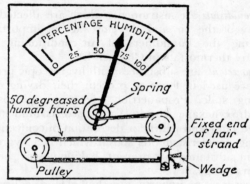

Figure 6.13. Interior of a hair hygrometer

Normal humidity is between 60 and 70 per cent and this amount is suitable for body comfort.

APPLICATIONS OF HUMIDITY

1. Textiles used in furnishings, bedding, and clothing (namely wool, cotton, and rayons) have natural hygroscopic properties. Wool and cotton clothing can absorb perspiration and feel warm next to the skin. Wool and cotton carpets, curtains, and furnishings, being made of hygroscopic materials, control the humidity of a room. This is evident in a lounge furnished in these materials compared to one furnished in non-hygroscopic plastic and artificial materials. The cool low-absorbent nature of man-made fibres is also evident in clothing made of these materials.

2. Ventilation, air conditioning, and heating are essentially complementary systems. A building can be well heated, but without good ventilation and air conditioning it can create an unpleasant, dry, heavy atmosphere causing bodily discomfort.

Air entering large buildings passes through the conditioning and heating systems as follows:

(*a*) Filters first remove airborne dust, smells, and some microbes.

(*b*) Heaters warm the air. In hot climates, refrigerators are substituted for heaters.

(*c*) Humidifier water sprays add moisture to the air.

(*d*) Large ventilating fans now drive the air through

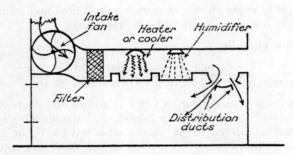

Figure 6.14. Air-conditioning system

tubes or ducts to reach individual rooms and halls (Figure 6.14).

3. *Humidistats* are instruments which are affected by the humidity of the air and therefore are of importance in controlling the humidifiers of air-conditioning plants. (Compare thermostats in Chapter 4.)

4. *Humectants* are substances with hygroscopic properties which are used in foods to prevent their drying out and becoming stale. Propanetriol (glycerine), glucose, and hexahydroxyhexane (sorbitol) are used as humectants in prepared jams and jellies for decoration of confectionery.

Baking powder contains starch which is a hygroscopic, desiccant substance that prevents baking powder becoming damp in storage.

5. *Steaming* is an important method of food cookery which is aimed at preserving food flavour, shape, and colour. Proving cabinets provide the humidity for proving yeast flour doughs in a warm moist atmosphere.

6. *Flour* is hygroscopic and should therefore be kept in a dry storage bin. During the milling of flour, the atmospheric humidity is controlled to prevent the clogging of milling machinery with damp, sticky flour.

DAMP

The four main causes of damp are; (*a*) rising damp, (*b*) condensation, (*c*) penetrating damp, (*d*) hygroscopic damp.

(*a*) *Rising damp* or capillary damp has been described on page 17, in relationship to capillarity. This form of damp is overcome by the insertion of an injected damp-proof course (D.P.C.), or the use of passive electro-osmosis described on page 47 for houses built without a D.P.C.

(*b*) *Condensation damp* is due to humid air in contact with cold surfaces and subsequent condensation of the liquid water. It can be prevented by improving ventilation, insulation of walls and windows, the provision of electric heaters or central heating heaters beneath windows. Paraffin and gas heaters which can operate without flues will both *add water* vapour as products of combustion.

(*c*) *Penetrating damp* is due to a defective structure in the building, such as the entry of water through cracks in the walls, missing roof tiles, blocked rainwater pipes and gutters, damaged window and door frames. Apart from repair, walls can be waterproofed by water repelling silicone paints (see page 16).

(*d*) *Hygroscopic damp* is due to certain hygroscopic salts present as impurities or contaminants of plaster, the salts attract water by their hygroscopic property to show damp patches which vary with the degree of air humidity. This can be overcome by removal of the affected plaster and replacement with new plaster and the use of silicone water repelling paints.

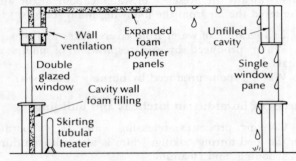

Figure 6.15. Condensation damp prevention

SUGGESTIONS FOR PRACTICAL WORK

1. Obtain some pork fat and render it using the dry-heat and hot-water methods.

2. Compare the rate of evaporation of steam from boiling water in an open saucepan and a covered saucepan. Weigh two identical pans containing the same amount of water and determine the loss in weight after a period of 15 minutes and 30 minutes. Repeat the experiment comparing evaporation rates from a shallow frying pan and covered saucepans.

3. Using a thermometer (mercury-in-glass) determine the coldest and warmest parts of the refrigerator cabinet.

4. Obtain some solid carbon dioxide but do not handle it with the fingers. Note how it sublimes in room temperature.

5. Prepare a freezing mixture from crushed ice and sodium chloride, and use it to prepare water ices or ice-cream.

6. Steam-distil some herbs, e.g. cloves, thyme, mint, or vanilla pods, in a litre flask, using the steam distillation apparatus described in this chapter (Figure 6.12).

7. Distil some milk using the vacuum distillation method described in this chapter. The flask should be surrounded by a hot-water bath: a naked Bunsen-burner flame should *not* be used to heat the flask.

8. Using a hair hygrometer, keep an hourly record of the humidity in a kitchen throughout a typical working day.

9. Leave dishes of known weight of the following substances exposed to the atmosphere of the laboratory for a period of days, then reweigh each item to determine any increase in weight: sugar, glucose, propanetriol (glycerine), mannitol, hexahydroxyhexane (sorbitol), flour, broken toffee or sugar confectionery, sodium hydrogen carbonate and dihyoxydroxybutanedioic acid (tartaric acid) mixture, starch, and powdered biscuits.

10. See *Experimental Science for Catering and Homecraft Students*, Practical work, 8.4, 11.4, 18.5, 21.5 and 23.4.

QUESTIONS ON CHAPTER 6

1. Explain the term melting. Describe how the melting point of lard and sugar can be determined. Why has toffee a lower melting point than pure sugar?

2. Define boiling. Give a brief account of how the boiling point of water is affected by (*a*) changing air pressure, and (*b*) the addition of dissolved salts. Show one example in each case of the application of these effects to cookery practice.

3. Describe a typical horizontal hot-water boiler as fitted in a building or hotel and construct a simple sketch showing the circulation system of hot water to wash-basins, baths, and radiators.

4. Define evaporation. What are the main factors which affect the rate of evaporation as it applies to laundry drying processes?

5. Give a brief illustrated account of the construction and method of operation of a gas-operated refrigerator.

6. Give a short account of: (*a*) vacuum drying; (*b*) quick freezing; and (*c*) slow freezing of foods.

7. What is meant by humidity? How is humidity measured? Give some applications of humidity and its effects in cookery processes.

8. What are humectants? Give an account of their uses.

9. Write short notes on: (*a*) ventilation; and (*b*) air conditioning.

10. Give reasons for the following statements:
(*a*) wool and cotton furnishings affect the air in a room;
(*b*) double glazing prevents condensation on windows;
(*c*) gas flames can indirectly produce ice.

MULTIPLE CHOICE QUESTIONS ON CHAPTER 6

1. Which of the following is most volatile liquid?
(*a*) water   (*c*) coconut oil
(*b*) brandy   (*d*) olive oil

2. Which of the following has a melting point of about 40°C?
(*a*) sodium chloride (salt)   (*c*) lard
(*b*) sugar   (*d*) starch

3. The heat required to change the state of a substance without raising its temperature is called:
(*a*) latent heat   (*c*) specific heat capacity
(*b*) conducted heat   (*d*) radiant heat

4. The change of state of a solid e.g. ice into a vapour or gaseous state without melting is called:
(*a*) evaporation   (*c*) condensation
(*b*) sublimation   (*d*) fusion

5. Which of the following causes water to boil at a temperature below 100°C?
(*a*) adding sugar to water
(*b*) adding salt to water
(*c*) boiling under high pressure, in pressure cooker
(*d*) boiling under reduced pressure, in vacuum evaporators

6. Heat is absorbed from warm food by one of the following components of an electric refrigerator:
(*a*) compressor   (*c*) condenser
(*b*) evaporator   (*d*) insulator

7. Perfumes and essential oils from herbs are extracted by:
(*a*) dry distillation   (*c*) filtration
(*b*) steam distillation   (*d*) sublimation

8. Which of the following components of the air can vary on a hot day?
(*a*) oxygen   (*c*) carbon dioxide
(*b*) nitrogen   (*d*) water

9. Hygroscopic dampness on walls in house rooms is caused by:
(*a*) capillary rise through porous plaster
(*b*) penetration of water through wall cracks
(*c*) chemical impurities in the plaster
(*d*) condensation of moisture on non-porous surface

10. Sublimation is an important process which occurs in:
(*a*) spray drying   (*c*) blast freezing
(*b*) freeze drying   (*d*) rendering

7 Electricity, circuits, and electrical terms

Electricity is a form of energy which can be used for heating, lighting, and power in industry and the home.

Matter is made up of tiny particles of electricity of two main kinds:

(*a*) Negative and very light *electrons*.
(*b*) Positive and heavier *protons*.

These particles join together in equal numbers to form neutral *atoms* (Figure 7.1).

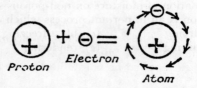

Figure 7.1. Electron and proton forming the hydrogen atom

When an electric *current* is flowing through a wire, it can be considered as a flow of very fast-moving electrons leaping from atom to atom in the wire (Figure 7.2).

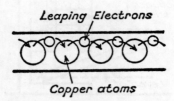

Figure 7.2. Electron flow or electric current

HOW ELECTRICITY IS MADE

(*a*) STATIC ELECTRICITY

Electrons can be removed from atoms by friction or rubbing.

Experiments

Tear up some tissue paper into tiny pieces. Rub a plastic comb or pen briskly along your sleeve, and hold it over the pieces of paper: they will leap up and cling to the plastic.

Obtain some polythene plastic sheet and smooth it out against a wall. Observe how the sheet of plastic will remain clinging to the wall.

When the plastic material is rubbed, electrons are drawn from the human body on to the plastic surface, which becomes *negatively* charged or rich in electrons. Similarly, the material that was rubbed has lost negative electrons and has become *positively* charged.

When the negatively charged pen or comb is held over the paper, there will be *attraction* of the paper towards the plastic material; similarly, the negatively charged polythene sheet will cling to the wall. Attraction takes place because unlike charges of electricity, positive and negative, are drawn towards each other in an attempt to neutralize one another.

APPLICATIONS

1. Dusting and polishing furniture surfaces will create charges of static electricity which in turn will attract dust and fluff particles. Silicone-containing polishes are important anti-static polishes.

2. Clothing and bedding become soiled by dirt and dust

particles attracted by the negative electrostatic charges which accumulate on the textile fibre surfaces by friction. Soiling is most noticeable on cuffs, collars, and hems or those parts of the garment subjected to the greatest friction or rubbing.

3. Many *fatal accidents*, especially to children, have been caused by plastic bags being drawn over the head; the bag clings to the face by electrostatic attraction and air pressure, causing suffocation.

4. Nylon, silk, and certain man-made textiles crackle and spark when removed from an ironing board after smoothing; the same effect is noticeable during undressing.

5. *Electro-osmosis* is a method of preventing rising damp due to electrostatic charges which attract damp. Continuous strips of copper are fixed into the wall and connected to rods in the earth drawing the charge away.

(b) ELECTRICITY FROM CHEMICAL CHANGES

A simple *electric cell* is made by dipping plates of copper and zinc into weak sulphuric acid. A torch bulb connected to the plates will light up, showing that an electric current is being produced. This is an example of electricity in motion: contrast the static electricity previously described.

The gradual extinction of the lamp shows that the current of electricity diminishes. This is caused by the accumulation of hydrogen bubbles on the copper plate, a process called *polarization* (Figure 7.3).

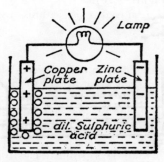

Figure 7.3. Simple electric cell

APPLICATIONS

1. *Dry batteries* (Figure 7.4) are modified forms of the simple electric cell. A rod of graphite carbon replaces the copper and a paste of ammonium chloride is used instead of sulphuric acid. Polarization is overcome by using a depolarizing mixture to remove the hydrogen bubbles; electricity is thus provided for a longer period. The case of the dry battery is made of zinc. These dry batteries give a convenient, compact, portable supply of electricity.

2. *Corrosion of metal.* Many establishments have a *zinc-coated* cistern tank connected to *copper* pipes. The water they carry is slightly acid and a current of electricity will flow between the copper piping and the zinc-coated cistern tank, which becomes paper thin by this *galvanic action.* The suspension of a bar of magnesium in the tank prevents the tank corroding, the bar becoming corroded instead.

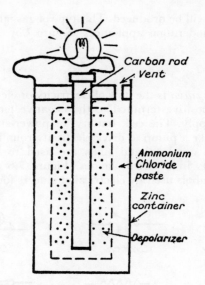

Figure 7.4. Dry battery

3. *Accumulators* are cells which can be filled or charged with electricity and then emptied or discharged when in use. Typical accumulators consist of a series of lead plates or grids, separated by sheets of wood or glass. The plates are immersed in battery acid, i.e. weak sulphuric acid.

Accumulators are a useful stand-by supply for emergency use in hotels, hospitals, and telephone exchanges.

(c) LARGE-SCALE GENERATION OF ELECTRICITY

The production of electricity from water, coal, oil, atomic energy, or wind in turbine generators will be considered in Chapter 10.

(d) QUARTZ-CRYSTAL SPARK GENERATOR

A charge of electricity can be produced by applying *pressure* to quartz crystals when sufficient electricity will be made to produce a spark which will light a gas appliance. On removing the applied pressure a further electric charge

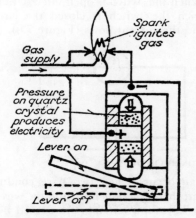

Figure 7.5. Crystal spark igniter

and spark will be produced. This type of gas igniter is fitted to many modern gas appliances (Figure 7.5).

CIRCUITS

An electric *circuit* is the flow of electricity or electric current from the positive terminal to the negative terminal of an electric supply. The cell, battery, or power-station generator acts like a pump to drive electricity round the circuit.

Symbols or shorthand signs are used to indicate the components in a circuit layout. Figure 7.6 shows some typical symbols used by electrical engineers for installation diagrams.

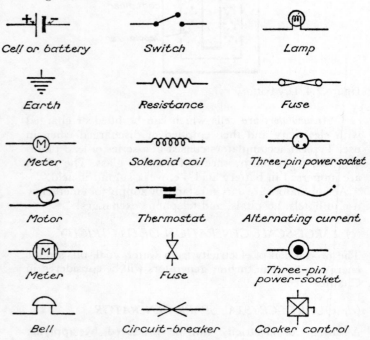

Figure 7.6. Electrical circuit symbols

A simple circuit, consisting of either a dry battery or low-voltage supply, a torch lamp, and a switch is shown in Figure 7.7. When the switch is open the circuit is said to be 'broken'. When the switch is closed the circuit is now 'complete' and the current flows (Figure 7.8).

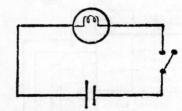

Figure 7.7. Broken circuit

A *short-circuit* occurs when two bare conducting wires touch together; there is a blue flash and the wires in contact burn (Figure 7.9). Short-circuits are caused by using old, frayed flexes or incorrectly connected flexes and plugs.

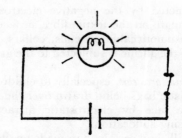

Figure 7.8. Complete circuit

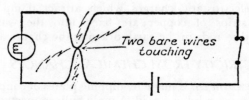

Figure 7.9. Short-circuit

Live and neutral wires

The domestic or hotel electric installation is supplied by a *feed*, *phase*, or *live* wire; there is also a *return* or *neutral* wire from the power-station generator. The live phase wire is covered with *brown* or *red* material and the neutral return with *blue* or *black* (Figure 7.10).

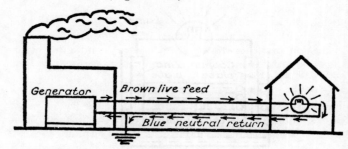

Figure 7.10. Live and neutral wire

CONDUCTORS AND INSULATORS

Construct a simple circuit as shown in Figure 7.11. Place different kinds of materials across the terminals and note which cause the lamp to light, i.e. which complete the circuit.

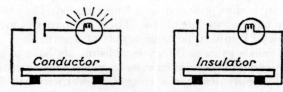

Figure 7.11. Conductor and insulator circuits

Conductors will allow electricity to pass and cause the lamp to light. Examples are copper, silver, iron, aluminium, brass, graphite carbon. Water, the human body, and soil conduct to a lesser extent.

Insulators do not allow electricity to pass through them. Examples are wood, rubber, plastics, porcelain, cotton, waxed paper, wool and air.

APPLICATIONS OF CONDUCTORS AND INSULATORS

1. *Switches* are inserted into the live wires of a circuit (Figure 7.12). The insulated plastic handle or *dolly* controls the on–off mechanism. Protection from electric shock is also afforded by the plastic cover, porcelain base, or cotton pull-cord. The conducting metal parts are of copper alloy or silver, the conducting wires being screwed into brass terminals.

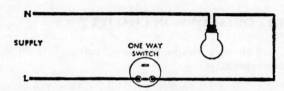

Figure 7.12. Circuit with switch in the live wire

2. *Cables and flexible cord insulation* consist mainly of plastic, rubber, cotton, or waxed paper wrapped round the stranded wire conductors; the latter are of pure copper wire coated with tin to prevent corrosion. The cable and flex insulation prevents the live and neutral conducting wires touching and causing a short-circuit; it also protects people from electric shock.

3. *Electrical appliances*, such as food mixers, have a plastic bodywork. Similarly, the handles of electric frying pans, kettles, and coffee percolators are made of plastics to protect the user from electric shock from a faulty appliance.

4. *Electric plugs and socket outlets* have plastic insulated bases and covers whereas the terminals and conducting pins are made of brass.

5. *Automatic thermostats* and time switches have silver contacts. This is because the frequent electric sparking would rapidly burn out the copper if it were used.

6. *Pull-cord ceiling switches* are safety devices for use in bathrooms, toilets, or in places such as kitchens where switches may be handled with wet hands or near to water or water pipes.

Electric shock

Electric shock can result in severe burns, shock, and – in extreme cases – death. It can be caused (*a*) by touching a bare live wire through a frayed flexible cord; (*b*) by handling electrical appliances which are live; (*c*) by handling appliances and fittings with wet hands. Everyone should make a special point of learning how to treat electric shock. It could help save a life.

MEASUREMENT OF ELECTRICITY

THE VOLT

The *volt* (abbreviated V) is the unit used in measuring electric *pressure*, it is measured by a *voltmeter*.

An electric mains supply or a battery act like a pump that drives the electricity round the circuit at a definite pressure or *voltage*. This can vary from the 1·5 V of a dry cell to the greater voltage of the house mains supply of 250 V, although smaller or larger voltages are known.

VOLTAGES OF VARIOUS ELECTRICAL SUPPLIES

Electricity supply	Voltage
Single dry cell	1·5
Bicycle or torch battery	3
Transistor radio batteries	3–9
Car-battery accumulator	12
Continental mains supply	110–120
Standard mains voltage for domestic use in Great Britain	240
Mains voltage for large hotel and institution kitchens and factories (i.e. small sub-stations)	400
Voltage in pylon cables	132 000

In Great Britain the domestic voltage supply varies from one part of the country to another and is between 210 and 250 V. It is therefore important to state the voltage of your supply when ordering new equipment. The voltage of an electrical installation is stamped on the name-plate of the electricity meter.

Continental and many foreign electrical appliances operate on 110–120 mains voltage and these appliances are destroyed if connected to the British 240-V supply.

THE AMPERE

The *ampere* is the unit of rate of *flow* of electric *current*; it is measured by an *ammeter*. Ampere is abbreviated to A or sometimes amp. A vacuum cleaner takes about 1 A whereas an electric cooker can take 30 A; this indicates that more electricity flows through a cooker than a vacuum cleaner.

The current or number of amperes flowing in an electric appliance governs the size and choice of:

(*a*) *Switches* are available in 2, 5, 15, and 30 A sizes.

(*b*) *Flex and cables* are available in 2, 5, 10, 15, and 30 A sizes.

(*c*) *Plug and socket outlets* are now available in one standard size consisting of square-pin plug tops fitted with individual fuses.

THE OHM

The *ohm* is the unit of *resistance*, the force which *opposes* electricity flowing through a conductor. The abbreviation for ohm is the Greek letter Ω (omega).

Conductors such as copper and brass offer little resistance to the flow of electricity. Non-conductors or *insulators*, like wood, rubber, and plastics, have a high resistance and prevent the flow of electricity.

Experiment

Using the circuit of Figure 7.7, connecting a small torch lamp, 1·5 V, to a torch cell or 1·5-V low-voltage supply, and it will burn brightly. Obtain a coil of thin Nichrome wire, which is wound on a bobbin, and connect it to the lamp and cell; the lamp hardly lights up, if at all. The long coil of thin Nichrome wire has a *high* resistance, whereas the ordinary thicker circuit connecting wires have a *low* resistance.

Conclusion: Long, thin wires have a high resistance, particularly those made of Nichrome wire. Thick conducting wires have a lower resistance, hence their use for carrying electricity in flexes, cables and overhead pylon cables.

APPLICATIONS OF RESISTANCE

1. Heater elements for cookers, room heaters, etc., are made of thin high-resistance Nichrome, a nickel-chromium alloy.

2. Control switches for increasing and decreasing the heat in cookers and room heaters, the volume in radio sets, or for dimming lights, are essentially long thin Nichrome wires whose effective length is increased or decreased, hence altering the flow of electric current.

SUGGESTIONS FOR PRACTICAL WORK

1. Compare the effect of using a dry duster for polishing a small article of furniture, e.g. a coffee table, with the polishing of an identical article using silicone-containing polishes.

2. Saw a dry battery in half (with a hacksaw). Draw and describe its appearance.

3. Obtain a contractor's building plan for the electrical services lay-out and note the symbols used.

4. Obtain a *one-way switch*, i.e. an ordinary on–off switch which controls one lamp, dismantle it, and note its conducting and insulating parts. *Two-way switches* are used to control lights in halls and passage-ways so that they can be switched on or off from either of two positions; a bed-head light can be similarly controlled by two two-way switches. Examine how two-way switches work.

5. Check the situation of all *pull-cord* switches in a large establishment.

6. Gather together a number of electrical appliances to see if the operating voltage and amperage are recorded on the makers' metal plates; these are usually fixed to the back of the appliance.

7. A visit to the electrical accessories counter of a chain store should prove of interest to see the range of plugs, sockets, switches, flexes, cables and lamp sizes available.

QUESTIONS ON CHAPTER 7

1. What is static electricity? Discuss its main effects in the home.

2. Describe how electricity can be produced by chemical action. State how this has an important effect in the corrosion of metals. What is done to overcome this corrosion?

3. Briefly outline the structure, use, and care of acid battery accumulators.

4. Give a list of electric appliances found in a well-equipped kitchen. Select one appliance and describe the insulators and conductors which enter into its make-up.

5. Explain the term voltage. Give a brief summary of voltages needed to operate different items of electrical equipment.

6. Explain the term ampere. Why is it important to know the amperage of an appliance?

7. A householder has taken delivery of a new washing machine which has no cable or flex connected to it. State what size flex, plug, and socket outlet he would need to purchase.

8. A young married couple received the following appliances: coffee percolator, radio, two-bar electric fire, and reading lamp. What size flex and plug should be connected to each of these items?

MULTIPLE QUESTIONS ON CHAPTER 7

Figure 7.13 shows a simple electric circuit connected to an appliance labelled 4.

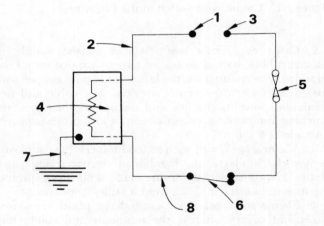

Figure 7.13

1. Which sequence of numbers shows the correct current flow to complete a circuit?
   (*a*) 1, 2, 8, 5, 3   (*c*) 1, 2, 7, 6, 3
   (*b*) 3, 5, 8, 2, 1   (*d*) 3, 5, 8, 4, 7
2. The terminal labelled 1 is called the:
   (*a*) neutral terminal   (*c*) phase terminal
   (*b*) live terminal   (*d*) feed terminal
3. The conductor labelled 2 will have an insulation which is coloured:
   (*a*) brown   (*c*) red
   (*b*) blue   (*d*) green
4. The weakest part of the circuit shown in the figure, which acts to serve as a safety device is labelled:
   (*a*) 4   (*c*) 6
   (*b*) 5   (*d*) 7

5. The part referred to in Question 4 is called the:
    (*a*) guard   (*c*) flex
    (*b*) fuse   (*d*) element

6. The part of the circuit shown in Figure 7.13 which offers the highest resistance to current flow is:
    (*a*) 3   (*c*) 5
    (*b*) 4   (*d*) 6

7. Which of the following *cannot* be located at the part labelled 5?
    (*a*) cartridge link   (*c*) miniature circuit breaker
    (*b*) rewirable fuse   (*d*) filament lamp

8. The colour of the insulation found on the conductor labelled part 7 in Figure 7.13 is:
    (*a*) red/black   (*c*) grey/green
    (*b*) brown/blue   (*d*) green/yellow

9. The name given to the conductor labelled 7 is:
    (*a*) earth   (*c*) neutral
    (*b*) aerial   (*d*) phase

10. The arrangement of items in Figure 7.13 is called:
    (*a*) an open circuit   (*c*) short circuit
    (*b*) an incomplete circuit (*d*) complete circuit

8   Electrical power and heat

Electrical power is measured in units called *watts*. A watt equals one *joule* per second. The power, or the rate at which an electric appliance delivers its *energy* in the form of heat or light, depends on the rate of flow of the current (*amperes*) and the electric pressure (*volts*). Current flow and electric pressure are related as follows:

$$\text{watts} = \text{amperes} \times \text{volts}$$

i.e.
$$\text{amperes} = \text{watts} \div \text{volts}$$

$$\text{volts} = \text{watts} \div \text{amperes}$$

The watt (W) is the smallest unit of electrical power. The *kilowatt* (kW) is the larger unit and is equal to 1 000 watts.

1 kilowatt = 1 000 watts = 3·6 megajoules/hour (see page 25)

A megawatt (MW), is a much larger unit, equal to 1 000 kW or 1 000 000 W.

LOADING OR WATTAGE

Loading and *wattage* are terms used to describe the *rating* or number of watts used by an electric appliance. Examples of different wattage values can be seen in electric lamps; for example, the 150-W filament lamp burns very brightly compared to a 5-W nursery night-light lamp. A one-bar (1 kW) electric fire gives out only half as much heat as a two-bar (2 kW) fire. Small wattage indicates that the appliance will use *little* electricity whereas high wattage indicates high consumption.

Experiment
To find the wattage of an electric appliance: a competent electrician will assemble the circuit shown in Figures 8.1 and 8.2. The appliance is plugged into the universal 13-A socket and the wall-socket switch turned on. The readings of the 10-A ammeter and 0–250-V voltmeter are noted. Switch off the current at the wall-socket switch and *then* remove the appliance. For additional safety, the appliance can be connected to a switched socket outlet.

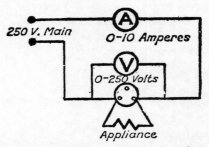

Figure 8.1. Circuit for finding wattage of appliance

Determine the amperage of a variety of appliances. The voltage pressure should remain the same for all determinations.

The wattage of the appliance can now be calculated from the formula:
$$\text{watts} = \text{amperes} \times \text{volts}.$$

Example
An electric kettle is connected to a 240-V mains supply and takes a current of 8·4 A. Calculate the loading of the kettle.

Since watts = volts × amperes and volts = 240, amperes = 8·4

Wattage of kettle = 240 × 8·4 = 2 kW or 7·2 MJ/hour

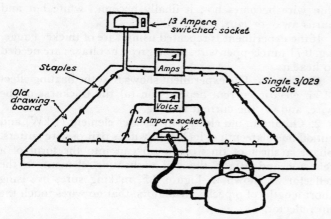

Figure 8.2. Experiment to determine wattage of an appliance

UNITS OF CONSUMPTION OF ELECTRICITY

The unit of consumption of electricity is the *kilowatt-hour* (kWh). It is also called the Board of Trade unit or simply the *unit* and is equal to 1 000 W of electricity flowing for 1 hour:

$$1 \text{ kWh or unit} = 1\ 000 \text{ W for 1 hour}$$

The heat energy (in joules) from an electric heater = watts multiplied by seconds. (1 hour = 3 600 seconds.)

Thus

$$1 \text{ kWh} = 1\ 000 \text{ W} \times 3\ 600 \text{ sec} = 3\ 600\ 000 \text{ J} = 3 \cdot 6 \text{ MJ}$$

To *calculate the number of units used by an appliance in one hour*:

$$\text{Units or kilowatt-hours consumed} = \frac{\text{wattage or loading}}{1\ 000}$$

Example

How many units or megajoules does a 12 000-W cooker use in 1 hour?

$$\text{Units} = \frac{\text{wattage}}{1\ 000} = \frac{12\ 000}{1\ 000} = 12 \text{ units (or } 43 \cdot 2 \text{ MJ/hour)}$$

ELECTRICITY METERS

The *electricity meter* records the number of *megajoules* or *kilowatt-hours* of electricity used. A domestic electrical installation usually has one meter, situated on the outside wall of modern houses, thus dispensing with the need for the meter-reader to enter the house. A large establishment may have a master meter with meters installed elsewhere in various departments.

HOW TO READ THE ELECTRICITY METER

1. The modern, easy-to-read, *cyclometer* electric meter resembles the milometer of a car: the figures are read off directly. This type is rapidly replacing the old fashioned four-dial meter.

2. For older type four-dial electric meters read the larger dials from left to right. Each dial hand should be read as indicating the figure it has *last* passed and not the one it is nearest to. If the hand is between two figures, write down the lower figure, with the exception of 0 and 9 when you should write down 9. See Figure 8.3.

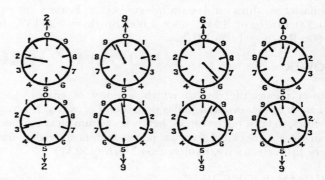

Figure 8.3. Meter reading

To find the number of units of electricity consumed subtract the first meter reading from the second meter reading. For example, if the reading on 1 May is 2 960 units and a later reading on 13 May is 2 999 units the total number of units used is:

Second reading (13 May)	2 999
First reading (1 May)	2 960
Units consumed	39

The meter can be a useful check on how much electricity a particular appliance is using. Turn off all electric appliances in the home and observe whether the disc on the meter has stopped rotating: this indicates that the electricity supply is at a standstill. Read the meter and turn on the appliance, connecting it to a power socket convenient to the meter. Allow the appliance to operate for a fixed length of time, e.g. 15, 30 or 60 minutes; take meter readings at these intervals and calculate the number of units the appliance uses in 1 hour.

COST OF ELECTRICITY

The cost of electricity varies from one part of the country to another. The individual tariffs or the methods of charging for electricity also vary from one regional electricity board to another and the board will give full details on request.

The approximate cost of operating an electric appliance can be calculated as follows:

$$\begin{array}{l}\text{Cost of operating} \\ \text{an appliance}\end{array} = \frac{\text{wattage}}{1\ 000} \times \begin{array}{l}\text{number of} \\ \text{hours used}\end{array} \times \begin{array}{l}\text{rate} \\ \text{per unit}\end{array}$$

HEAT RATE OUTPUT OF HEATING APPLIANCES

The heat output of electric, gas, or oil appliances is indicated in megajoules per hour with the kilowatt equivalent in brackets, allowing comparison of the performances of different appliances. For example a three bar electric fire has an output of 10·8 MJ/h (3 kW), as do a radiant gas fire and a large paraffin heater.

$$1 \text{ kW} = 3{\cdot}6 \text{ MJ/h} \qquad 2 \text{ kW} = 7{\cdot}2 \text{ MJ/h}$$

Heat outputs of gas and paraffin heaters were previously reckoned in British thermal units (Btu) per hour, large radiant gas fires and paraffin convector heaters giving 10 300 Btu/h, or 3 kW, since 1 000 Btu/h = 0·29 kW, or 1 000 Btu/h = 1·055 MJ/h.

POWER

Power means the rate at which a motor or engine does work. It is measured in joules per second or watts. Electric motors, in fans, refrigerators, heaters, vacuum cleaners, and hair-dryers are called *fractional* power motors since they use very little electricity, namely 0·54 MJ/h (150 W).

HUMAN BODY POWER

The human body needs *power* in order to stay alive and also in order to do *work*. Human body power is normally measured in megajoules per *day*. An adult male at complete rest, doing absolutely nothing but lie quietly in bed, needs 7 MJ or 2 kW per *day*. This power is used for the basic body functions of breathing, digestion and so on, and amounts to 80 watts per hour or the power used per hour by a *reading lamp* bulb. (See also Chapter 24, *Human body energy reserves*, page 186.)

HEATING EFFECT OF AN ELECTRIC CURRENT

The following experiments demonstrate the production of heat by an electric current and show the principles that govern the heating effect of an electric current.

Experiments
A competent electrician should assemble all demonstration circuits.

1. Prepare a thin piece of wire from a length of 1-A fuse wire. Attach it between two iron nails fixed to a wooden board as in Figure 8.4. Connect the board to a switch and a source of variable low-voltage supply. Adjust the voltage to 2 V and press the switch; repeat the experiment at 4, 6, 8, 10, and 12 V. As the voltage is increased, or stepped up, the

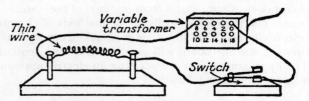

Figure 8.4. Experiment to show heating effect of an electric current

thin wire becomes hot; it finally becomes white hot and burns away or *fuses*.

If the experiment is repeated using wire of thicker gauge, e.g. 0·71 mm copper wire, much greater voltages are needed to heat it.

Conclusion: The experiment shows that the heating effect of an electric current depends on (*a*) the thickness of the wire, and (*b*) the current flowing.

2. Obtain an old electric-fire heater element (1 kW) and cut off one-sixteenth of its length with a pair of wire cutters. Shape a sheet of tin from a tin can into the form of a reflector and attach the coil of heating element to the reflector as shown in Figure 8.5, making sure, by using short lengths of pipeclay insulators, that no wires touch the tin reflector.

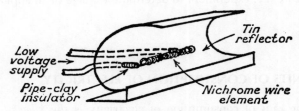

Figure 8.5. Miniature electric fire

Connect the miniature electric fire to a source of variable low-voltage supply and step up the voltage until the heater element wires glow bright red.

Conclusion: Electric-fire element wire is made of a nickel-chromium alloy called *Nichrome*, which has a very high resistance to the flow of electric current. This high resistance is responsible for the heating effect.

Summary:
The heating effect of an electric current depends on:
1. Resistance or resitivity of the conductor.
2. Thickness of the wire.
3. Voltage and amperage of the current.

APPLICATIONS OF THE HEATING EFFECT

1. Local or room heaters
Many room heaters have heating elements made up of high-resistance Nichrome wire, wrapped or embedded in such insulating materials as fireclay, magnesium oxide, or mica.

(*a*) Storage heaters use off-peak and cheap electricity supply. The heater elements are embedded in blocks of fireclay, which are good heat absorbers; the heat is retained in the fireclay blocks by the surrounding insulation of glass wool and the whole appliance is housed in an attractive metal or polished wooden case. In the daytime, heat is released by natural and forced convection through metal grills and by radiation (Figure 8.6).

(*b*) Electric floor warming is similar to the storage heater. The heating-element wires are laid in concrete, the heat rising from the floor by convection; cheap off-peak electricity is used to heat the concrete of high thermal capacity.

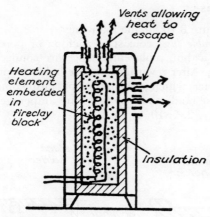

Figure 8.6. Storage heater

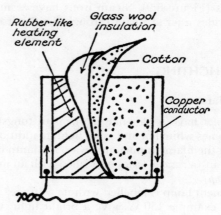

Figure 8.8. Flexible heating element

2. *Water heaters*

Water heaters are mainly of the immersion type, where the heater element is inserted into the hot-water storage tank. Immersion heaters consist of Nichrome wire element surrounded by magnesium oxide insulation and an outer copper sheath (Figure 8.7). A similar form of heater is used in an electric kettle.

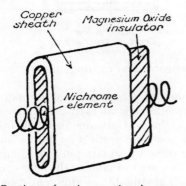

Figure 8.7. Portion of an immersion-heater element

Oil-filled radiators usually have a heater element of the immersion type fitted to the base of the appliance.

3. *Flexible electrical heating elements*

Flexible electrical heating elements are used for a variety of purposes, which include blankets, carpet underfelt, panel heaters, ceiling and even wallpaper heaters.

The elements are polyester coated with carbon-impregnated rubber which conducts electricity but because of its high resistance produces heat. The material is coated on glass cloth and electricity is led into the heating element through strips of copper foil or through wire sewn on to the material. In electric blankets the heating element is covered with insulating material, i.e. glass cloth and cotton (Figure 8.8).

4. *Cooking appliances*

Ovens are heated by tubular heaters similar in structure to the immersion-type heater, i.e. a Nichrome wire embedded in magnesium oxide and surrounded by a copper sheathing.

Radiant cooking rings are again coiled forms of the tubular oven heater with a highly-polished reflector backing plate.

Boiling or hot plates consist of a coil of Nichrome wire embedded in magnesium oxide and surrounded by an iron plate to provide heat by conduction, in contrast to radiant cooking rings which supply heat mainly by radiation.

Grills are either Nichrome wire elements fixed on fireclay supports and backed by a highly-polished reflector plate, or Nichrome wire elements within a silica tube backed by a polished reflector plate and called infra-red cookers. All radiant heaters give infra-red rays.

Rotisseries or roasting spits have either the open-type, fireclay-supported heating element or a silica-tube sheathed element, the radiated heat being reflected on to the rotating food from highly polished reflectors.

5. *Laundry appliances*

Wash boilers and washing machines contain a water-heating element similar to that of an electric kettle.

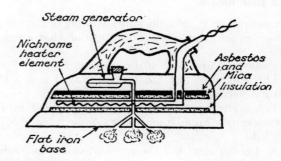

Figure 8.9. Electric-iron

Electric-iron heater elements consist of Nichrome wire sandwiched between two insulating sheets of mica; the heat is transferred to the flat iron base by conduction, a layer of asbestos preventing conduction of heat to the handle and upper parts (Figure 8.9). Steam irons have a small boiler which provides a jet of steam through the flat iron base.

ELECTRIC LIGHTING

Filament lamps

Filament lamps have a hair-like filament of tungsten metal which becomes white hot and gives light in addition to heat. To prevent the filament burning away, the lamp has all the air drawn out (a *vacuum lamp*) or is filled with an inert gas (a *gas-filled lamp*).

The filament lamp is labelled with its wattage; large watt values, for example 150 W, give a bright light, whereas a 60-W lamp gives a less brilliant light.

In addition to wattage, the operating voltage is marked on the lamp. This should be the same as the mains supply voltage indicated on your electricity meter. If the mains voltage is too much for a lamp the light it produces will be brighter than expected but its life will be reduced. Similarly, if the voltage is less than the stated value the lamp will provide a dimmer light but its life will be increased.

FUSES

A *fuse* is by design the *weakest* part of the electrical installation. If too much current is flowing through a circuit cable it may become very hot; if the cables are laid under wooden floorboards or near to wood the heat could start a fire. The fuse is therefore a safety device to protect the consumer from fire and from damage to electrical appliances.

A fuse consists of a thin piece of tinned copper wire supported in a non-conductor holder. The melting or *blowing* of fuse wire can be demonstrated using the same apparatus as in Figure 8.4.

Why a fuse blows

When an appliance suddenly stops working or the lights on one floor go out, this is a good indication that a fuse has blown.

The following are some of the reasons:

1. The appliance flex has become frayed and a short-circuit has occurred.

2. Too many appliances have been plugged into one power socket via an adaptor. See example 2, page 57, and Figure 8.12.

3. A light point has been overloaded by running appliances other than lamps from a lamp-holder socket. This is a very dangerous practice.

4. A faulty appliance with stray conducting wires has short-circuited.

5. There is an old, corroded fuse wire in the fuse holder. The tin coating serves to prevent corrosion.

Types of fuse

Refer to Figure 8.10 for the following:

(*a*) *Rewireable fuses* consist of a china or porcelain fuse holder with a thin, replaceable fuse wire connected to the brass screws. After rewiring, the fuse holder is pushed into the fuse carrier, which is the basic part of the domestic fuse box. The fuse holder has the fuse-wire amperage indicated on it, namely, 2, 5, 10, or 15 A.

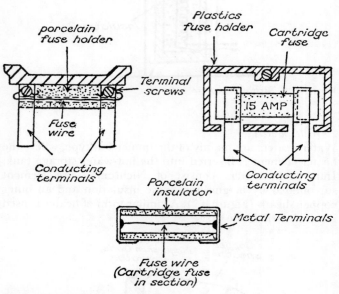

Figure 8.10. Rewireable and cartridge fuses

(*b*) *Cartridge* or *link fuses* consist of a small cylinder of porcelain with metal caps at each end and with the fuse wire inside the cylinder. Cartridge fuses are fitted into the fuse holders of some domestic fuse boxes and they are always found in standard square-pin fused plugs and fused wall switches. They are available in the following sizes: 2, 5, 10, 15, and 30 A, identifiable by different colours. Once a cartridge fuse blows, it must be discarded and replaced by a new one.

Fuse sizes are measured in amperes and fuse wire can be purchased for 2, 5, 10, 15, and 30 A. The domestic fuse box can conveniently have a small card of fuse wire attached to it.

How to calculate fuse size

It is important to be able to calculate the right size of fuse to fit either a standard fused plug or a fuse box. Replacing a fuse with one having a higher rating than normal can lead to fires and to electric shocks.

The following formula is used to calculate fuse rating:

Since   Watts = amperes × volts

Therefore $\text{Amperes} = \dfrac{\text{watts}}{\text{volts}}$

Assuming that the mains voltage is 250, then

$$\text{Fuse size} = \frac{\text{wattage of appliance or circuit}}{250}$$

Examples

1. Calculate the fuse rating for a 6-kW electric cooker operating from a 250-V main supply.

$$\text{Fuse size} = \text{wattage} \div 250$$
$$\text{Wattage of cooker} = 6\ 000$$

Therefore $\text{Fuse rating} = \dfrac{6\ 000}{250} = 24\ \text{A}$

A large cooker of this type would be fitted with a 30-A fuse switch.

2. The following appliances are connected to a 13-A standard fused plug: electric kettle, 1 kW; electric fire, 2 kW; and coffee percolator, 750 W. What happens when all appliances are in operation together?

$$\text{Total wattage} = 3\ 750\ \text{W}$$

Therefore $\text{Fuse size} = \dfrac{3\ 750}{250} = 15\ \text{A}$

The total current is 15 A, i.e. 2 A greater than the fitted cartridge fuse, and therefore the fuse will blow.

3. A portable 2-kW electric fire requires a cartridge fuse. Calculate the correct size.

$$\text{Fuse size} = \frac{2\ 000}{250} = 8\ \text{A}$$

Since 8-A cartridge fuses are not available, a 10-A fuse should be fitted.

How to replace a fuse

1. Switch off the main supply at the consumer's fuse unit.
2. Remove the fuses from the fuse carrier and examine each one in turn.

If the fuse wire has *parted* in the middle, the power point is over-loaded and fewer appliances should be connected or the correct cartridge fuse fitted to the plug. If the fuse wire has *burnt away*, this is caused by a short-circuit and the appliance or its flex is faulty or frayed; therefore, repair the appliance or replace the flex. Cartridge fuses do not show any visible signs of blowing and they must be tested using the torch battery and lamp circuit shown in Figure 8.11.

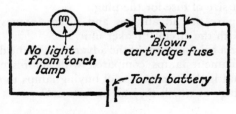

Figure 8.11. Testing a blown fuse

3. For rewireable fuse holders replace with fuse wire of the amperage indicated on the fuse holder. Wrap the fuse wire clockwise under the brass screw-head and screw up

tightly. If cartridge fuses are required, see that one of the correct amperage is inserted in the carrier.

4. Replace the fuse in the fuse carrier and turn on the main switch. If the fuse blows again, remove the faulty appliance and have it repaired.

Note. Occasionally there is a *general power* failure and this will be experienced by your neighbours. If your establishment is the only one affected, the *main fuse* belonging to the electricity board has blown; only the board can repair this.

CIRCUIT-BREAKERS

Modern circuit-breakers are rapidly replacing the fuse unit because of their simplicity and safety. The circuit-breaker unit resembles a row of switches each labelled with circuit amperage. If a circuit or appliance is faulty, the circuit-breaker switch turns *itself* off: the faulty circuit will be shown by the switch in the *off* position. The circuit is now restored by turning the switch to the *on* position.

TIME SWITCHES

Time switches are clockwork-operated switches which turn a circuit on or off at a pre-set time. They are fitted into cooker, heater, lighting, and water-heater circuits, and are particularly useful in the home or in a large establishment for the economic control of electricity.

FLEXES AND CABLES

Flex is a flexible electric wiring for connecting to electric appliances and is made up of three conductors covered with coloured insulation, *brown* for live, *blue* for neutral, and *yellow and green* for the earth. The three conductors are wrapped together in a plastic, rubber, or a braided cotton sheath.

Two core flexes with brown and blue coloured conductors are *without* an earth conductor and are only for use for connecting to certain well insulated appliances.

Cable is also three cored but has thick strands of conductors used by electricians for wiring the house circuits up to the socket outlets. They are frequently carried in conduits or hidden below the floor boards. See Figure 8.12 for explanation of cable overloading leading to fire.

Selecting flex

Flexes are available in several sizes depending on the amount of current used by the electric appliance. Thin flexes will only stand a small amperage, whilst thicker flexes will take a greater amperage. The correct size of flex is calculated in the same way as the appliance fuse:

$$\text{Flex size} = \text{Appliance wattage} \div 250$$

The flex sizes available are 3, 6, 10, 15, and 20 amperes. For example a 2 kW electric fire requires the following three core flex:

$\text{Flex size} = 2\ 000 \div 250 = 8$, or 10 ampere being the nearest suitable size.

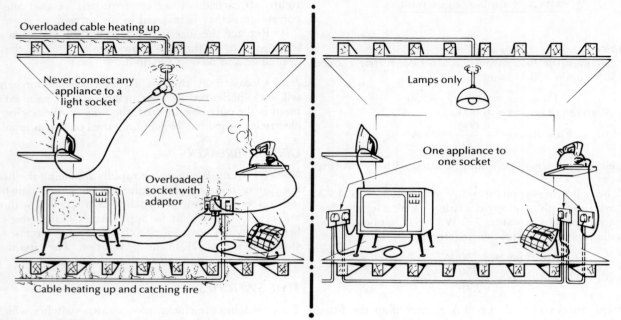

Figure 8.12. Overloading causes fire

SUGGESTIONS FOR PRACTICAL WORK

1. Locate the position of your main fuse box or circuit-breaker unit. Note the electricity board's fuse box with a metal seal, immediately below the meter. You must not interfere with either the meter or the board's fuse box.

2. Check all the cartridge fuses in the appliance plugs in your home and see how many are fitted with 13-A fuses where 2 or 5 A should be fitted.

3. Obtain some old fuse boxes and practise rewiring the fuses.

4. Examine different electric appliances, reading their wattage ratings from the manufacturers' labels. Obtain catalogues and descriptive literature and note how many refer to the watt rating of the electrical appliances.

5. If your kitchens have a separate electricity meter, make a note of the reading before work starts for the day and take the reading again before close-down. Make a rough calculation of electrical cost at 5p per unit.

QUESTIONS ON CHAPTER 8

1. Explain in a few words the meaning of: (*a*) ampere; (*b*) voltage; (*c*) wattage; (*d*) kilowatt; and (*e*) kilowatt-hour.

2. Explain what is meant by watt rating or loading of an electric appliance and outline how it can be measured. Give the watt rating of two heating, two laundry, and one cooking appliance.

3. Draw the four dials of an electric meter which reads 9 762 kWh. Outline how a knowledge of reading the meter can be of value to the consumer.

4. Find out the types of tariff which are in operation in your electricity board area.

Calculate the cost of electricity for the following appliances for the times stated, if electricity costs 1p per unit:

A cooker, 6 kW	6 hr
Washing machine, 3 kW	2 hr
Water heater, 3 kW	4 hr

5. Describe an experiment to show that an electric current can produce a heating effect. What factors are of importance in producing heat from an electric current?
   Draw a simple sketch to show how an electric-kettle heater element operates.

6. Give a brief review of electrical appliances used for room heating. Describe briefly their method of heat production and how the heat is transferred.

7. Describe how you would determine the watt rating of an electric kettle which has no manufacturer's label.

8. What are fuses? What are the main causes of fuses blowing? A 2-kW electric fire is connected to a standard fused plug for operation on 240-V main supply: calculate the correct size of fuse for the plug.

9. Compare the advantages and disadvantages of the fuse box with the circuit-breaker unit.

10. Give a brief account of the advantages of the different types of filament lamps compared with fluorescent-tube lights. What is the importance of buying lamps to suit the mains voltage at which they are to be used?

MULTIPLE CHOICE QUESTIONS ON CHAPTER 8

1. All of the following items are in continual use for one hour: a 1 kilowatt electric fire, 3 kilowatt washing machine,

Figure 8.13

500 watt hairdryer and a 1·5 kilowatt ironing machine. How many units of electricity will be used in 1 hour:

(a) $4\frac{3}{4}$ units   (c) 6 units

(b) 5 units   (d) 10·5 units

Figure 8.13 shows the reading of clock face dials in an electric meter.

2. The reading on the meter shown in Figure 8.13 is:

(a) 8 4 2 7   (c) 9 4 2 7

(b) 9 5 3 7   (d) 8 5 2 7

3. Which appliance in continual use for 1 hour consumes the greatest amount of electricity:

(a) television set   (c) two bar electric fire

(b) hairdryer   (d) electric blanket

4. The label on a washing machine reads: 240 v, 3kW, 50 Hz, 13 amp. How many units of electricity will it use in 1 hour:

(a) 3   (c) 50

(b) 13   (d) 240

5. A one bar electric fire is labelled 240 volts, 4·2 amp. Its wattage will be:

(a) $240 \times 4.2 = 1\,008$ (c) $4.2 + 240 = 244.2$

(b) $240 - 4.2 = 235.8$ (d) $240 \div 4.2 = 60$

6. A domestic ring circuit is protected by a 30 ampere fuse. What is the total maximum number of 3 kilowatt electric fires that can be connected to the 30 ampere wiring circuit and used at the same time:

(a) one   (c) three

(b) two   (d) four

7. The electric flex size for connection to a 1·5 kilowatt electric kettle on 240 volt main is:

(a) 3 ampere two core   (c) 10 ampere two core

(b) 3 ampere three core   (d) 10 ampere three core

8. Which of the following flex is the most suitable for a metal table lamp if it is to hold a 150 watt lamp at 240 volt main supply?

(a) 3 ampere two core   (c) 10 ampere two core

(b) 3 ampere three core   (d) 10 ampere three core

9. The entire electricity supply to your home suddenly goes off, but your neighbours' houses continue to have an electric supply. The reason for this breakdown is:

(a) a power station generator breakdown

(b) your service cutout fuse blowing

(c) your power circuit fuse blowing

(d) your lighting circuit fuse blowing

10. Which can be connected safely to a lamp-holder bayonet fitting socket?

(a) one-bar electric fire   (c) electric iron

(b) three-bar electric fire   (d) none of these

9   Electrical safety, circuits, and repairs

EARTHING

Earthing is a method of safeguarding against electric shock in the event of a fault developing in an appliance or plug.

A thunder cloud becomes charged with static electricity which is discharged at a great voltage towards the earth as lightning, the moist air acting as a conductor. Lightning is a hazard to tall buildings and can be overcome by fitting copper lightning conductors, strips which carry the electricity safely to earth (Figure 9.1). The electricity takes the shortest path to earth through the copper metal strip of low resistance.

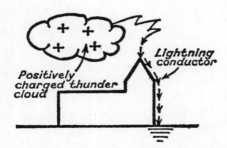

Figure 9.1. Electricity travelling towards the earth

As stated in Chapter 7, electricity enters a residence at 240 V pressure, through a *brown* insulated phase or live wire and returns to the power station by way of the *blue* insulated return or neutral wire (Figure 9.2). If a brown insulated live wire were to break and make contact with the metal frame of the appliance, the frame would become live. If a person touched the live appliance, the electricity would flow through the body to the earth, since the human body offers a shorter route to earth; severe electric shock would result (Figure 9.3).

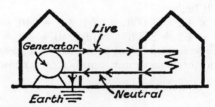

Figure 9.2. Neutral return wire to earth

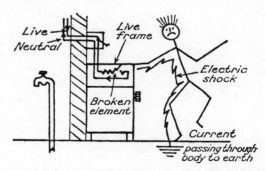

Figure 9.3. Electric shock from a non-earthed appliance

Many appliances are fitted with a safety earth wire. This is a thick copper wire of low resistance covered with a *green/yellow* insulation, and forms the third component of a three-core flexible cable, the other two being the brown live and blue neutral conductors. One end of the green/yellow earth wire is connected to the frame of the appliance, the other to earth by way of a metal cold water pipe or copper plate buried in the earth. If the appliance becomes live, the current will now flow rapidly to the earth through the earth wire and not through the human body which now offers a greater resistance to the electric current (Figure 9.4). *Note*: plastic water pipes cannot be used to earth a circuit.

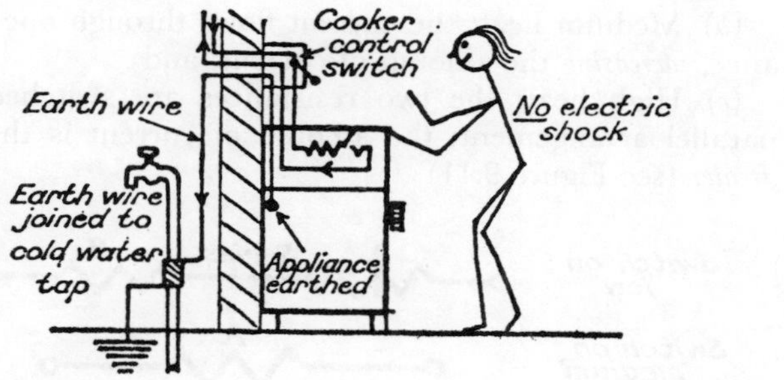

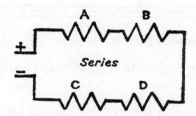

Figure 9.4. Earthed electric appliance

Because of short-circuiting, a live appliance usually blows the fuse which acts as a further safety device.

PLUGS AND SOCKET OUTLETS

Plugs and sockets are available in various types and sizes.

(*a*) Two-pin plugs have live and neutral connecting terminals only and are not provided with a safety earth device. They are found mainly in electric shavers with well insulated plastic bodies.

(*b*) Three-pin plugs and sockets are all provided with a safety earth pin which is usually the largest pin of the three.

(1) *Round* three-pin plugs and sockets were available in 2, 5, and 15 A sizes and were not fitted with fuses. They succeeded the early two-pin plug, and as electrical appliances were developed, increased in size with the greater current requirements. The disadvantage of the round three-pin system is the presence of differently sized socket outlets in a room necessitating inconveniently long flexes. These plugs and sockets are now obsolete.

(2) The *flat* three-pin or fused standard plug and socket is available in one size only and is used in all modern electrical installations or ring circuits.

PROTECTIVE DEVICES FOR USERS OF ELECTRICITY

The main protective devices can be summarized as follows:

(*a*) *Insulation* (see Chapter 7) protects the consumer from shock by means of non-conducting insulating materials. Food mixers are not fitted with an earth wire since their bodywork is of plastic insulating material.

(*b*) *Fuses* (see Chapter 8) prevent both shock and fire by virtue of being thin, easily melted wire, and the weakest link in the circuit.

(*c*) *Earthing* protects the consumer from electric shock by means of the thick, copper earth wire.

(*d*) *Guards* fitted to all exposed heating elements of fires

and other appliances prevent electric shock and fire caused by direct contact.

SERIES AND PARALLEL CIRCUITS

(*a*) Series circuits consist of appliances or resistances linked one after the other in a circle (Figure 9.5).

Figure 9.5. Series circuit

Experiment

Arrange six 1·5-V torch lamps in series as shown in Figure 9.6 and connect the circuit to a variable low-voltage supply. Note the voltage required to produce the normal lamp brightness. Remove one lamp and note how the circuit is broken, all the other lamps being extinguished.

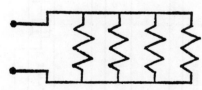

Figure 9.6. Lamps in series

Conclusion: The joining of lamps or appliances in series calls for an increased voltage; the total resistance of the circuit equals the *sum* of each separate resistance.

Series circuits have few applications apart from Christmas tree lighting circuits.

(*b*) The parallel circuit arrangement of appliances or resistances is shown in Figure 9.7.

Figure 9.7. Parallel circuit

Experiment

Arrange four 1·5-V torch lamps as shown in Figure 9.8 and connect them to a 1·5 V low-voltage supply. Remove one lamp and note how those remaining continue to burn brightly.

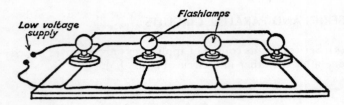

Figure 9.8. Lamps in parallel

APPLICATIONS OF PARALLEL ARRANGEMENT

1. Lighting

Lighting circuits in electrical installations are made up of lamps and lamp holders wired together in parallel as shown in Figure 9.9. Decorative festoon lighting employs a parallel circuit.

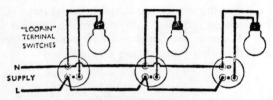

Figure 9.9. Lamps and switches in parallel

2. Power socket outlets

Power socket outlets are also arranged in a parallel circuit as shown in Figure 9.10.

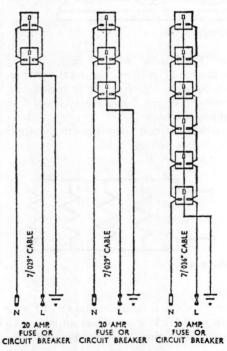

Figure 9.10. Power-points in parallel

3. Three-heat switches

Three-heat switches with low-, medium-, and high-heat settings are used to control the heater unit in cooker ovens, hot plates, and room heaters. A three-heat switch consists of two resistances through which the current flow as follows:

(*a*) Low heat: the current flows through two resistances in series, thus *reducing* the amount of current;

(*b*) Medium heat: the current flows through one resistance, *increasing* the amount of current; and

(*c*) High heat: the two resistances are switched to a parallel arrangement; the amount of current is therefore *greater* (see Figure 9.11).

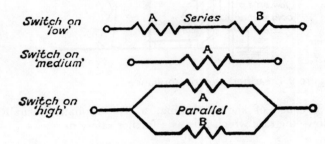

Figure 9.11. Three-heat switch circuit

4. Circuits in the home

(i) *Old-type distributive system*

(*a*) Electricity enters the home from the street through the electricity board's fuse box which is always closed and sealed (see Figure 9.12).

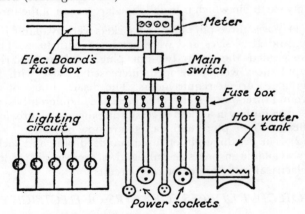

Figure 9.12. Old-type distributive circuit

(*b*) All current used in the installation is measured by the board's meter.

(*c*) A large fuse box, or in some cases an array of small fuse boxes, supplies the lighting and power socket outlets.

(*d*) The lights are in a parallel circuit controlled by a 5-A fuse.

(*e*) Power socket outlets are connected separately to their individual fuses. Old electrical circuits may have many socket outlets of 2, 5, and 15 amperes, and a random arrangement of cable installed over a period of time.

(ii) *Modern ring circuit*

The modern circuit (see Figure 9.13) consists of a compact consumer's fuse unit or circuit-breaker unit controlled by a mains switch.

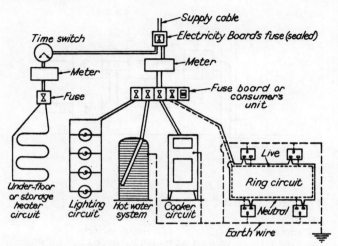

Figure 9.13. Modern ring-circuit installation

(a) The *lighting circuit* arranged in parallel is controlled by a 5-A fuse or 5-A circuit-breaker.

(b) Electric cookers have an individual 30-A fuse or 30-A circuit-breaker.

(c) Immersion *water heaters* also have an individual 30-A fuse or 30-A circuit-breaker.

(d) The ring circuit supplying the *power socket outlets* is controlled by a 30-A fuse or 30-A circuit-breaker.

The main features of the ring circuit are:

1. All plugs and socket outlets are of the *same* size, namely standard, flat-pin fused plug and socket. Therefore all plugs are interchangeable.

2. Each plug has its *own fuse*, a contribution to safety. A faulty appliance will blow its own plug-top fuse only.

3. Less cable is needed to install a ring circuit as compared with the old distributive type.

4. Appliances need have only short flex.

5. Up to twenty socket outlets can be installed in a ring circuit, and *spurs* may be added. A room may have as many power outlets as are required.

(e) *Off-peak* space heating circuits are controlled by a time switch clock set to provide a flow of current at the off-peak times 7 p.m.–7 a.m., the quantity of current used being measured by a separate meter. Off-peak storage heat circuits are controlled by single fuse or circuit-breaker units.

Time switches are useful devices to control lighting, heating, and cooking appliances, and are rapidly gaining favour.

SIMPLE ELECTRICAL REPAIRS

The following suggestions are given as a guide for simple first-aid repairs.

1. How to wire a three-pin plug

(a) Strip back, for about 5 cm, the outer insulation of the cord to expose the brown, green/yellow, and blue insulated wires.

(b) Strip off 1 cm of insulation from all three wires.

(c) If the wire is to be fixed under a screw-head terminal, make a fishtail end as in Figure 9.14; otherwise twist the bare wires to prevent splaying for insertion into the terminal hole.

(d) Connect up the wires as follows:

Brown wire to live pin L (or P phase), *blue* wire to neutral pin N, and *green/yellow* wire to earth pin E. Make sure all terminals are screwed firmly down to make a tight contact.

Figure 9.14. Stages in wiring a three-pin standard fused plug

Fatal accidents can occur if the conducting wires are not connected correctly. Always ensure that the wire insulation reaches the connecting terminal to prevent short-circuits caused by bare wires touching.

If the colour scheme is other than brown, blue, and green/yellow, *do not* attempt to connect it, but call in an electrician. Do not use cables or flexes with other colour codes without first consulting a competent electrician.

(e) The cord grip screws should be tightened up in order to hold the flex firmly.

(f) Replace the fuse of correct size and reassemble the plug top.

The round three-pin plug is connected in a similar manner, the conducting wire being wound clockwise on to the terminals.

A two-pin plug should not be connected to any appliance other than those with completely insulated plastic bodywork, such as food mixers, electric shavers and hair-dryers.

Plug pins which heat up in use should have all terminal connections tightened firmly; heating of plug pins is caused by loose connections.

2. How to wire a non-metal or plastic lamp holder

(a) Switch off the electricity at the mains.

(b) Dismantle the lamp holder and thread the flex through the cover.

(c) Strip off 1 cm of the insulated covering from the two conducting wires and twist the ends clockwise to prevent splaying.

(d) Insert the bare wires into the terminal holes, and tighten the screws firmly. Carefully cut away any projecting bare wire.

(*e*) Hook the flex under the small lugs to take the weight of the lamp and shade which otherwise will pull the wires from the terminals.

(*f*) Screw down the lamp holder cover, insert the shade and screw up the shade support ring leaving a slight slackness to allow for thermal expansion.

Note: Metal lampholders require connection to earth.

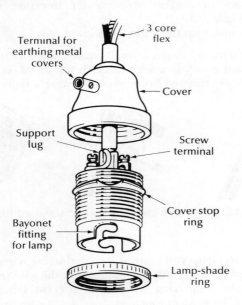

Figure 9.15. Lampholder connections

QUESTIONS ON CHAPTER 9

1. An efficiently operated electrical installation should never require fuse replacement! Comment on this statement and state how you would prevent fuses blowing.

2. Give a summary of the main methods by which a consumer of electricity is protected against fire and electric shock.

3. What is meant by the earthing of an appliance? Make a list of rules to observe when handling electric appliances.

4. Explain the following terms, giving examples in each case: (*a*) simple circuit; (*b*) parallel arranged circuit; (*c*) series arranged circuit; (*d*) short-circuit; and (*e*) ring circuit.

5. Give a simple illustrated account of the modern electrical installation in a home.

6. Compare the advantages of the modern ring circuit with the disadvantages of the old distributive circuit.

7. Draw a simple plan of a small hotel electrical installation and construct a list of instructions regarding electrical safety for the establishment.

8. Draw a universal three-pin plug illustrating the colour of the wiring. State the purpose of each of the three pins.

9. An electric fire connected to a plug does not heat up when switched on at the wall socket. State the probable reasons for its failure.

10. What purpose does a fuse serve? Describe the main features of a standard fused plug.

MULTIPLE CHOICE QUESTIONS ON CHAPTER 9

Figure 9.15 shows how electricity comes into a house and the items it must pass through before reaching sockets and lights.

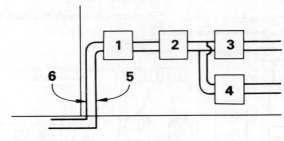

Figure 9.15

1. The part labelled 2 in Figure 9.15 is the:
   (*a*) fuse box   (*c*) service cutout
   (*b*) meter   (*d*) main switch
2. One of the two wires labelled 5 or 6 allows the flow of electricity from the power station to the home wiring through a wire called the:
   (*a*) earth wire   (*c*) neutral wire
   (*b*) live wire   (*d*) return wire
3. The main switches could be located in two of the following labelled parts:
   (*a*) 1 and 2   (*c*) 3 and 4
   (*b*) 1 and 6   (*d*) 2 and 5
4. House electric wiring, usually hidden below floorboards, behind ceilings and skirtings, is called the:
   (*a*) flex   (*c*) conduit
   (*b*) cable   (*d*) sheathing
5. There are normally four circuits connected to a domestic consumer's unit. Which circuit takes a maximum of 5 amperes:
   (*a*) cooker circuit   (*c*) lighting circuit
   (*b*) water heating circuit   (*d*) power socket circuit

Figure 9.16 shows lamps arranged in different circuits.

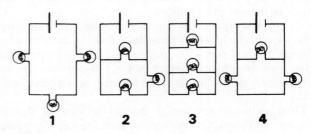

Figure 9.16

6. Which of the four circuits shown in Figure 9.16 has all its lamps arranged in series:
   (*a*) 1   (*c*) 3
   (*b*) 2   (*d*) 4

7. Which of the circuits shown in the figure have all the lamps arranged in parallel:
   (*a*) 1   (*c*) 3
   (*b*) 2   (*d*) 4

8. If one lamp fuses or becomes faulty in each of the circuits shown in the figure, in which circuit will *all* the lamps fail to light up:
   (*a*) 1   (*c*) 3
   (*b*) 2   (*d*) 4

9. Which electric circuits in the home takes the least amperage when all circuits are fully operative:
   (*a*) lighting   (*c*) cooking
   (*b*) water heating   (*d*) power

10. Houses built since 1950 will have socket outlets of the following type only:
   (*a*) 2 ampere two round holes
   (*b*) 5 ampere three round holes
   (*c*) 13 ampere three rectangular holes
   (*d*) 15 ampere two round holes

10   Electric generators, motors, and electronic cooking

We have seen that electrical *energy* can be converted into heat and light. In this chapter, we consider how an electric current produces *magnetism* or *electromagnetism*. This has important applications in electric motors and motor-driven appliances.

MAGNETISM

Magnetism is the power shown by such metals as iron, steel, cobalt, and nickel of attracting iron filings towards themselves.

PROPERTIES OF MAGNETS

1. Dip a bar magnet into iron filings and note how the iron filings gather in clusters at the ends or *poles* of the magnet.

2. Obtain a magnetic compass, made up of a needle magnet over a compass card. Note how the compass needle always comes to rest in the same position. The magnetic pole that points to the north is called the north seeking magnetic pole.

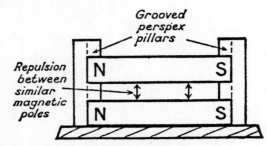

Figure 10.1. Magnetic levitation apparatus

3. Using the apparatus in Figure 10.1 arrange the magnets as shown. It will be seen that there is *repulsion* between similar magnetic poles and *attraction* between opposite poles, north and south – *like* poles repel each other; and *unlike* poles attract each other.

4. Place a piece of paper over a bar magnet and carefully sprinkle iron filings on it. Tap the paper gently and note how the iron filings arrange themselves into a pattern showing the *magnetic field* of the magnet (Figure 10.2).

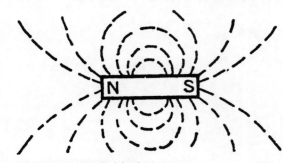

Figure 10.2. Magnetic field of a magnet

MAKING MAGNETS

Steel, cobalt, and nickel alloys are used to make *permanent* long-lasting magnets. Soft iron, as used for nails and wrought-iron work, magnetizes easily, but soon loses its power.

A steel sewing needle stroked several times in the same direction with a permanent magnet becomes magnetic.

The *electromagnet* is employed to make a magnet using a current of electricity. A coil of cotton-insulated copper wire, the *solenoid*, is wrapped round a soft iron 150-mm nail, the coil being connected to a source of low-voltage current (see Figure 10.3). When the current flows it will be seen that iron filings, tacks, or nails are drawn towards the soft iron nail or electromagnet core. When the current ceases, they fall back into the dish.

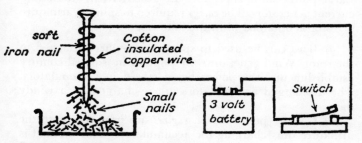

Figure 10.3. Simple electromagnet

(*a*) If more turns are wound around the solenoid more iron filings can be picked up because the electromagnetism has now been increased.

(*b*) If the electric current or voltage is increased with more batteries, increased electromagnetism results.

(*c*) The electromagnet has magnetic poles similar to a bar magnet, as shown in Figure 10.4. The south pole shows a *clockwise*, the north pole an *anti-clockwise* direction of current flow when viewed endwise.

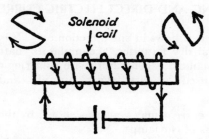

Figure 10.4. Polarity of a solenoid coil

APPLICATIONS OF ELECTROMAGNETISM

1. Electric bells

Electric bells (Figure 10.5) operate by means of a solenoid which attracts a piece of soft iron connected to a hammer. This strikes the bell at the same time switching *off* the current. The spring-operated soft iron springs back to its original position, switching *on* the current and causing the hammer to strike the bell, owing to the electromagnetic attraction of the solenoid.

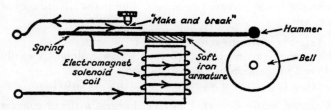

Figure 10.5. Electric-bell circuit

The tone and pitch of the bell can be altered by adjusting the make and break screw or by slackening the retaining screw on the bell. Chime bells operate similarly, the bell being replaced by two tubes of different length.

2. Circuit-breakers

These operate by means of a spring-loaded electromagnetic mechanism (see page 57) which comes into operation when too much current flows through the switch coil. This is the case when circuits are overloaded with too many appliances.

3. Lift or electromagnetic brakes

Electricity flowing through the coil magnetizes it, attracting the iron plate which meanwhile presses against the brake drum spring. When the current is switched off the electromagnetism ceases and the strong brake drum spring presses the brake shoe against the brake drum, thus halting the movement of the lift (Figure 10.6).

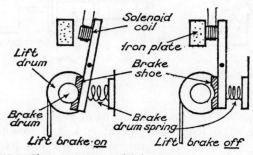

Figure 10.6. Electromagnetic lift-brakes

INDUCED ELECTRIC CURRENTS

Obtain a solenoid coil of many turns of cotton-insulated wire and connect it to a *galvanometer*, which is a very sensitive current-detecting device.

Push a strong bar magnet into the solenoid coil and note the deflection of the galvanometer needle. Withdraw the magnet and again note the deflection of the galvanometer. An *induced* electric current (see Figure 10.7) has been made by moving a strong magnet within a stationary solenoid coil.

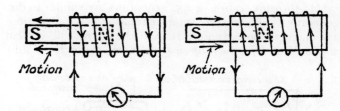

Figure 10.7. Induced electric current

Motion or mechanical energy has been converted into electrical energy. The *direction* of the flow of electric current alters as the magnet enters and leaves the coil; such a current is described as an *alternating* current (a.c.).

Repeat the experiment keeping the bar magnet stationary but moving the coil over the magnet. The electromagnetic circuit is the opposite of an induced electric current circuit in which electricity flowing in one direction or direct current (d.c.) is used. In this experiment magnetism has been used to make an alternating current (a.c.).

ELECTRIC GENERATORS

Electric generators or dynamos are of two kinds depending on the type of electricity made:

(*a*) *Direct current* or d.c. generators, consist basically of a coil of insulated wire, the *armature*, which rotates rapidly between the poles of a strong magnet. The induced electric current is picked up from the copper split-ring commutator by means of graphite carbon *brushes* (Figure 10.8).

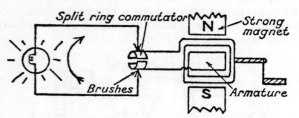

Figure 10.8. Direct-current dynamo or generator

Experiment

Obtain an old G.P.O. telephone hand-generator as used in the older-type telephone switchboard, and mount on a wooden board as in Figure 10.9. Turn the handle at different speeds and note the changing brilliance of the lamp. Dismantle the generator and notice the two large permanent magnets and the coiled armature.

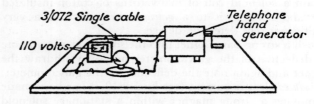

Figure 10.9. Telephone hand generator

(*b*) *Alternating current* or a.c. generators are similar to d.c. generators in having an armature rotating between stationary magnetic poles (Figure 10.10). The alternating current is picked up by a two-*slip-ring* conductor through graphite

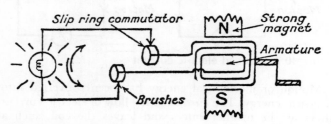

Figure 10.10. Alternating current

carbon brushes. Coaxial slip-rings are found on large-scale electric generators.

LARGE-SCALE GENERATION OF ELECTRICITY

Large power-stations produce a.c. electricity in alternating current generators. The *energy* required to spin the armature or rotor is obtained from the following sources:

(*a*) *Wind* can be used to spin a wind-wheel attached to the rotor. Wind generators are popular in isolated country establishments, the power being stored in accumulators. The discharged accumulators are re-charged on a windy day.

(*b*) Gas- or petrol-driven *engines* are used to rotate the armature thus charging the accumulators. This method is used for isolated buildings and also for motor-cars and ships.

(*c*) *Turbine* generators have a large turbine wheel consisting of many turbine blades. The wheel is rotated either by a jet of high-pressure water, as in hydroelectric power-stations (H.E.P.), or by high-pressure steam from boilers fired by coal, gas, oil, or atomic energy. The rapidly rotating turbine wheel spins the armature. Most large power-stations have turbine generators.

ALTERNATING AND DIRECT ELECTRIC CURRENTS

1. *Direct current* flows in one direction only. It is obtained from chemical dry batteries, accumulators, battery chargers, and dynamo d.c. generators with split-ring commutators. It is used in cars, ships, aircraft, and isolated buildings.

(*a*) Direct current may waver as shown by the fluctuating brightness of car lamps.

(*b*) It is difficult to change the voltage of a d.c. current for distribution purposes.

(*c*) D.c. current causes arcing or sparking across switch terminals which burns away switch contacts and causes interference on radio and television.

2. *Alternating current* flows in a rapidly changing direction. If the direction of flow alters 50 times per *second* its frequency is described as 50 cycles per second or 50 hertz (Hz). One hertz = one cycle per second.

Alternating current is produced by alternator generators fitted with coaxial *slip-rings* as, for example, in large-scale turbine electric generators. Approximately 90 per cent of all consumers have a.c. supplies; the remainder are supplied with d.c. from private generators. The main advantages of a.c. are:

(*a*) it is easier to generate on a large scale;

(*b*) it gives an electric current whose voltage is easily altered in *transformers* for distribution;

(*c*) a.c. current does not cause arcing in switches.

Note. A.c. mains-operated battery chargers *rectify* or convert the a.c. into d.c. to charge accumulators. Accumulators cannot be charged directly from unrectified alternating current.

Electric clocks

All power-station generators revolve at the same speed and therefore produce a.c. supply at the same frequency of 50 Hz. They are therefore similarly timed or synchronous. The electric clock or synchronous electric clock has a small electric motor which revolves in step with the 50 Hz frequency of the generator, the movement being transmitted through gear wheels to the dial hands.

Many large buildings are fitted with a master pendulum clock connected to a number of slave clocks. The master clock sends out an electric current every half minute. This current operates electromagnetic devices which cause the dial fingers to move forward.

PHOTOELECTRICITY OR ELECTRICITY FROM LIGHT

When light falls between two different metals, one of which is coated with *selenium*, a small electric current is produced which can be magnified in an amplifier (Figure 10.11). This cell finds many applications:

(*a*) Automatic door openers controlled by motors driven by electricity from the amplifiers.

(*b*) Fire alarms powered by electricity from the photo-electric cell activated by the flames.

(*c*) Boiler fire controls operated by a photoelectric cell either by the colour or brightness of the flame or the colour of the smoke issuing from the chimney.

(*d*) Burglar alarms.

(*e*) Colour measuring instruments (colorimeters) for food and textiles.

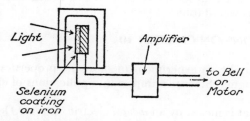

Figure 10.11. Photoelectric circuit

Transformers

The transformer is an apparatus for changing the voltage of an a.c. electric current. There are two main types, step-up and step-down transformers.

Step-up transformers convert current from a *low* to a *higher* voltage. They are found in power-stations, where the generated voltage is stepped up from 11 000 V to 132 000 V in order that the electricity can be pumped over a widespread network more economically.

Step-down transformers convert from a *high* to a *lower* voltage. For example, the 132 000 V in the main distribution network must be gradually stepped down to reach the

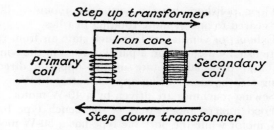

Figure 10.12. Transformer structure

consumer at 240 V. Many large buildings have small sub-stations which change the main voltage from 440 V to 240 V.

The transformer consists of two insulated copper coils wrapped around a soft iron former or core. Step-up transformers take in low-voltage current through the primary coil which has a small number of turns and produce a high-voltage current in the secondary coil which has a large number of turns (Figure 10.12). The step-down transformer operates in reverse.

Electric motors

The action of an electric motor is the *reverse* of that of a dynamo or generator, i.e. electrical energy is converted into motion or mechanical energy.

$$\text{Motion} \xrightarrow[\text{generator}]{\text{Dynamo}} \text{Electricity}$$

$$\text{Electricity} \xrightarrow{\text{Motor}} \text{Motion}$$

The electric motor (Figure 10.13) consists of an *armature* rotating between strong magnets which are normally electromagnets. The electric current is passed into the *commutator* of the armature by way of the carbon graphite *brushes*. This type of electric motor is used for all portable household appliances. Their motors consume little electricity, for example 50 W for a fractional-power motor. Fractional power motors are also called *universal* motors since they are designed to operate on a.c. or d.c. supplies.

Motor-driven appliances

1. Vacuum cleaners have 200-W motors connected to fans which suck in air and dust. The fan is also connected by a belt to a rotating brush and beater.

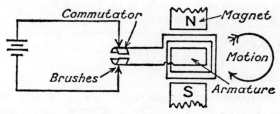

Figure 10.13. The electric motor

2. Floor polishers have a vertically mounted 200-W motor geared to one or more rotating brushes.

3. Exhaust or ventilating fans suck stale air from rooms and are usually mounted in a panel of glass in the window. Table and desk fans rotate in the opposite direction, blowing air, the motor being approximately 40 W.

4. Sewing machines are driven by a 40-W motor.

5. Food mixers and beaters of the bench type have a 200-W motor while the portable type has a 50-W motor.

6. Washing machines have an agitator and wringer driven by a 300–400-W motor.

7. Compressor-type refrigerators are driven by a 250-W motor.

8. Spin-dryers are driven by a 200-W motor which causes the perforated container to rotate and throw out the evaporated water by centrifugal action.

MICROWAVE ENERGY AND ELECTRONIC COOKERS

Microwaves are forms of electromagnetic energy similar to infra-red, radar, and radio waves (see page 73). The microwaves are generated by a *magnetron* valve at a very *high frequency*, 2 400 MHz, and wave-length of 12 cm which show the following properties when they strike food or other materials.

(*a*) Certain materials such as foods will *absorb* microwaves, this causes the food particles or molecules to vibrate rapidly and heat up. The depth to which the microwaves penetrate is about 3 cm, the heat generated passing beyond this depth by *conduction* of heat.

(*b*) Glass, china, and paper, will allow the microwaves to be *transmitted* through them without any heating occurring, consequently these materials are used to support the food during microwave cooking.

(*c*) *Reflection* of microwaves will occur on metal surfaces such as the oven lining, or from metal pans and cooking foil, these materials cannot be used for supporting food in microwave ovens.

Microwave oven construction

The magnetron valve radiates its microwaves which strike the moving metal blades of a *stirrer*, which evenly distributes the electromagnetic waves within the cooker interior, coupled with reflection from the oven lining. Shelves in the oven are of glass allowing free transmission to reach the food. The oven walls and door are specially constructed to prevent the escape of any microwaves outside the cooker, as they are known to be harmful to the body if it is exposed to large doses of this radiation.

The wattage of the oven for domestic use is between 400–1 300 W.

Cooking effects

1. Microwave ovens will poach, boil, or steam and do certain kinds of baking. The cooking is fairiy uniform throughout, but there is no surface browning or crust formation unless the cooked food is browned by infra-red radiation.

2. It is a rapid means of cooking, for example a 2 kg chicken takes between 50 and 15 minutes to cook depending on the oven wattage, being most rapid with the higher wattage oven. Traditional gas or electric ovens would take about 90 minutes in comparison.

Thin, sliced or small portions of food will cook more quickly than thicker portions which are more than 5 cm thick.

3. Apart from being used to *defreeze* deep frozen foods rapidly, it can also be used to *reheat* previously cooked, blast frozen foods directly on the plates, making it suitable for institutional cooking.

Safety

If exposed excessively to microwave radiation, the human body is liable to develop disorders of the eyes or damage the reproductive organs, this has been shown to happen with experimental animals.

In order to prevent leakage of microwaves the oven should not be operated empty or with metal dishes. The door should be closed gently as slamming or banging may cause leakage. Regular servicing is essential to check for microwave leakage.

SUGGESTIONS FOR PRACTICAL WORK

1. Examine an electric bell and set up a circuit to operate it.

2. Obtain a surplus, G.P.O. telephone hand-generator and set it up as shown on page 68.

3. Contact your local electricity board in order to visit a near-by power-station.

QUESTIONS ON CHAPTER 10

1. Describe an experiment to show the properties of an electromagnet. State two important applications of electromagnets.

2. What is meant by an *induced* electric current? Describe how it can be demonstrated.

3. Explain the terms alternating and direct current and how they are produced.

4. Describe how a fractional power motor works. Describe how any two motor-operated appliances work.

5. Give a brief account of microwave cooking ovens. Compare this method of cooking with traditional electric ovens.

6. Write short notes on: (*a*) transformers; (*b*) amplifiers; (*c*) synchronous electric clocks; (*d*) circuit-breakers; and (*e*) lift-brakes.

7. State the main advantages of microwave cookers for the large-scale caterer.

8. Give a brief account of photoelectric cells and their applications.

9. An electric meter nameplate is stamped 230 V, 50 Hz

a.c., total amperes = 60. Explain the meaning of these terms.

10. How does the electric motor work? Describe three motor-driven appliances together with their approximate wattages.

MULTIPLE CHOICE QUESTIONS ON CHAPTER 10

Figure 10.13 shows a current carrying coil of insulated copper wire between two strong magnets.

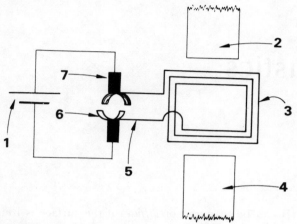

Figure 10.13.

1. The circuit shown in Figure 10.13 shows the structure of an electric:
   (*a*) generator   (*c*) transformer
   (*b*) motor   (*d*) dynamo

2. The rotating coil part labelled 3 in Figure 10.13 is called the:
   (*a*) connector   (*c*) stator
   (*b*) armature   (*d*) commutator

3. The contact brushes are shown as the part labelled:
   (*a*) 2   (*c*) 6
   (*b*) 4   (*d*) 7

4. The contact brushes in Figure 10.13 are made of:
   (*a*) nylon   (*c*) hog bristle
   (*b*) charcoal   (*d*) graphite

5. The contact brushes connect directly with the following:
   (*a*) commutator   (*c*) armature
   (*b*) stator   (*d*) shaft

6. The house main supply is 240 volt and a door bell circuit operates on 12 volts. Which of the following will change the main voltage to meet the needs of the bell circuit:
   (*a*) transformer   (*c*) adaptor
   (*b*) rectifier   (*d*) accumulator

7. One of the following 2 pin socket outlets is fitted with a transformer:
   (*a*) bathroom razor socket
   (*b*) main radio socket
   (*c*) electric clock socket
   (*d*) electric standard lamp socket

8. A length of cotton-insulated copper wire through which a current flows when it is coiled into a cylinder longer than its width, is called a:
   (*a*) resistance   (*c*) heater element
   (*b*) solenoid   (*d*) thermostat

9. Which rod, when inserted into the item in Question 8 would become a magnet?
   (*a*) glass   (*c*) ebonite
   (*b*) perspex   (*d*) iron

10. Which operates by an electromagnet:
   (*a*) electric kettle   (*c*) electric bell
   (*b*) electric blanket   (*d*) electric lamp

11 Illumination and acoustics

LIGHT

Light is a form of *energy* produced, for example by (*a*) the sun, (*b*) atomic energy (the atom bomb produces a blinding light), (*c*) electricity, and (*d*) burning fuels. Sunlight is the main energy source for all living things. See *photosynthesis*, page 169.

All light travels in *straight lines* or rays; this can be demonstrated by means of the raybox. A further example is a beam of sunlight passing through a small opening into a darkened room. The straight edge of the beam is easily observed.

PROPERTIES OF LIGHT

When a beam of light strikes a surface, three things can happen to it, according to the nature of the surface (Figure 11.1).

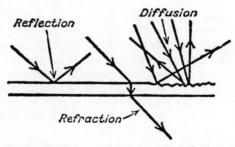

Figure 11.1. Reflection, refraction, and diffusion of light

1. The ray of light can be *reflected* from a polished surface.
2. It can pass into and through the material, being bent in the process by *refraction*.

3. It can be scattered or *diffused* if the surface is rough and also be absorbed.

Reflection

Light rays striking a smooth, polished surface are reflected in accordance with the laws of reflection. This states that the angle formed by the incident ray equals the angle formed by the reflected ray (Figure 11.2). This can be proved experimentally by reflecting a single beam from a raybox on to a flat plane mirror and measuring the angles of incidence and reflection.

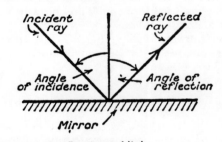

Figure 11.2. Law of reflection of light

APPLICATIONS OF REFLECTION

(1) *Mirrors* are made of highly-polished sheets of glass coated on the back with a reflecting layer of silver metal or tin and mercury amalgam. The reflecting layer is protected from moisture by a coat of paint or varnish. Highly-polished stainless steel can also be used but is susceptible to damage by scratching.

A cloth dampened with methylated spirits is most suitable for restoring the gleaming surface of a mirror.

(2) How you see yourself in a mirror. All objects give out rays of light which travel towards the mirror and are reflected. The reflected rays now enter the eye which sees an image as if from the back of the mirror (Figure 11.3). Figure 11.4 shows the lateral inversion of the image in a mirror by means of which ink prints on blotting paper can be read.

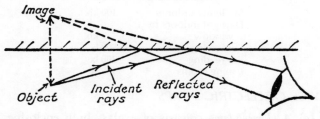

Figure 11.3. Formation of an image in a plane mirror

Figure 11.4. Lateral inversion

(3) Transparent mirrors are fitted in large stores as security observation windows. They allow observers in a dark room to see through into a well-lit room, while those being observed see only their reflection. Transparent mirrors are made of polished glass with a thin, reflecting metal surface backed by a sheet of glass.

(4) Curved mirrors are of two kinds:

(a) *Concave* mirrors in which the reflecting surface curves *inwards*. They are used to magnify an object being suitable for shaving and cosmetic mirrors.

(b) *Convex* mirrors whose reflecting surface curves *outwards*. They are used as decorative mirrors to give a panoramic view of a room.

Refraction

Refraction is the *bending* of a beam of light as it passes from one medium to another, for example from air to glass

APPLICATIONS OF REFRACTION

(1) *Refractometers* are instruments used to measure the percentage strength of sugar solutions used in making jam, syrup, and confectionery. The degree of refraction and hence the sugar solution strength is indicated on the refractometer scale.

(2) *Ribbed glass* is often used for lighting basements and such rooms as toilets, making them much lighter than with plain glass windows. The light rays are refracted to light up parts of the room other than the floor.

Diffusion

The scattering of light rays by such rough surfaces as curtain material, upholstery, and matt paint finishes prevents the glare associated with highly-polished, reflected surfaces. Dull, roughened surfaces are also described as light-absorbing surfaces.

COMPOSITION OF LIGHT

Mirrors with bevelled edges or pendant prism chandeliers produce an attractive rainbow effect when incident light plays on them. This is called a *spectrum* and can be projected on to a screen using the apparatus illustrated in Figure 11.5.

A hollow glass prism containing carbon disulphide produces a more distinct spectrum than by means of a solid glass prism. This experiment shows that white light can be split up or *dispersed* into a variety of colours collectively called the spectrum:

White light = spectrum (ROYGBIV)
- Red
- Orange
- Yellow
- Green
- Blue
- Indigo
- Violet

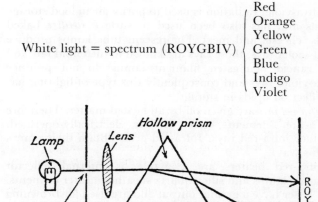

Figure 11.5. Formation of a spectrum

COLOURS

When white light falls upon an object certain colours are absorbed while the colour observed is reflected. For example red roses *absorb* all the spectrum colours but *reflect* the red. White *objects* reflect all the colours of the spectrum which together produce white. Black objects *absorb* all the spectrum colours and none is reflected.

Food and textiles colour can be measured in *colorimeters* by reflecting *one* coloured light from a spectrum on the food sample, the reflected light being measured in a photoelectric cell (Figure 10.11, page 69).

ULTRA-VIOLET, INFRA-RED, AND X-RAYS

The sun, together with radio-active substances, is undergoing continuous decomposition or *fission*, during which heat, light, and rays called electromagnetic rays are produced. The heat and light of the sun are obvious to all but the invisible electromagnetic waves need description.

Scientists have discovered the existence of rays outside the visible spectrum. Those beyond (*infra* means below) the red are called infra-red and those beyond the violet are called ultra-violet (*ultra* means beyond). As they have electric and magnetic properties they are collectively called electromagnetic rays or waves.

The electromagnetic waves contained in sunlight are:

Radio waves also include microwaves for cooking	Infra-red	Visible spectrum (ROYGBIV)	Ultra-violet	X-rays Gamma (γ) rays

Ultra-violet rays are present in sunlight and will travel through *clean* air towards the earth. Smoke-laden air will *prevent* the rays reaching the earth. Ultra-violet rays are beneficial to the body since they produce vitamin D in the skin.

Ultra-violet radiation is used to purify air in food storage rooms and has also been used to surface *sterilize* baked foods, cheese, and meat. Fluorescent tube lamps produce ultra-violet rays, these rays are known to turn lipid fats and oils rancid. Tungsten filament lamps do not produce ultra-violet rays and consequently this type of lighting has no effect on lipids in storage.

Infra-red rays are given off by all heated matter. Therefore all heater elements, gas-, oil- or electrically-operated, produce infra-red rays. Infra-red grills obtain their names in this way.

Infra-red heaters are available as internal reflector infra-red lamps and silica quartz sheathed heater elements. The latter have a greater output and are used for browning microwave cooked food.

Ordinary glass used in homes allows infra-red rays to penetrate them but unfortunately ultra-violet rays cannot pass through to sterilize the air. *Vita-glass* however will allow ultra-violet ray penetration and is therefore frequently used for sanatoria where the beneficial effect of the sun is enjoyed without exposure to the wind.

X-rays and γ-rays or ionizing radiation from radio-active materials can be used to destroy bacteria or sterilize foods containing bacteria. X-rays and γ-rays from radio-active material also damage and destroy living cells of plants and animals after long exposure.

The use of γ-rays and X-rays for preserving and storing food has limitations: the flavour, colour, and smell can change (see pages 204 and 211).

Different dose levels of *irradiation* produce different degrees of food sterilization.

ELECTRIC LIGHTING

Artificial lighting should provide sufficient illumination to allow people to work free from *eyestrain* and to provide comfort without glare. Good lighting reduces the risk of accidents.

Measurement of illumination

Illumination is measured in units called *lux* (lx) the amount of light falling on one square metre per second; 1 000 lx = 1 kilolux (klx).

ILLUMINATION VALUES OF LIGHT

Nature of light	Lux
Sunlight outdoors	100 klx
Daylight indoors by a window	2 klx
For sewing	500 lx
For reading	300 lx
Dining rooms	150 lx

TYPES OF ELECTRIC LAMPS

(*a*) A *filament lamp* consists of a glass bulb enclosing a tungsten wire of high electrical resistance. It glows white hot as electricity flows into it. The bulb contains inert argon to prevent the filament burning away and so reducing the life of the lamp. There are two main types of filament lamp: (1) Clear glass lamps, which give a harsh, bright light with sharp shadows. They are suitable for display or for an enclosed fitting; (2) Pearl lamps in which the inside bulb surface is roughened to provide a *diffused*, soft light. Silica-coated lamps give an even softer light.

Lamps should be of the correct operating voltage as the lamp's life will be shortened and its illumination faulty on unsuitable voltages. (See page 56.)

(*b*) *Fluorescent lamps* give three to four times as much light as a filament for with the same quantity of electricity, its life being approximately three times as long. The quality of its light is nearest to daylight.

When first switched on the fluorescent lamp produces ultra-violet rays, which in turn cause the powder lining the tube to fluoresce as white visible light. When sunlight (natural ultra-violet rays) falls on materials laundered with special *whiteners*, they fluoresce making the garment look whiter.

Lamp fittings

Lamp fittings (see Figure 11.6) serve either to reflect or diffuse light or act in a combined capacity as reflector and diffuser.

1. *Reflector fittings* give 90 per cent downward light with pearl lamps.

2. *Diffuser fittings* are of translucent material and enclose the lamp.

3. *Semi-indirect light fittings* are translucent inverted bowls which give partly diffused and partly reflected light, the latter from the ceiling or wall surface; 60–90 per cent is upward directed light.

4. *Indirect reflector fittings* are inverted reflectors in which the light is cast on to a ceiling or wall; 90 per cent is upward directed light.

GLARE

Glare is discomfort caused by bright light entering the eyes. Its main causes are:

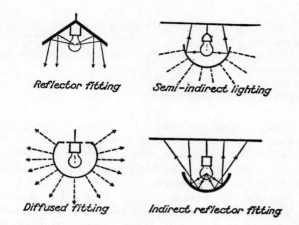

Figure 11.6. Light fittings

(*a*) Reflection from shiny surfaces such as mirrors, gloss painted walls and ceilings, and highly-polished wood and chrome furniture and fittings.

(*b*) Unshaded lamps with clear glass filament bulbs.

Glare can be prevented by the following methods which provide soft, diffused illumination:

(*a*) Walls and ceilings should have a roughened or matt surface of light-absorbent substances.

(*b*) Furniture and fittings should not be polished but be upholstered with rough light-absorbent materials.

(*c*) Curtains and other drapes help to provide diffused lighting.

(*d*) Warm-coloured paints in matt finish should be used. Post-Office red, crimson, middle brown and sage green reflect light least, while white, cream, and lemon have high reflecting values.

(*e*) Opal or pearl lamps should be used in open lamp fittings. Clear glass bulbs are suitable for diffuser-type fittings.

(*f*) Lamps can be set behind pelmets, the light being reflected on alcoves and curtains.

(*g*) Lights, or small pearl lamps fitted with diffuser shades, can be arranged beside a mirror to prevent light shining directly on to a person but on to the mirror itself.

Good restaurants will take care that glare is eliminated by diffused lighting producing relaxed, comfortable surroundings.

SOUND AND ACOUSTICS

Sound, like heat and light, is a form of *energy*, demonstrable when certain sounds cause wine glasses and windows to shatter. Sound is produced by materials in motion. The vibration of a tight string or wooden ruler will create a sound, as does the vibration of the diaphragm in a radio or telephone loudspeaker. All sound travels in the form of waves which resemble the ripples formed by dropping a stone into calm water.

PROPERTIES OF SOUND

Sound behaves much as heat and light, in that it can be reflected, conducted, absorbed, and refracted.

1. Reflection

Sound waves are reflected from polished, smooth surfaces as are heat and light waves and they obey the same law of reflection.

APPLICATIONS OF REFLECTION

1. Echoes result from the reflection of sound from smooth, hard surfaces of walls, floors, and ceilings. The sound is said to *reverberate* as it does when someone sings in a tiled bathroom.

2. Sound waves can be reflected intentionally by means of reflecting boards, thus directing music or speech from a stage into an auditorium.

2. Conduction

Different substances conduct sounds differently. Metals are excellent conductors of sound, while non-metals such as wood, plastics and wool are poor conductors. Air is a very poor conductor and a vacuum will not conduct sound at all (compare heat).

APPLICATIONS OF CONDUCTION

1. Sound is conducted through a building by way of metal, water and gas pipes, illustrated by the disturbance caused when maintenance work is being carried out on the pipe system (Figure 11.7).

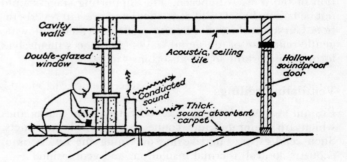

Figure 11.7. Building acoustics

2. Entry of sound into buildings from outside is prevented by double-glazed windows, cavity walls, doors, and ceilings, the non-conducting air acting as an insulator.

Absorption of sound is achieved through the use of felt, curtains, and other materials containing air-spaces. Panels of light, plastic material filled with tiny holes are excellent for this purpose. Certain expanded plastics resembling solid foams incorporate air cells which have effective sound-absorbing properties.

APPLICATIONS OF ABSORPTION

1. Acoustic ceiling and wall panels of cork, wood, and plastics are excellent sound absorbers, particularly if made of a soft-, rough-surfaced material with pores throughout. Such panels are used in modern buildings, to overcome the reverberations from plaster walls, metal doors, and windows.

2. Soft furnishings, curtains, carpets and upholstered furniture absorb sound considerably. Hard-tiled floors and gloss-painted walls and ceilings and expanses of glass will cause reverberation, which is a major hazard to health. Kitchens should be fitted with acoustic surface materials to reduce the inevitable reverberation.

BUILDING ACOUSTICS

Loud noise is a hazard to health, causing headaches, tiredness, irritability, and even deafness (see Figure 11.7). Buildings should therefore be designed to muffle noise, using some of the following methods:

(*a*) Surfaces of walls, ceilings, floors, etc., should be roughened or matt to diffuse sound waves. Acoustic tiles or panels of porous, plastic cork or asbestos are attractive and popular. Porous acoustic plaster may be used for music rooms.

(*b*) Soft furnishings, carpets, curtains, and upholstered furniture absorb sound.

(*c*) Cavity walls, double-glazed windows, and hollow doors are effective against noise from the street.

(*d*) Plastic instead of metal piping reduces the conduction of sound through the water and gas service systems.

(*e*) Halls used for performing music, plays or for speaking are usually specially designed, using sound-absorbing and insulating materials to reduce the reverberation of the music or speech. The supporting stage should not be hollow but of solid construction to prevent reverberation. Curved surfaces are a feature of concert halls allowing gentle reflection of the sound waves. Audiences themselves form an important sound-absorbing factor.

Ventilating ceilings

Restaurants and kitchens can be fitted with ceiling tiles which are perforated and connected to ventilating ducts. Such ceilings are effective in combining the functions of acoustic control, thermal insulation, and ventilation.

SUGGESTIONS FOR PRACTICAL WORK

1. Obtain a raybox and use the apparatus to demonstrate the reflection of light rays from (*a*) plane; and (*b*) curved mirrors.

2. Examine the lighting system in your home or in a hotel, and determine whether (*a*) it is adequate and safely lit; and (*b*) that comfortable lighting conditions prevail without glare.

3. Examine your kitchen and determine ways of reducing noise in it, using sound-absorbing surfaces or other methods.

4. Visit a concert hall and note how the architecture and design promote good acoustic powers.

QUESTIONS ON CHAPTER 11

1. Explain what is meant by reflection, refraction, diffusion, and dispersion of light rays.

2. What are the main causes of light glare? Give a summary of the methods used to promote diffused lighting in the home or in a restaurant.

3. Describe the various electric lamps for domestic lighting purposes. Briefly explain how lamp fittings affect the illumination of a room. What lighting arrangements would you suggest for a lounge?

4. Suggest suitable lighting arrangements for a (*a*) kitchen; (*b*) passageway; (*c*) dining area; and (*d*) bedroom and dressing area.

5. Write a short account of the uses of ultra-violet rays, infra-red rays, X-rays, and ionizing gamma radiation.

6. 'Noise is a serious hazard to health.' Suggest methods for reducing noise and for sound absorption in dwellings.

7. 'Sound and heat insulation are complementary systems.' Discuss this statement and indicate its truth with reference to modern buildings.

8. Enumerate what you regard are the important factors which contribute to comfortable surroundings in a residence and how they can be achieved.

9. Give an account of kitchen design with reference to ventilation, lighting, walls, ceilings, windows, and floors.

10. Compare and contrast the advantages and disadvantages of an all-gas kitchen with that of an all-electric kitchen.

MULTIPLE CHOICE QUESTIONS ON CHAPTER 11

1. Figure 11.8 shows the various bands of rays or waves in their relationship to light. Which numbered band indicates the position of the radiant heat rays?

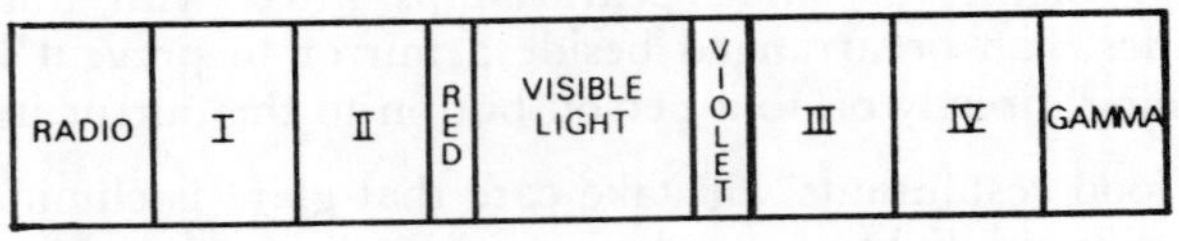

RADIO	I	II	R E D	VISIBLE LIGHT	V I O L E T	III	IV	GAMMA

Figure 11.8.

   (*a*) I   (*c*) III
   (*b*) II   (*d*) IV

2. In which band are the microwaves located:
   (*a*) I   (*c*) III
   (*b*) II   (*d*) IV

3. Which of the following bakes food without forming a brown crust:
   (*a*) infra-red rays   (*c*) microwaves
   (*b*) convection   (*d*) conduction

4. One of the following dish materials is unsuitable for use with the heating method referred to in Question 3:

(*a*) glassware   (*c*) earthenware
(*b*) paperware   (*d*) metalware

5. Which one of the following is the source of the heat used in the method of cooking referred to in Question 3:

(*a*) an X-ray tube   (*c*) magnetron valve
(*b*) aerated gas burner   (*d*) nichrome wire element

6. Which light fitting needs earthing?

(*a*) plastic lampholder   (*c*) plastic ceiling rose
(*b*) brass lampholder   (*d*) wooden pendant fitting

7. Which rooms must have a pull cord ceiling switch for the lights?

(*a*) bedroom   (*c*) bathroom
(*b*) sitting room   (*d*) lounge

8. An electric single coil filament lamp has a lamp life of about:

(*a*) 10 to 20 hours   (*c*) 1 000 to 2 000 hours
(*b*) 100 to 200 hours   (*d*) 10 000 to 20 000 hours

9. Which is the poorest conductor of sound?

(*a*) water   (*c*) air
(*b*) glass   (*d*) brass

10. Which wall surface is a good reflector of sound?

(*a*) glazed tiles   (*c*) wall paper
(*b*) wooden panels   (*d*) tapestry hangings

PART II

Chemical Aspects

INTRODUCTION – CHEMICAL ASPECTS

In this part the *chemical composition* of substances and materials used as energy sources from food and fossil fuels, cleaning preparations, structural, furnishing, bedding, china and ceramic materials is studied. In addition, it is essential to know of any *chemical changes* affecting chemical composition of these commodities and materials which occur in use, processing or by cooking.

12   Foundations of chemical knowledge

Chemistry is the study of the behaviour and composition of matter. All foods are made up of chemical substances which undergo chemical changes when cooked in an oven or digested within the body. The cooking of meat and vegetables induces chemical changes making them more palatable; similarly the leavening action of baking powder is a straightforward chemical change, as is the conversion of starch into sweet sugars by digestion.

Cookery is a science requiring a knowledge of chemistry. This is evident from the variety of cooking products and food additives available as cooking oils, fats, colourings, sweeteners, tenderizers, flavourings, creaming agents, preservatives, etc. Each is carefully prepared after painstaking research.

It is therefore essential for trained cooks to understand chemical science in order to appreciate the chemical nature of foods and the changes achieved on cooking. Home-workers should also know about cleansing agents and textiles used in the home and how the latter respond to the effects of heat, light, water, and chemical cleansing agents.

CLASSIFICATION AND PROPERTIES

The orderly collection and arrangement of knowledge is the basis of scientific study. The *properties* are the first thing to learn about a substance, meaning that a substance is classified according to (*a*) physical properties, appearance, taste, etc., and (*b*) chemical properties.

Physical properties include the appearance, taste and such measureable factors as specific gravity, boiling and melting points, elasticity and viscosity.

Chemical properties indicate the behaviour of the substance when burnt or treated with other chemical substances.

PHYSICAL AND CHEMICAL PROPERTIES OF GRANULATED SUGAR AND LARD

Property	Granulated sugar	Lard
Physical properties		
State	White, crystalline solid	White, non-crystalline solid
Taste	Sweet	Bland, tasteless
Smell	None	None to slight
Melting point	160°C	36°–39°C
Relative density	1·5	0·91
Viscosity	None	Viscous
Chemical properties		
Action of water	Dissolves rapidly	Insoluble
Tetrachloromethane (Carbon tetrachloride)	Insoluble	Soluble
Action of heat	Melts and changes to a dark-coloured mass of caramel at high temperature	Melts and produces an unpleasant smelling, irritating vapour of propenal (*acrolein*) at high temperature
Keeping qualities	Keeps indefinitely	Becomes rancid with objectionable smell and taste
Boiling with sodium hydroxide solution	No action	Forms a soap
Acids, e.g. ethanoic acid (vinegar)	Change to *invert* sugar	No change
Digestion	Quickly digested	Slowly digested

CHEMICAL AND PHYSICAL CHANGES

The table shows that sugar undergoes certain changes but different from those of lard, and this difference in behaviour accounts for their different properties. The changes are of two kinds.

(*a*) physical changes which are temporary, no new substances being formed. For example, to dissolve lard in tetrachloromethane (carbon tetrachloride) produces a change in physical state, but the lard is recoverable on evaporating the tetrachloromethane;

Note: tetrachloromethane is a toxic liquid with a vapour harmful to the eyes and the body.

(*b*) chemical changes which are permanent, usually involving the generation of heat, and in which the product cannot revert to its original form. The lard can be heated to form a new substance propenal (*acrolein*), or the lard can catch fire producing gases not reconvertible by any simple, chemical method.

Examples of physical changes

1. Boiling water.
2. Freezing of foods.
3. Dissolving sugar in water.

All these are physical changes involving a change of state; they are easily reversed and no new substance is formed.

Examples of chemical changes

1. The heating and cooking of most foods.
2. The toasting of bread.
3. Heating baking powder.

These are chemical changes involving a change in the chemical composition of the food. They are not easily reversed by chemical means.

ELEMENTS, COMPOUNDS, AND MIXTURES

All chemical substances can be classified into either elements, compounds, or mixtures.

Chemical elements

Elements are the *simplest* forms of matter and are the substances that combine to make all known compounds and mixtures. All foodstuffs, textiles, and cleansing materials are composed of chemical elements, sugar, for example containing carbon, hydrogen, and oxygen.

For convenience, elements are given symbols in the form of one or two letters, which represent *one atom* of the element. The symbol is usually the first letter or letters of the name of the element: H for hydrogen, O for oxygen, or Ca for calcium. The initial letter is always a capital. Some symbols have been derived from the Latin names, since early scientists used Latin in speech and writing. Iron (Fe from the Latin *Ferrum*), Copper (Cu from *Cuprum*), Sodium (Na from *Natrium*), and Potassium (K from *Kalium*) are instances.

Metals and non-metals

All chemical elements are divided into two sub-classes, namely metals and non-metals, as in the table. *Metals* have a lustre and can be polished and are good conductors of heat and electricity. *Non-metals* have no lustre and are non-conductors or insulators of heat and electricity (except graphite carbon).

IMPORTANT METAL ELEMENTS IN FOOD AND HOUSECRAFT CHEMISTRY

Name	Symbol	Name	Symbol	Name	Symbol
Aluminium	Al	Magnesium	Mg	Silver	
Arsenic	As	Manganese	Mn	(Argentium)	Ag
Calcium	Ca	Mercury		Sodium	
Chromium	Cr	(Hydrargyrum)	Hg	(Natrium)	Na
Copper	Cu	Nickel	Ni	Tin	
Gold	Au	Platinum	Pt	(Stannum)	Sn
Iron	Fe	Potassium		Zinc	Zn
Lead		(Kalium)	K		
(Plumbum)	Pb				

IMPORTANT NON-METAL ELEMENTS IN FOOD AND HOUSECRAFT CHEMISTRY

Name	Symbol
Bromine	Br
Carbon	C
Chlorine	Cl
Fluorine	F
Hydrogen	H
Iodine	I
Nitrogen	N
Oxygen	O
Phosphorus	P
Silicon	Si
Sulphur	S

Uses of the elements

1. Cooking utensils are made of copper, iron, and aluminium.

2. Plated tableware can be of silver, copper, gold, or chromium deposited on a nickel-silver alloy by electrolytic methods producing the well-known E.P.N.S., electroplated nickel-silver ware.

3. Nutritional elements or elements that enter into the composition of food are: carbon (C), hydrogen (H), oxygen (O), phosphorus (P), sulphur (S), and nitrogen (N), while the following elements are *mineral* elements needed in small or *trace* amounts: sodium (Na), potassium (K), calcium (Ca), magnesium (Mg), iron (Fe), chlorine (Cl), iodine (I), manganese (Mn), copper (Cu), and fluorine (F).

4. The human body is composed by per cent of the following chemical elements:

Oxygen	65	Sulphur	
Carbon	18	Sodium	
Hydrogen	10	Chlorine	
Nitrogen	3	Magnesium	Less
Calcium	2	Iron	than
Phosphorus	1	Manganese	1 per cent
		Copper	
		Iodine	
		Cobalt	
		Zinc	

The chemical elements in the human body must be supplied by the food and drink it consumes.

IMPORTANT ELEMENTS IN FOODS

Element	Foods containing the element, and recommended daily amounts for adults (see also Appendix B and C)
Carbon (C)	All foods contain carbon. Fats are particularly rich
Hydrogen (H)	Found in all foods and water
Oxygen (O)	Present in all foods and water
Phosphorus (P)	Present in meat, fish, and dairy products; plentiful in yeast extract
Sulphur (S)	Is an important ingredient of meat, fish, and dairy products. Present in large amounts in horseradish and in carrageen moss, the latter being used as a thickening agent. Bad eggs.
Nitrogen (N)	Is an essential component of fish, meat, dairy products, and peas and beans. Soya flour contains a high percentage
Calcium (Ca)	Present in large amounts in milk, cheese, watercress, and spinach. Daily intake 500–1 200 mg
Magnesium (Mg)	This element is found in all green vegetables, in carrageen moss, beans, and broccoli in large amounts, 200–300 mg daily
Iron (Fe)	Present in liver, kidney, beans, peas, wheat germ, almonds, and spinach. Large amounts in curry powder. Daily intake 6–15 mg
Sodium (Na) and Chlorine (Cl)	Are usually found together forming sodium chloride or table salt. Meat and vegetable extracts are rich in these elements. Daily intake as 'salt', 5–8 g, daily
Copper (Cu)	Raw liver, Brazil nuts, and cocoa are particularly rich in copper, 2–4 mg daily
Potassium (K)	Present in nearly all foods. Large amounts in coffee, meat and vegetable extracts
Iodine (I)	Present in seafish and in iodized table salt, 0·1 to 0·4 mg daily
Fluorine (F)	Present in seafish and added to drinking water, 0·25 to 1·5 mg daily
Cobalt (Co)	Present in liver. It is important against the development of anaemia
Manganese (Mn)	Present in tea, wheat germ, oatmeal flour, and cocoa
Zinc (Zn)	Found in wheat germ, cocoa, oysters, and liver, 2·0 mg daily
Chromium (Cr)	Yeast and animal origin foods, 20–50 µg daily

CHEMICAL COMPOUNDS

Chemical compounds are substances formed by the chemical union of two or more chemical elements:

element + element = compound

For example, when the elements iron and sulphur are heated together, a chemical change takes place, and a *chemical compound*, iron(II) sulphide, is formed:

Iron + sulphur = iron(II) sulphide
(element) (element) (compound)

The component elements of iron(II) sulphide cannot be separated by means of a magnet, since the atoms of sulphur and iron are joined together by strong chemical bonds.

MIXTURES

Mixtures are made up of two or more substances, elements or compounds, present in different amounts and easily separable:

Element iron + element sulphur = mixture of iron and sulphur

Compound iron sulphide + element sulphur
= mixture of iron(II) sulphide and sulphur

Iron filings can be removed from any mixture by means of a magnet.

All raw and unrefined foods are *mixtures* of different compounds. Unrefined sugar juice from sugar cane or sugar beet is a *mixture* of many different compounds which produces a single compound of pure sugar or *sucrose* on refining. Milk and flour are also mixtures of many different compounds which can be *partly* separated by various dairy processes and by milling. Food chemistry therefore is concerned with the composition of food mixtures and the effect of cooking on their components.

Synthesis

This is a process of building up a compound from its *elements*. Many chemical compounds can be synthesized. Such plastics as polyamides and polyesters are produced in this way. Chemical science has not yet achieved the synthesis of a foodstuff, attempts to synthesize cane sugar for instance having failed.

Analysis

This is the process of breaking down a chemical compound into its component elements. The analysis of cane sugar reveals it to be a compound of carbon, hydrogen, and oxygen. All information concerning the chemical composition of food has been obtained by chemical analysis.

Chromatography is a method of analysis using paper for separating mixtures of chemical compounds. It is employed in protein analysis.

CHEMICAL FORMULAE AND EQUATIONS

All matter consists of tiny particles called *atoms*. The different elements are made up of their own kind of atoms, those of sulphur for example differing from those of iron in size and weight. The lightest atom is that of hydrogen. The *atomic weight* of an element is the ratio of the weight of its atom compared with that of the hydrogen atom.

ATOMIC WEIGHTS OF SOME ELEMENTS

Element	Symbol	Atomic weight
Hydrogen	H	1
Carbon	C	12
Oxygen	O	16
Sulphur	S	32
Iron	Fe	56
Curium	Cm	242

Atoms do not usually exist on their own in the *free state*. They tend to join together into a more permanent relationship in the form of *molecules*, which is the smallest part of a compound or element which *can* exist in the free state:

Atom + atom = molecule of a compound

Radicals

These are groups of atoms that do not normally exist on their own in the free state. For example hydrogen carbonate, chloride, nitrate, and sulphate are *acid radicals* which can exist in the free state only when linked to metal radicals such as calcium or magnesium or other metals.

Formulae

Formulae are the chemist's shorthand system for describing the composition of molecules. A molecule of hydrogen is written as H_2, a molecule of water as H_2O. These formulae show that hydrogen consists of one element only, two atoms of which form a *stable* molecule which can exist in the free state. Similarly the stable molecule of water consists of two different elements, hydrogen and oxygen.

$$H + H = H_2, \text{ a molecule of hydrogen}$$
$$H + O + H = H_2O, \text{ a molecule of water}$$
$$C_{12}H_{22}O_{11} = \text{ a molecule of cane sugar}$$

VALENCIES OR COMBINING POWERS OF IMPORTANT ELEMENTS AND RADICALS

Valency	Element or radical
Univalent (One-armed)	Elements: H, Ag, Na, and K Radicals: $-OH$ (Hydroxyl) and $-HCO_3$ (hydrogen carbonate), $-NO_3$ (nitrate), $-Cl$ (chloride), and NH_4- (ammonium)
Bivalent (Two-armed)	Elements: O, S, Ca, Mg, and Zn Radicals: $=CO_3$ (carbonate), $=SO_4$ [sulphate(VI)], and $=SO_3$ [sulphate(IV)] (sulphite)
Trivalent (Three-armed)	Elements: N, and Al Radical: $\equiv PO_4$ [phosphate(IV)]
Tetravalent (Four-armed)	Elements: C and Si

Sodium hydrogen carbonate is made up of the elements sodium, hydrogen, carbon, and oxygen; its formula is *not* $NaHCO$, but $NaHCO_3$. The symbols $Na- -HCO_3$ show the 'arms' or combining powers of the sodium and hydrogen carbonate radical. Each arm must be connected to another and cannot hang free. The sodium arm joins the hydrogen carbonate radical arm to form $NaHCO_3$, sodium hydrogen carbonate:

$$Na- -HCO_3 \text{ or } NaHCO_3$$

Water is written H_2O, since the oxygen is bivalent (two-armed), and the hydrogen one-armed or univalent.

$$H- -O- -H \text{ or } H_2O$$

Sodium chloride (common salt) is written as $NaCl$ because each radical has one arm or is univalent.

$$Na- -Cl \text{ or } NaCl$$

How to write the formula of a compound

1. Remember the chemical name of the compound.
2. Remember the symbols for the elements or radicals.
3. Write the symbol of the *metal first*, followed by the symbol of the non-metal or radical.

$$\text{Formula} = \text{metal} + \text{radical}$$

4. The number is written last.

Examples

(1) Calcium carbonate (chalk) is $CaCO_3$. The calcium is two-armed as is the carbonate, CO_3 radical. Therefore we write

$$Ca= =CO_3 \text{ or } CaCO_3$$

(2) Sodium carbonate (washing soda) is Na_2CO_3. Thus two univalent sodium atoms are needed to combine with the bivalent carbonate radical arms:

$$\left. \begin{array}{l} Na- \\ Na- \end{array} \right\rangle CO_3 \text{ or } Na_2CO_3$$

(3) Ammonium hydrogen carbonate or German baking powder is NH_4HCO_3. The one-armed ammonium radical is joined to a one-armed hydrogen carbonate radical:

$$NH_4- -HCO_3 \text{ or } NH_4HCO_3$$

(4) Sodium sulphate(IV) used as potato whiteners, is Na_2SO_3. The bivalent sulphate(IV) radical must have two univalent one-armed solution radicals connected to it:

$$\left. \begin{array}{l} Na- \\ Na- \end{array} \right\rangle SO_3 \text{ or } Na_2SO_3$$

IONS AND IONIZATION

When salt or sodium chloride is dissolved in water the molecule of $NaCl$ breaks up by *ionization* into positively charged Na^+ ions called *cations*, and negatively charged Cl^- ions called *anions*.

$$\begin{array}{ccc} & NaCl & \\ \swarrow & & \searrow \\ Na^+ & & Cl^- \\ \text{cation} & & \text{anion} \end{array}$$

Mineral salts in the diet will therefore be available to the body cells in this form as *ions*.

EQUATIONS

Equations are useful to describe chemical changes briefly. They can involve both formulae and words:

$$Fe + S = FeS$$

This equation shows that iron joins with sulphur to form iron sulphide.

$$CaSO_4 + \text{sodium soap} = Na_2SO_4 + \text{calcium soap}$$

This is a mixed formula and word equation stating that when sodium soap is added to calcium sulphate there is a chemical change in which sodium sulphate and a calcium soap are formed.

Note. You will encounter many formulae and names of chemical compounds in later chapters. Remember as many as possible since all are connected with cookery or housecraft. Chemical changes should be remembered and written as word equations with the exception of the simpler formula equations.

Variable valencies

A chemical element may have more than two valencies, e.g. copper has valencies of 1 and 2 shown as Cu(I) and Cu(II). Also radicals, e.g. sulphate SO_4(IV) and SO_4(VI) with valencies of 4 or 6.

SUGGESTIONS FOR PRACTICAL WORK

1. Examine and note the appearance of the following chemical elements: carbon, sulphur, calcium, magnesium, iron, cobalt, and manganese. Also ask to be shown samples of phosphorus, potassium, and sodium which are *dangerous* and must not be handled.

2. Separate the components of baking powder. Stir some baking powder into cold water, allow to stand, and note how some of the mixture is insoluble. Filter the solution and dry the filter paper in an oven at 110°C. The insoluble ingredient of the baking powder mixture is *starch* or perhaps flour.

3. Separate the main components of flour. Take about three tablespoonsful of flour and make into a stiff dough-ball. Place the dough in a small muslin bag and knead and squeeze the bag in some water in a litre beaker. Note how the white *starch* enters the water, leaving behind the sticky *gluten*.

4. Examine the labels of various packed food and confectionery products and note the names of any chemical ingredients.

5. See *Experimental Science for Catering and Home Craft*, Practical work 1.1 to 1.4, 2.5, 2.6 and 22.3.

QUESTIONS ON CHAPTER 12

1. Give four examples in each case of chemical and physical changes encountered in cookery and housecraft.

2. Write the formulae of five chemical compounds used in the kitchen.

3. Explain the following terms, giving examples in each case: (*a*) metals and non-metals; (*b*) elements; (*c*) mixtures; (*d*) compounds; and (*e*) symbols.

4. Name ten chemical elements and state in which foodstuffs they occur.

5. Name a mixture used in cookery. State its main ingredients and briefly describe how they can be separated.

6. Explain the terms: (*a*) analysis; (*b*) synthesis; and (*c*) photosynthesis.

7. Write the formulae for: sodium hydrogen carbonate, calcium sulphate, calcium carbonate, magnesium sulphate, and sodium chloride.

MULTIPLE CHOICE QUESTIONS ON CHAPTER 12

1. Most foods are complex chemical substances called:
   (*a*) organic compounds   (*c*) inorganic elements
   (*b*) inorganic compounds   (*d*) mixtures of elements

2. Chemical elements are given simple shorthand means of identification called:
   (*a*) signs   (*c*) formulae
   (*b*) symbols   (*d*) recipes

3. The daily requirement of the main chemical element needed for healthy teeth and bones is:
   (*a*) 5 milligram   (*c*) 5 microgram
   (*b*) 500 milligram   (*d*) 50 microgram

4. The chemical inorganic element closely linked with energy-giving chemical substances in muscles and living cells is:
   (*a*) sulphur   (*c*) phosphorus
   (*b*) magnesium   (*d*) potassium

5. Which of the following foods contains the greatest amount of the mineral needed for red blood cell formation:
   (*a*) white sugar   (*c*) golden syrup
   (*b*) brown sugar   (*d*) treacle molasses

6. The daily requirement of the element needed for formation of red blood cells is:
   (*a*) 5 to 15 kg   (*c*) 5 to 15 mg
   (*b*) 50 to 150 μg   (*d*) 50 to 150 g

7. If a person is on a low sodium diet which of the following are forbidden:
   (i) vinegar   (v) potassium chloride
   (ii) baking powder   (vi) sugar
   (iii) pepper   (vii) meat extract
   (iv) baking soda   (viii) bacon

   (*a*) i, iii, iv, vi   (*c*) ii, iv, vii, viii
   (*b*) ii, iv, v, vii   (*d*) iv, v, vi, vii

8. If a food sample is placed in a crucible and heated strongly over the bunsen burner flame shown in Figure 12.1

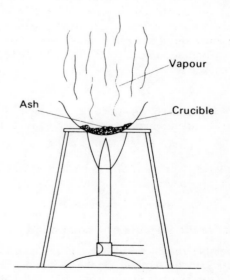

Figure 12.1.

which two of the following chemical elements will be burnt away and enter the vapours:

(i)	phosphorus	(iv)	carbon
(ii)	calcium	(v)	potassium
(iii)	iron	(vi)	hydrogen

(a)	i, ii	(c)	iv, vi
(b)	iii, iv	(d)	v, vi

9. The solid ash remaining in the crucible is moistened with hydrochloric acid and a clean platinum wire dipped in the moistened ash and placed in a lighted bunsen burner flame. The flame becomes coloured yellow/orange. This indicates the original food sample contained the chemical element:

(a)	sulphur	(c)	iron
(b)	sodium	(d)	phosphorus

10. Lead ethanoate (acetate) paper turns black when held in the vapours from a heated mixture of soda lime (sodium, calcium hydroxides) and dried egg. This shows the presence of one of the following elements in the egg:

(a)	carbon	(c)	hydrogen
(b)	nitrogen	(d)	sulphur

13 The air: oxidation and reduction

OXYGEN

Oxygen (formula O_2) is one of the most abundant elements and forms 50 per cent of the earth's crust.

Preparation

Hydrogen peroxide (H_2O_2) is rich in oxygen, which can be released by means of manganese dioxide:

$$\text{Hydrogen peroxide} = \text{water} + \text{oxygen}$$

$$2H_2O_2 = 2H_2O + O_2$$

Experiment

Note: Chemical experimental work should be *demonstrated* by a *qualified* instructor.

Set up the apparatus shown in Figure 13.1. Carefully allow the 20-volume hydrogen peroxide (H_2O_2) to fall drop by drop on to the powdered manganese dioxide in the flask. The large-scale preparation of oxygen is from liquid air.

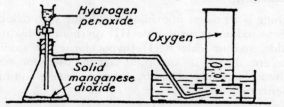

Figure 13.1. Laboratory preparation of oxygen from hydrogen peroxide

Properties

Oxygen is a colourless gas with no smell or taste. If a glowing piece of wood is plunged into a gas-jar of oxygen, it will relight and burn very brightly.

Experiment

Obtain samples of the *non-metals* carbon, sulphur, and phosphorus and the *metals* sodium, magnesium, and calcium. Heat a small portion of each gently in a deflagrating spoon and plunge it into a gas-jar of oxygen. Test the contents of the gas-jar, to which a little water has been added, with *neutral litmus* solution or paper.

OXIDES

Oxides are formed by the union of an element with oxygen, a process called *oxidation*. There are two main types of oxides *acid* and *basic*, classified according to their action with water and litmus *indicator*.

Acid and basic oxides

Oxidation
Element + oxygen = element oxide

THE FORMATION OF OXIDES

Acid oxides	Basic oxides
Formed from non-metals, such as C, S, and P	Formed from metals such as Na, Ca, and Mg
Carbon dioxide (CO_2)	Sodium oxide (Na_2O)
Sulphur dioxide (SO_2)	Calcium oxide (CaO)
Phosphorus oxides	Magnesium oxide (MgO)
Acids	**Bases**
Formed from acid oxides with water and turn litmus *red*	Formed from basic oxides with water and turn litmus *blue*
Carbonic acid (H_2CO_3)	Sodium hydroxide ($NaOH$)
Sulphuric acid (H_2SO_4)	Calcium hydroxide ($Ca(OH)_2$)
Phosphoric acid (H_3PO_4)	Magnesium hydroxide ($Mg(OH)_2$)

Conclusion:

Metal + oxygen = basic (metal) oxide
Non-metal + oxygen = acidic (non-metal) oxide

Neutral oxides

Neutral oxides do not change the colour of neutral litmus and are therefore neither acid nor basic. An example is water (H_2O).

Peroxides

These oxides readily lose oxygen on heating, e.g. hydrogen peroxide.

OXIDATION

Oxidation is the process of *addition of oxygen* to an element or compound or *removal* of hydrogen. The table shows some of the more important oxidation processes and their meanings.

OXIDATION PROCESSES

Oxidation process	Definition	Example
Combustion	Process in which substances join with oxygen forming oxides, heat, and light	Burning of fossil fuels, wood, coal, petrol, etc.
Explosion	A process of *rapid* combustion	Explosion of coal gas and gunpowder
Aerobic respiration	Process of liberating energy from food by means of oxygen. Carbon dioxide and water are byproducts.	Breathing or plant and animal respiration
Bleaching	Process of adding oxygen to a coloured chemical compound and changing it into a colourless compound	Textile and flour bleaching
Rusting	The slow process of adding oxygen to iron in the presence of water to form rust or iron oxides	Rusting of iron

APPLICATIONS OF OXIDATION

1. Flour

Milled flour has a slight yellow tinge which can be removed by oxidation. Early methods of flour bleaching involved prolonged storage and slow oxidation by the oxygen of the air. This process also improved the baking qualities of the flour and was called the *ageing* process. The process is now hastened by the use of flour oxidizing chemicals which add oxygen. The reagents which mature the flour include ammonium persulphate, sulphur dioxide, and potassium bromate.

2. Food packaging

Coffee, dried milk, and malted milk preparations are packed in evacuated tins, the air being removed by a vacuum pump and replaced by either carbon dioxide, hydrogen, or nitrogen as *air excluders*.

3. Food preservation

Canning and bottling involve creating an air-free space above the contents. Similarly certain oily foods such as fish, butter, and margarine keep longer if packed closely together to reduce the amount of air between the items.

4. Anti-oxidants

Fats, particularly cooking fat, butter, and margarine become rancid and objectionable in smell and taste if kept too long. The fats become rancid by oxidation because of contact with the air and can be preserved by adding a chemical compound – the *anti-oxidant* (see Appendix A, E300 onwards).

5. Enzymatic browning of foods

Apples, potatoes, fruits, and vegetables turn brown rapidly when the cut surfaces are exposed to the air. The main cause is the oxygen of the air but the *enzymes* in the plant cells contribute also. Solutions of sodium sulphate(IV) (sulphite) and potassium dihydroxybutanedioate (cream of tartar) are used as *whiteners* to prevent this *enzymatic browning*. Immersion in cold previously boiled water will hinder the browning process.

6. Disinfectants and antiseptics

Most harmful microbes are destroyed by high concentrations of oxygen. Oxygen-rich and oxidizing chemicals are therefore used in such disinfectants as hydrogen peroxide, potassium chlorate(VII), potassium manganate(VII) or 'Condys fluid', and sodium chlorate(I) (hypochlorite) or bleach preparations. Good ventilation or aeration provides ample oxygen for purposes of hygiene. Water supplies are purified by aerating the water with air or oxygen. (See pages 204 and 206.)

7. Bleaching

Bleaching is a process of oxidation utilizing such oxidizing agents as sodium peroxoborate(III) (perborate), hydrogen peroxide, sodium chlorate(I) (hypochlorite) or sunlight, which are the most important agents used for textile bleaching. *Flour* is bleached by chlorine dioxide and nitrogen peroxide.

NITROGEN

Nitrogen is an important component of air, being present to the extent of four-fifths or 80 to 78%.

Nitrogen gas (formula N_2) is obtained from a cylinder of

compressed nitrogen gas (Figure 13.2). The large-scale preparation of nitrogen is from liquid air.

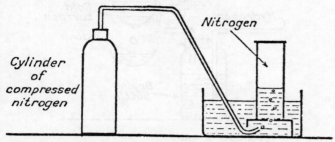

Figure 13.2. Laboratory preparation of nitrogen

Properties

Nitrogen is a colourless gas with no taste or smell. Nitrogen is chemically lazy or *inert*. It does not allow things to burn in it, with the exception of magnesium metal. The gas has no action on litmus indicator and is therefore neutral.

Uses

1. Nitrogen is used to provide an inert atmosphere in packaged potato powder, dried coffee, milk, meat, and malted milk to prevent the development of rancid flavours.
2. The most important application is in the manufacture of ammonia, nitric acid, and for fertilizer production.
3. *Liquid nitrogen* is sprayed on foods for *quick freezing*.

THE AIR

The air or atmosphere forms a layer many kilometres high surrounding the earth. We shall now consider its chemical composition.

Experiments

1. Sprinkle a few iron filings inside a long, graduated, glass tube, plug it lightly with cotton wool, and invert it in a jar of water. Put the apparatus aside for a week, allowing the iron filings to rust (oxidation). As the rusting occurs, oxygen is used up and the level of the water rises inside the tube by one-fifth (Figure 13.3).
2. Place a lighted candle in a dish and float it in a trough of water (Figure 13.4). Cover with a bell-jar and note how the level of the water rises inside the bell-jar as the oxygen is removed by combustion (oxidation).

Note. When measuring the final levels of water inside the tube or bell-jar, equalize the water levels inside and out by adding water to the outer container.

Conclusion: The two experiments show that approximately one-fifth of the air is oxygen which is used up during rusting and combustion. The remaining four-fifths is nitrogen and inert, taking no part in either process.

AIR IS A MIXTURE

The average composition of air is:

| Nitrogen | 78% | Inert gases | 1% |
| Oxygen | 21% | Carbon dioxide | 0·03% |

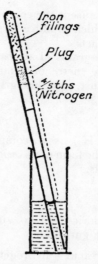

Figure 13.3. Demonstration of composition of air using iron filings

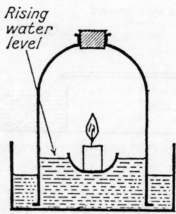

Figure 13.4. Demonstration of the composition of air using a burning candle

with variable amounts of dust, micro-organisms, chemical waste gases, and moisture.

Air is considered to be a mixture and *not* a compound, because its composition *varies* from time to time, and each component can be *separated* by simple methods.

Nitrogen in the air serves to dilute the oxygen and slow down the oxidation processes.

Inert gases are those with no chemical properties such as helium, neon, argon, and krypton. They are used for filling electric lamps and for advertising signs.

Carbon dioxide enters the air by the respiration of plants and animals and by the combustion of fuels. The proportion in the air remains fairly constant, since living plants use it in their feeding process, *photosynthesis*. In addition some of the gas dissolves in rain, river, and sea water.

Air pollution

The pollution of air by chimney smoke and chemical waste gases is a continuous hazard to health, causing chest disorders. The main cause is the combustion of raw coal in domestic fireplaces which produce tarry smoke in contrast to that of smokeless fuels.

Approximately 100 grams of atmospheric dirt fall each year on every square metre of a large industrial town, composed of mixed dust, soot, fine grit, and ash.

HYDROGEN

Hydrogen (formula H_2) is a comparatively abundant chemical element in the form of its *compounds*, which include water, foods, and fuels.

Preparation

Add dilute hydrochloric acid to zinc metal using the apparatus shown in Figure 13.5:

Zinc + hydrochloric acid = hydrogen + zinc(II) chloride
$$Zn + 2HCl = H_2 + ZnCl_2$$

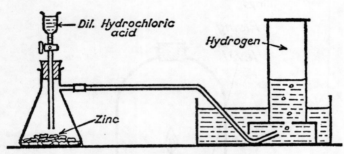

Figure 13.5. Laboratory preparation of hydrogen

Properties

Hydrogen is a colourless gas with no taste or smell, extremely light, and of low density.

Experiments

1. Pass a stream of hydrogen gas through a clay pipe dipped into soap solution. The light soap bubbles of hydrogen will rise to the ceiling.

2. Collect half a large test tube of hydrogen, ignite the gas and note how it burns with a pop. This is a test for the presence of hydrogen.

3. Hydrogen means 'water maker'. The origin of the name can be shown by passing hydrogen or natural gas, which contains hydrogen, through a gas-drying bottle containing concentrated sulphuric acid (see Figure 13.6). The gas is then lit after making certain all *air* has been flushed out of the apparatus and that only hydrogen gas is issuing, and the flame allowed to impinge on the cold surface of the flask. Droplets of water collect in the dish. To prove that it is water, determine its boiling point which is 100°C. This experiment demonstrates the *synthesis* of water from hydrogen and oxygen:

Hydrogen + oxygen from air = water or hydrogen oxide
$$2H_2 + O_2 = 2H_2O$$

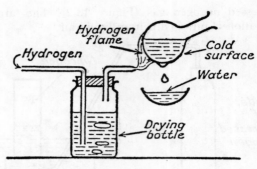

Figure 13.6. Synthesis of water

REDUCTION

Reduction is the *removal* of oxygen from a compound or the process of adding hydrogen, and is the opposite of oxidation.

Experiment

Place black copper(II) oxide (basic oxide) in the apparatus shown in Figure 13.7. Pass a stream of coal gas or hydrogen over the heated copper oxide. Note how the red copper metal appears after the oxygen has been removed. In addition droplets of *water* appear in the cooler parts of the tube:

Copper(II) oxide + hydrogen = copper + water
$$CuO + H_2 = Cu + H_2O$$

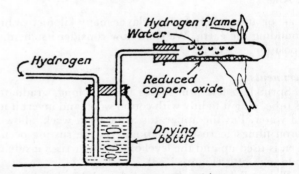

Figure 13.7. Reduction of copper(II) oxide

APPLICATIONS OF REDUCTION

1. Hydrogenation or hardening of edible lipid oils

Solid fats can be produced from the *liquid* oils of maize, cottonseed, sunflower, and the whale, by bubbling hydrogen through the lipid in the presence of powdered nickel which acts as a catalyst in the *hydrogenation* process. This process is used in the manufacture of cooking fats and margarine. Hydrogenation causes *saturation* of the double bonds in the lipid molecule (see page 114).

2. Flour quality

White flour which has been oxidized produces a strong, resilient, elastic dough. Wholemeal or brown flours produce a soft, inelastic dough because of the *reducing* properties of the chemicals and enzymes present in the wheat germ or added malt extract or vitamin C.

3. Anti-oxidants (see Appendix A)

These are *reducing* agents which prevent fats and margarine becoming rancid and prevent the browning of fruits and vegetables in air. A form of vitamin C, erythorbic acid also has strong reducing properties.

4. Reducing bleaches

Certain colours or stains cannot be bleached or oxidized, but are changed into colourless compounds by means of a reducing agent, a substance that removes oxygen. Sodium hexaoxodisulphate(V) (dithionite) ($Na_sS_2O_4$) and sodium methanal sulphoxylate ($NaHSO_2.HCHO.2H_2O$) are the most important reducing bleaches for fabrics. The bleaching action depends on the formation of sulphur dioxide (SO_2) which extracts the oxygen to yield sulphur trioxide (SO_3) and finally sulphuric acid (H_2SO_4).

SUGGESTIONS FOR PRACTICAL WORK

1. Obtain a brownish flour of 85 per cent extraction, and mix 10 g of it with 1 g of potassium bromate. Place it in a labelled screw-cap bottle alongside a sample of untreated brown flour. Leave for a fortnight and observe whether any bleaching has occurred.

2. Obtain some ripe apples and peel off the skin *under* water. Cut the apples into 1-cm cubes, placing some in: (a) a glass dish in air; (b) in cold *boiled* water; (c) in cold tap water; (d) in water containing potassium dihydroxybutanedioate (cream of tartar); (e) in water containing ethanoic acid (vinegar); and (f) in water containing sodium sulphate(IV) (sulphite). Compare the rates at which browning develops.

3. Place lightly greased white tiles in a quiet position on an outside window ledge and note the accumulation of atmospheric dirt.

4. Investigate the conditions required for the rusting of iron. Obtain six 5-cm nails, cleaning them with fine emery paper.

(a) Insert two in a test tube containing a little water.

(b) Insert two in a test tube containing boiled water (from which the air has been removed) and cover the water with a layer of paraffin oil.

(c) Place the rest in a stoppered test tube containing anhydrous calcium chloride.

Leave the test tubes for a week and then observe which conditions allow the iron to rust.

5. See *Experimental Science for Catering and Homecraft Students*, Practical work 7.1, 10.3, 15.1, 23.3, 84.1, 84.2 and 85.3.

QUESTIONS ON CHAPTER 13

1. What is meant by the terms *oxidation* and *reduction*? Give examples of these processes in cookery and laundry work.

2. Write brief notes on (a) anti-oxidants, and (b) the ageing process of flour.

3. Describe an experiment to demonstrate the composition of air. What measures would you undertake to contribute to cleaner air in cities?

4. Describe briefly the preparation of hydrogen and give some of its more important properties. State what is meant by hydrogenation of oils.

5. Write short notes on: (a) potato whiteners; (b) vacuum packaging of foods; (c) rancidity; (d) potassium bromate; and (e) reducing bleaching agents.

6. Describe the various types of oxide encountered and how they react with water and an indicator.

7. Write a brief account of two of: (a) air pressure; (b) clean air; (c) chemical composition of air; (d) humidity of air; and (e) effect of air on foodstuffs.

MULTIPLE CHOICE QUESTIONS ON CHAPTER 13

1. Which shows the composition of the air we exhale or breathe out?

	Oxygen %	Nitrogen %	Carbon dioxide %
(a)	78	21	0·03
(b)	17	79	4
(c)	20	0·03	79
(d)	3·5	79·5	17

2. The normal composition of the fresh air we inhale or breathe in is:

	% Oxygen	% Nitrogen	% Carbon dioxide	% Rare gases
(a)	20	0·03	78·97	1
(b)	78	1·97	20	0·03
(c)	20	0·03	1·97	78
(d)	20	78·97	0·03	1

3. Which chemical element forms water on combustion in air?

(a) carbon   (c) sulphur
(b) hydrogen   (d) phosphorus

4. Which fuel does *not* form sulphur dioxide gas on combustion?

(a) natural gas
(b) bituminous house coal
(c) smokeless solid fuels
(d) light central heating oil

5. A muslin bag containing one of the following materials is inserted on the end of a plastic rod inside a test tube of air inverted in a container of water. It is seen that after a time the level of water rises up inside the tube due to the **removal** of one component of the air by the:

(a) sulphur powder   (c) sand
(b) iron filings   (d) sawdust

6. Which component of the air is removed in the experiment referred to in Question 5?

(*a*) oxygen   (*c*) argon

(*b*) nitrogen   (*d*) carbon dioxide

7. The process of adding hydrogen or removal of oxygen from a compound is called:

(*a*) oxidation   (*c*) combustion

(*b*) synthesis   (*d*) reduction

8. One of the following is used to provide an inert atmosphere in packaged dried foods:

(*a*) oxygen   (*c*) chlorine

(*b*) nitrogen   (*d*) hydrogen

9. Soft or liquid lipids are hardened by the process of

(*a*) oxidation   (*c*) bleaching

(*b*) hydrogenation   (*d*) combustion

10. Which of the following will *not* contain oxygen liable to cause potatoes to become discoloured?

(*a*) cold fresh tap water

(*b*) boiled cooled tap water

(*c*) fresh sea-water

(*d*) hydrogen peroxide solution

14 Acids, bases, and salts

ORGANIC AND INORGANIC COMPOUNDS

Chemical compounds can be divided into two main groups, *organic* and *inorganic*. Organic compounds are those of *carbon* or chemical compounds derived from living plants or animals. Inorganic compounds are derived from non-living minerals.

ORGANIC AND INORGANIC COMPOUNDS

Organic compounds	*Inorganic compounds*
From plants and animals, e.g. sugar from sugar beet and sugar cane	From rocks and minerals, e.g. sodium chloride, sand, and iron
They char or blacken easily on heating	Do not char on heating
All contain carbon	Contain elements other than carbon
Melt readily at low temperatures	Melt at high temperatures
Do not ionize	Ionize readily (see page 84)

ACIDS

Acids usually contain hydrogen exchangeable with a metal to form a *salt*. Organic or alkanoic acids contain hydrogen in a *carboxylic acid* ($-COOH$) group.

Example

Hydrogen gas is made by adding dilute hydrochloric acid (HCl) to the metal zinc (Zn) (see Chapter 13). The hydrogen of the acid is replaced by the zinc to form the salt zinc(II) chloride ($ZnCl_2$):

$$Zn + 2HCl = ZnCl_2 + H_2$$

Zinc + hydrochloric acid = zinc(II) chloride + hydrogen

Examples of *inorganic* acids are hydrochloric acid (HCl), nitric acid (HNO_3), and sulphuric acid (H_2SO_4), obtained from rock salt, salt-petre, and sulphur *minerals* respectively. Typical *organic* acids are ethanoic (acetic;. 2: hydroxypropane tricarboxylic (citric), and 2-hydroxypropanoic (lactic), obtained from vinegar, lemon, and sour milk respectively.

Properties of acids

1. Acids have a sour taste: sour milk 2-hydroxypropanoic (lactic) acid, and lemons 2-hydroxypropane tricarboxylic (citric) acid. Some organic acids, for example octadecanoic (stearic) acid, do not have this taste.

2. Most acids will turn litmus indicator, a vegetable dye, *red*.

3. Acids are corrosive and dissolve cotton and linen. Inorganic acids are *strong* with corresponding corrosive strength. Organic acids are *weak* and are less corrosive.

All organic acids have a $-COOH$ carboxylic acidic group.

4. Acids will *neutralize* bases and alkalis to form salts and water. If sodium hydroxide solution is added to hydrochloric acid containing red litmus, the indicator will gradually become pale blue or neutral as the salt sodium chloride and water are formed:

$$Acid + base = salt + water$$

Hydrochloric acid + sodium hydroxide = sodium chloride + water

IMPORTANT ACIDS AND THEIR USES

Acids	Appearance and Properties	Uses
Inorganic acids		
Hydrochloric (HCl)	Colourless liquid with a strong smell	Making other chemical compounds. Stomach juices contain 1%
Nitric (HNO₃)	Yellow liquid with a strong smell	Dyes, fertilizers, and explosives
Sulphuric (H₂SO₄)	Oily liquid with no smell	Battery acid, fertilizers, and synthetic fibre manufacture
Phosphoric (H₃PO₄)	Syrupy liquid	Jams, jellies, and fruit juices
Organic (alkanoic) acids		
Ethanoic (acetic) (CH₃COOH)	Colourless liquid with a characteristic smell. Its pure form is glacial acetic acid	Used to remove blue and to brighten coloured fabrics. Vinegar for pickling. Forms in dough during yeast fermentation
Ascorbic	White solid	Vitamin C
Benzene carboxylic (benzoic)	White solid	Food preservative
Carbonic (H₂CO₃ = CO₂ + H₂O)	Carbon dioxide soluble in water	Aerated mineral water and soda water
2-hydroxypropane-tricarboxylic (citric)	White solid	Found in citrus fruits. Flavours jellies and cordials, and prevents browning of apples and potatoes
2-aminopentanedioic (glutamic)	Solid	Found in soy sauce and flour. It intensifies food flavours
2-hydroxypropanoic (lactic)	Syrupy liquid	Found in sour milk. Flavouring for soft drinks and sauces
2-hydroxybutanedioic (malic)	Solid	Present in apples, prunes, and cherries. Used in jams and jellies
Ethanedioic (oxalic) COOH | COOH	White solid *Poisonous and toxic to skin and eyes*	Found in rhubarb leaves with smaller amounts in the leaf stalks. Used for stain removal and cleaning brass-ware
2,3-dihydroxybutane-dioic acid (tartaric)	White solid	Found in fruits. Used in baking powder, and as a flavour in jams and jellies

5. When acids are added to sodium hydrogen carbonate, bubbles of carbon dioxide gas are produced. Mix together small amounts of 2-hydroxypropane tricarboxylic (citric) acid and sodium hydrogen carbonate and stir them into warm water. Note the rapid production of CO_2 gas or *effervescence*.

Acid rinses

Weak solutions of ethanoic (acetic) acid or vinegar, are used to remove deposits of calcium soaps from fabrics washed in hard water. The acid also neutralizes the remaining alkali of the soap. Coloured garments are brightened by rinsing in dilute ethanoic acid (vinegar).

BASES

Bases are the oxides or hydroxides of *metals*.

Example

Calcium burnt in oxygen forms white calcium oxide (CaO), a base which partly dissolves in water forming calcium hydroxide $(Ca(OH)_2)$:

$$\text{Calcium} + \text{oxygen} = \text{calcium oxide}$$
$$2Ca + O_2 = 2CaO$$

$$\text{Calcium oxide} + \text{water} = \text{calcium hydroxide}$$
$$CaO + H_2O = Ca(OH)_2$$

ALKALIS

Alkalis are bases which *dissolve readily* in water. Examples are sodium hydroxide (caustic soda) (NaOH) and potassium hydroxide (KOH) (caustic potash).

Properties of bases and alkalis

1. All have a bitter taste similar to soap.
2. They are soapy to touch.
3. They turn litmus indicator *blue*.
4. They *neutralize* acids to form salts and water.
5. Bases and alkalis are corrosive. Strong alkalis will dissolve wool, silk, and rayons.
6. They form soap with plant and animal oils or fats (see page 128).

SOME IMPORTANT BASES AND ALKALIS

Base or alkali	Properties	Uses
Ammonium hydroxide (NH₄OH)	Ammonia gas (NH₃) dissolves readily in water to form ammonium hydroxide: $NH_3 + H_2O = NH_4OH$ The strongest solution of ammonia has an R.D. of 0·880 and is called Eighty-eight ammonia. Never smell the liquid and always handle with *care* – poisonous and corrosive.	1. To soften hard water 2. As a rinse to remove acids 3. Cleaning brass and copperware 4. Cleaning upholstery 5. Grease remover for textile materials
Calcium oxide (CaO) (Burnt lime)	White solid that combines with water giving out considerable heat (exothermic reaction) forming calcium hydroxide (Ca(OH)₂) (slaked lime): $CaO + H_2O = Ca(OH)_2$	1. Water softener 2. Preparation of gelatine (see page 124)
Calcium hydroxide (Ca(OH)₂) (Lime water)	Clear liquid that turns cloudy in air	For the treatment of skin, bones, and sinews for gelatine extraction
Potassium hydroxide (KOH) (Caustic potash)	White solid, very hygroscopic	1. Soft or toilet soap manufacture 2. Grease remover for ovens, sinks, and drains
Sodium hydroxide (NaOH) (Caustic soda)	White hygroscopic solid	1. Household soap manufacture 2. Grease remover for ovens, sinks, and drains 3. Paint remover

ORGANIC BASES

The organic bases are called *amines*, which contain the functional amino group-NH_2. The important organic bases are called *purines* (adenine and guanine) and *pyrimidines* (cytosine and uracil), which are components of the living cell nucleus, nucleic acids. Amino groups are present in the molecules of all amino acids (see page 122).

NEUTRALIZATION

Neutralization consists of the interaction of an *acid* and a *base* or alkali to form a *salt* and *water*:

$$\text{Acid + base} \quad \overset{\text{neutralization}}{=} \quad \text{salt + water}$$

Experiment

Place 25 cm³ of bench dilute hydrochloric acid in a beaker with litmus indicator. Fill a burette with bench dilute sodium hydroxide and add the acid until the litmus is just turning blue. At this point the solution is neutral:

$$\underset{\text{acid}}{\text{Hydrochloric}} + \underset{\text{hydroxide}}{\text{sodium}} = \underset{\text{salt}}{\text{sodium chloride}} + \text{water}$$

$$HCl \quad + \quad NaOH \quad = \quad NaCl \quad + H_2O$$

APPLICATIONS OF NEUTRALIZATION

Neutralization is frequently used in laundry practice to remove acidic or alkaline residues.

(*a*) Ethanoic (acetic) acid removes alkaline residues caused by soap or the hard water calcium soap deposits which make coloured fabrics lustreless.

(*b*) Ammonium hydroxide rinses remove the acidic residue after using sodium chlorate(I) (hypochlorite) bleaches or after employing an acid stain remover.

HYDROGEN ION CONCENTRATION OR pH

When an acid is added to water it splits up into two parts: (*a*) hydrogen ions, and (*b*) the acid radical ions.

$$\underset{\text{hydrochloric acid}}{HCl} = \underset{\text{hydrogen ion}}{H^+} + \underset{\substack{\text{chloride ion} \\ \text{(acid radical)}}}{Cl^-}$$

The symbol pH describes the number of hydrogen ions present, or the *acidity* or *alkalinity* of a solution. The pH system is a scale which runs from pH1 to pH14, from extremely strong *acid* to extremely strong *alkali*.

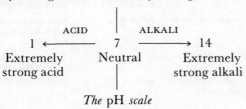

The pH *scale*

THE pH SCALE

Pure water is pH7 or *neutral*. Acidity is found between pH1 and pH7. Alkalinity is found between pH7 and pH14. A solution of pH7 would be weakly alkaline while a solution of pH5 would be weakly acid.

Measurement of pH

The pH of a solution can be determined by:

(*a*) the colorimetric 'Universal Indicator' test papers which give a range of colours for different pH values;

(*b*) the electrometric pH apparatus which measures the pH of a solution by electrical means giving a direct reading on a graduated pH scale.

APPLICATIONS OF pH

1. Cake mixing

Cake texture alters with pH. Low pH gives cakes a fine texture, high pH a coarse texture. The high pH value of alkalinity is obtainable with excess sodium carbonate or sodium hydrogen carbonate. Cakes with a low pH keep fresh longer, the rate of staling being slowed down.

Fruit cake pH = 4·5–5·0 (slightly acid)
Sponge cake pH = 7·5 (*very* slightly alkaline)

2. Jam making

The setting of jam takes place at a low pH of 3·5. Therefore small amounts of acid, such as hydroxypropane tricarboxylic (citric) or dihydroxybutanedioic (tartaric) acids, must be added to such fruits as strawberry which do not set or gel easily.

3. Laundry

The pH of solutions for washing depends on the detergent used. Mild alkali soaps give a pH of 8–10 (causing them to sting the eye), while a soapless detergent can have a pH approaching *neutral*.

Strong alkali wash water may have a pH of 10 to 11 and is mainly used for white cotton and linen. Wool, silk, rayon, and coloured fabrics require a pH between 7 and 8.

4. Cooking vegetables

Raising the pH of the cooking water of vegetables retains the green colour but destroys the vitamins of the B group and C (ascorbic acid). Sodium hydrogen carbonate is frequently used for this purpose.

5. Food digestion

An *acid* pH of between 1 and 2 is needed to digest food in the *stomach*. A *slightly alkaline* pH 7 to 8 is needed to digest food in the *intestine*.

	pH	
Acid	2	Lemons, vinegar
	3	Apples, mineral waters
	4	Soda water, fruit cake
	5	Bread
	6	Eggs, milk, potatoes, and flour
Neutral	7	Chocolate
Alkaline	8	Egg whites
	9	Soda bread

SALTS

Salts are produced when the *hydrogen* of an acid is replaced by a metal or ammonium (NH_4) radical. All salts consist of two parts: (*a*) the metal or ammonium radical, and (*b*) the acid radical:

Salt = metal or ammonium radical + acid radical

Sodium chloride (common salt) is NaCl= Na^+ Cl^-

metal   acid

radical   radical

TYPES OF SALT

The majority of salts are *neutral* and are called normal salts, examples being sodium chloride and magnesium sulphate. Others show an *acid* reaction and usually contain hydrogen. For example potassium *hydrogen* ethanedioate (oxalate) and potassium *hydrogen* dihydroxybutanedioate (tartrate) are salts formed by the incomplete replacement of the hydrogen of the two acids:

Dihydroxybutanedioic (tartaric) acid + potassium hydroxide

= potassium hydrogen dihydroxybutanedioate (tartrate) + water

The acid salt potassium hydrogen dihydroxybutanedioate (tartrate) can now act as an acid, and will neutralize potassium hydroxide to form a normal salt, potassium dihydroxybutanedioate tartrate:

Potassium hydrogen dihydroxybutanedioate (tartrate) + potassium hydroxide

= normal potassium dihydroxybutanedioate (tartrate) + water

SOME IMPORTANT SALTS AND THEIR USES

Phosphates: the salts of phosphoric acid are one of the most important substances in the human body, being components of bones and teeth, muscles and nerves. They are important components of the living cell *nucleus*, nucleic acids. Phosphate is also an *energy-rich* radical which provides living cells with their energy needs by way of the compound adenosine triphosphate (or ATP) (see page 186).

Salt	Appearance and properties	Uses
Normal salts		
Ammonium chloride (NH_4Cl)	White solid	For fireproofing. Yeast stimulant and food
Calcium phosphate $Ca_3(PO_4)_2$ Calcium carbonate $CaCO_3$ Calcium sulphate $CaSO_4$	All white solids	All are flour additives. Yeast food
Potassium salts: Chloride (KCl)	White solid	As an alternative to common salt, sodium chloride, in salt free diets
Iodide (KI)	White solid	Iodine supplement in iodized table salt
Nitrate(V) [saltpetre] (KNO_3)	White solid	Curing bacon and ham
Nitrate(III) [nitrite] (KNO_2)	White solid	Meat pickle, preservative for canned meats
Bromate ($KBrO_3$) and Iodate (KIO_3)	White solid	Flour maturers and improvers
Sodium compounds: Chloride (NaCl)	White solid	Meat pickle preservative. Fish curing agent. Aid to digestion
Nitrate(III) [Nitrite] ($NaNO_2$)	White solid	Meat pickle preservative
Sulphate(IV) [Sulphite] (Na_2SO_3) or hydrogen sulphate(IV) [bisulphate] ($NaHSO_3$)	White solids	Potato whiteners or browning preventers. Bleaching agent
Phosphate	White solid	Mineral supplement in flour
Heptaoxidiphosphate [Pyrophosphate]	White solid	Added to potato powder to prevent browning on cooking
Sulphate(VI) (Na_2SO_4) (Glauber salts)	White solid	Ingredient of soapless detergent washing powder
Acid salts		
Sodium hydrogen carbonate ($NaHCO_3$)	White solid	1. Baking powder 2. Mild alkali for laundry work
Ammonium hydrogen carbonate (NH_4HCO_3)	White solid	German baking powder, cream cracker biscuits
Sodium aluminium sulphate, S.A.S.	White solid	Acid component of baking powder in U.S.A.
Disodium dihydrogen heptaoxidiphosphate (pyrophosphate) ($Na_2H_2P_2O_7$)	White solid	Acid component of baking powder
Calcium hydrogen phosphate ($Ca(H_2PO_4)_2$)	White solid	Acid component of baking powder
Potassium hydrogen ethanedioate (oxalate) [Salts of lemon]	White solid	Iron stain remover *Poisonous*
Potassium hydrogen 2,3-dihydroxybutanedioate (tartrate) [Cream of Tartar]	White solid	Acid component of baking powder
Alkali-producing salts		
Sodium carbonate (Na_2CO_3) [Washing soda. Soda ash]	White solid Crystalline powder	Medium alkali for laundry purposes. Water softener and varnish remover
Sodium hydrogen carbonate ($NaHCO_3$)	White solid	Mild alkali for laundry work. Baking powder ingredient
Sodium silicate. ['Water glass']	Syrupy liquid	1. Egg preserver. 2. Paint stain remover
Sodium hexatrioxophosphate (hexametaphosphate) [Calgon]	White solid	Water softener

SUGGESTIONS FOR PRACTICAL WORK

1. Test samples of substances by heating small quantities on a metal plate or spatula to see whether they are inorganic or organic.

2. Place 5 cm^3 of a solution of sodium hydrogen carbonate in six test tubes. Add small amounts of dilute solutions of organic acids also dilute hydrochloric, to each test tube and note any effervescence.

3. Take a clean porcelain spotting dish and place a few drops of the following in different parts of it: saliva, tapwater, soapy water, vinegar, water containing soapless detergent, and a colourless cordial (lemonade). Add a piece of Universal Indicator paper to each sample and compare the colour produced with the colour card supplied with the Universal Indicator to determine the pH value of each.

4. Prepare dilute solutions of the following salts and test their reaction to neutral litmus or B.D.H. Universal indicator paper: sodium chloride, sodium hydrogen carbonate, sodium carbonate, sodium dihydrogen heptaoxidophosphate (pyrophosphate), potassium hydrogen dihydroxybutanedioate (tartrate), and sodium silicate.

5. See *Experimental Science for Catering and Homecraft Students*, Practical work 2.1 to 2.6, 3.1 to 3.3.

QUESTIONS ON CHAPTER 14

1. Give examples of: (*a*) two acids; and (*b*) two bases that are used in catering. What is the difference between a base and an alkali?

2. Explain what is meant by neutralization. Give two examples of the application of neutralization to laundry work.

3. Give a list of the important properties of acids and bases. Give named examples of two acids used in cookery and two alkalis used in laundry work.

4. What is meant by the term pH? State briefly a method of measuring the pH of a fruit juice. Indicate how a knowledge of pH is important in food preparation.

5. How are salts formed? Give named examples of: (*a*) neutral salts; (*b*) acid salts; and (*c*) alkali-forming salts, stating their uses in institutional management.

6. Write short notes on the following substances indicating their uses in the kitchen or laundry: (*a*) ethanedioic (oxalic) acid; (*b*) ammonium hydroxide; (*c*) potassium bromate; (*d*) sodium nitrate(III) (nitrite); and (*e*) sodium aminopentanedioate (glutamate).

7. Give an account of some of the alkalis used for laundry work and state which fabrics are suited to the alkalis you mention.

8. State which foods produce: (*a*) an acid reaction; (*b*) an alkaline reaction; and (*c*) a neutral reaction on an indicator.

9. Give two examples of the use of each of the following substances in laundry work: (*a*) sodium carbonate; (*b*) vinegar; (*c*) ammonium hydroxide; and (*d*) sodium sulphate(VI).

MULTIPLE CHOICE QUESTIONS ON CHAPTER 14

1. The correct name for this chemical change

ACID + BASE = SALT + WATER:
- (*a*) reduction
- (*b*) oxidation
- (*c*) neutralization
- (*d*) decomposition

2. Which of the following is an organic compound?
- (*a*) cane sugar
- (*b*) sand
- (*c*) sodium chloride
- (*d*) sodium nitrite

3. Which of the following is a normal neutral salt:
- (*a*) sodium aluminium sulphate
- (*b*) sodium hydrogen carbonate
- (*c*) sodium chloride
- (*d*) calcium hydrogen phosphate

4. One of the following is an oxidising agent used for ageing flour:
- (*a*) sodium hydrogen carbonate
- (*b*) potassium bromate
- (*c*) calcium carbonate
- (*d*) iron sulphate

5. Water has a pH value of:
- (*a*) pH 1
- (*b*) pH 3
- (*c*) pH 5
- (*d*) pH 7

6. Cream crackers, scones and soda bread all have a pH of approximately:
- (*a*) pH 1 to 2
- (*b*) pH 4 to 5
- (*c*) pH 6 to 7
- (*d*) pH 8 to 9

7. The pH of the foods in Question 6 is mainly due to the large amounts of one of the following ingredients:
- (*a*) carbon dioxide
- (*b*) starch
- (*c*) sodium carbonate
- (*d*) dihydroxybutanedioic (tartaric) acid

8. Which of the following can cause the red colour of beetroots and red cabbage to change to blue?
- (*a*) hydroxypropane tricarboxylic (citric) acid
- (*b*) sodium hydrogen carbonate
- (*c*) sodium chloride
- (*d*) ethanoic (acetic) acid

9. A fruit cake will have a pH value of approximately:
- (*a*) pH 1 to 2
- (*b*) pH 4 to 5
- (*c*) pH 7 to 8
- (*d*) pH 9 to 10

10. The cause of the pH value of a fruit cake as in Question 1 is mainly due to:
- (*a*) the baking soda
- (*b*) dried fruit
- (*c*) flour
- (*d*) sugar

15   Carbon, the key element

We have previously referred to organic chemistry as the study of carbon compounds. We shall now consider the chemistry of the element carbon noting how it forms a vast number of chemical compounds important in food and household science.

The element carbon (C) is found in different physical forms called *allotropes*; for example diamond, graphite, and non-crystalline carbon.

(*a*) *Diamonds* as jewellery are well known.

(*b*) *Graphite* is a form of carbon which feels greasy when rubbed between the fingers. For this reason graphite is an important component in lubricants. It is used in electric-motor brushes, cast-iron polish and the lead of pencils.

(*c*) *Amorphous or non-crystalline carbon*, includes charcoal, lamp-black, soot, animal charcoal, and coke.

Charcoal is obtained by heating vegetable substances, wood, sugar or biscuits, in the absence of air.

Experiments

1. Moisten a little cane sugar in an evaporating dish with a few drops of concentrated sulphuric acid. Heat the dish gently and observe the change in colour of the sugar and the final formation of a dense mass of pure sugar charcoal.

2. Using the apparatus in Figure 15.1 heat some wood shavings or dried biscuits in the test tube. Ignite the gases produced and observe the charcoal residue that remains.

3. Animal or bone charcoal is prepared by heating bones in the absence of air in the apparatus shown in Figure 15.1.

Properties

Animal or bone charcoal can remove coloured impurities from solutions; it is therefore used to prepare white

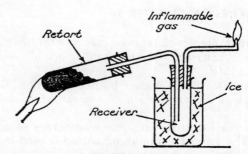

Figure 5.1. Apparatus for distilling substances in the absence of air

crystalline sugar from brown sugar. Flueless extractor fume hoods contain a tray of charcoal to remove cooking odours.

Experiment

Dissolve brown sugar or a little caramel in water and add a pinch of animal charcoal. Boil for 2–3 minutes and filter the hot solution.

Caramel is the dark brown colouring prepared by heating sugar above 160°C with a small amount of ethanoic acid. It is used in gravies, malted vinegar, and proprietary types of flour, sauces, soft drinks and canned foods.

FUELS

Three main sources are available for the production of heat: atomic power, coal and its by-products, and petroleum products.

1. ATOMIC POWER

Atomic power depends on the disintegration or *fission* of radio-active materials into other materials, the fission process giving out great heat which in turn is utilized to produce electricity.

2. COAL AND ITS BY-PRODUCTS

Formation of coal. Coal is formed by the decay of plant remains under extreme pressure and in the absence of air, for this reason it is called a *fossil fuel*.

Wood containing 50 per cent carbon is converted into *peat* (60 per cent carbon). This poor-quality fuel is in turn changed into brown coal (67 per cent carbon), and subsequently into bituminous coal (88 per cent carbon), and finally anthracite (94 per cent carbon):

TYPES OF COAL

1. *House or bituminous coal* contains 60–88 per cent carbon, and burns with a bright flame producing some smoke. Heat content of energy value is 13 to 30 MJ/kg, depending on group.

2. *Welsh dry steam coal* contains 90 per cent carbon; it burns slowly producing very little flame and smoke. Energy value is approximately 33 MJ/kg.

3. *Anthracite* contains 94 per cent carbon; it burns very slowly producing barely any smoke or flame. This coal should be used in special anthracite grates and stoves. Its energy value is 33 to 35 MJ/kg.

Smokeless fuels

Since the introduction of the Clean Air Act, it has become essential to produce little smoke by using smokeless fuels, fuels of high carbon content and few volatiles. The following are the main types of smokeless solid fuels:

(*a*) *Natural smokeless* solid fuels, anthracite, and Welsh dry steam coal.

(*b*) *Coke*, a by-product of the carbonization of coal in coal gas preparation has an energy value of 29 MJ/kg.

(*c*) *Controlled-carbonized coke*; a flame producing coke with more volatile ingredients than ordinary coke, energy value 25 MJ/kg.

(*d*) *Carbonized ovoids and briquettes* made from crushed coal mixed with pitch and heated under pressure to reduce the content of volatiles, have energy values of 31 MJ/kg.

COAL GAS

Coal gas can be made in the laboratory by heating bituminous household coal in the absence of air, in the apparatus shown in Figure 15.1. The products obtained by this process are: (*a*) coal gas, (*b*) coke, (*c*) coal tar, and (*d*) ammonia liquor (which turns litmus blue).

NATURAL GAS

The traditional method of making gas from coal has now been displaced by the supply of natural gas from pockets of the gas found below the ground, these may be located *alone*, or above petroleum in oil wells. The UK supply of natural gas comes from gas wells below the sea and is piped ashore to supply almost 90% of the gas users at the time of writing.

The natural gas supply is distributed through a system of pipelines 1 m in diameter, passing to smaller diameter pipes and ultimately through the narrow *service* pipe into the home. (See Figure 2.7, page 12.)

Natural gas may be stored in existing gasholders, or in a liquified form in underground chambers, or in gas cylinders as a portable means of gas supply for isolated buildings.

Natural gas has an energy value of 34 megajoules (MJ) per cubic metre (m^3), in comparison to the lower energy value of coal gas 18 megajoules per cubic metre, consequently existing gas burning appliances had to be altered due to the high energy value of natural gas. Alterations being carried out to the appliance governor, and fitting special burners to provide an aerated flame.

THE GAS FLAME AND THE BUNSEN BURNER

The Bunsen burner is an essential part of all gas appliances, particularly cookers and ranges. The burner consists of an injector jet surrounded by a hollow tube, with a movable collar which controls the entry of air to supply the burning gas (Figure 15.2).

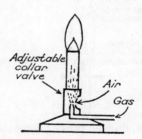

Figure 15.2. The Bunsen burner

Experiment

1. Close the collar of the Bunsen burner and light the gas. Note the luminous flame. Hold a porcelain dish in the flame and observe how a deposit of black soot collects on the cold surface.

2. Insert a pin through the head of a live match and suspend the match in the centre of the tube. Open the collar of the burner, light the gas and observe how the match remains unlit.

3. Light the Bunsen burner, leave the collar open, and slowly turn the gas down. Note how the flame lights back, or *strikes back*, down the burner tube causing a slight pop and is extinguished.

4. Take an empty ½-kg syrup tin, puncture the lid and bottom of the tin. Fill the tin with gas and light it through the opening in the lid. Note how the luminous flame disappears into the tin causing a loud detonation. This is another version of striking back.

Types of gas flame

1. The fishtail, luminous, or neat flame (Figure 15.3) was the type of burner used in coal gas fires and water heaters. This type of burner cannot be used in natural gas appliances.

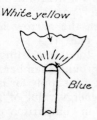

Figure 15.3. Fishtail or luminous flame

2. The *aerated* Bunsen flame (Figure 15.4) is the type of flame in all natural gas appliances. The air drawn in through the ports of the collar is called primary air. With the natural gas it forms a mixture which burns with a blue flame at the outer cone. The inner green-coloured cone consists of *unburnt* gas. Natural gas appliances are all fitted with aerated Bunsen burners as part of the appliance conversion process.

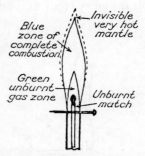

Figure 15.4. Aerated Bunsen burner flame, with live match in unburnt-gas zone

The air surrounding the aerated flame contributes to the combustion process by supplying *secondary* air which forms a very hot, barely visible mantle around the edge of the flame. It is important that the aerated gas flame *just* touch the bottom of a pot thus allowing use of the hottest part of the flame. Gas jets turned full on merely waste heat and gas (see Figure 5.11).

Striking back

When a gas flame strikes back with a pop the cause is either the gas supply being turned down or blocked injector jets. The injector jets of a gas appliance must be kept clean.

3. PETROLEUM AND ITS PRODUCTS

Petroleum or rock oil is the main source of mineral oils. Petroleum is found underground in many parts of the world and was originally formed millions of years ago from the remains of tiny organisms resembling shellfish. Petroleum is therefore an organic substance and fossil fuel.

All the oils and gases obtained by the refining of crude petroleum are composed of *hydrogen and carbon*, and are called *hydrocarbons*. See page 105.

The table shows some of the main products obtained when petroleum is distilled.

PETROLEUM PRODUCTS

Product	Uses
Natural gas	1. Gas for cooking, lighting, and heating 2. Used for making soapless detergents
Petrol or gasoline	1. Motor fuel 2. Used for making grease solvent
Paraffin or kerosene	For heating, cooking, and lighting, energy value 44 MJ/kg
Diesel oil	Heavy engines
Light and heavy fuel oils	For firing boilers and heating systems
Petroleum jelly	Skin protection and rust preventative
Paraffin wax	For grease-proof paper and cake-cups
Pitch	For water-proofing roofing felts and damp-proof courses. Making carbonized ovoids and briquette fuels

FOOD GRADE WHITE MINERAL OIL

This is a highly purified form of medicinal liquid paraffin which has no food value. It is used as an additive for dried fruits to prevent fruits clumping or sticking together.

It is harmful in large doses as a laxative, since it dissolves the lipid soluble vitamins A and D, which then pass out of the body in the faeces (see page 158).

CARBON MONOXIDE

Carbon monoxide (formula CO) is a highly poisonous gas with no colour or smell, and thus offers no warning of its presence.

Properties

1. Carbon monoxide can form a permanent compound with the haemoglobin of the blood, called *carboxy-haemoglobin*. This causes death from oxygen shortage due to carbon monoxide poisoning.

2. Carbon monoxide burns with a blue flame. It is one of the main components of coal gas and is *not* found in natural gas.

FORMATION OF CARBON MONOXIDE

Carbon monoxide is formed when a carbon-containing fuel such as paraffin, coal, or petrol burns in an *insufficient* supply of air or oxygen. It is produced by:

(*a*) Exhaust fumes from motor-cars. (It is dangerous to run a car engine in a garage with closed doors.)

(*b*) Coal, gas, and paraffin oil appliances burning with

either no flue or an inefficient flue chimney. The gas appliance should have a flue to remove waste gases.

(*c*) The use of heating appliances in areas which do not have a good supply of air for combustion. Sealing off all draught inlets to a room containing an oil or coal gas burning appliance results in the exhaustion of oxygen and the formation of carbon monoxide fumes.

CARBON DIOXIDE

Carbon dioxide (CO_2) is present in the air to the extent of 0·03 per cent. It derives from (*a*) *combustion* of carbon-containing fuels, and (*b*) *respiration* of plants and animals.

Preparation of carbon dioxide in the laboratory

Place a little calcium carbonate ($CaCO_3$) in a flask and add dilute hydrochloric acid (Figure 15.5). Fill a few gas-jars with the gas. Insert a burning taper into a gas-jar and note how the gas extinguishes the flame. Carbon dioxide will not allow things to burn in it and so is used as a fire extinguisher.

Calcium hydroxide solution test

Half fill a large test tube with clear calcium hydroxide ($Ca(OH)_2$) (lime water). Bubble in the carbon dioxide gas and note how the lime water turns milky due to the formation of *insoluble* calcium carbonate:

$$\text{Calcium hydroxide [lime water]} + \text{carbon dioxide} = \text{insoluble calcium carbonate} + \text{water}$$

$$Ca(OH)_2 + CO_2 = CaCO_3 + H_2O$$

If more carbon dioxide is bubbled through the milky-coloured liquid it will gradually become *clear*, following the formation of *soluble* calcium hydrogen carbonate (see Figure 15.5):

$$\text{Calcium carbonate} + \text{and water} + \text{carbon dioxide} = \text{soluble calcium hydrogen carbonate}$$

$$CaCO_3 + H_2O + CO_2 = Ca(HCO_3)_2$$

This reaction is used as a test for carbon dioxide.

Carbonic acid (H_2CO_3)

Pass some carbon dioxide gas into a test tube containing water and blue litmus indicator. The indicator turns red showing an acid, namely carbonic acid (H_2CO_3), has been formed:

$$\text{Water} + \text{carbon dioxide} = \text{carbonic acid}$$

$$H_2O + CO_2 = H_2CO_3$$

CARBONATES AND HYDROGEN CARBONATES

Carbonic acid (H_2CO_3) contains two replaceable hydrogen atoms and so can form two salts, the carbonates $CO_3 =$ and the acid salt hydrogen carbonate $HCO_3 -$. These radicals have valencies of two and one respectively. Hydrogen carbonates were formerly called bicarbonates.

(*a*) *Soluble* carbonates are those of sodium, potassium, and ammonium: Na_2CO_3, K_2CO_3, and $(NH_4)_2CO_3$.

(*b*) *Insoluble* carbonates are those of calcium and magnesium: $CaCO_3$ and $MgCO_3$.

(*c*) Hydrogen carbonate salts, for example those of sodium, potassium, calcium, magnesium, and ammonium hydrogen carbonates are *soluble* in water.

(*d*) All carbonate and hydrogen carbonate salts when treated with an acid produce carbon dioxide.

Experiment

Mix a little hydroxypropane tricarboxylic (citric) acid with samples of calcium carbonate, sodium carbonate, and sodium hydrogen carbonate. Add water and note any effervescence. Test the gas using a glass tube containing calcium hydroxide (Figure 15.6).

(*e*) Hydrogen carbonate salts give carbon dioxide on *heating* gently. Carbonate salts produce carbon dioxide at very high temperatures only.

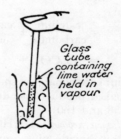

Figure 15.6. Testing for carbon dioxide gas with lime water held in glass tube

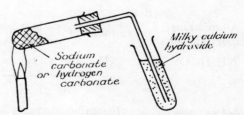

Figure 15.7. Effect of heat on carbonates and hydrogen carbonates

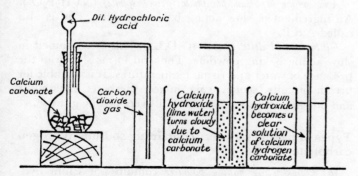

Figure 15.5. Laboratory preparation of carbon dioxide and action of the gas on lime water

Experiment

Heat sodium hydrogen carbonate and sodium carbonate in the apparatus shown in Figure 15.7. Observe the effect of the issuing gases on the calcium hydroxide solution.

Action of heat on sodium hydrogen carbonate

Sodium hydrogen carbonate breaks down when heated into sodium carbonate (Na_2CO_3) evolving carbon dioxide and water vapour:

$$\text{Sodium hydrogen carbonate} = \text{sodium carbonate} + \text{carbon dioxide} + \text{water vapour}$$

$$2NaHCO_3 = Na_2CO_3 + CO_2 + H_2O$$

Calcium hydrogen carbonate $Ca(HCO_3)_2$ is similarly decomposed when the clear solution is boiled:

$$\text{Calcium hydrogen carbonate} = \text{calcium carbonate} + \text{carbon dioxide} + \text{water}$$

$$Ca(HCO_3)_2 = CaCO_3 + CO_2 + H_2O$$

USES OF CARBON DIOXIDE AND ITS SALTS

1. Mineral water and soda water

Carbon dioxide dissolves in water forming a weak acid solution of carbonic acid with its characteristic acid taste. Soda water is prepared by releasing carbon dioxide into water, while mineral waters contain added sugar or saccharine, flavouring and colouring agents.

2. Baking powders and baking soda

(a) *Baking soda* or sodium hydrogen carbonate $NaHCO_3$ liberates carbon dioxide when heated causing the batter or dough to rise:

$$\overset{\text{Heat}}{\underset{\text{baking soda}}{\text{Sodium hydrogen carbonate}}} = \text{calcium carbonate} + \text{carbon dioxide} + \text{water}$$

$$2NaHCO_3 = Na_2CO_3 + CO_2 + H_2O$$

The residue of sodium carbonate or soda affects the taste and colour of the baked product and destroys vitamins B and C (see pages 158 and 160).

(b) *Ammonium hydrogen carbonate* NH_4HCO_3 produces *twice* the volume of carbon dioxide plus ammonia as ordinary baking soda, sodium hydrogen carbonate, and so is used for choux pastry, biscuits, and éclairs.

$$\overset{\text{Heat}}{\text{Ammonium hydrogen carbonate}} = \text{ammonia} + \text{carbon dioxide} + \text{steam or water}$$

$$NH_4HCO_3 = \underbrace{NH_3 + CO_2 \qquad H_2O}_{\text{All gaseous}}$$

(c) *Baking powders* are basically mixtures of sodium hydrogen carbonate and an acid-reacting material, together with starch or flour.

The acid-reacting ingredient releases carbon dioxide when water is added, further gas being released when the mixture is heated. The flavour of the baked product is not affected by any soda (Na_2CO_3) residues since they are prevented from forming by the acid-reacting ingredient:

$$\text{Sodium hydrogen carbonate} + \text{acid-reacting ingredient} = \text{salt} + \text{carbon dioxide} + \text{water}$$

The flour or starch present in the baking powder serves to keep the mixture dry; a damp baking powder would soon lose its efficiency. When baking powder alone is strongly heated it chars, since the starch or flour decomposes at high temperatures.

Preparation of a simple baking powder

Weigh out 22 g of potassium hydrogen dihydroxybutanedioate (cream of tartar), and 10 g of sodium hydrogen carbonate. Mix thoroughly. Careful weighing is necessary to balance acid and alkaline ingredients to prevent distortion of the flavour. Stir up some of the mixture with water and note the evolution of carbon dioxide

$$\text{sodium hydrogen carbonate} + \text{potassium hydrogen dihydroxy butanedioate} = \text{sodium potassium dihydroxy-butanedioate} + \text{carbon dioxide} + \text{water}$$

$$NaHCO_3 + KHC_4H_4O_6 = NaKC_4H_4O_6 + CO_2 + H_2O$$

Acid-reacting ingredients of baking powder

Some old-fashioned ingredients were: sour milk, hydroxypropanoic (lactic) acid, vinegar, ethanoic (acetic) acid, and lemon juice, hydroxypropanetricarboxylic (citric) acid. Nowadays 28–30 per cent sodium hydrogen carbonate is mixed with varying amounts of acid-reacting ingredients:

Dihydroxybutanedioic acid (tartaric) acid. This is the acid ingredient of grapes, and is used in rapid acting baking powder.

Potassium hydrogen dihydroxybutanedioate (tartrate) cream of tartar. Slightly slower acting than dihydroxybutanedioic (tartaric) acid.

'Phosphate' or calcium dihydrogen phosphate ($Ca(H_2PO_4)_2$). This is an ingredient of slow acting baking powders; it is also called A.C.P. (acid calcium phosphate).

Acid sodium heptaoxodiphosphate (pyrophosphate) ($Na_2H_2P_2O_7$). An ingredient of slow acting baking powders, and is also called A.S.P.

Gluconic acid delta lactone (G.D.L.). This is contained in slow acting baking powders. The acid forms slowly in the presence of water and rising temperatures. It is suitable for bread, biscuits, scones, cake mixes, sherberts, doughnuts and doughs – it leaves a residue of sweet tasting glucose.

Types of baking powders containing sodium hydrogen carbonate

(a) *Quick-acting baking powders* contain potassium hydrogen dihydroxybutanedioate (cream of tartar), dihydroxybutanedioic (tartaric) acid or calcium dihydrogen phosphate (A.C.P.), and sodium hydrogen carbonate. A large amount of gas is released on *moistening*.

(*b*) *Slow acting baking powders* contain acid sodium heptaoxidophosphate (pyrophosphate) (A.S.P.), sodium hydrogen carbonate, and gluconic acid delta lactone (G.D.L.), most of the gas being released on *baking*.

(*c*) *Double action baking powders* are mixtures of both quick and slow acting ingredients. Thus the carbon dioxide is liberated partly on *moistening* the mixture and partly on baking. This is the mixture most suited for *domestic* use, while the quick and slow acting powders are used in large-scale bakeries.

3. Self-raising flour

This flour contains salt, sodium hydrogen carbonate, and calcium dihydrogen phosphate or acid sodium heptaoxidophosphate (pyrophosphate) as the acid-reacting agent.

4. Sherbet

This preparation usually consists of a mixture of sugar, sodium hydrogen carbonate, and either hydroxypropane tricarboxylic (citric) or dihydroxybutanedioic (tartaric) acid, together with vanilla, chocolate, or banana flavour. Gluconic acid delta lactone (G.D.L.) gives it a bland flavour.

5. Sodium hydrogen carbonate

This is used in cooking to preserve the green colour of vegetables, but it destroys any vitamins B and C present.

6. Gas storage

Fruits and certain vegetables are still *alive* after harvesting and they respire until they are fully *ripe*. The ripening process is slowed down if the air in the store has *less* oxygen, by *increasing* the carbon dioxide content to about 2–3%. In this way fruits are stored over long periods of up to 4 months.

Experiments

1. To compare the rate of reaction of different baking powders:

Take the white of one egg, mix with $200\,cm^3$ of water, allow to stand and pour off the clear liquid into a $250\,cm^3$ beaker, discarding the cloudy residue. Place 5 g of different baking powders in tall density jars or $250\,cm^3$ measuring cylinders. Add $25\,cm^3$ of the egg white solution to the baking powder, stir 2 or 3 times *only*, and allow the mixture to foam. Measure the greatest height attained by the foam. The heights of the different foams measures the comparative reactivities of the baking powders.

2. Typical recipes for baking powders:

(*a*) Potassium hydrogen dihydroxybutanedioate
(cream of tartar)   48 g
Sodium hydrogen carbonate   28 g
Cornflour   21 g
Dihydroxybutanedioic (tartaric) acid   3 g

(*b*) Calcium dihydrogen phosphate   32 g
Sodium hydrogen carbonate   28 g
Cornflour   40 g

FIRE EXTINGUISHERS

All fire extinguishers act in the same way by forming a blanket over the fire, thus sealing off the oxygen of the air. Water however serves to cool the fire. Some of the main types of first-aid fire extinguishing agents are:

(*a*) *Water*, from taps, buckets, pumps, and soda acid extinguishers. The soda acid extinguisher resembles a quick-acting baking powder in that an acid is released into a solution of sodium carbonate, producing carbon dioxide. The pressure of the gas drives a spray of soda acid and water over the fire (see Figure 15.8).

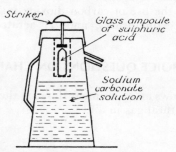

Figure 15.8. Soda-acid fire extinguisher

(*b*) *Carbon dioxide extinguishers* are cylinders full of carbon dioxide which serves to form a heavy blanket over the fire.

(*c*) *Dry powder extinguishers* discharge a cloud of powdered sodium hydrogen carbonate which, in contact with the heat of the fire, produces carbon dioxide. Ordinary sand can also be used to smother a fire, as can an asbestos blanket.

(*d*) *Vaporizing liquid extinguishers* contain tetrachloromethane (carbon tetrachloride) (T.C.M.) or chlorobromomethane (C.B.M.), which are liquids producing heavy non-inflammable vapours.

(*e*) *Foam extinguishers* resemble soda acid extinguishers but also include a soap-like foaming agent called saponin.

SUGGESTIONS FOR PRACTICAL WORK

See *Experimental Science for Catering and Homecraft Students*, Practical work 17.1 to 17.5 and 19.5.

QUESTIONS ON CHAPTER 15

1. What is natural gas and how is it made? Describe the structure of the flame and burner found in: (*a*) the gas cooker; and (*b*) the gas convector heater.

2. Give an account of the Bunsen burner. What is the cause of striking back in a Bunsen burner?

3. Discuss the safety measures you would take when using gas and electric appliances.

4. Describe the preparation of carbon dioxide in the laboratory. What is the effect of the gas on lime water? What are its main properties and uses?

5. Give the chemical formula for sodium hydrogen carbonate. What is the effect on sodium hydrogen carbonate and sodium carbonate of: (*a*) heat; (*b*) ethanoic acid; and (*c*) dihydroxybutanedioic acid.

6. State the composition of simple baking powder. Describe three different types of baking powder and their uses.

7. Write short notes giving the proper chemical names for the following: (*a*) washing soda; (*b*) baking soda; (*c*) baking powder; (*d*) self-raising flour; (*e*) soda water; and (*f*) gluconic acid delta lactone.

8. Give a short account of how carbon monoxide can be formed and its physiological effect.

9. Give an account of chemical raising agents describing how and why they are used. Why are some chemicals unsuitable as raising agents?

10. Discuss the use of carbon dioxide in: (*a*) refrigeration; (*b*) fire extinguishers; and (*c*) aerated or mineral waters.

MULTIPLE CHOICE QUESTIONS ON CHAPTER 15

Figure 15.9 shows an experiment showing the flue products on burning natural gas in air:

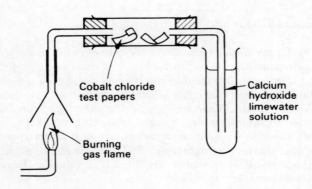

1. Which of the following will cause the cobalt chloride papers to change colour from blue to pink?

(*a*) heat   (*c*) carbon dioxide
(*b*) water   (*d*) sulphur dioxide

2. Which of the following would cause the calcium hydroxide (lime water) to change from a clear colourless liquid?

(*a*) heat   (*c*) carbon dioxide
(*b*) water   (*d*) sulphur dioxide

3. The change seen to occur in Question 2 would be seen as the solution of calcium hydroxide (lime water):

(*a*) turns orange   (*c*) turns white
(*b*) turns black   (*d*) turns red

4. If natural gas burns without sufficient air one of the following poisonous gases will be formed:

(*a*) carbon dioxide   (*c*) methane
(*b*) carbon monoxide   (*d*) sulphur dioxide

5. The component of baking powder which releases a gas when it is heated alone is:

(*a*) dihydroxybutanedioic (tartaric) acid
(*b*) sodium hydrogen carbonate
(*c*) starch
(*d*) potassium hydrogen dihydroxybutanedioate (cream of tartar)

6. The leavening of a sponge cake is mainly due to:

(*a*) chemical action   (*c*) yeast fermentation
(*b*) steam   (*d*) lipid vapourization

7. The chemical name of baking soda is:

(*a*) sodium carbonate
(*b*) sodium hydrogen carbonate
(*c*) ammonium hydrogencarbonate
(*d*) dihydroxybutanedioic (tartaric) acid

8. A chemically aerated cake is given a soapy bitter taste by one of the following:

(*a*) dihydroxybutanedioic (tartaric) acid
(*b*) ethanol
(*c*) sodium carbonate
(*d*) starch

9. Petroleum oil is mainly composed of chemical compounds called:

(*a*) carbohydrates   (*c*) carbonates
(*b*) hydrocarbons   (*d*) lipids

10. Petroleum is a material which provides:

(*a*) essential oils   (*c*) lipid oils
(*b*) mineral oils   (*d*) resin oils

16   Hydrocarbons and carbohydrates

HYDROCARBONS

The hydrocarbons are organic compounds containing the element carbon and hydrogen only. There are two main kinds (a) saturated and (b) unsaturated hydrocarbons.

Saturated hydrocarbons or *alkanes* have names ending in -ane. For example methane, ethane, propane, butane, octane, nonane, decane, dodecane, hexadecane, and octadecane are called *paraffin hydrocarbons*.

The formulae of the first two are:

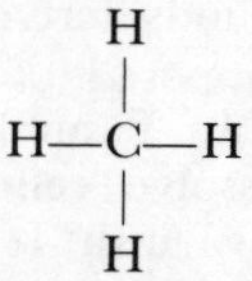

Methane
(CH_4)

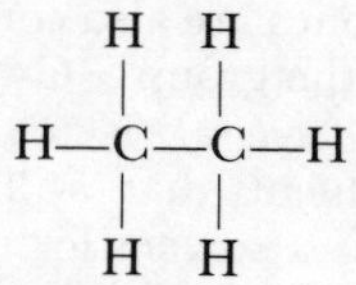

Ethane
(C_2H_6)

Unsaturated hydrocarbons, the *alkenes* and *alkynes*, have names ending in -ene or -yne: ethene (ethylene), propene (propylene) and ethyne (acetylene). Their main point of distinction is the presence of *double* and *triple* bonds which allow them to react with such chemicals as hydrogen. This property is of importance in the *hydrogenation* of unsaturated lipids. The formulae of ethene (ethylene) and ethyne (acetylene) are:

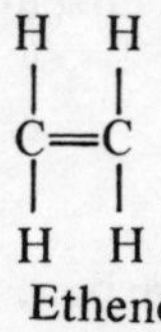

Ethene
(ethylene)
(C_2H_4)

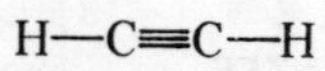

Ethyne (acetylene)
(C_2H_2)

Certain *aromatic* hydrocarbons have the carbon atoms arranged in the form of a ring of six carbon atoms:

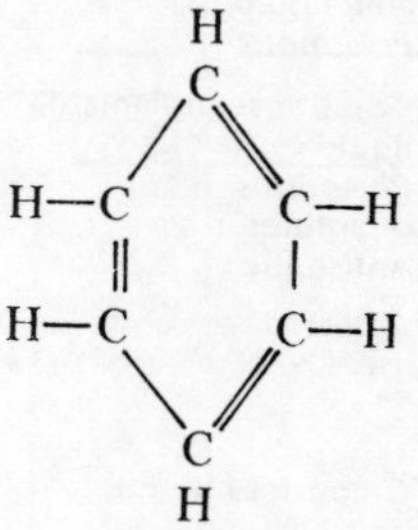

Benzene
(C_6H_6)

USES OF IMPORTANT HYDROCARBONS

Hydrocarbon	Use
Methane (CH_4)	Component of town and natural gas
Propane (C_3H_8) and butane (C_4H_{10})	Present in bottled gas
Pentane and hexane	Petrol or gasoline is a good solvent for grease and coal tar
Propene (propylene)	Making polypropylene plastics
Ethene (ethylene) (C_2H_4)	Manufacture of Terylene and such plastics as polythene or polyethylene. It is produced by ripening fruits and is used to hasten ripening in storage.
Benzene (C_6H_6)	An excellent grease and coal tar solvent. Inflammable
Methyl benzene (toluene) ($C_6H_5CH_3$)	Grease solvent. Used in the estimation of water in foods
Terpenes	Components of citrus fruit essential oils (see page 117)

ALCOHOLS – ALKANOLS

The alcohols or alkanols are organic compounds containing the elements carbon, hydrogen, and oxygen. They all contain the −OH *hydroxyl* group resembling water and alkalis in this respect. Examples are:

$$CH_3-OH \text{ methanol (methyl alcohol)}$$
$$C_2H_5-OH \text{ ethanol (ethyl alcohol)}$$
$$C_3H_7-OH \text{ propanol (propyl alcohol)}$$

Note. Water H−OH   Sodium hydroxide Na−OH

Properties of alcohols

1. They do not affect litmus.
2. They are flammable liquids.
3. They form *esters* or salts with acids:

$$\text{Alcohol + acid = ester + water}$$

This process of esterification is similar to the neutralization process between acids and bases.

USES OF IMPORTANT ALCOHOLS

Alcohol	Appearance and properties	Uses
Methanol (methyl alcohol) (CH₃OH) from the distillation of wood	Colourless, inflammable liquid *Poisonous*	Denaturization of ethanol
Ethanol (ethyl alcohol) (C₂H₅OH) (see page 215)	Colourless, inflamable liquid *Poisonous* in large quantities Antiseptic	1. Wines and spirits 2. Solvent for lacquer in varnish 3. Surgical spirit 4. Transfer, ball-pen ink, and chlorophyll stain remover 5. Mirror and window cleaner
Propanol (propyl alcohol)	Colourless liquid	Window and mirror cleaner
Propane 1,2,3,triol (glycerol) (C₃H₅OH) By-product of soap manufacture	Sweet, syrupy liquid, very hygroscopic	1. Preserving fruits 2. Humectant in confectionery to keep in moisture 3. Tea, coffee, and cocoa stain remover
Hexahydroxyhexane (sorbitol)	White solid	Sweet tasting sugar substitute

ESTERS

Esters are formed by esterification when organic acids react with organic alcohols:

Ethanoic acid +   ethanol = ethyl ethanoate + water
[Acetic acid + ethyl alcohol =   ethyl acetate + water]

Experiment

Take 5 cm³ of ethanol (ethyl alcohol) and 3 cm³ of glacial ethanoic (acetic) acid and add a few drops of concentrated sulphuric acid. Warm the mixture on a water bath for 5–10 minutes, then pour into a large beaker of cold water. Note the pleasant smell of the ethyl ethanoate (ethyl acetate) ester.

Properties of esters

Esters are mainly neutral liquids with pleasant, fruity smells and are therefore frequently used as synthetic flavouring agents in banana, apple and pineapple essences.

USES OF IMPORTANT ESTERS

Ester	Appearance and properties	Uses
Methylbutyl ethanoate (amyl acetate)	An inflammable liquid	1. Pear drops essence 2. Nail varnish remover 3. Cellulose paint thinner
Methylpropyl ethanoate (butyl acetate)	Liquid	Cellulose paint thinner
Phenylmethyl ethanoate (benzyl acetate)	Liquid	Strawberry flavour
Methylbenzene dicarboxylate (dimethyl phthalate)	Liquid	Fly and midge repellent
Ethyl ethanoate (ethyl acetate)	Liquid	Rum flavour. Cellulose paint stain remover
Ethyl hydroxypropanoate (ethyl lactate)	Liquid	Grape flavour

Alkanals and alkanones – aldehydes and ketones

Alkanals or aldehydes are compounds formed from alcohols and contain the functional-CHO aldehyde group. Some important aldehydes are:

Ethanal (acetaldehyde) is associated with the flavour of apples.

Benzenecarbaldehyde (benzaldehyde) is found in synthetic almond and cherry flavours.

Methanal (formaldehyde) is an unpleasant smelling liquid used for preserving plants and animals and for air sterilization.

Vanillin is an important aldehyde component of vanilla essence. Ketones are also compounds derived from alcohols and contain the group −C=O.

Propanone (acetone) is a highly flammable ketone or alkanone solvent that will dissolve cellulose ethanoate (acetate), it is a solvent for nail varnish. It also forms with other substances and collects in the urine of *diabetic* and starving people.

Phenols

Phenols are a group of compounds containing the −OH group and have acid properties.

Hydroxybenzene (phenol or carbolic acid) is a disinfectant and is also used in the manufacture of plastics.

Methylphenols (cresols) are important components of the disinfectant *lysol.* Tocopherols (vitamin E), benzene tricarboxylic (gallic) acid and methoxybenzene (anisole) are phenolic antioxidants – see page 153.

CARBOHYDRATES

Carbohydrates are compounds of carbon, hydrogen, and oxygen. Carbohydrates are formed in green plants by the process of *photosynthesis* from sunlight energy and the simple raw materials carbon dioxide and water.

The carbohydrates are providers of energy for the human body and with proteins and lipids form one of the three major food groups.

Types of carbohydrates

There are three main classes of carbohydrates, *monosaccharides* or simple single sugars, *disaccharides* or double sugars, and *polysaccharides* or starches.

1. *Monosaccharides*. The most important monosaccharides have six carbon atoms in the molecule with a general formula $C_6H_{12}O_6$. The chief monosaccharides are glucose, fructose, galactose, and mannose. The names of all carbohydrates finish in -ose. The *pentose* sugars $C_5H_{10}O_5$ have five carbon atoms, as in *ribose*.

2. *Disaccharides*. The most important disaccharides have twelve carbon atoms in the molecule with a general formula $C_{12}H_{22}O_{11}$. This is two hydrogen atoms and one oxygen atom less than two molecules of a monosaccharide:

$$\frac{\text{Two monosaccharide}}{\text{molecules}} - \text{less water} = \frac{\text{one disaccharide}}{\text{molecule}}$$

$$2 \times C_6H_{12}O_6 \quad - \quad H_2O \quad = \quad C_{12}H_{22}O_{11}$$

The important disaccharides are sucrose, maltose, and lactose.

3. *Polysaccharides*. The polysaccharides have large, chain-like molecules all formed by uniting many molecules of a monosaccharide sugar. Each monosaccharide molecule joins with another with the *elimination* of a molecule of water:

Monosaccharide Monosaccharide Monosaccharide

less H_2O less H_2O

$C_6H_{10}O_5$ $C_6H_{10}O_5$ $C_6H_{10}O_5$

Polysaccharide

Poly means *many*; therefore polysaccharide will mean many sugar molecules together. This prefix is also used in connection with naming plastics. The important polysaccharides are dextrins, starch, glycogen, inulin, and cellulose. (See also pages 122, 138 and 144.)

CHEMICAL PROPERTIES OF CARBOHYDRATES

1. Sweetness

Sweetness is the common property of all monosaccharide and disaccharide sugars, the order of *increasing* sweetness being lactose, maltose, glucose, sucrose, invert sugar, and fructose. The polysaccharides or starches have no sweet tasting properties.

2. Solubility in water

All monosaccharide and disaccharides are readily soluble in cold and hot water. Inulin is the only polysaccharide soluble in hot water, while starch, dextrin, and gum dissolve with difficulty. Cellulose is insoluble in water.

3. Reducing properties (see page 90)

Many sugars have *reducing* powers or the property of removing oxygen from another substance. *Fehlings* solution, made by mixing equal volumes of Fehlings A and B solutions, is essentially a solution of soluble copper(II) *oxide* (CuO). This solution can be affected by reducing agents which form a red, cloudy precipitate of copper(I) oxide (Cu_2O), the reducing agent having removed an oxygen atom from the two copper(II) oxide molecules, leaving one molecule of cuprous oxide:

$$\begin{matrix} CuO \\ CuO \end{matrix} + \text{reducing agent} = \begin{matrix} Cu \\ Cu \end{matrix}\!\!>\!\!O + O$$

Deep blue Fehlings solution   Red precipitate of copper(I) oxide   Oxygen removed

Experiment

Place 5 cm^3 of Fehlings A solution in a test tube, and add 5 cm^3 of Fehlings B solution. Mix by shaking the test tube. Sprinkle a little glucose into the mixture and warm the test tube *gently*. Observe the appearance of the reddish-yellow precipitate of copper(I) oxide indicating the reducing properties of the sugar.

Sugars with reducing properties are glucose, fructose, lactose, maltose and pentoses. The polysaccharides and sucrose have no reducing properties.

4. Action of heat

Strong heat causes the sugars to melt and burn. The sugars easily char or caramelize above 160°C.

5. Hydrolysis

This is the reaction of a compound with water. Many organic compounds react with water which is essential in boiling and steaming. If the sugars are boiled with water containing a little acid or alkali, the reaction is hastened.

Experiment

Dissolve 10 g of sucrose (cane sugar) in 100 cm^3 of water, and add 1 cm^3 of concentrated hydrochloric acid. Boil the solution for 5–10 minutes. Allow to cool and neutralize the mixture by adding a few drops of sodium hydroxide solution until it is neutral to litmus. Test the solution with Fehlings and note how the sucrose, after hydrolysis, produces the red precipitate whereas ordinary sucrose has no effect. During hydrolysis a molecule of water is added to the carbohydrate molecule:

Disaccharides $C_{12}H_{22}O_{11}$

$$C_{12}H_{22}O_{11} + H_2O \xrightarrow{\text{Hydrolysis}} 2C_6H_{12}O_6$$

Cane sugar   Monosaccharide molecules

The disaccharides break down into monosaccharides.

Polysaccharides ($C_6H_{10}O_5$) many times over.

$$—C_6H_{10}O_5—C_6H_{10}O_5—C_6H_{10}O_5—$$

$$\text{plus} \quad \downarrow \quad \text{water}$$
$$H_2O \qquad H_2O$$

$$C_6H_{12}O_6 + C_6H_{12}O_6 + C_6H_{12}O_6$$

Monosaccharide molecules

The polysaccharides break down into monosaccharides.

Conclusion: Hydrolysis of disaccharides and polysaccharides with dilute acid or alkali forms monosaccharides.

Digestion of carbohydrates is a process of hydrolysis taking place in the presence of digestive enzymes acting as catalysts. (See page 183.)

Sugar inversion. This is the process of hydrolysis of cane sugar producing a mixture of glucose and fructose monosaccharides, both of which are reducing sugars.

$$\text{Sucrose} + H_2O \underset{\text{Hydrolysis}}{=} \text{glucose} + \text{fructose}$$

The mixture of glucose and fructose is called *invert sugar*, and is sweeter than ordinary cane sugar. Invert sugar is found in honey, golden syrup, jam, boiled sweets, and toffee. Jam making and sweet making require the presence of *acids* such as dihydroxybutanedioic (tartaric) acid or ethanoic acid (vinegar) to bring about the inversion or hydrolysis of the sucrose. The inversion produces softer confectionery, important in making soft toffee, the *crystallization* of sugar is controlled by weak acids called *sugar doctors.*

USE OF IMPORTANT MONOSACCHARIDES

Monosaccharide	Occurrence	Uses
Glucose, also called dextrose, grape sugar, and blood sugar	Normal sugar of the blood. Found in all sweet fruits	1. Fruit drinks 2. Confectionery manufacture 3. In soluble coffee powder to make it free-flowing
Fructose, also called laevulose or fruit sugar	Found in all ripe fruits	Component of invert sugar, honey, and boiled sweets. Manufactured by the hydrolysis of inulin.

Glucose manufacture

Two main glucose sweeteners are available:

1. Glucose is made by the *complete* hydrolysis of cornflour starch and is a white *solid* or powder used in sugar confectionery, soft drinks, and ice-cream.

2. *Liquid glucose* or *starch syrup* is made by the *partial* hydrolysis or cornflour starch; it is a mixture of glucose and other disaccharides. Liquid glucose is available as a *syrupy liquid* for jam making, canned fruits, ice-cream, cakes, and table jellies. Jams made with it set quicker.

PREPARATION OF SUGAR – SUCROSE

1. From sugar cane

Sugar cane grows to a height of 4 m or more, the sugar

USES OF IMPORTANT DISACCHARIDES

Disaccharides	Occurrence	Uses
Maltose, or malt sugar, formed of two glucose molecules	Found in germinating barley seeds or malt	Malt extract is made by treating germinating barley with hot water. Brewing of beer (see page 215)
Sucrose, cane or beet sugar. Formed of one glucose and one fructose molecule	Sugar canes, sugar beet or maple bark	Confectionery, soft drinks and rum manufacture. Jams and preserves. Sweet-curing hams and bacon. Sucrose provides some of the body needs of carbohydrate.
Lactose, milk sugar formed of glucose and galactose	Milk	Tablet making

being present within a soft fibre of the stems to the extent of 14–17 per cent.

(*a*) The sugar cane is cut up by shredding knives, crushed between rollers, and sprayed with water to assist the sugar extraction. The cane juice thus produced contains 18–21 per cent sugar.

(*b*) The sugar cane juice is now treated with lime to remove the ethanedioic (oxalic) and 2-hydroxypropane tricarboxylic (citric) acids.

(*c*) Evaporation of the juice is performed in multiple evaporators using steam from boilers fired with *bagasse*, the sugar fibre remaining after sugar extraction.

(*d*) The concentration juice is boiled in steam-heated evaporating pans until crystallization is complete. This results in *massecuite*, a mixture of raw sugar and molasses.

(*e*) Centrifugal spinning separates the raw sugar from the molasses. The sugar is then refined.

2. From sugar beet

(*a*) The beets are washed before passing into machines which slice them into *cosettes* containing 15 per cent sucrose.

(*b*) The sugar is extracted from the cosettes by the process of diffusion (see page 18). Fresh water continuously circulates around the sugar beet to extract the sugar in the diffuser plants.

(*c*) The sugar juice is treated with calcium oxide to remove ethanedioic (oxalic) and 2-hydroxypropane tricarboxylic (citric) acids, and then treated with carbon dioxide to eliminate any calcium oxide which has combined with sugar to form calcium sucrate.

(*d*) After filtration the juice is concentrated in multiple evaporators and vacuum evaporated to induce crystallization. The raw sugar and syrup massecuite are separated in centrifugal spinners.

Sugar refining

This is the process of purifying raw sugar.

(*a*) *Affination* is the first stage consisting of washing away in centrifugal spinners the molasses present in the brown raw sugar.

(*b*) The washed sugar is dissolved in water and treated with calcium oxide and carbon dioxide gas. The calcium carbonate formed is used as a filter agent and is removed by filter presses, giving an amber-coloured solution.

(*c*) Animal bone charcoal (see page 98) is now used to decolorize the amber-coloured solution which thus emerges colourless from the vertical charcoal cisterns.

(*d*) The clear solution is boiled in *vacuum* evaporating pans until it is suitably crystallized. This is essential to prevent caramelization of the sugar produced by high temperatures.

(*e*) The crystallized sugar is spun in centrifugal separators and the damp sugar dried in granulators in a current of hot air.

Molasses

This is the treacle-coloured, bitter flavoured by-product consisting of 67% sucrose. The molasses can be made into rum or further purified to produce syrup. Refiners' syrups, golden syrup and treacle, contain 70 and 60 per cent sucrose respectively, together with invert sugar and useful amounts of *iron* and calcium are present in the molasses and treacle.

USES OF IMPORTANT POLYSACCHARIDES

Polysaccharides	Occurrence	Use
Cellulose, made up of glucose molecules (See also page 147)	Cell walls of all plants, forms the *dietary fibre* of vegetable diets	1. Cellulose is the main component of cotton, linen, jute, paper, and wood 2. Cellulose fibres, rayon, and cellulose acetate 3. Powdered cellulose is indigestible and is used to provide bulk in weight-reducing foods 4. Compounds of cellulose used as thickening and creaming agents
Dextrins (British gum)	Derivative of starch and wheat, e.g. formed by toasting bread	Made by roasting dry starch forming a crust in baked bread and cakes. Used as adhesives on stationery for sizing carpet backs, and textile finishing. Coffee extracts. An adhesive for wall-papers
Glycogen (animal starch) composed of glucose molecules	Liver, oysters, meat and also in mushrooms and yeast	Important foodstuff and component of liver
Inulin composed of fructose molecules	Found in Jerusalem artichokes	*Soluble* in hot water

USES OF IMPORTANT POLYSACCHARIDES

Polysaccharides	Occurrence	Use
Pectin composed of galacturonic and mannuronic acids	Pectin substances cement together the cell walls of plants. Found in under-ripe fruits. Strawberry, raspberry, and cherry are short of pectin. Apple, plum, seville orange and seaweed are rich in pectin	Setting agent for jams and jellies. Fruits must be under-ripe since pectin breaks down into pectic acid in *ripe* fruits making them soft and of poor setting quality

PECTIN

Pectin is commercially produced by extracting the substance from apple pulp or orange skin pith. The extract is treated with salts to precipitate the crude pectin which is washed, filtered, then dried and packed as a powdered solid. The gelling power of pectin is due to the formation of a sponge-like network by its molecules which support the water and sugars within the framework.

Acids are essential to the formation of a pectin jelly, a pH of 3·3 giving the best results. Below this the jelly has poor setting qualities. The acids may be already present in the fruit or can be added, as in jam making, as hydroxypropane tricarboxylic (citric) or dihydroxybutanedioic (tartaric) acid. Sugars are needed to form soft tender jelly.

Experiment

A simple method of showing the relevant amounts of pectin in fruit juices is to take about 5 cm³ of fruit juice and add an equal volume of clear industrial ethanol and to observe the quantity of pectin precipitated. A comparison of the juice from under- and over-ripe fruits can be made.

STARCHES

1. *Ordinary Starch* comes from ordinary varieties of maize, rice, sorghum, plants and also from wheat, tapioca and potato. The starch granules are found in the plant storage cells, surplus monosaccharides being converted into starches.

The ordinary starch granule consists of two polysaccharides:

(*a*) 20 to 30 per cent water soluble *amylose*

(*b*) 70 to 80 per cent insoluble *amylopectin*.

Ordinary starches form *gels* with water.

2. *Waxy Starch* comes from different varieties of plants called waxy maize, waxy rice and waxy sorghum. The granules of these waxy starches are composed entirely of *amylopectin* and do not contain any amylose.

Ordinary starch = Amylopectin (70–80 per cent) + Amylose (20–30 per cent)

Waxy starch = Amylopectin (100 per cent)

Waxy starches with water form clear mucilaginous *pastes*.

Chemical test

(i) Dissolve a few crystals of iodine [care:– corrosive to

skin and eyes, and poisonous] in a solution of 10 per cent potassium iodide. Add a few drops to a starch solution which turns blue-black. Boil the mixture and note the disappearance of the coloration. On cooling the colour reappears.

(ii) Add a few drops of iodine solution to *waxy* starches, such as waxy cornflour and waxy rice. A *red* stain appears, showing amylopectin.

Hydrolysis of starch

When starch is treated with dilute hydrochloric acid and boiled it produces glucose, this process being used in large-scale manufacture.

$$\text{Acid hydrolysis}$$
$$\text{Starch} \longrightarrow \text{glucose}$$

When starch is treated with α-amylase enzyme or malt extract the process of hydrolysis takes place as below, giving dextrin, maltose, and finally glucose (see page 215).

$$\text{Starch} \rightarrow \text{dextrin} \rightarrow \text{maltose} \rightarrow \text{glucose}$$

Partial hydrolysis occurs on boiling starchy foods such as potatoes. The change from starch to maltose also occurs in potatoes on long storage giving them a sweet taste. Potatoes that have been frozen also have a high sugar content which adversely affects their keeping quality. Potatoes with a high sugar content yield potato chips with a pleasing brown colour.

Starch production

The main raw material for starch production is maize or cornflour. Potatoes, wheat, and rice are also used.

1. The maize kernel is wet-milled to separate its four main components, starch, gluten, fibre, and germ. The final product is a suspension of pure starch in water or starch slurry.

2. This is spun in centrifuges and the damp starch dried in a stream of warm air in a flash drier. Then the product is bagged.

MODIFIED STARCHES

These are starches which have been treated by heating or by chemical action.

1. *Acid Modified Starch* is made from ordinary starch that has been treated with acid and is used for making fruit gums.

2. *Oxidized Starches*, made from ordinary starch treated with hypochlorite reagents, are used for making tender confectionery gums.

3. *Cross Linked Starch*, made from waxy starches treated with phosphate esters, give starches used in canned fruit pie fillings.

4. *Starch Phosphates* are modified starches readily soluble in cold water used in fruit pie fillings and wallpaper pastes.

5. *Precooked Starches* are made from ordinary or waxy starches by cooking on heated rollers. They are used mainly in 'instant' puddings and creams, and soups.

Uses of starch

1. Maize starch is the basis of cornflour for custard, blancmange and as a thickener for sauces and puddings.

2. Laundry starch. The choice of a starch for laundry purposes depends on the size of the starch grains. The small grain of rice can penetrate between the threads of the fabric producing stiffness *within* the fabric, as compared to stiffness on the *surface* using potato or wheat starch. The latter stiffness is rather rigid and brittle.

3. Waxy starches which give clear mucilaginous pastes find use in white sauces, puddings, and canned fruit pie fillings (see page 134).

GUMS AND MUCILAGES

Gums are the secretions of plants found on leaves, roots, and barks. Chemically gums are mixtures of monosaccharides and polysaccharides, and are composed of carbon, hydrogen, and oxygen. Seaweeds and mosses produce slimy secretions known as *mucilages*. Gums and mucilages swell in the presence of water and mix freely with it. Preparations containing gums and mucilages tend to go mouldy and should therefore contain a *preservative*. Natural gums find considerable use as food emulsion *stabilizers*, and as non-nutritive food *thickeners*.

ORIGIN AND USES OF GUMS AND MUCILAGES

Gum or mucilage	Origin	Uses
Arabic gum	Formed on *acacia* tree barks of North Africa	1. A thickener and creaming agent for gum confectionery 2. Stiffener for silk and rayon 3. Adhesive
Tragacanth gum	Forms as a wound on the bark of a shrub in Turkey – *Astrogalus*	1. Creaming agent for salad cream 2. Stiffener for delicate fabrics
Ghatti gum	Forms on stems of certain plants in India *Anogeissus*	Thickener for creams. Stiffener for fabrics
Karaya gum	Found in India – *Sterculia* plant	Similar to gum tragacanth though cheaper
Locust bean gum	Sweet tasting, bean-like fruit of carob tree – *Ceratonia*	Used to thicken puddings, salad creams, and ice-creams. Locust beans were the popular sweetmeat of children in the 1930s
Agar-agar	Red seaweed mucilage from Japan	Gels for soups, jellies, ice-cream, and meat pastes
Alginates	Brown seaweed extracts	Similar to agar-agar
Carrageen	Irish Moss, a seaweed extract – *Chondrus*	Mucilage and an emulsifier for beverages
Guar gum	Seeds of *Cyanopsis*	Ice-cream stabilizer or thickener.

DIETARY FIBRE

Plant *cell walls* (see page 167) are composed of several different substances, which include the main material *cellulose*, or *lignin* (the main component of wood) (page 152), and the *gums*, *mucilages* and *pectins* previously described. *All* these substances together form what is called *dietary fibre*. The non-fibrous gums and pectins are partly digested, but the fibrous lignin and cellulose are indigestible in the human gut. Synthetic *methyl cellulose* (see page 134) is an indigestible substance used in weight-reducing dietary preparations.

EFFECT OF COOKING ON CARBOHYDRATES

1. Hydrolysis

Acids will produce hydrolysis of sugars as in jams and sugar boiling. The pectin of fruits will be hydrolysed by acids and cause thickening of the fruit juices.

Polysaccharides will hydrolyse, for example some potato starch will change into maltose. Heat will change starch into dextrin on the outer crust of bread and cakes.

2. Heat

High temperatures will cause the cereal grains to burst, as evident in making popcorn from maize grains and in the preparation of various breakfast cereals. Similarly treated starch will gel quicker, an important factor in sauce, custard, and blancmange preparation and to an extent in the making of laundry starch. Starch gelatinizes in the presence of water at about 70°C, a suitable temperature for custard and cornflour sauce preparation. Dry heat of 160°C turns starch brown and causes it to become dextrinized. See sugar boiling, paragraphs 5 and 10.

3. Cooked starchy foods

These are more easily digestible as the grains of starch are ruptured.

4. Vegetable foods

These are softened by breaking down the intercellular cementing substances and also by weakening of the cellulose walls of the cells.

5. Sugar confectionery

Sucrose is the main ingredient, together with liquid glucose syrup and honey. Sweets or candy which contain *crystallized* sugar include fondants and fudges, while *non-crystalline* confectionery includes boiled sweets, toffees and brittles.

The *sugar boiling* cooking process (see following paragraph) results in an *increasing* sugar concentration as the sugar solution reaches *higher* temperatures. At 100°C the dissolved sugar concentration is 82%, and at 150°C it is 95%. Caramelization occurs at higher temperatures.

SUGGESTIONS FOR PRACTICAL WORK

1. Observe the effect of heating small amounts of the following substances individually in hard glass test tubes: (*a*) propanetriol (glycerine); (*b*) starch; (*c*) sucrose; (*d*) glucose.

2. Perform simple tests showing the solvent properties of: (*a*) ethanol (methylated spirit) and ball-pen stains; (*b*) propanetriol (glycerine) and coffee stains; (*c*) methyl butylethanoate (amyl acetate) as a nail varnish remover; and (*d*) (acetone) as a solvent for cellulose ethanoate (acetate) and nail varnish propanone.

3. Test the following sugars using Fehlings solutions: glucose, fructose, maltose, and sucrose.

4. Extract the juices from the following: potato, carrot, apple, cabbage, and germinated barley grains. Test each of the juices with Fehlings solution.

5. Shake up small quantities of cornflour or laundry starch, rice, and potato starch with a little water in individual test tubes. Place samples on a cavity slide and examine the starch grains under a microscope. (The experiment can be demonstrated by using a micro-projector.)

6. To test for the presence of starch in different foodstuffs add a few drops of iodine solution to soaked or fresh pieces of: onion scale, potato, carrot, turnip, bread, cake, biscuit, flour, and baking powder.

7. *Browning of potato chips*. Cut some potatoes, preferably new ones, into chips. Fry some in deep fat in the normal manner. Before frying immerse some in glucose solution and some in sucrose solution. Note the effect of the sugars on the browning. Fry some potatoes which have been stored in the freezing compartment of a refrigerator.

8. *Preparation of hard-gum pastilles*. Weigh out the following:

Gum arabic	180 g
Sugar	120 g
Glucose	32 g
Hydroxypropane tricarboxylic (citric) acid	1 g
Lemon essence and colouring as required	

Dissolve the gum in 80 cm³ of water and heat over a steam bath. Dissolve the sugars and acid in 60 cm³ of water and heat over a steam bath. Mix the two solutions together and simmer for 30 min; add colouring and filter the solution through a sieve. Allow it to cool in shallow metal dishes.

9. A de-icer for windows and windscreens can be made from a mixture of 30 g propanetriol (glycerine) and 70 cm³ propanol (propyl alcohol).

10. Sugar boiling temperatures:

Mix together 100 g sucrose and 20 cm³ of water and heat slowly in a 250 cm³ beaker, observing changes in the physical condition at the different temperatures:

Temperature	Sugar boilers' description	Use
115°C	Soft ball	Marzipan
121°C	Hard ball	Nougat

Temperature	Sugar boilers' description	Use
138°C	Crack	Meringues
160°C	Hard crack	Toffee and spun sugar
193°C	Caramel	Coffee and gravy colour

11. 'Hokey Pokey': when the temperature of the boiled sugar reaches 160°C add 5 g of a mixture of equal amounts of sodium hydrogen carbonate and potassium hydrogen dihydroxybutanedioate (cream of tartar), with vigorous stirring. Pour the golden-yellow foaming mass into greased metal dishes to cool. Note how the cooling mass can be pulled into threads of spun sugar.

12. See *Experimental Science for Catering and Homecraft*, Practical work 4.1 to 4.4, 18.1 to 18.4, 19.1 to 19.5 and 20.1 to 20.4.

QUESTIONS ON CHAPTER 16

1. What is a carbohydrate? Name three members of each of the following groups: monosaccharides; disaccharides; and polysaccharides.

2. What is the difference between a hydrocarbon and a carbohydrate? Give three examples of each and their uses in catering.

3. Write short notes on (a) ethanol; (b) polyethene (poly ethylene); (c) ethene (ethylene); (d) propanone (acetone); and (e) ethyl ethanoate (ethyl acetate).

4. What are reducing sugars?

5. Explain the term hydrolysis of carbohydrates. Give three examples of this process in cookery practice.

6. What does photosynthesis mean? Give an account of the products of photosynthesis and their uses in food.

7. Give an account of the importance in cookery of: (a) pectin; (b) agar gum; (c) dextrin; and (d) liquid glucose or starch syrup.

8. Describe the production of sucrose from sugar cane and its subsequent refining. Give three examples of the use of sucrose in catering.

9. Describe how you would examine foodstuffs for the presence of: (a) glucose; (b) starch; (c) water; and (d) carbon.

10. Describe a chemical experiment to show the inversion of sucrose. Give the names of some substances which contain invert sugar.

MULTIPLE CHOICE QUESTIONS ON CHAPTER 16

Figure 16.1 shows a stage in the testing of a food for carbohydrates, the following questions are concerned with this figure and test.

1. During the test a deep blue coloured copper reagent forms a brick-red to orange coloured precipitate due to the chemical reaction of one of the following reducing sugars:
(a) starch   (c) sucrose
(b) glucose   (d) cellulose

2. The water bath in the diagram should be kept at a temperature of:

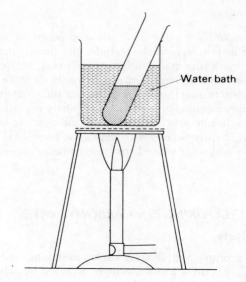

Figure 16.1

(a) 0°C   (c) 40°C
(b) 20°C   (d) 100°C

3. The test for the presence of reducing sugars in foods is called the:
(a) iodine test   (c) Sudan III test
(b) Benedicts test   (d) Millons test

4. In order for the cane sugar to be hydrolysed, the same apparatus may be used but one of the following must be added to the sugar solution:
(a) water
(b) sodium chloride
(c) sodium hydrogen carbonate
(d) hydrochloric acid

5. The hydrolysis of cane sugar produces:
(a) glucose   (c) fructose and lactose
(b) glucose and fructose   (d) maltose

6. Which of the following food samples will display a blue black colour when treated with iodine solution?
(a) melon   (c) potato
(b) egg   (d) tripe

7. Carbohydrates are composed of the chemical elements:
(a) nitrogen carbon and hydrogen
(b) carbon, hydrogen and oxygen
(c) carbon, hydrogen, oxygen and nitrogen
(d) carbon, hydrogen, oxygen, nitrogen and phosphorus

8. One of the following is the chemical formula for a carbohydrate:
(a) C_2H_5OH (c) H_2O
(b) CO_2 (d) $C_6H_{12}O_6$

9. Select a complex carbohydrate or polysaccharide from the following:
(a) maltose   (c) lactose
(b) cellulose   (d) fructose

10. Lactose is a sugar found in:
(a) malt   (c) fruits
(b) sugar beet   (d) milk

17 A variety of oils

LIPIDS OR PLANT AND ANIMAL OILS AND FATS

Plant and animal oils and fats, also called *lipids*, are available from a wide range of sources as shown by the table.

PLANT AND ANIMAL LIPIDS

Plant oils and fats	Animal oils of fats
Coconut oil – normally a *solid* in temperate climates	Butter fat
Corn or maize germ oil	Cream
Copra or coconut oil	Cod-liver oil
Cottonseed oil	Dripping fat
Groundnut or peanut oil	Halibut oil
Linseed oil	Herring oil
Olive oil	Lard
Palm kernel solid fat	Mutton fat
Rape seed oil	Whale oil
Soya bean oil	
Sunflower oil	
Wheat germ oil	

EXTRACTION OF LIPIDS

(a) Animal lipids

Animal fats are obtained by heat-rendering. *Dry-rendering* is the method of heating the fat to 50°C, to allow the fat to melt and separate from the fat cell (see Figure 6.1).

Wet-rendering consists of the lipid material being heated with water in an open pan, or heated with steam in pressure cookers or autoclaves (see page 39). This method is used for lard and fish oils.

(b) Vegetable lipids

Crushing is the method used for groundnuts, palm kernels, and coconuts. The seed is cleansed, crushed, then cooked to burst the fat cells. Pressing of the cooked meal expels the oil to leave a residue of seed cake for animal feeds.

Solvent extraction. The crushed seed is mixed with a solvent such as *trichloroethene* (*trichloroethylene*) which extracts the oil. The solution is distilled to separate oil and solvent, the latter being re-used.

Experiment

To extract peanut oil:

Crush some peanuts in a mortar and cook the product over a water bath for 15 minutes. Place the cooked meal inside the Soxhlet thimble and reflux with trichloroethene (trichloroethylene) over a steam bath for 30 minutes (see Figure 17.1). Carefully distil the trichloroethene extract over an electric mantle or a steam bath. The groundnut oil will remain as an oily residue in the distilling flask.

LIPID REFINING

The crude vegetable oil and animal fats obtained by these extraction methods contain impurities which affect the flavour, colour, and smell. They are removed by *refining* to give a colourless, tasteless, and odourless oil, the process being summarized as follows:

(*a*) Neutralization with sodium hydroxide removes the acid impurities.

(*b*) Bleaching using fullers' earth or animal charcoal removes the coloured impurities.

(*c*) Deodorization, the removal of strong smells and

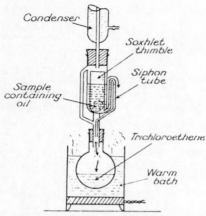

Figure 17.1. Soxhlet apparatus for extraction of oils and fats from nuts and other foods

flavours, is achieved by steam distillation under low pressure (see page 42).

CHEMICAL COMPOSITION OF LIPIDS

1. All animal and plant oils or fats are made up of carbon, hydrogen, and oxygen. They contain *more* carbon than the carbohydrates and are therefore valuable energy providing foods. Fats provide 37 kJ per gram compared to the 17 kJ per gram of carbohydrates (see page 26).

2. Natural lipids may be regarded as salts, or more correctly esters of fatty, or alkanoic acids, and propanetriol (glycerine), and are also described as *glycerides* or *triglycerides*:

Fatty acid + $\dfrac{\text{propanetriol}}{\text{(glycerine)}} = \dfrac{\text{oils and fats or esters of fatty}}{\text{acid and propanetriol (glycerine)}}$

Olive oil is mainly an ester of propanetriol (glycerine) and the fatty acid octadec-9-enoic (oleic) acid; the compound formed is also called propanetriol triolein:

Olive oil, propaneoctadec-9-enoate triolein = $\dfrac{\text{propanetriol}}{\text{(glycerine)}} + \dfrac{\text{octadec-9-enoic}}{\text{(oleic acid)}}$

The chemical formula of olive oil could be shown in a *simple* manner by representing the propanetriol (glycerol) molecule as

$$\left[\begin{array}{l} -\text{OH} \\ -\text{OH} \\ -\text{OH} \end{array}\right.$$

and the fatty acid as H.F.A.

The formation of a lipid from propanetriol (glycerine) and fatty acids could be shown as:

$$\left[\begin{array}{l} -\text{OH} \\ -\text{OH} \\ -\text{OH} \end{array}\right. + \begin{array}{c} 3\text{H.F.A.} \\ \text{Alkanoic} \\ \text{acid} \end{array} = \left[\begin{array}{l} -\text{F.A.} \\ -\text{F.A.} \\ -\text{F.A.} \end{array}\right. + 3\text{H}_2\text{O}$$

Propanetriol (Glycerine)   Lipid

3. *The physical state* of natural lipids is dependent on their chemical composition. At room temperature (20°C) lipids which are *liquids* are called oils and those which are *solid* are called fats.

Some lipids are composed of fatty acids with many *double bonds*, resembling those in ethene (ethylene) described on page 105. They are called *unsaturated* fatty acids or unsaturated oils; cottonseed, groundnut, and corn oil are examples. The unsaturated oil double bond can react with hydrogen gas and become *saturated* forming a solid fat, a chemical change important in fat manufacture:

Liquid	Hydrogenation	Solid
Unsaturated oil + Hydrogen	=	Saturated fat

$$\begin{array}{ccc} \overset{\displaystyle H\ \ H}{\underset{\displaystyle |\ \ \ |}{-C=C-}} + H_2 & \underset{=}{\overset{\text{Catalyst}}{=}} & \overset{\displaystyle H\ \ H}{\underset{\displaystyle |\ \ \ |}{-C-C-}} \\ & & \underset{\displaystyle H\ \ H}{|\ \ \ |} \end{array}$$

Unsaturated double bond   Saturated bond

Linoleic (octadeca*di*enoic) and *linolenic* (octadeca*tri*enoic) fatty acids are polyunsaturated fatty acids PUFA, having 2 and 3 double bonds respectively in their molecules. Since *linoleic* acid cannot be made in the human body, it is also called the *essential fatty acid* or Vitamin F, because it affects the condition of skin and hair.

Erucic (docosenoic) acid found in mustard and rape seed oil is a harmful unsaturated fatty acid known to affect animal heart muscle.

The *saturated* fatty acids forming the solid fats are mainly octadecanoic (stearic), hexadecanoic (palmitic), dodecanoic (lauric), and butanoic (butyric) acids, and are the main components of lipids from animal sources, excepting fish oils.

Experiment

To find the melting point of a fat.

Draw melted fat into capillary tubes by sucking as with a pipette. Cool and rapidly seal one end of the tubes in a Bunsen flame. Cool the sealed tubes under running cold water or in ice.

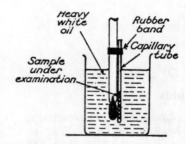

Figure 17.2. Melting-point apparatus

Mount the tube alongside the bulb of a mercury thermometer using small rubber bands. Immerse the thermometer in a beaker of cold water and heat gently continuously stirring the water to maintain an even temperature throughout (see Figure 17.2). Observe the temperatures when the fat begins to melt and when the last fat particle turns to liquid. Repeat several times to obtain average values.

The melting points of lard, cooking fat, coconut oil, butter, and margarine can then be determined and their melting points compared.

4. *High temperatures* cause oils and fats to decompose into fatty acids and propanetriol (glycerol), a process called 'lipid splitting':

$$\begin{array}{ccc} \lceil F.A. & & \lceil OH \\ & heat & \\ \mid F.A. & \rightarrow & \mid OH + 3F.A. \\ & & \quad\quad Alkanoic\ acid \\ \lfloor F.A. & & \lfloor OH \\ Oil\ or\ fat & & Propanetriol \\ & & (glycerol) \end{array}$$

This breakdown occurs when a fat is repeatedly used for frying purposes. Old frying fat can be clarified by heating it with sodium hydrogen carbonate dissolved in water. The water removes the soluble propanetriol (glycerine) and the sodium hydrogen carbonate *neutralizes* the free fatty acids, the clarified fat solidifying above the aqueous solution:

$$\begin{array}{l} \quad\quad\quad\quad Propanetriol \rightarrow water \\ \quad\nearrow \quad\quad\quad (glycerine) \\ Old\ fat \\ \quad\searrow \\ \quad\quad fatty\ acids \rightarrow sodium \rightarrow sodium\ salts\ of \\ \quad\quad\quad\quad\quad\quad hydrogen \quad fatty\ acids\ or \\ \quad\quad\quad\quad\quad\quad carbonate \quad 'soaps' \end{array}$$

If the temperature rises or the fat burns, the unpleasant, irritating odour of *propenal* (acrolein) $CH_2 . CH . CHO$ is now detected, caused by the thermal decomposition of the glycerine:

$$\underset{}{\overset{Heat}{Fat \longrightarrow}} propanetriol\ (glycerine) \overset{High}{\underset{temperature}{\longrightarrow}} propenal\ (acrolein) + water \\ + \\ fatty\ acid$$

$$\begin{array}{l} CH_2OH \\ \mid \quad\quad\quad Heat \\ CHOH \longrightarrow \quad CH_2—CH—CHO + 2H_2O \\ \mid \quad\quad\quad\quad\quad Propenal\ (acrolein) \\ CH_2OH \\ Propanetriol\ (glycerine) \end{array}$$

Experiment

Place a little mutton fat on a metal plate and heat strongly. Note the colour of the burning fat flame and the odour of propenal (acrolein).

SMOKE AND FIRE POINTS OF COOKING OILS

When an oil or fat is heated strongly above the frying temperatures, normally between 180° and 195°C, the oil gives off a thin bluish smoke at the smoke point, usually 25°–40°C *above* the normal frying temperatures. The blue *smoke point* indicates that the oil is beginning to *decompose*. At higher temperatures (340°–360°C) the oil may catch fire and burn.

Corn or maize oil has a *normal frying temperature* range between 180° and 195°C, the smoke point is 232°C, while the fire point is 360°C. Vegetable oils have higher smoke and frying temperatures than animal fats. The smoke point is lowered by the addition of such *creaming agents* as propanediol octadecanoate (glyceryl monostearate).

Smoking fat is *not* a true measure of frying temperatures; a thermometer should be used with a thermostat to maintain the temperature. The keeping quality of the cooking fat will be maintained provided the frying temperature range is not exceeded.

The smoke points of some fats and oils are:

Vegetable oils: soya bean oil, pure peanut oil 243°C, cottonseed oil 236°C, and corn oil 232°C.

Animal oils and fats: fresh lard 222°C, butter 201°C, and used lard 191°C. Beef dripping 163°C.

Lard that has been used frequently contains a large amount of free fatty acids which lower the smoke point. They can be removed with sodium hydrogen carbonate as in the clarifying process.

Experiment

To find the smoke point of a frying oil:

Place some frying oil in a small porcelain evaporating dish and suspend a thermometer in the oil. Heat the dish gently until the oil produces the thin bluish smoke and note the temperature. Compare the smoke points of pure corn and olive oils with those of lard, dripping, and manufactured cooking fats, and oils containing creaming agents such as high-ratio fats.

5. *Hydrolysis.* The interaction of an oil or fat with water to form propanetriol (glycerine) and fatty acids can be achieved by *lipase enzymes* during the digestive process or by heating under pressure. The latter method is used in the steam-rendering process for animal fat (see page 128).

$$Oil\ or\ fat + water \overset{Heat}{=} fatty\ acid + \underset{(glycerine)}{propanetriol}$$

6. *Saponification,* the process of soap making, involves boiling together an alkali and an oil or fat to form *soaps*. Surfaces washed with soda or alkali before painting must be *neutralized* with ethanoic or other weak acid as the alkali will combine with the paint oils forming soap which will prevent the paint clinging to the surface (see page 128).

7. *Rancidity.* The spoilage of oils and fats and the development of unpleasant odours and tastes in lipid products is the result of a number of causes:

(*a*) The lipids can *absorb* odours of paint, mothballs, fire-lighters, perfumes from air sprays, polishes, and disinfectants.

(*b*) Oxygen from the air can *oxidize* the unsaturated fats producing objectionable flavours. The oxygen adds on to the double bond of the unsaturated fats forming *oxyns* or rancid products:

$$\begin{array}{ccc} \overset{\displaystyle H}{\underset{\displaystyle |}{}} \overset{\displaystyle H}{\underset{\displaystyle |}{}} & & \overset{\displaystyle H}{\underset{\displaystyle |}{}} \overset{\displaystyle H}{\underset{\displaystyle |}{}} \\ -C==C- & + \text{ oxygen} = & -C-C- \\ & & \overset{\displaystyle |}{\underset{\displaystyle O-O}{}} \end{array}$$

unsaturated oil

oxyns

Sunlight and ultra-violet rays from fluorescent tube lamps hasten the process of rancidity. Tungsten filament lamps do not affect the process. Traces of such metals as copper and iron act as catalysts.

(*c*) Hydrolytic rancidity described in 5 above.

Anti-oxidants are used to prevent the development of rancidity. They are *reducing agents* which remove oxygen; methyl propylhydroxy methoxybenzene (butylated hydroxy anisole B.H.A.) is one of the permitted anti-oxidants added to fat and margarine. Vitamins C and E are naturally occurring antioxidants. (See pages 91, 153 and Appendix A.)

Storage of fats in cool, dark, odourless places is vital; non-metal containers or glass or porcelain prevent contamination by iron or copper.

LIPID PRODUCTS (SEE APPENDIX B)

1. *Cooking, frying, and salad oils.* These products are mainly refined cottonseed, corn, olive, safflower, and groundnut oils either individually or in carefully blended mixtures. They are *winterized* or cooled to 7°C to crystallize any solid fats which might cloud the oil when used in winter.

2. *Margarine* is manufactured from a blend of refined groundnut, whale, coconut, palm, and palm kernel oils. The liquid groundnut and whale oils are hydrogenated at 140°–180°C using hydrogen and a nickel catalyst to produce white fats rich in PUFA polyunsaturated oils. The oil ingredients are mixed with ripened milk, salt, emulsifying agents, and Vitamins A and D. A yellow dye is also added and the mixture homogenized carefully. The method of chilling affects the fat crystals thus forming hard or soft consistency margarines for different purposes.

3. *Cooking fats or shortening.* The refined oils are blended with fats and hydrogenated oils to produce a composition of the desired melting properties. Plasticizing or chilling follows to provide the correct form of fat crystals and fat consistency. Air or nitrogen is blown into the cooling blended oils to produce a whitened effect while the blend is agitated or puddled. Finally the cooking fat is tempered or stored at a temperature of 25°–30°C for three days.

(*a*) *All-purpose* cooking fat is used for pastry and cake making, and also for frying.

(*b*) *High-ratio shortening fat* contains added creaming agents propanediol octadecanoate (glyceryl monostearate) and diglycerides which increase the creaming powers of fats intended for use in *high-sugar*-content confectionery. High-ratio fats gives confectionery a higher ratio of sugar to flour than that obtainable with all purpose cooking fat.

Propanediol octadecanoate (glyceryl monostearate (G.M.S.)), a white powder, and a monoglyceride, is used as an *emulsifier* in fats, bread, cakes, and as a tin-greasing agent. Diglycerides are also used for their creaming powers.

Margarines, fats, and shortenings containing the mono- and diglycerides are liable to *spatter* when heated and therefore may contain such anti-spattering additives as lecithin.

4. *Lard* or hog fat is available in three types, dry-rendered, leaf lard, and prime steam lard.

(*a*) *Dry-rendered lard* is obtained by melting the hog fat and has a high smoke point.

(*b*) *Leaf lard* is obtained from hog fat lining the body cavity and is dry-rendered.

(*c*) *Prime steam lard* is the popular domestic type and is obtained by steam extraction in autoclaves.

Other derivatives of lard are: *hydrogenated* lard treated with hydrogen and nickel to saturate the unsaturated fatty acids, thus forming a fat with a high smoke point used for bread fattening; and *interesterified* lard, or lard in which the fatty acid groups are reshuffled between the propanetriol (glycerine) molecules by heating with a catalyst. This is a lard derivative with excellent creaming powers used in commercial cake making.

5. *Butter* is made by separating cream, which contains some 30 per cent butter fat, and pasteurizing it. Churning causes the butter fat globules to come together and form butter. This contains some 80 per cent butter fat and buttermilk, which is drawn off. Salt is added to the butter to improve its flavour and keeping quality. (See also page 196.)

$$\text{Milk} \longrightarrow \text{cream} \longrightarrow \text{butter} \longrightarrow \text{buttermilk}$$

separated milk

+ salt

packed butter

RELATED LIPID COMPOUNDS

Lecithin is a fatty substance of propanetriol (glycerine), fatty acids, choline, and phosphoric acid, and is found in egg yolk, soya bean, peanut, and maize. Its uses are to prevent spattering in fats, and as a creaming agent for chocolate, salad cream, and white flour.

Cholesterol is an alcohol associated with animal oils and fats. Deposits of cholesterol within the arteries cause blockage of the arteries (see page 189).

Phytosterols are the alcohols found in vegetable oils and fats and do not affect the arteries. Such oils are therefore recommended for dietary purposes instead of animal fats.

Ergosterol, found in yeasts and fungi, is changed into Vitamin D_2 by sunlight or ultra-violet light (see page 160).

Vitamin F, the essential fatty acid, linoleic acid, this PUFA or polyunsaturated fatty acid is found in sunflower, safflower, and maize corn oil. The acid has a beneficial effect on the skin, hair, and nails.

Maize oil or maize germ oil. Maize grains provide starch and maize germ; the latter is rich in lipid which is expelled on crushing. The maize germ oil is filtered, refined, cooled, and finally distilled to provide a clear, odourless, maize germ oil used for cooking purposes.

WAXES

Waxes are obtained either from plant or animal sources. Carnauba wax from Brazilian palm oil, a plant source, and beeswax from honeycombs, an animal source, are examples respectively. Waxes are hard non-greasy solids which do not leave grease marks on paper as do ordinary lipids.

Chemical composition of waxes

Waxes do *not* contain propanetriol (glycerine). They are compounds of certain fatty acids and fatty alcohols such as tetradecanol, hexadecanol, octadecanol and dodecanol and are described as esters.

$$Wax = fatty\ acid + fatty\ alcohol$$

Beeswax or tetradeconyl
hexadeconoate = hexadecanoic + tetradecanol
(myricyl palmitate)　(palmitic acid)　(myricyl alcohol)

Spermaceti or hexadecanyl
dodecanoate = dodecanoic + hexadecanol
(cetyl laurate)　(lauric acid)　(cetyl alcohol)

Paraffin wax is not a true wax but a mixture of solid *hydrocarbons*.

USES OF IMPORTANT WAXES

Wax	Appearance	Uses
Carnauba wax	Hard, yellow, waxy solid from the leaves of the Brazilian palm	For all wax polishes used for furniture, floors, shoes, cars and for toughening other softer waxes. Candles
Candelilla	White solid from Mexican candelilla shrub	Polishing waxes
Beeswax	White, waxy solid	Polishing wax and for waxing cotton and silk thread. Candles
Spermaceti	White, crystalline solid from the head of the whale	Polishing wax
Lanolin	A yellow, sticky solid from sheep fleece	For skin creams and water proofing wool. Lanolin is mainly a mixture of fatty acids, alcohols plus cholesterol

Beeswax and spermaceti are used as non-stick reagents as a coat inside cooking pans, and also to give sweets a glossy coat.

The grey bloom on grapes is due to a fine coating of wax, and the waterproof quality of the human hair and skin is due to *sebum*, the natural secretion of the skin. *Synthetic waxes* used for polishes and as waterproofing agents are made from such hydrocarbons as polyethene wax and Fischer-Tropsch wax.

RESINS

Resins are secretions produced by insects and from the bark of such *conifers* as pine and Christmas trees. Resins are mixtures of essential oils and resin, and are called *oleo-resins*.

Some important resins

Turpentine is a component of the turpentine gum secretion from pine trees. It is distilled to provide spirits of turpentine for paints and polishes, and *rosin* for paint and textile sizing and soap manufacture. *Copal* gum from Central Africa is used mainly for varnish manufacture.

Lac is a resin secreted by an Indian insect from which shellac is obtained. It is used for making French polish by dissolving it in methylated spirits. Lacquer is the resin obtained from trees in Japan and China and is employed in lacquering furniture in the oriental style.

Purified *shellac* is used to glaze sweets.

Oleoresins are also obtained from peppers and ginger by solvent extraction (see page 118).

WAX POLISHES

A wax polish provides a surface with a layer of hard transparent wax with water-repelling properties and attractive lustre. These polishes are available as paste, liquid, and silicone waxes (see page 16).

Paste waxes are mixtures of natural waxes and white spirit, the latter a by-product of petroleum refining. The white spirit evaporates leaving a thin film of wax. Liquid waxes are thin creams of wax with an emulsifying agent and water. Silicone waxes contain the compounds composed of silicon and oxygen atoms linked in long-chain molecules. These compounds have a low surface tension making the wax easy to apply and are also water-repelling. These compounds can be incorporated in paste or liquid waxes.

Experiment

To prepare a paste wax polish:

Obtain:　5 g　Carnauba wax
5 g　Beeswax
15 g　Paraffin wax
95 cm^3　White spirit or turpentine

Melt the ingredients in a 500 cm^3 beaker over a steam bath. Blend and allow the mixture to cool, stirring frequently.

HYDROCARBONS OR MINERAL OILS

Petroleum or rock oil and coal tar are the main sources of hydrocarbons or mineral oils (see Chapter 15). None is used in foods except white mineral oil added to dried fruits. Liquid paraffin dissolves vitamin A and D and causes vitamin deficiency in respect of these vitamins; it is a permitted additive in dried fruits (see pages 100 and 158).

USES OF IMPORTANT HYDROCARBONS

Hydrocarbon or derivative	Appearance	Uses
Benzene and Methylbenzene (toluene)	Flammable liquid	Dissolves oils and fats. Paint remover
Tetrachloromethane (carbon tetrachloride) (CCl_4)	Non-flammable liquid	1. Fire extinguishers 2. Grease solvent
Tetralin	Flammable liquid	Paint remover
Trichloroethene (trichloroethylene)	Liquid with toxic vapour	1. Solvent for oils and fats 2. Dry-cleaning fluid
White spirit (mixture of hydrocarbons)	Flammable liquid	1. Thinner for paints 2. General-purpose grease stain remover 3. Polish manufacture

ESSENTIAL OILS

Natural flavourings, apart from those which are the result of cooking meat and other foods, are due to essential oils produced by oil glands of plants found in many fruits, and vegetables but more so in herbs and spices.

Herbs are soft stemmed plants which produce flavourings mainly because of the following chemical components;

Thymol (hydroxy methylethyl methylbenzene) – thyme, and origanum; *eugenol* – West Indian bay; *menthol* – garden mint, and peppermint.

Spices are mainly tropical plants produced from barks, flowers, fruits, seeds and roots or rhizomes; they include peppers, nutmeg, aniseed, cinnamon, cloves, and saffron, whose flavour is due to several different aromatic chemicals.

Essential oils in foods

Essential oils together with other chemical components of herbs and spices, when added to food as flavourings, provide *colour* as in paprika, and turmeric, *flavour* in all herbs and spices, and also act as *antioxidants* possibly due to the high vitamin C ascorbic acid content as for example in dry parsley.

Herb and spice preparations

1. *Dried and ground* the traditional method of collecting plants and using simple drying methods leaves much to be desired in the way of cleanliness of the dried product which is often contaminated with dust soil, and may have a high bacteria content. The flavour may vary from source to source, and the use of ground and powdered preparations tends to speck the food and give rise to 'hot spots' with a strong spice or herb flavour.

2. *Essential oils* are hygienic, clean, and highly concentrated liquid extracts obtained by steam distillation, crushing, solvent extraction, or the use of cold fat enfleurage extraction. As they are so concentrated, essential oils must be diluted for culinary use and provide flavours closely resembling the original herb or spice.

3. *Essences* are prepared by dissolving the concentrated essential oils in ethanol, propanediol (propylene glycol), or propane-2-ol (isopropyl alcohol). Vanilla essence is made by extracting the essential oil with ethanol. *Synthetic* essences are prepared from a combination chemical substance such as esters, alkanals (aldehydes) and alkanones (ketones) with added colouring. *Vanillin* is a synthetic form of vanilla.

4. *Oleoresins* are either highly concentrated solid or thick viscous liquid extracts of spices with a very strong complete flavour that must be *diluted* for culinary use. They may be diluted as essences in a solvent such as ethanol or isopropanol, or as *emulsions* with water and gum acacia.

5. *Dispersed preparations* are dry powder preparations of herb or spice oleoresin extracts blended with sodium chloride, glucose, or starch, to give a dry, hygienic, preparation of uniform flavour, easily dispersed in food mixtures without specking or providing hot spots as with traditional dried herbs and spices.

6. *Encapsulated preparations* are prepared by enclosing a tiny amount of highly concentrated herb or spice extract, in solid, liquid or gaseous form, inside a coating of edible gum. This provides a free running powder, with a sealed-in flavour which can be stored for long periods without flavour loss. The encapsulated spices have flavours almost ten times as strong as that of the natural dried preparation.

7. *Crystallized* preparations involve the preservation of the herb or spice in concentrated sugar syrups, as in the case of angelica stems, ginger rhizomes and cherry fruits.

8. *Liquers* such as Curacao, Kirsch, Maraschino, Noyau and Orgeat, are sweetened solutions of alcohol, the particular flavour being mainly due to soluble essential oils.

Capillaire syrup is a pleasing flavoured infusion of a fern in orange water (see page 215).

Perfumery

Perfumes are blends of scent-producing substances, the main components being:

(*a*) essential oils:

(*b*) artificial or synthetic compounds, mainly pleasant-smelling esters (see page 106);

(*c*) animal products such as ambergris, civet cat extract, and musk which prolong the perfume aroma;

(*d*) the liquid *solvent* in which all the ingredients are dissolved is either methanol or ethanol.

SUGGESTIONS FOR PRACTICAL WORK

To make floor polish: melt together the following ingredients over a steam-heated water bath, allowing the mixture to solidify in tins:

70 g White spirit – Care: Highly Flammable
18 g Paraffin wax (52–54°C)
 8 g Carnauba wax
 4 g Montan wax

QUESTIONS ON CHAPTER 17

1. What causes rancidity of lipid oils and fats and how can it be controlled?

2. What is meant by the smoke point of a cooking oil or fat?

3. Give a brief account of the occurrence of four natural lipid oils and fats explaining simply the extraction process for one of them.

4. Describe the chemistry of the composition of lipids. Outline the effect of the following on natural lipids: (*a*) heat; (*b*) steam; (*c*) digestive enzymes; and (*d*) hydrogen.

5. What is the difference between the frying temperature, the smoke point, and the fire point of a fat?

6. Write short notes on: (*a*) propanediol octadecanoate (glyceryl monostearate) (G.M.S.); (*b*) anti-spattering agents; (*c*) cholesterol; and (*d*) essential fatty acids.

7. Describe briefly the manufacture of cooking oils, cooking fats, and margarine.

8. Give an account of the composition of lard, its extraction, and important derivatives.

9. What are the essential oils? Describe their importance in cookery.

10. What are the essential points to observe in fat storage?

11. See *Experimental Science for Catering and Homecraft Students*, Practical work 5.1 to 5.3, 23.1 to 23.5, 24.1 to 24.3.

MULTIPLE CHOICE QUESTIONS ON CHAPTER 17

1. Lipids, also known as oils and fats, contain a greater percentage of one of the following chemical elements compared to the other food nutrients:
  (*a*) carbon   (*c*) hydrogen
  (*b*) oxygen   (*d*) nitrogen

2. Lipids are composed of the following chemical compounds:
  (*a*) amino acids and water
  (*b*) fatty acids and propanetriol
  (*c*) glucose
  (*d*) hydrocarbons

3. The chemical elements which compose a lipid oil, are:
  (*a*) hydrogen and oxygen
  (*b*) carbon and hydrogen
  (*c*) carbon, hydrogen and oxygen
  (*d*) carbon, hydrogen, oxygen, nitrogen and sulphur

4. The highest proportion of unsaturated lipids is found in one of the following:
  (*a*) lard   (*c*) butter
  (*b*) peanut oil   (*d*) cream

5. What is the maximum number of fatty acid molecules that can be joined with a single molecule of propanetriol (glycerine) in a lipid?
  (*a*) one   (*c*) three
  (*b*) two   (*d*) four

6. Lipids become rancid through the action of one of the following:
  (*a*) oxygen   (*c*) nitrogen
  (*b*) hydrogen   (*d*) carbon dioxide

7. Lipids break down by their reaction with water during high temperature cooking, or by the action of enzymes. The chemical reaction is called:
  (*a*) neutralization   (*c*) oxidation
  (*b*) hydrolysis   (*d*) hydrogenation

8. Lipid oils and fats when strongly heated break down and produce a burnt fat smell due to the following:
  (*a*) propanetriol (glycerine)   (*c*) propenal (acrolein)
  (*b*) hydrogen sulphide   (*d*) carbon dioxide

9. A sample of rancid lipid oil in neutral ethanol (ethyl alcohol) requires 5 ml of 0.1 M aqueous sodium hydroxide to neutralize it. In comparison, a fresh sample of lipid oil requires no sodium hydroxide to neutralize it. The addition of sodium hydroxide to the rancid oil indicates that it contains:
  (*a*) alkaline soap   (*c*) mineral acids
  (*b*) amino acids   (*d*) fatty acids

10. A pale brown solution of bromine is decolourized by adding a few drops of sunflower oil. This test shows that:
  (*a*) bromine is a bleaching agent
  (*b*) sunflower oil is a bleaching agent
  (*c*) bromine is an unsaturated compound
  (*d*) sunflower oil is an unsaturated compound

18 Proteins

Proteins are essential components of all living cells, and vital substances for life. Plants and animals synthesize different proteins within living cell structures called *ribosomes*, using raw materials called amino acids.

Different $\xrightarrow[\text{(condensation)}]{\text{RIBOSOMES}}$ different

amino acids proteins

Plant protein *differs* in composition from animal protein. Plants can make all their protein from simple raw materials. Animals need certain amino acids, present in their *food*, to make all their protein.

The table lists important proteins and the foods containing them.

IMPORTANT PROTEINS AND THEIR OCCURRENCE

Protein	Occurrence	Protein	Occurrence
Actin	Lean meat	Lactalbumin	Milk
Casein	Milk	Legumin	Peas and beans
Collagen	Skin and bones	Myosin	Lean meat and muscle
Elastin	Tough meat and tendons	Ovalbumin	Egg white
Gluten	Wheat flour dough	Pepsins	Stomach gastric juice
Gelatin	From skin, tendons, and bone	Prolamin	Wheat and barley
		Reticulin	Muscle, kidney, liver
Glycinin	Soya bean	Rennin	Milk
Haemoglobin	Blood	Tuberin	Potatoes
Insulin	Pancreas or sweetbread	Vitellin	Egg yolk
Keratin	Hair, feathers, and nails	Zein	Maize

Note. Albumin (or albumen) is a term describing egg white and its component proteins, viz. ovalbumin, ovoglobulin, and vitellin (see page 195).

CLASSIFICATION OF PROTEINS

Proteins can be classified according to two systems: first on their *chemical composition* and second on their *function*.

1. Classification by chemical composition

Proteins can be subdivided into *simple* and *conjugated* or joined proteins. Some important simple proteins are:

(*a*) *Globular proteins* in which the molecule tangled chain globular in shape as in egg albumin, blood albumin, and zein of maize.

(*b*) *Fibrous proteins* which have a molecule resembling a fibre either as a coil or simply extended chain. Fibrous protein molecules will give the protein distinct *elastic* properties evident in wool and hair *keratin*, in muscle actin and *myosin*, in tendon or cartilage *elastin*, and in dough *gluten*. The extended, fibre molecule has little elasticity as seen in skin *collagen* and silk *fibroin* (see page 146).

Conjugated proteins are composed of a protein portion, usually globular, with a *non-protein* portion which can be a sugar or lipid. Some important conjugated proteins are:

(*a*) *Phospho-protein* the non-protein group is phosphoric acid as in *casein* of milk and egg vitellin, and ovovitellinin.

(*b*) *Nucleo-proteins* the non-protein is *nucleic* acid and is found in the nuclei of cells.

(*c*) *Metallo-protein* the non-protein group is a metal such as iron in *haemoglobin* of blood.

(*d*) *Lipo-protein* found in eggs and animal cell membranes, composed of combined lipid and protein molecules.

2. Classification by function

Proteins have three uses: to build new body tissues, to take part in or control chemical changes within the cell, and to act as essential nutrients.

(*a*) *Structural proteins.* Muscle, skin, tendons, ligaments, bones, and other animal cell structures are formed of the fibrous proteins, collagen, myosin, elastin, reticulin and keratin.

(*b*) *Physiologically active proteins.* These take part in vital chemical and metabolic processes within the living cell and are mainly enzymes, hormones, nuclei, blood plasma, and haemoglobin.

(*c*) *Nutrient proteins.* These are proteins essential in the human diet, providing certain *essential amino acids* which cannot be synthesized within the body cells.

SUMMARY

1.

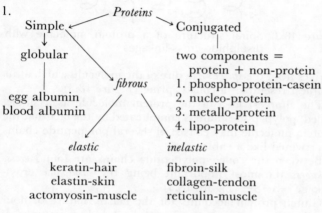

2.

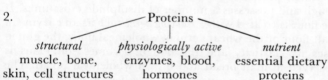

CHEMISTRY OF PROTEINS

Proteins are amongst the most complicated chemical compounds known to the food chemist, and contain the chemical elements carbon, hydrogen, oxygen, sulphur, nitrogen, and some phosphorus:

$$\text{Proteins} = \text{C, H, O, P, S, and N}$$

Experiments

To indicate the chemical elements present in protein:
    The tests can be performed on gluten, gelatine, dried egg white, or albumin, soya bean flour or powdered fishmeal.

1. Carbon and hydrogen

Mix a little of the *dry* protein material with *dry* copper(II) oxide and heat the mixture in a test tube (Figure 18.1). The carbon present in the protein is oxidized by the copper(II) oxide to form carbon dioxide, which turns calcium hydrox-

ide milky. The hydrogen present in the protein will be oxidized to form water which condenses in the cooler parts of the tube:

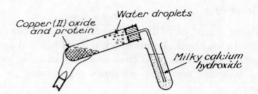

Figure 18.1. Testing for carbon and hydrogen in protein

Carbon in protein + oxygen from copper(II) oxide = carbon dioxide

Hydrogen in protein + oxygen from copper(II) oxide = water

Note. This test can also be applied to carbohydrates and fats to demonstrate the presence of carbon and hydrogen.

2. Nitrogen

Nitrogen is the vital element in all proteins. It can be detected by mixing powdered protein with sodium and calcium hydroxides (soda lime) and holding a red litmus paper in the vapours which smell faintly of ammonia:

$$\text{Nitrogen in protein} + \frac{\text{sodium hydroxide and calcium}}{\text{hydroxide (soda lime)}} = \frac{\text{ammonia}}{\text{gas}}$$

3. Sulphur

The presence of sulphur can be proved by holding a filter paper soaked in lead ethanoate (acetate) in the vapour emitted when the protein is heated with soda lime:

$$\text{Sulphur in protein} + \begin{array}{c}\text{sodium and}\\\text{calcium hydroxides}\\\text{(soda lime)}\end{array} = \begin{array}{c}\text{hydrogen sulphide}\\\text{[blackens lead}\\\text{ethanoate (acetate)]}\end{array}$$

Alternatively protein, particularly eggs, if allowed to putrefy, will produce an unforgettable odour of hydrogen sulphide (H_2S)! The amino acids methionine, cystine and cysteine contain sulphur.

4. Phosphorus

Phosphorus can be detected in phosphoro-proteins such as casein using sophisticated methods described in textbooks of practical organic chemistry.

5. Oxygen

There is no suitable, simple, chemical method for detecting oxygen in proteins, lipids, or carbohydrates.

COMPOSITION OF PROTEINS

The percentage of the elements present varies with the protein, but an average composition is: carbon 53, oxygen 22, sulphur 1, hydrogen 7, nitrogen 16, and phosphorus 0·5 per cent.

Experiments

Tests for proteins and certain amino acids

The following tests produce characteristic colours in the presence of proteins and certain amino acids.

1. Millons test

Place about 2 cm³ of Millons reagent in a test tube, add a little protein and boil. A pink/dark red colour will appear in the presence of amino acid *tyrosine* found in most proteins. Millons reagent contains mercury salts and is highly *poisonous*.

2. Biuret reaction

Add a few drops of potassium hydroxide to a solution of protein such as egg white, followed by a few drops of copper(II) sulphate solution. A violet/blue colour results in the presence of *peptide linkages* found in protein.

3. Xanthoproteic test

Add 5 cm³ of concentrated nitric acid to 5 cm³ of protein solution and boil the mixture to produce a yellow colour which turns orange on adding ammonium hydroxide, when *tyrosine* and *tryptophan* amino acids are present, as in almost all proteins.

4. Coagulation

Many proteins coagulate on heating. This is shown clearly when a solution of egg white is heated gently, or when the skin forms on heated milk and milk puddings.

PROTEIN MOLECULES

The protein molecule is very large being made up of smaller units called *amino-acids*. When a protein undergoes hydrolysis – a reaction with water on boiling with acid – the molecule breaks down into its simple *amino-acids* which can be separated by *chromatography*. These have both basic and acidic properties due to the $-NH_2$ *amino* basic group and *carboxylic*$-COOH$ acid group of the molecule.

Figure 18.2 represents an amino-acid molecule, the arrow head represents the basic $-NH_2$ group while the tail represents the acidic $-COOH$. Many of these units can be linked into long chains by the *neutralization* reaction between acid carboxyl and basic amino-group and subsequent elimination of water (see Figure 18.2). The link formed between the amino-acid units in the chain, the $-CONH-$ group, is called a *peptide* link and forms a *polypeptide chain*. Protein molecules can be built up from some twenty-two *different* amino-acid units, the selection resulting in a variety of protein molecules and molecular structures.

Many fibrous proteins have elastic properties seen in lean meat or muscle which can contract or extend; the skin on milk puddings; in flour dough owing to the protein gluten, and the rubbery nature of cheese. This elastic property

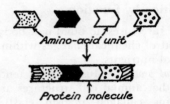

Figure 18.2. The linkage of amino-acids to form protein molecules

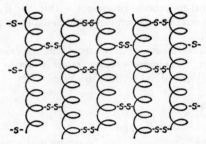

Figure 18.3. Spiral structure of a protein molecule with disulphide cross-linkages

derives from the *spiral* structure of the molecule which at its simplest resembles a coiled spring (Figure 18.3).

The simplest idea of the protein molecule as a single, coiled, polypeptide chain is complicated by the fact that the protein molecule may consist of several polypeptide chains intertwined like a cable.

Between the coiled polypeptide chains are found *cross-linkages*, the most important being the *disulphide* cross-linkage $-S-S-$ (Figure 18.3).

Gluten protein accounts for the elastic nature of flour dough and possesses a number of disulphide cross-links. If the flour is treated with a *reducing agent* such as an enzyme in malt flour or the wheat germ of wholemeal flour, the gluten loses its elasticity and the dough becomes soft. This is observed in malt bread and brown wholemeal bread. The loss of elasticity is due to the *reduction* of the disulphide linkage and subsequent breakdown of the cross-linkage to form *sulphydryl* groups.

Conversely the treatment of gluten protein with *oxidizing* agents produces stable disulphide cross-links from any unstable sulphydryl groups. This gives the flour strong properties with such flour oxidizing agents as benzoyl peroxide, chlorine dioxide, potassium bromate, and potassium iodate.

ESSENTIAL AMINO-ACIDS

Proteins are built up from twenty-two different amino-acids, *ten* being necessary for body-building purposes in a *growing* person though a fully-grown adult requires only *eight*.

The *essential* eight for an adult are: Isoleucine, methionine, tryptophan, leucine, phenylalanine, valine, lysine, and threonine.

Growing children need also arginine and histidine.

These eight amino acids *cannot* be synthesized in the

human body from other substances containing nitrogen, and *must* be available in the different *food* proteins. *Methionine* is the essential amino acid often present in the smallest amount in most plant and animal foods; its *absence* from the diet can be as serious as a diet *without* any protein.

Cystine and tyrosine are amino-acids which reduce the requirements of phenylalanine and methionine, and are therefore sometimes considered essential, bringing the total to *twelve*.

Some of the non-essential amino acids are: alanine, aspartic acid, cysteine, glycine, glutamic acid, hydroxyproline, proline, and serine.

BIOLOGICAL VALUE OF PROTEINS

The biological value of a protein food is measured by the percentage of protein available for growth and body repair. Eggs have a biological value of 100 per cent indicating that all the contained protein is utilizable. Peanuts have a value of 45 per cent meaning that 55 per cent is not available. Milk and eggs are staple foods for young animals and their high biological value would be expected.

Foods containing all essential amino-acids are described as having high biological value or as *complete* proteins and include protein of animal origin such as milk, meat, fish, cheese, and eggs. Foods deficient in essential amino-acids are called low biological value proteins. Such foods as vegetables, nuts and gelatine fall into this class.

Thus young growing people require sufficient animal as well as vegetable protein to provide body-building amino-acids. A strict *vegan* diet of low biological value protein would not yield enough tryptophan and lysine amino-acids for such purposes. A *lactovegetarian* diet includes milk and milk products and so contains high biological value proteins to supplement the low biological value protein of vegetables.

$$\text{Biological value of protein (B.V.)} = \frac{\text{Protein used by the body}}{\text{Protein taken into body as food}} \times 100$$

PROPERTIES OF PROTEIN

1. Denaturation

Denaturation is a *change* in *natural state* of a protein; it is a mild process which can cause a soluble protein to lose some of its solubility through exposure to ultraviolet radiation, *mild* acid (vinegar) or alkali, raised temperature, or presence of ethanol (wines). Enzymes lose their digestive activity when temperature rises above blood heat.

Coagulation is a *permanent* change, causing proteins to become completely *insoluble* due to the effect of strong acids, alkali, other chemicals and *high* temperatures, as in egg boiling and flour dough baking.

Heat coagulates meat protein sealing in the juices, while the denatured protein fibres shorten producing the shrunken appearance of a cooked joint. Gelatin is denatured at temperatures above 65°C, a fact vital when making meat galantine.

Beating an egg white is an example of denaturation by agitation; excessive beating causes the solid sheets of denatured protein to break up and the foam collapses. Air whipped into eggs and cream causes stretching of the protein molecule resulting in denaturation.

Poisons cause denaturation of the proteins of the living cells of animals making them unavailable for the processes of life. The function of egg white as a poison *antidote* is that it is denatured by such poisonous substances as salts of mercury and lead. The egg white combines with them rendering them harmless to the body.

The process of denaturation causes the disorganization of the orderly protein molecule. Coagulation of the protein involves loss of solubility; coagulated egg white for example is no longer soluble in water.

Coagulation of proteins is a two-stage process: (*a*) denaturation or alteration of the molecular structure by heat, agitation, acids, poisons, or freezing; and (*b*) coagulation and precipitation of protein.

Freezing foods containing protein draws water out of the protein molecule resulting in it being denatured.

Acids denature protein in milk forming a *clot*, whilst acid in meat marinades causes the muscle protein to elongate and helps the meat protein to bind with more water.

Texture of meat, fish and egg proteins alter on denaturation, making them easier to digest.

2. Hydration

Proteins in contact with water swell considerably to form *hydrates*. Gelatine in cold water does not dissolve, but swells, owing to hydration. If this hydrated gelatine is warmed it goes rapidly into solution. It is preferable to let gelatine stand for several minutes in cold water to allow hydration before heating. Flour proteins, namely *glutenin* and *gliadin*, when mixed with water hydrate to form elastic *gluten*.

3. Hydrolysis

Hydrolysis or *proteolysis*, the breakdown of proteins into peptides and amino acids, can be achieved either *chemically* using water and alkali, or *biologically* using water and enzymes. *Protein hydrolysates* are present in meat and yeast extracts, and include flavoursome peptones and amino acids products of hydrolysis.

PROTEIN — PROTEOSES — PEPTONES — POLYPEPTIDES — AMINO ACIDS

Largest molecule ↓   PROTEOLYSIS / HYDROLYSIS   Smallest molecule ↑

PROTEINS AND THE COOKING PROCESS

All proteins undergo changes during the cooking process through dry heat or moist heat; the table summarizes the main changes.

Browning of food is either *enzymatic*, see page 88, or *nonenzymatic*. Caramelization of heated sugars is a nonenzymatic browning of food, whilst the interaction between sugars and amino acids is a further example, also called

EFFECT OF COOKING ON PROTEINS

Protein	Cooking process	Effect
Egg white, ovalbumin	1. Dry or moist heat 2. Agitation followed by heat	1. Coagulation as for boiled, fried, and poached eggs 2. Coagulation as for meringues
Gluten, wheat flour dough protein Gluten = gliadin + glutenin	Dry or moist heat	Extension and coagulation of protein molecule to form a framework supporting the starch component of the baked food
Meat proteins, collagen and elastin	Dry or moist heat	Collagen and elastin fibre molecules contract causing shrinkage of meat. Meat with plentiful connective tissue becomes tough with dry heat or roasting
Globulins and albumins of meat	Moist heat, stewing	They dissolve to form soluble protein enriching the stock
Milk lactalbumin, lactoglobulin	Dry heat	The protein coagulates and forms the skin on milk and milk puddings
Cheese	Dry heat as in toasted cheese	Coagulation of cheese protein to form tough, rubbery and ultimately crisp, cheese protein
Fish	Dry or moist heat	Produces the breakdown of the collagen protein connecting the muscle segments, giving flakiness to cooked fish. A large amount of fish protein is soluble in water.

'Maillard Browning', as occurs in roasting potatoes and meat.

FOOD BROWNING IN COOKING

1. *Fast browning* occurs in
(a) grilling of aerated food
(b) frying of non aerated food surface
(c) griddle cooking.
2. *Slow browning* occurs in roasting and baking
3. *Negligible browning* in
(a) micro-wave cooking
(b) pressure cooking, stewing, steaming, casserole cooking, coddling, braising, and potbaking.

GELATINE

Gelatine is produced by the hydrolysis of *collagen*, the protein present in such connective tissues as skin, bones, ligaments, hornpiths, sinews and cartilage. It is also found in the tougher portions of meat such as shin, neck, calves' feet, and pigs' trotters. When these collagen materials are boiled with water the soluble gelatine is dissolved and sets to a jelly on cooling.

$$\text{Collagen + water} \xrightarrow[\text{Hydrolysis}]{} \text{gelatine}$$

Gelatine is a *mixture* of proteins and amino-acid compounds, its main protein component being called *gelatin*. Gelatine is totally lacking in the essential amino acid *tryptophan*, hence its low biological value.

When gelatine is placed in water it adsorbs water molecules and hydrates (up to ten times its own weight). It is advisable to add granulated gelatine to cold water and allow the solution to stand for several minutes before heating, preferably in a steam bath. Prolonged heating destroys the setting power of gelatine.

GELLING POWER

The setting of a gelatine jelly is dependent on a number of factors:
1. The *concentration* of gelatine in the solution should not be less than 6 per cent.
2. The *temperature* for setting is between 13° and 0°C. Rapid cooling may induce the formation of stiff lumps.
3. Higher sugar content in a jelly produces a strong gel, whilst certain flavouring agents, if present in sufficient quantity, may cause hardening of the gel.
4. Proteolytic *enzymes* in the body rapidly digest gelatine and for this reason it is frequently included in a convalescent diet. Such enzymes as *bromelin* found in fresh pineapples and used as a meat tenderizer will prevent the setting of a gelatine jelly. Fresh pineaples are best omitted from a jelly or if essential should be heated above blood heat to destroy the active enzyme. This is done during the sterilization process of canning.

Gelatine finds wide applications in the food industry for table desserts, confectionery, ice-cream, and for meat products in the following capacities: (a) thickening agent for soups and cream; (b) clarifying wines and fruit juices; (c) setting agent for ice-cream and marshmallows; and (d) glaze for baked confectionery.

Gelatine is frequently included in gastric disorder diets and diabetes. Its hydrating property is used for absorbing water from the intestine to give a feeling of fullness useful in certain weight-reducing foods.

CELL NUCLEUS PROTEINS

Certain animal body cells have a large *cell nucleus* (see page 167), liver, kidney, sweetbread and brain. Game and certain fish roes are examples. The cell nucleus is made up of *nucleoprotein*, which consists of two main components, a *protein* and *nucleic acids*.

The nucleic acids consist of *phosphate*, *pentose*, sugars (ribose or deoxyribose) and *organic bases* (purines or pyrimidines) (see page 95).

Digestive enzymes called *nucleases* digest the nucleic acids in the stomach and small intestine.

$$\text{Nucleic acids} \xrightarrow[\text{enzymes}]{\text{nuclease}} \text{pentose sugars} + \underset{\substack{\text{(purines and} \\ \text{pyrimidines)}}}{\text{organic bases}} + \text{phosphate}$$

Gout is a disease affecting bone joints, especially the big toe, and is partly caused by eating foods rich in purines and nucleic acids.

TVP – TEXTURED VEGETABLE PROTEINS

Textured proteins are food materials that can be used as substitutes or analogues instead of real meat, or can also be used to supplement or extend real meat. Textured proteins are manufactured mainly from plant protein such as soya bean, or wheat gluten or oil seed protein. Animal protein such as milk casein and egg albumen can also be used.

Soya bean protein is the main raw material used in textured protein manufacture, this is converted into a fibrous form having a high biological value of about 70%, almost the same BV as real meat by the addition of the amino acid methionine and other nutrients, vitamins B_2, B_1, B_{12} and iron.

1. Spun protein (see page 146)

This is textured protein manufactured by dissolving pure fat free soya bean protein in alkali to form a thick viscous 'dope' to which colour and meat-like flavour are added. This solution is then spun through spinnerets in a similar manner to the spinning of man-made and other regenerated fibres. As the solution or 'dope' emerges from the spinneret into an acid and salt bath it regenerates into long filaments which forms into a long hank and is then wound and stretched over rollers.

The spun protein fibres are bound together with fat, flour, additional flavours, nutrients and a filler which gels on heating in cooking. Afterwards the product is made up into meatlike products in slices, cubes, or granules, the final product has a protein content of 50%.

2. Expanded or extruded protein

A mixture of soya protein meal, water, flavour, and colour is partly cooked and passes under very high pressure whilst it is hot and in the form of a dough, through a narrow opening of an extruding or injection moulding machine. As the dough emerges through the opening it puffs or expands out providing an expanded form of protein fibre. This product is then cut up into short lengths, cooled, dried and packed.

3. Microbial or single cell protein (SCP)

This is a process of protein manufacture which involves the feeding of yeast moulds – *Fusarium*, on hydrocarbon oil waste or on waste carbohydrate material. The resulting growth of mould is then harvested and processed to produce a matted fibrous protein product which in the dry state contains over 45% of protein.

4. Leaf protein

Leafy vegetables contain between 3 and 5% of protein. This protein content can be extracted from grass, water weeds and tree foliage leaves, thus providing a useful source for textured vegetable protein production.

Uses of textured proteins

(*a*) Meat *substitutes* or *analogues* are primarily made from spun protein and are sold as products resembling meat steaks or rashers.

(*b*) Meat *extenders* involve expanded protein to extend otherwise normal meats in such preparations as beefburgers, pie fillings, minced meat, and sausages, thus reducing the amount of expensive real meat.

(*c*) Certain microbial protein is fed to cattle to produce real meat.

SUGGESTIONS FOR PRACTICAL WORK

1. Boil small portions of fish or meat in dilute sodium chloride solution and filter. Test the filtrate for protein with Millons reagent.

2. Investigate the effect of the following on the setting powers of gelatine:

(*a*) concentrations from 1 to 10 per cent of gelatine by weight;

(*b*) using a 6 per cent solution of gelatine investigate the effect of varying quantities of sucrose and of sodium chloride on the setting process.

3. Estimate the percentage crude gluten in a flour by taking 100 g of the flour and washing out the starch using a muslin bag as described on page 85.

Dry the crude gluten residue in a weighed evaporating basin at 105°C, when:

$$\text{Percentage crude gluten} = \frac{\text{weight of gluten residue}}{\text{original weight of flour}} + 100$$

4. See *Experimental Science for Catering and Homecraft Students*, Practical work 6.1 to 6.4, 15.2, 21.1 to 21.6.

QUESTIONS ON CHAPTER 18

1. Write a short essay on proteins with particular reference to their molecular structure and their occurrence. Give two chemical tests you would use to identify proteins in named foods.

2. Name four proteins and the foods in which they occur. Give a brief account of the molecular structure of a fibrous protein.

3. Explain the following: (*a*) amino acid; (*b*) peptide link; (*c*) polypeptide chain; and (*d*) disulphide link.

4. What affect have: (*a*) hydrolysis; (*b*) oxidation; and (*c*) reduction on the nature of proteins?

5. Give a brief account of the effect of cooking on the proteins of wheat, flour, meat, eggs, and milk.

6. Explain the terms denaturation and hydration with reference to proteins.

7. Give an account of gelatine, its preparation, and uses.

8. What are essential amino-acids? What are essential fatty acids?

9. Give a short account of the hydrolysis of lipids, polysaccharides, and proteins.

10. The body requires certain elements, five of which are present in proteins. Briefly state how you would detect the presence of two elements in a lipid, carbohydrate, or protein and indicate which are present in these foods.

MULTIPLE CHOICE QUESTIONS ON CHAPTER 18

1. Which part of the living plant cell shown in Figure 18.4 directly controls protein production?
   (a) I   (c) II
   (b) III   (d) IV

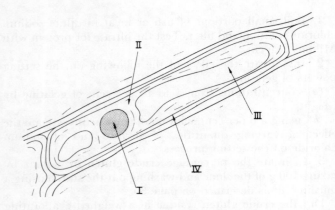

Figure 18.4

2. Which of the following turns red litmus paper blue?
   (a) carbon dioxide   (c) ammonia gas
   (b) water   (d) hydrogen sulphide gas

3. Which of the following when heated with soda-lime (sodium, calcium hydroxides) would cause neutral litmus paper, held in the vapours, to turn blue?
   (a) protein   (c) carbohydrate
   (b) lipid   (d) ethanol

4. A protein containing food heated with aqueous sodium hydroxide and copper(II) sulphate solution gives a violet colour. This test is called:
   (a) Millons test   (c) Xanthoproteic test
   (b) Biuret test   (d) Sakaguchi test

5. The attractive Maillard browning of many cooked foods is due to:
   (a) enzymes reacting with the food components
   (b) breakdown of the lipids during the heating
   (c) partial carbonization of the starch present in food
   (d) reaction between amino acid and sugars of food

6. Myosin is a protein mainly present in:
   (a) eggs   (c) hair
   (b) meat   (d) blood

7. Wheat contains the protein material called:
   (a) gluten   (c) lactalbumin
   (b) tuberin   (d) legumin

8. The amino acids are released from proteins by the process called:
   (a) hydrolysis   (c) oxidation
   (b) neutralization   (d) hydration

9. The chemical elements composing proteins are:
   (a) carbon, chlorine and hydrogen
   (b) carbon, hydrogen, calcium and oxygen
   (c) carbon, hydrogen, oxygen, iodine and nitrogen
   (d) carbon, hydrogen, oxygen, phosphorus, nitrogen and sulphur

10. The units which build up the protein molecule are called:
   (a) fatty acids   (c) glucose
   (b) amino acids   (d) propanetriol (glycerine)

19 Detergents and solutions

DETERGENTS

The word *detergent* is used to describe a substance that cleans surfaces or removes dirt. All detergents affect the surface tension of water and other liquids and being associated with surface activity are also called *surfactants*, or surface active agents. Surface soiling consists essentially of tiny particles of lipids, proteins, carbohydrates, soot, calcium salts, dirt, and dust clinging to the surface.

Some detergents employed in housecraft and catering are:

1. *Solvent detergents* or dry cleaners. These are liquid solvents which dissolve the greasy soil from an article.
2. *Abrasives* in powder, paste, or metal form.
3. *Powder* detergents such as French chalk.
4. *Soaps.*
5. *Alkaline detergents.*
6. *Soapless or neutral detergents.*
6. *Acidic detergents.*
8. *Enzymes.*

1. SOLVENT DETERGENTS

When sugar is added to water it slowly disappears or *dissolves* in the water forming a *solution* of sugar in water. The dissolved sugar is called a *solute*, and the water in which it dissolves the *solvent*:

$$\text{Solute} + \text{solvent} = \text{solution}$$

The solute consists of *ions* or *molecules*, invisible to the naked eye, forming a clear, transparent, uniform solution. The solute cannot settle nor can be filtered out. The only methods of recovery are evaporation, distillation, or crystallization.

Solvent detergents cleanse because the solute or soil dissolves in it. Grease will dissolve in petrol, paraffin or tetrachloromethane (carbon tetrachloride) while sodium chloride and sugar will dissolve in water.

CLASSIFICATION OF SOLUTIONS

(*a*) Solutions of *gases in liquids*: ammonia (NH_3) dissolves in water forming ammonium hydroxide (NH_4OH) or household ammonia. Carbon dioxide (CO_2) dissolves in water forming carbonic acid (H_2CO_3), the main ingredient of soda water and aerated mineral waters. Sulphur dioxide (SO_2) dissolves in water, forming sulphurous acid (H_2SO_3) a preservative for fruit and fruit juices. Air dissolves to some extent in tap water producing a certain flavour.

(*b*) Solutions of *liquids in liquids*: ethanol (ethyl alcohol) dissolves in water forming the alcoholic ingredient of wines and spirits. Propanetriol (glycerine) dissolves in water. Petrol dissolves or is *miscible* with paraffin.

(*c*) Solutions of *solids in liquids*: many solids dissolve in different solvents. Sugar dissolves in water forming *syrups*, and salt (sodium chloride) in water yielding *brine*. Stain removal is chiefly dependent on the solubility of the stain. The table describes what solutes dissolve in different solvents.

A general-purpose spotting agent for dry-cleaning and laundry work consists of equal parts of trichloromethane (chloroform), tetrachloromethane (carbon tetrachloride) and benzene. The mixture is *highly inflammable*.

SOLUBILITY

Solubility of a solute is defined as the weight in grams of the solute which dissolves in 100 g of a solvent to form a

IMPORTANT SOLVENTS AND SOLUTES

Solvent	Solutes or stains	Applications
Water is the commonest solvent	Most inorganic acids, bases, and salts dissolve in water. Fresh fruit and wine stains	Universal solvent for cookery dissolving mineral salts, carbohydrates, and certain proteins from foods forming soups, extracts, cordials, and infusions
Ethanol (ethyl alcohol) methylated spirits	Dissolves essential oils, castor oil, shellac, and certain dyes. Ball point pen and grass stain. Iodine and certain medicines	Removes varnish and lacquer. Strong spirits will remove French polish. Useful for cleaning mirrors and glassware. Transfer stain remover
Tetrachloromethane (carbon tetrachloride)	Dissolves animal, vegetable, and mineral oils and grease. Lipstick	Dry-cleaning suits. Grease stain remover. A *poisonous* vapour is produced when the solvent or vapour is heated. Always use in a well-ventilated area. It is non-inflammable being used in fire extinguishers
Trichloroethene (trichloroethylene)	Solvent oils, fats, grease, and paints	Mainly used in dry-cleaning industry. Strong anaesthetic. Use in well-ventilated area
Propanone (acetone)	Solvent for animal and vegetable oils and nail varnish	Nail varnish remover and useful ingredient for paint remover. Dissolves cellulose acetate fabric
Methylbutyl ethanoate (amyl acetate)	Solvent for celluloid and cellulose paint	Nail varnish and cellulose paint remover
Turpentine	Solvent for paint	Removing fresh paint stains and cleaning paint brushes. (Dry paint stain can be removed with sodium silicate)
Petrol and naphtha	Solvent for tar and pitch	Tar and pitch stain remover. Contact adhesive remover
Octadec-9-enoic acid (oleic acid)	Grease remover	Sodium silicate and oleic acid used for stubborn grease stain removal as on engineers' overalls
Propanediol (iso-propyl alcohol)	Solvent used instead of ethanol (ethyl alcohol)	For lacquer, varnish, French polish, and ball-pen ink stain removal
Ethoxyethane (ether)	Dissolves animal oils and fats	Not recommended for general use. Highly inflammable

saturated solution, or one in which no more solute will dissolve, at a given temperature.

The solubility of most solutes *increases* with rising temperature. Salt (sodium chloride) is the exception, its solubility remaining fairly constant at 36 g between 0°–50°C. It increases to 39 g only at 100°C. In dry cleaning *hot* trichloroethene solvent is used to remove the grease.

The solubility of gases shows a marked decrease in rising temperature. When water is boiled the tiny air bubbles collect on the side of the vessel in the early heating stages. This decreasing solubility is exploited in regard to sulphur dioxide in preserved fruits used in jam manufacture. During the boiling process the sulphur dioxide is driven off, leaving very little, between 20 and 100 parts per million in the final jam.

2. ABRASIVE DETERGENTS

These detergents contain abrasive materials such as powdered brick dust, pumice, china clay, silica, fine sand, or emery mixed with a little detergent powder. Scouring pads are composed of steel wool mixed with *rouge* or red iron(III) oxide and a little detergent powder. Their efficiency depends on the physical displacement of the soil together with the removal of some of the article's surface.

Experiment

To prepare an abrasive soap paste:

Dissolve 15 g of soap flakes in 45 cm^3 of hot water. Add 1 g of sodium carbonate then 40 g of finely powdered pumice, stirring until a stiff paste results.

3. DRY POWDER DETERGENTS

These preparations consist mainly of fullers' earth and French chalk or talc and are used mainly to absorb grease from unwashable fabrics such as coloured art needlework and suede jackets.

4. SOAPS

Soluble soaps are manufactured from such animal fats as mutton fat or tallow, and olive or palm kernel vegetable oils. The hot fats and oils are *hydrolysed* at high temperature and pressures with steam to produce fatty acids and propanetriol (glycerine):

$$\text{Oil or fat} \xrightarrow[\text{hydrolysis}]{\text{Plus water}} \text{fatty acid} + \text{propanetriol (glycerine)}$$

The fatty acids float to the top and are drawn off and converted into soaps by *saponification* on adding sodium hydroxide alone or in a mixture with potassium hydroxide. Octadec-9-enoic acid (oleic acid) is the main fatty acid formed by hydrolysis, which in turn forms sodium or potassium octadec-9-enoate (oleate) soap:

Fatty acid + sodium hydroxide = soluble sodium soap + water

$$\underset{\text{(oleic) acid}}{\text{Octadec-9-enoic}} + \underset{\text{hydroxide}}{\text{sodium}} = \underset{\text{(oleate)}}{\text{sodium octadec-9-enoate}} + \text{water}$$

Soaps can also be made by boiling caustic soda and oil or fats together to produce a mixture of soap and propanetriol (glycerine):

$$\underset{\text{vegetable oils}}{\text{Animal or}} + \underset{\text{hydroxide}}{\text{sodium}} = \underset{\text{soap}}{\text{soluble sodium}} + \underset{\text{(glycerine)}}{\text{propanetriol}}$$

This 'kettle method' has now been displaced by the previously described hydrolyser method.

SOAP ADDITIVES

Various substances are added to soaps depending on their intended use. The chief additives are:

(a) *Builders*; these increase the soap's cleansing efficiency and are added to household bar soap, soap powders, and laundry soaps. They include sodium carbonate, sodium heptaoxotetraborate (borax), sodium silicate, and sodium phosphates. These soaps are *not* suitable for toilet purposes or for washing delicate materials.

(b) *Perfumes* are added to toilet soaps and many soap powders.

(c) *Dyes* are included in most soap preparations but not in soap flakes and powdered soap.

(d) *Antiseptic* materials are included in certain toilet soaps to improve their natural germicidal properties.

(e) *Superfat* involves including an excess of fat to offset alkalinity. Lanolin or vegetable oils can be used.

Experiments

1. To prepare a soap powder:

Powdered soap	25 g
Sodium heptaoxotetra borate (borax) powder	50 g
Sodium hydrogen carbonate	15 g
Sodium carbonate	2 g

The powders are mixed together in a large tin, perfume being added if required.

2. To prepare soap:

Potassium hydroxide pellets	3 g
Water	160 cm³
Octadecanoic acid (stearic acid)	30 g

Dissolve the potassium hydroxide in the water and add the acid. Heat the mixture to 60°–80°C stirring continuously. Remove from the heat and stir the mixture vigorously until it is cool. Note its soapy feel and see if it forms a lather when a little is mixed with water. A leaflet on the laboratory preparation of soap together with other publications are available from Unilever Education Service.

5. ALKALINE DETERGENTS

These preparations in solid or liquid form attack food soils by their strong alkaline action. They consist mainly of sodium hydroxide, sodium carbonate, sodium silicate, and sodium phosphates. All should be used with extreme care when cleaning cookers, etc.

6. SOAPLESS NEUTRAL DETERGENTS

Soapless detergents are synthetic substances available for domestic, catering and laundry work. The first were made by treating such vegetable oils as olive and castor oils with sulphuric acid (H₂SO₄) to provide a *hydrogen sulphate* compound with acidic properties. These could be neutralized by alkali to form a neutral sulphated oil:

Olive or castor oils + sulphuric acid = acidic sulphated castor or olive oil + alkali = neutral sulphated castor or olive oil

Sulphonated castor oil is also called Turkey red oil.

Coconut oil is the ester of dodecanoic acid (lauric) which is the basic raw material for many soapless detergents.

Coconut oil = propanetriol (glycerine) + dodecanoic acid (lauric acid)

(a) The coconut oil is changed into dodecanol (lauryl alcohol) by a process of *reduction* using methanol (methyl alcohol) and hydrogen.

(b) The dodecanol (lauryl alcohol) is then treated with sulphuric acid forming dodecanyl (lauryl) hydrogen sulphate:

Coconut oil $\xrightarrow{\text{Reduction}}$ dodecanol (lauryl alcohol) $\xrightarrow{\text{Sulphuric acid}}$ dodecanyl hydrogen sulphate

(c) If the *acidic* dodecanyl (lauryl) hydrogen sulphate is treated with sodium hydroxide the white powder sodium dodecanyl (lauryl) sulphate can be obtained:

Dodecanyl (lauryl) hydrogen sulphate + sodium hydroxide = sodium dodecanyl (lauryl) sulphate + water

If ammonia or trihydroxyethylamine (triethanolamine) neutralize the acid dodecanyl (lauryl) hydrogen sulphate, viscous liquids of ammonium dodecanyl (lauryl) sulphate, and trihydroxyethylamine (triethanolamine) lauryl sulphate are produced:

Dodecanyl (lauryl) hydrogen sulphate + ammonia = ammonium dodecanyl (lauryl) sulphate + water

Dodecanyl (lauryl) hydrogen sulphate + trihydroxyethylamine (triethanolamine) = trihydroxyethylamine (triethanolamine) dodecanyl (lauryl) sulphate + water

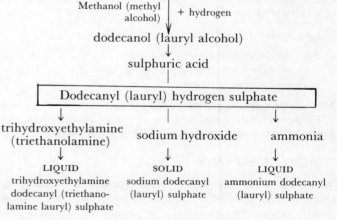

Since vegetable and animal oils and fats are valuable foodstuffs the use of petroleum by-products such as benzene, naphthalene, and alkane gases in detergent manufacture is more economical.

The liquid hydrocarbon *alkyl benzene* is treated with sulphuric acid to form the *alkyl benzene hydrogen sulphate*. This has acidic properties which can be neutralized with sodium hydroxide forming sodium alkyl benzene sulphate:

$$\text{Alkyl benzene} \xrightarrow[\text{acid}]{\text{Sulphuric}} \text{alkyl benzene hydrogen sulphate}$$

$$\downarrow \text{Sodium} \mid \text{hydroxide}$$

$$\text{sodium alkyl benzene sulphate}$$
$$\text{a solid or paste}$$

IMPORTANT SOAPLESS DETERGENT PRODUCTS

1. *Soapless synthetic powders* contain sodium alkyl or sodium dodecanyl (lauryl) benzene sulphonates, with additives. Builders to improve cleansing power include sodium phosphates and sodium carbonate. Carboxy methyl cellulose (C.M.C.) is also included to prevent the emulsified dirt being redeposited on the fibre. Perfumes and whitening agents are also components. Sodium sulphate(VI) (Glauber's salt) is frequently added to act as a bulky filler.

2. *Clear liquid soapless detergents* are solutions of such liquid detergents as trihydroxyethylamine dodecanyl (triethanolamine lauryl) sulphate, and tridecyl sulphate diluted with water. Salt is added to increase viscosity.

3. *Detergent sterilizers* contain quaternary ammonium compounds and are intended for light-duty cleansing and sterilization. They are employed to clean food-processing equipment, dishes, cutlery, and crockery. Many are used for sterilization after using heavy-duty detergents.

4. *Structuring agents*, which are also called *emulsifiers* and *stabilizers* (see Appendix A), are surfaceactive detergents made from sugars and propanetriol (glycerols) and fatty acids. These edible substances are used as crumb-softeners, dough improvers and anti-staling agents in baked bread, biscuits and cakes. *Sucrose stearate*, made from sucrose and stearic (octadecanoic) acid, is one example of a sucrose *ester* of a fatty acid.

To prepare a soapless detergent powder:

Sodium dodecanyl (lauryl) sulphate	50 g
Sodium heptaoxotetraborate (borax) powder	40 g
Sodium carbonate powder	10 g

Mix the powders together in a large tin.

These two preparations are suitable as dish-washing detergents, but not for laundry or toilet purposes.

7. ACID DETERGENTS

These are cleansing agents for descaling and removing calcium salts from W.C. pans and cookers. They consist mainly of sodium chlorate(I) (hypochlorite), sodium persulphate, sodium hydrogen sulphate, and chlorinated isocyanuric acid.

8. ENZYMES

These are proteolytic enzymes, attacking protein stains, blood, egg, etc., and function at 38°–45°C (hand hot).

WATER

Homes and catering establishments receive supplies of water from mountain reservoirs, artesian wells, boreholes, rivers, and wells or springs filled in the first place with rain water.

Types of natural water

1. *Rain water* is very pure if it falls through *clean* country air away from the sea. Town rain water contains suspended soot and dust, with dissolved gases mainly carbon dioxide, sulphur dioxide, and oxides of nitrogen. All rain water contains dissolved carbon dioxide.

2. *Mountain reservoir* or upland surface water is rain water from mountains collected in streams to fill a dammed valley. Its quality depends on whether it passes over cultivated or uncultivated land, or whether the underlying rock is insoluble or partly soluble limestone. Upland surface water is wholesome and palatable.

3. *Spring water* has sparkling clarity and purity, produced by slow filtration through sand and clay. Most contain dissolved substances which make the water very wholesome. The spring waters of Bath, Harrogate, and Leamington contain dissolved salts of medicinal value, while the natural *mineral waters* of Vichy, Appollinaris, Evian, Seltzer and Vittel, contain carbon dioxide and alkaline salts.

4. *Well water* is underground water brought to the surface by the natural water pressure of artesian wells, or by mechanical means. Shallow wells are liable to contamination by sewage.

5. *River water* may contain dissolved and suspended impurities, the former depending on the rocks forming the river bed, and the latter on sewage and other waste discharged into the river. This water must be purified before drinking.

6. *Sea water* contains many dissolved salts of sodium, potassium, and magnesium, the main being some 2·5 per cent of sodium chloride. Solar distillation and demineralization are methods of purifying sea water for drinking purposes.

HARDNESS OF WATER

Water which, with soap, produces a lather persisting at least five minutes is called *soft*. Hard water will not readily give a lather with soap because certain salts are dissolved in it. The salts have entered the water from the rock bed over which it passed. 65 per cent of the water supplies in the British Isles is hard, of which 45 per cent is classified as *very* hard. Hard water is of two main kinds (*a*) temporary, and (*b*) permanently hard water.

TEMPORARY HARDNESS

Temporary hardness is caused by the soluble salts of calcium and magnesium *hydrogen carbonates* entering the water by the action of rain water containing dissolved carbon dioxide flowing over chalk or limestone which is mainly calcium carbonate.

$$\begin{array}{c}\text{Magnesium or}\\ \text{calcium carbonate}\\ \text{MgCO}_3 \text{ or CaCO}_3\end{array} + \begin{array}{c}\text{carbon}\\ \text{dioxide}\\ \text{CO}_2\end{array} + \begin{array}{c}\text{water}\\ \text{H}_2\text{O}\end{array} = \begin{array}{c}\text{magnesium or}\\ \text{calcium hydrogen carbonates}\\ \text{Mg(HCO}_3)_2 \text{ or Ca(HCO}_3)_2\end{array}$$

Solutions of hydrogen carbonates are alkaline, the term *alkaline hardness* is used instead of temporary hardness. Temporary hard water is softened by *boiling*, when a calcium and magnesium carbonate *scale* is formed. This chemical change is the reverse of the equation above.

PERMANENT HARDNESS

Permanently hard water contains calcium and magnesium *sulphates* dissolved from rocks as the rain water flowed over them. This hardness *cannot* be removed by boiling and is alternatively called *non-alkaline* hardness:

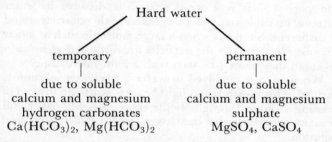

Combined together temporary and permanent hardness are called *total hardness*.

DISADVANTAGES OF HARD WATER

1. *Curd*, or calcium or magnesium *soap* formation, is one of the main disadvantages of hard water. When sodium octadec-9-enoate (oleate) or octadecanoate (stearate), *soluble* soap, is added to hard water, a flocculent *insoluble* soap of sticky calcium octadecanoate (stearate) or octadec-9-enoate (oleate) soap is produced:

$$\begin{array}{c}\text{Soluble soap}\\ \text{sodium octadec-9-}\\ \text{enoate (oleate)}\\ \text{or octadenoate}\\ \text{(stearate)}\end{array} + \begin{array}{c}\text{calcium}\\ \text{salt,}\\ \text{hard}\\ \text{water}\end{array} = \begin{array}{c}\text{insoluble}\\ \text{calcium octadec-9-}\\ \text{enoate (oleate)}\\ \text{or octadecanoate}\\ \text{(stearate) curd}\end{array} + \begin{array}{c}\text{sodium salt}\\ \text{dissolved in}\\ \text{soft water}\end{array}$$

Calcium and magnesium octadecenoate (stearate) or octadec-9-enoate (oleate) are *insoluble* soaps which cling to the fibres of textiles, giving a grey appearance and damaging the texture. This insoluble soap appears as a tide line in bath water and clings to the hair and skin. Repeated rinsing does not dislodge it. Ethanoic (acetic) acid is frequently used as an acid rinse. The adhesive nature of sticking plaster is due to zinc soaps.

2. *Scale* of insoluble calcium and magnesium carbonate is deposited on the heater elements in kettles, immersion heaters, and boilers. Hot-water pipes become blocked causing waste of fuel through overheating and damage to boiler tubes through unequal heating.

Scale can be removed from kettles with a 70 per cent solution of methanoic (formic acid) (H.COOH). The acid liberates carbon dioxide from calcium and magnesium carbonates:

$$\begin{array}{c}\text{Calcium}\\ \text{carbonate}\end{array} + \begin{array}{c}\text{methanoic acid}\\ \text{(formic acid)}\end{array} = \begin{array}{c}\text{carbon}\\ \text{dioxide}\end{array} + \begin{array}{c}\text{calcium}\\ \text{methanoate + water}\\ \text{(formate)}\end{array}$$

ADVANTAGES OF HARD WATER

1. Hard water is palatable and is frequently used in aerated waters and beers. Water from the rivers Thames and Trent is used by the breweries.

2. The dissolved salts of calcium are of importance in bone and teeth formation.

3. Fluoridation, the addition of fluoride salts to the water, helps to strengthen teeth and prevent decay.

Experiment

To measure the total hardness of water.

Put 70 cm^3 of water to be tested in a 250 cm^3 conical flask. Standard soap solution (Clark's) from a 50 cm^3 burette is added. The flask is shaken after each addition of preferably 1 cm^3, and allowed to stand for 5 minutes to determine whether a permanent lather has been achieved which shows that the hardness has been removed.

The amount of standard soap solution in cubic centimetres, *less* 1 cm^3, gives the degrees of hardness of the water solution: Cubic centimetres of soap $- 1$ cm$^3 \equiv$ degrees of hardness of the water on Clark's scale.

MEASUREMENT OF TOTAL WATER HARDNESS

Hardness of water is usually measured in degrees Clark; 1 cm^3 of Clark's standard soap solution is equal to 1 degree Clark of 1 part of calcium carbonate per 1 000 000 parts of water.

1 cm^3 Clark's standard soap solution = 1 degree Clark
 = 1 part calcium carbonate per million parts of water

If, for example, the amount of standard soap solution added to 70 cm^3 of water was 12·5 cm^3, the degrees of hardness would be $12·5 - 1 = 11·5$ degrees of hardness. This is equivalent to 11·5 parts of calcium carbonate per million parts of water.

Very hard water can be between 100° and 200° Clark. When testing them 25 cm^3 is diluted with 75 cm^3 of *distilled* water and the titration proceeded with as previously. The degree of hardness is calculated by subtracting 1 cm^3 and multiplying the answer by 4:

Soap titration for very hard water $- 1$ cm^3 = answer $\times$ 4

A titration of 20 cm^3 soap will equal $20 - 1 = 19 \times 4 = 76°$ hardness.

METHODS OF SOFTENING WATER

Hardness of water is due to *both* temporary and permanent hardness; natural waters are rarely affected by one cause only. Methods of water softening are:

1. *Soapless detergents* are most suitable in hard water areas because the calcium and magnesium salts formed are *soluble*:

$$\text{Sodium dodecanyl (lauryl) sulphate} + \text{calcium salt in hard water} = \text{calcium dodecanyl (lauryl) sulphate (soluble)} + \text{sodium salt in soft water}$$

Soaps will produce the insoluble calcium soaps. This can be demonstrated by adding soap solution to one beaker of hard water (a 2 per cent solution of magnesium sulphate) and a solution of sodium dodecanyl (lauryl) sulphate to another. The first beaker forms a cloudy precipitate while the second remains clear.

2. Sodium carbonate (Na_2CO_3), *washing soda*, is suitable for permanent hard waters. The carbonate radical of the washing soda is exchanged for the sulphate radical in the hard water:

$$\text{Calcium or magnesium sulphate} + \text{sodium carbonate} = \text{calcium or carbonate (insoluble)} + \text{soluble sodium salt in soft water}$$

Sodium carbonate and trisodium hydrogen carbonate sodium sesquicarbonate are ingredients of many laundry washing powders and bath salts.

3. *Clark's* method using calcium hydroxide ($Ca(OH)_2$) removes *temporary* hardness due to hydrogen carbonates. It does not affect permanent hardness due to soluble sulphates:

$$\text{Calcium hydrogen carbonate (soluble)} + \text{calcium hydroxide} = \text{calcium carbonate (insoluble)} + \text{soft water}$$

4. Calcium hydroxide and sodium carbonate, *lime-soda*, process is a combination of methods 2 and 3 frequently used in laundries, factories, and for softening boiler feed water. Water so softened has a hardness of 2°–4° Clark.

5. *Sequestrants*, such as sodium hexatrioxophosphate(V) (hexametaphosphate) and sodium tripolyphosphate, soften water without forming a scum. They are ingredients of laundry and washing-up powders and are added before using soap or washing powder, being employed in laundries using water of hardness below 50° Clark.

6. *Ion-exchange process* or zeolite process. The hard water is passed through a tower packed with natural or synthetic *zeolite* ion-exchange materials. The calcium or magnesium ions in the water exchanges with sodium ions in the zeolite. The process continues until no more sodium ions remain:

$$\text{Sodium ion zeolite} + \text{calcium or magnesium ion (hard water)} = \text{calcium ion zeolite} + \text{sodium salt (soft water)}$$

Periodically the exhausted ion-exchange material is regenerated by flushing the tower with a solution of sodium chloride which replaces calcium with sodium ions:

$$\text{Calcium ion zeolite} + \text{sodium chloride} = \text{sodium ion zeolite} + \text{calcium chloride}$$

The water-softener unit is fitted into the main water system, close to its point of entry into the premises. Zeolite-softened water is usually 0°–2° Clark.

7. *Demineralizing process* involves passing the hard water through a bed of synthetic demineralizing resin; it is a two-stage process. Its main advantage is the resin's capacity to remove chlorides from water, thus making it possible to purify sea water.

Stage 1. The hydrogen carbonate sulphate, and chloride ions in the water are changed into their corresponding acids carbonic (H_2CO_3), sulphuric (H_2SO_4), and hydrochloric (HCl) by receiving hydrogen ions from the resin.

Stage 2. The acids are now absorbed by the demineralizing resin to leave pure, soft water. This process yields water of 0° of hardness, similar to distilled water.

COLLOIDS

On page 127 it was noted that salts dissolve in water forming invisible *ions*. Such solutions are therefore clear and transparent. Similarly when a large molecule such as sugar dissolves in the water the particles are dispersed as *molecules* so small they cannot be seen with a light microscope.

When soap is dissolved in water a *translucent* solution is formed. This means that a light beam is scattered instead of passing straight through. If the solution is filtered it still remains translucent or opalescent, and is called a *colloidal* solution.

The difference between a true solution and a colloidal solution is in the size of the particles of the solute. Colloidal particles can only be seen because they reflect light rays. Figure 19.1 shows how a microscope is used to observe colloidal particles.

If a little cocoa powder is stirred with water it becomes cloudy and will not permit a beam of light to pass through

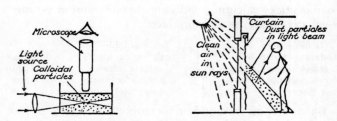

Figure 19.1 Colloidal solutions and Tyndall effect

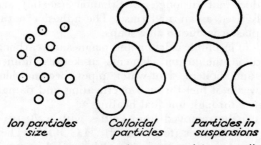

Figure 19.2. Approximate diameters of ions, colloid, and suspension particles

it. This is a *suspension* of cocoa powder which rapidly settles as a sediment above which the water is clear. By contrast colloidal particles do not settle (Figure 19.2).

SOLUTIONS, COLLOIDS, AND SUSPENSIONS

Solution	Colloidal solution	Suspension
Clear transparent liquids; beam of light passes through	Opalescent and translucent; some light reflected from colloid particles	Opaque
Solute consists of molecules or ions not observable through a microscope	Large molecules only observable through an electron microscope or by light scattering	Easily seen with an ordinary magnifier or microscope
Passes through ordinary filter papers, parchment and cellophane	Passes through ordinary filter papers but *not* through parchment and cellophane	Cannot pass through filter papers of any kind
Example: sugar syrup	Example: soap in water or egg white	Example: cocoa in water

IMPORTANT COLLOIDAL SOLUTIONS

All colloidal solutions consist of (*a*) the *disperse* phase, the substance broken up into tiny particles, and (*b*) the *dispersion* medium, the liquid or solid in which dispersion

USES OF IMPORTANT COLLOIDAL SOLUTIONS

Colloidal solution	Dispersion medium	Disperse phase	Occurrence
Sol, i.e. solid in liquids	Water	Starch	Laundry starch
	Water	Gelatine	Jelly that has *not* set
	Water	Tea or coffee	Infused tea or coffee
	Water	Soap	Soap solution
	Water	Proteins	Proteins in living cells of meat and other foods
Emulsion, i.e. liquid in liquids	Water	Butter fat	Milk
	Vinegar	Olive oil	Mayonnaise
	Butter fat	Water	Butter, cream and processed cheese
	Hardened vegetable oil	Water	Margarine
Foam, i.e. gas in liquids	Butter fat	Air	Whipped cream
	Egg white	Air	Beaten egg white
	Water	Carbon dioxide	Beer foam
Gel, i.e. liquid in solids	Solid gluten	Water	Baked bread
	Solid gelatine	Water	Jelly that has *set*
	Casein	Water	Cheese
Aerogel or solid foam, i.e. gas in solids	Gluten	Carbon dioxide	Baked bread and sponge cakes (see Gel)
	Gelatine	Air	Marshmallows
	Solid in fats	Air	Ice-cream
	Coagulated albumen	Air	Meringue and souffles
Smoke or fog, i.e. solids in gas	Air	Soot and dust	Smoke or fog; chimneys

occurs. Colloidal solutions are *heterogeneous*, not of the same composition throughout; a true solution is *homogeneous*.

The table lists some important colloidal solutions found in food preparation and laundry work.

EMULSIONS

An emulsion is a colloidal solution of tiny particles of one liquid suspended in another. Milk is an emulsion of droplets of butterfat suspended in water. It soon settles into two layers, a process which can be speeded up using a *centrifuge* as in the centrifugal separator in creameries.

If ethanoic acid (vinegar) and olive oil are shaken together an emulsion is formed which rapidly settles into two layers. To prevent this an *emulsifying agent* must be added. Egg yolk containing the protein *vitellin* and *lecithin*, a fatty substance, are employed to make salad-cream emulsions. Emulsions are therefore composed of two mutually insoluble liquids held in a colloidal solution by means of an emulsifying agent:

Liquid A (ethanoic acid) + liquid B (olive oil)
+ emulsifying agent (egg yolk)
↓
Emulsion of oil in water (salad-cream)

Emulsions are of two main types;

(*a*) *water in oil* or W/O, a little water is the disperse phase in a large amount of oil which is the dispersion medium. For example butter, 12 per cent water in 83 per cent lipid oil.

(*b*) *oil in water* or O/W, a little oil is the disperse phase in a large amount of water which is the dispersion medium. For example milk is 3 per cent lipid oil in 87 per cent water.

EMULSION TYPES IN FOOD

	per cent lipid	per cent water
1. *Oil in water*		
Milk	3	87
Single cream	18	82
Double cream	48	52
Whipping cream	35	65
Ice-cream	10	60
Gravies, soups, some sauces	Variable composition	
2. *Water in oil*		
Butter and margarine	83	16
Mayonnaise	78	16

EMULSIFYING AGENTS (see Appendix A)

Emulsifying agents include a range of natural and synthetic chemical products which serve in the uniform dispersion of oils in water to form food *emulsions*. These substances are given the serial numbers E400 and E483 on food labels. *Stabilizers* and *thickeners*, which maintain the emulsions, are similar substances and are included in the same serial number range above E400 (see Appendix A).

The table lists some important emulsifiers used in food preparation and for cleansing purposes.

USES OF IMPORTANT EMULSIFIERS (E400–483)

Emulsifier	Use
Natural products	
Gums, e.g. arabic, tragacanth, agar and karaya	Confectionery, sauces, and salad-creams
Egg yolk containing lecithin	Chocolate confectionery, salad-creams, meringues, custards, and white flour
Carrageen or Irish moss	Thickener and emulsifier for soups and sauces
Gelatine	For ice-cream
Chemical reagents or derived products:	
Propanediol octadecanoate (glyceryl monostearate (G.M.S.)), a white powder	Ice-cream and in shortening fats to improve creaming properties. Improves the keeping quality of bread
Methyl ethyl cellulose (Edifas A), a white powder	Emulsifying agent for imitation creams and foams
Methyl cellulose (Methofas)	Instead of starches and natural gums as an emulsifier and thickener, for bakery products, sauces, gravies, and syrups
Sodium carboxy methyl cellulose (Edifas B), a white powder	Stabilizes emulsions in ice-creams, sauces, and confectionery products
Alginates or salts of acid derived from seaweeds	Emulsifier for imitation cream and ice-cream
Bile salts	Produced by the liver, serving to emulsify oils and fats within the intestine, thus offering a greater surface for digestion

GELS

Gels are important colloidal solutions made up of liquids in a solid dispersion medium. Table jellies are made by dissolving solid gelatine in hot water to form a colloidal *sol*. On cooling the table jelly sets into a *gel* consisting of a network of solid gelatine with water trapped within it. Other foods which are gels are porridge, baked custards, flour dough, jams, and batters. Rice and tapioca puddings and starch solution are also gels. Proteins are mainly found in the gel condition in cells of plant and animals; for example dried peas imbibe water as does dry gelatine. Meat consists of protein in a gel condition.

On long standing gels lose water, shrink and separate from their containers as seen in table jelly and baked custards. Baked bread is a gel with water within the solid gluten fibres. When bread stands it sweats because the gluten fibres get larger, squeezing water out. This process of water separating from gels is called *syneresis* and is frequently due to the strong acidity (pH below 3·0).

STARCH GELS

Ordinary starches from maize, wheat, rice, sorghum and arrowroot, which have granules containing *amylose* and *amylopectin*, will form *gels* in water.

Waxy starches from waxy maize, waxy rice, and waxy sorghum do not form a gel with water, but instead form clear, *mucilaginous* pastes (see page 109).

Consequently the selection of the correct starch or starch-rich ingredient is necessary in making gels or mucilages in cookery processes.

Retrogradation

Amylose molecules present in ordinary starches are responsible for forming gels. Under certain conditions of baking, freezing, or even at room temperature, the amylose molecules link up with each other through intermolecular bonds – this process is called *retrogradation*. During the process of retrogradation the gel *shrinks* and water is squeezed out. As more and more amylose molecules join together, more water is squeezed out by syneresis.

Jellies are seen to 'weep', and bread 'sweats' and stales, through retrogradation.

The rate of retrogradation of starch gels is dependent on temperature and size of the starch molecules. Crumb softeners slow down retrogradation in bread (see page 130).

Freeze-thawing

Retrogradation occurs during freezing of starch-thickened gravies, sauces and puddings. The thawed food shows 'weeping' and a 'curdled' appearance through syneresis and retrogradation (see page 42).

1. *Ordinary starch* gels of cornflour, wheat, rice etc., show gel shrinkage, syneresis and retrogradation. Cornflour, wheat and sorghum are more prone than other starches.

2. *Waxy maize* and other waxy starches, since they do not form gels, will not display syneresis or retrogradation.

3. *Modified starches* will form either clear gels or mucilages depending on the starch from which they are formed. These will show varying syneresis and retrogradation, particularly in freeze-thawing.

Effects of other substances on starch gels

1. *Sugar* slows the rate of starch granule swelling. Since sugars compete for water with starch, the sugar should be added after the gel has formed.

2. *Acids* from fruit juices cause hydrolysis of starch and thinning of the gel. Consequently acid components could be added after gel formation, or by using more starch.

3. *Proteins* present either as a component of the starch-rich component, wheat flour, or from added eggs and milk, improve the freeze-thaw stability of the gel.

4. *Flavours* are absorbed by starches and this can be effectively used in removing for example excessive spice flavours.

WATER IN FOODS

Water is a very abundant compound and is found to varying extents in different foods. The water may be in the cell sap of plants and easily removable with centrifugal juice extractors or by dehydration, using heat or vacuum drying.

The dehydrated product can easily be reconstituted by adding water. The water in a food can be held in close combination with the proteins, carbohydrates, and fats and be only removable with difficulty. This is seen in the combined water of egg white.

Experiments

To determine the water content of foods.

Method 1. Grated or finely divided foods such as cheese, potatoes, and cabbage are carefully weighed into an evaporating dish. They are heated in an oven at 100°C or over a steam bath until there is no further loss in weight. The percentage water is calculated from the loss in weight compared to the original weight of the food.

Method 2. Place a weighed amount of butter or margarine in the water-estimation apparatus containing methylbenzene (toluene) (see Figure 19.3). Heat the flask with an electric mantle and observe the separation of water in the graduated side limb of the apparatus. The percentage volume of water separating is then calculated.

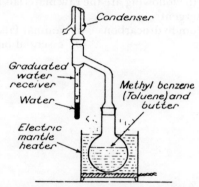

Figure 19.3. Apparatus for determining the water content of foodstuffs

For example 1 cm³ of water is produced from 10 g of butter. Since 1 cm³ of water equals 1 g the percentage water in butter is:

$$\tfrac{1}{10} \times 100 = 10 \text{ per cent}$$

DEHYDRATION OF FOOD (see also page 40)

Several methods are used in drying and preserving food by dehydration.

1. *Sun drying* is a traditional method for fruits, fish, and meat.

2. *Air drying* involves the passing of the food along tunnels through which hot air currents flow in the opposite direction. A 'fluidized bed' may also be used in which hot air rises from the perforated base of a trough and is used to dry peas and diced vegetables.

Spray drying is suitable for liquids and fluid extracts such as milk and coffee. The liquid is sprayed down a tower to meet a current of hot air which evaporates the liquid causing the dry powder to be deposited lower down the drying tower.

Roller drying involves the coating of hot rotating drums with a pasty viscous mass of the food, such as potatoes, this dries out rapidly as a thin layer on the drum and is scraped away by sharp knife edges.

3. *Vacuum freeze drying* is used to dehydrate coffee extract which is first deep frozen and then placed in vacuum chambers where it is gently heated sufficiently for the ice to *sublime*, changing into water vapour without passing through the liquid stage. The applied vacuum sucks away the water vapour leaving a light, brittle, crumblike texture.

Properties of dehydrated foods

Dehydrated foods show *hygroscopic* properties and will draw in moisture if stored exposed in humid conditions.

If lipids are present in the dehydrated foods it is necessary to destroy the *lipase* enzyme by heating to prevent the development of *enzymatic* rancidity. Similarly *oxidative* rancidity is prevented by storing the dehydrated foods in sealed packets containing an atmosphere of carbon dioxide or nitrogen gas or by vacuum packing.

SUGGESTIONS FOR PRACTICAL WORK

See *Experimental Science for Catering and Homecraft Students*, Practical work 8.1 to 8.4, 11.4, 25.1 to 25.4, 66.1 to 66.2, 67.1 to 67.3, 68.1 to 68.3, 69.1 to 69.5.

QUESTIONS ON CHAPTER 19

1. Explain why different parts of this country have water of varying degrees of hardness. What are the advantages and disadvantages of hard and soft water? Explain the nature of the scum which appears when soap is added to water. Describe two ways of softening water for household purposes.

2. Compare the advantages and disadvantages of soaps and soapless detergents.

3. How are the disadvantages of hard water overcome in laundering?

4. Write short notes on the composition of: (*a*) toilet soap; (*b*) soap flakes; (*c*) liquid soapless detergents; and (*d*) soap powders.

5. How would you deal with the following stains: (*a*) raspberry juice; (*b*) ball-pen ink; (*c*) grass; (*d*) lipstick; and (*e*) tar.

6. Write short notes on: (*a*) tetrachloromethane (carbon tetrachloride); (*b*) sodium octadec-9-enoate (oleate); (*c*) propanone (acetone); (*d*) trihydroxyethylamine dodecanyl (triethanolamine lauryl) sulphate; and (*e*) sodium hexatrioxophosphate (V) (hexametaphosphate).

7. Give a brief account of the laboratory method for determining the total hardness of water.

8. What are colloidal solutions? Give four examples of such solutions encountered in cookery.

9. What is an emulsion? Give a short account of the main emulsifying agents used in food preparation.

MULTIPLE CHOICE QUESTIONS ON CHAPTER 19

1. A 200 g portion of fresh bread weighed 140 g when dried at 100°C. The percentage water in the fresh bread is:
   (a) 15%   (c) 45%
   (b) 30%   (d) 70%

2. Protein containing foods such as bread, are able to hold the water in the form of a:
   (a) foam   (c) suspension
   (b) gel   (d) emulsion

3. A water which is permanently hard will show a white cloudiness when it is:
   (a) boiled
   (b) viewed in a glass tumbler
   (c) mixed with soap detergent
   (d) mixed with soapless detergent

4. Which one of the following clear samples of water will turn cloudy or milky in appearance when boiled?
   (a) sea water   (c) temporary hard water
   (b) rain water   (d) permanent hard water

5. The cloudiness or milky precipitate which forms on boiling the water in Question 4 could be due to:
   (a) sand   (c) clay
   (b) chalk   (d) salt

6. Which two of the following cause permanent hardness of water and are not affected by boiling the water?
   (i) calcium sulphate
   (ii) magnesium sulphate
   (iii) calcium carbonate
   (iv) magnesium carbonate
   (v) calcium hydrogen carbonate
   (iv) magnesium hydrogen carbonate
   (a) i, ii   (c) iv, v
   (b) iii, iv   (d) v, vi

7. Which of the following is an example of a gel or liquid in a solid phase?
   (a) bread   (c) milk
   (b) butter   (d) table jelly

8. Which of the following is an example of an emulsion?
   (a) beaten egg white   (c) salad cream
   (b) table jelly   (d) bread

9. Coffee extract is available as fine granules which have been prepared by the following dehydration process:
   (a) fluidized bed   (c) sundrying
   (b) freeze drying   (d) roller drying

10. Which of the following are the raw materials for making a soapless detergent?
    (a) petroleum hydrocarbons   (c) animal fats
    (b) enzymes   (d) essential oils

20 Metals, plastics, and paints

METALS

The most common metals used in catering and housecraft are iron, copper, aluminium, steel, and tin. Tableware and ornamental articles are made from silver, gold, chromium, nickel, and copper. Many metals used are in the form of *alloys* or mixtures of different metals; brass is an alloy of copper and zinc. Stainless steel is a mixture of iron and chromium together with a little nickel. Other important alloys are:

> Brass = copper + zinc
> Bronze = copper + tin
> Stainless steel = iron + chromium + nickel
> Solder = lead + tin
> Pewter = tin + copper + antimony

PROTECTION OF METALS

Most metals are subject to the corrosive action of oxygen, water, acids, and alkalis or to the effects of certain chemical compounds such as hydrogen sulphide.

Food acids present in pickles, grapefruit, oranges, lemons, and rhubarb have acid properties, usually about pH 3·7. Most fruits acids of plums, apples, and blackcurrants together with tomatoes, have a pH of 4·5–3·7. Fruit acids can attack and corrode the *tin* and *solder* layers of tinplate used in canning.

Alkalis such as sodium hydroxide and salts with alkaline properties such as sodium carbonate will corrode some metal utensils. Silver will blacken by the chemical action of hydrogen sulphide present in the air or food, and copper will turn green in moist air. The table summarizes the main methods of preventing metal corrosion.

PREVENTION OF METAL CORROSION

Methods	Example
Using metals resistant to corrosion	
Gold is not attacked by any domestic substance. But gold corrodes in contact with mercury due to amalgamation	Well-known use of pure gold and gold-plated metal articles
Silver is blackened by compounds of sulphur	Cutlery and plated tableware
Aluminium resists most reagents except alkali sodium hydroxide and sodium carbonate. It rapidly corrodes if it contains iron as an impurity. A protective coating of aluminium oxide develops which should *not* be removed.	Cast aluminium pans, kettles, pudding basins, and saucepans. Washing machine tubs are of aluminium so strongly alkaline powders should not be used.
Copper is corroded by food acids. Cooking utensils are coated inside with a layer of tin	Copperware is widely used in catering
Covering the metal	
Painting with metal primer red lead or zinc chromate paint for iron and steel. Aluminium and iron are covered with zinc chromate primer. Lead and copper are best left unpainted.	For painting iron gutters, and down-pipes. Metal windows are mainly aluminium or aluminium alloys
Electroplating. The metal is coated with chromium, silver, gold, or cadmium by electrolysis	Tableware and cutlery are electro-plated with silver or a nickel-silver alloy. E.p.n.s. means electroplated nickel-silver
Galvanized or sherardized metalware. Iron can be coated with a thin layer of zinc metal	Such domestic hardware as buckets, bowls, bins, and baths. Attic cistern tanks and roofing sheets. Galvanized ware should

Methods	Example
	not contain food since zinc is attacked by food acids and alkalis
Tinware consists of sheet iron or steel coated with tin. Tinned copperware has a thin layer of tin that prevents copper dissolving in contact with food acids. (See lacquered ware.)	Food containers, baking tins, funnels, and colanders. Tinned copper saucepans, frypans, and jam pans. Tinware can be cleansed with sodium carbonate
Vitreous enamels have coats of opaque glass fused on to iron. They chip easily and cheap enamels may contain antimony which causes chemical food poisoning	Enamelled working surfaces and oven surfaces. Saucepans, pie dishes, and baking dishes. Grey enamelware is not suitable for food preparation
Plastic coated metalware. Saucepans and frypans are coated with a non-stick surface of Fluon or polytetrafluorethylene (P.T.F.E.)	Used for frypans and saucepans and for coating metal rollers in bakeries
Lacquered ware. Brass and copperware are lacquered with transparent shellac. Such articles should not be cleansed with an abrasive polish	Lacquered ornamental copper for brassware. Cans for food are lacquered internally with gum and gum resin

Alloys

Stainless steel alloys of iron and chromium are resistant to all cooking and domestic cleansing agents	For working surfaces, sinks, draining boards, boiling pans, and steamers. Frequently used for basins, bowls, and cutlery. Stainless steel cooking pans have *copper* bases to improve heat conduction of the poorer conducting stainless steel

Iron

Iron, the oldest metal used for cooking pots, is still popular. Ironware such as frypans is case hardened by heating sodium chloride, in the pan	Frypans, kettles, griddle irons, and baking sheets. Ironware is best cleansed on the *inner* surface only. The black outside will absorb heat

Lead

Lead in buildings is rapidly being displaced by copper and plastics for piping and cistern tanks, etc.	Lead piping frequently caused lead poisoning in beer by hard water supplies

Experiments

1. Effect of food acids and alkalis on metals:

Obtain strips measuring 7.5×1 cm of iron, stainless steel, copper, tinned iron (tin can), zinc, galvanized iron, and aluminium. Immerse a strip of metal in vinegar, rhubarb juice, lemon juice, apple juice, 5 per cent sodium carbonate, and a control test of water. Compare the effects of immersion of the different metals after a period of one day and one week.

2. Effect of detergents and cleansing agents on metals:

Immerse strips of metals as before in vinegar, 5 per cent ethanedioic (oxalic) acid, dilute ammonium hydroxide, 10 per cent sodium carbonate, 10 per cent sodium hydroxide, a proprietary detergent, soap solution, and a control test of water. Compare the immersed metals for signs of corrosion or tarnishing, after a period of one day or a week.

METAL POLISHES (see page 128)

Metals are cleansed by the abrasive action of powdered whiting, iron(II) oxide or fine-grade abrasives such as silica and powdered brick. The abrasive removes the tarnished outer layers of the metal exposing a new surface. Many metal polishes contain ammonium hydroxide which removes any metal oxides, particularly those of copper from copper and brassware. Ethanedioic acid (oxalic acid) is frequently used for cleansing brass and copperware; this substance is poisonous and should be used with care.

Ethanol (methylated spirits) is a component of metal and glass polishes, hastening the evaporation of the polish to leave a deposit to be buffed up with a cloth.

Recipe for glass or metal polish

Calcium carbonate (abrasive whiting) or iron(III) oxide (jeweller's rouge)	6 g
Ethanol (methylated spirits)	15 cm^3
0.880 Ammonium hydroxide	2 cm^3
Trihydroxyethylamine (triethanolamine)	2 cm^3
Water	75 cm^3

Add the trihydroxyethylamine (triethanolamine) to the mixture of water, ammonium hydroxide, and ethanol. Sprinkle in the powdered abrasive and stir thoroughly.

Metal polish: plate butler's recipe

Calcium carbonate (ceiling whitening)	10 g
0.880 Ammonium hydroxide	2 cm^3

Mix the above ingredients with water to a creamy paste, and add sufficient water soluble blue dye to produce a dark blue mixture.

The mixture is applied to silverware with a stiff paint brush, allowed to dry overnight, then washed in soapy water, rinsed and polished with a soft chamois leather.

PLASTICS OR SYNTHETIC RESINS

Plastics, in marked contrast to metals, do not rust, tarnish, or corrode and have in many cases a flexibility and softness that makes them quiet to handle, as against the clatter of metal.

Plastics or synthetic resins vary greatly in their physical properties, from the hard brittle phenolmethanal resin (Bakelite) to transparent acrylic (perspex) and from flexible polythene to inflammable cellulose nitrate (celluloid).

CHEMISTRY OF PLASTICS

Proteins, polysaccharides and plastics are called *polymers*. They have large molecules in the form of long chains made up of units repeated throughout the chain. The units are called *monomers*. A polymer is composed of repeated monomers:

Polymer = monomer + monomer + monomer

Polythene is a plastic polymer of 1 000–20 000 ethene (ethylene) (C_2H_4) molecules joined together. The monomer is ethene (ethylene) and the final polymer is called polyethene (polyethylene).

Poly means many and *mono* means one, and therefore polyethene (polyethylene) is composed of many linked ethene (ethylene) monomers.

The formula for ethene (ethylene) is $H_2C=CH_2$, indicating the presence of a double and therefore unsaturated bond (see pages 105 and 114). Such unsaturated compounds can link up with similar molecules and form saturated chains:

$$CH_2=CH_2 + CH_2=CH_2 + CH_2=CH_2$$
ethene (ethylene) + ethene (ethylene) + ethene (ethylene)

$$-CH_2-CH_2-CH_2-CH_2-CH_2-CH_2-$$

polythene (polyethylene)
polymer

The process of forming a polymer from monomers is called *polymerization*.

Plastic monomers. Many different substances are used as the monomer for synthetic resin or plastic manufacture. The table lists some in common use.

USES OF IMPORTANT MONOMERS

Monomer	Polymer of plastic and trade name
Ethene (ethylene) (C_2H_4)	Polyethylene of polythene. Alkathene, Telcothene
Chloroethene (vinyl chloride) (CH_2CHCl)	Polychloroethene, Polyvinylchloride P.V.C. Corvic, Welvic, and Vynide
Phenylethene (styrene) ($C_6H_5CH_2CH$)	Polystyrene. Polyphenylethene
Propene (propylene) (CH_3CH_2CH)	Polypropylene. Propathene
Tetrafluorethene (CF_2CF_2)	Polytetrafluorethene P.T.F.E. Fluon
Methyl methylpropenoate (methyl methacrylate) ($CH_2C(CH_3)COOCH_3$)	Polymethacrylate. Perspex. Polymethyl methylpropenoate
Hexamethylene hexanamide (hexamethylene-adipamide)	Polyhexamethylene adipamide. Polyhexamethylene hexanamide. Nylon 66
Methyl pentene	Polymethylpentene, TPX

CLASSIFICATION OF PLASTICS

Plastics are divided into two main groups, *thermoplastic* and *thermosetting* resins.

1. THERMOPLASTIC RESINS

These resins soften when heated to become more or less liquid and harden on cooling. They can be reshaped by the repeated application of heat. Many thermoplastic resins are *soluble* in acetone, alcohol, benzene, carbon tetrachloride, nail varnish, turpentine, and petrol. Acids and alkalis have little effect on them. The table summarizes the more important thermoplastic resins, their method of manufacture, and uses.

USE OF IMPORTANT THERMOPLASTIC RESINS

Thermoplastic resin	Chemical name	Uses	Affected by
Polypropylene	Polypropene	Washing machine and refrigerator cabinets, water closet cisterns	Hot solvents but resistant to most chemicals. Abrasives and bleach not to be applied
Polyethylene	Polythene (high and low density)	Buckets, basins, cups, bins, bowls, and containers for washing up liquids, etc.	Warm solvents such as petrol, and benzene. No abrasives to be used. Protect from direct heat. Melts at 110°–115°C
Styrene	Polyphenylethene	Wall tiles, trays, dishes, and refrigerator linings	Propanone (acetone), turpentine, tetrachloromethane (carbon tetrachloride), paraffin, petrol, and essences. Softens at 80°–100°C
Cellulose ethanoate (acetate)	Cellulose ethanoate (acetate) made from cellulose and acetic acid	Photographic film, cellulose paints	Boiling water, nail polish, propanone (acetone), strong acid, alkalis, hydrogen peroxide, and esters
Celluloid	Cellulose nitrate	Toys	Highly inflammable. Propanone (acetone), acid, and alkalis
Nylon 66	Polymerized hexamethylene hexanamide	Fibre materials for stockings, carpets, etc. Packing foods, brushes and pan scourers	Strong acids and hydrogen peroxide. No abrasive cleaners should be used. Softens at 210°–250°C
Acrylic	Polymerized methyl methylpropenoate	Lamp shades, baths and kitchen sinks, roof lighting, and trays	Propanone (acetone), ethanol (alcohol), perfumes, benzene, tetrachloromethane (carbon tetrachloride), nail varnish, and turpentine. Abrasives damage. Softens at 100°C
Polychloroethene	Polychloroethene	Floor tiles, curtains, upholstery, rainwear, garden pools, and hoses. Wiring insulation	Propanone (acetone), benzene esters, essences, nail varnish, and chlorate (I) bleach. Softens at 80°C. Do not use abrasives
P.T.F.E.	Polytetrafluorethene	Non-stick lining for pans	Cannot withstand direct heat, i.e. decomposes at 400°C. Resistant to chemicals
Plastic foams	Polyurethane	Sponges, paddings, and stiffeners for clothing, cushion fillings, carpet underlays, and furniture	Propanone (acetone), benzene, tetrachloromethane (carbon tetrachloride)

2. *THERMOSETTING RESINS*

These are resins which cannot be reshaped or remoulded by heating. Heating causes them to char and blister. Most are unaffected by solvents but *are* attacked by acids and alkalis. They are mostly brittle. The table summarizes their more important properties and uses.

USES OF IMPORTANT THERMOSETTING RESINS

Resins	Chemical composition	Uses	Affected by
Casein	Casein from milk protein	Brush and cutlery handles, buttons	Strong acids and alkalis. Not harmed by household chemicals and solvents
Melamine, *Formica*, *Warerite*	Melamine methanal (formaldehyde)	Switch covers, plugs, sockets, cups, plates, saucers and working surfaces for tables	Strong acids and alkalis. No abrasives to be used. Not harmed by household chemicals and solvents
Phenolic, *Bakelite*	Phenol methanal (formaldehyde)	Telephone, radio and television cabinets, and toilet seats. Electrical switches and accessories. Not suitable for food containers because of their phenolic odour	Strong acids and alkalis. No abrasives to be used. Unaffected by household chemicals
Carbamide (urea)	Carbamide-methanal (urea formaldehyde)	Brighter colours than phenolics. Electrical equipment, buttons, and food containers	Strong acids and alkalis. No abrasives to be used. Unaffected by household detergents and solvents

Experiments
A scheme for identifying common plastics

1. To distinguish between thermoplastic and thermosetting plastics:

Attempt to pare off a sliver of plastic from the sample using a sharp knife. Thermoplastic resins produce a *continuous slice* whereas thermosetting resins yield only *powdery chips*. Heat an iron nail and apply it to the plastic; thermoplastic resins melt while thermosetting resins char and blister.

2. Identification of thermosetting resins:

Hold a lighted match to a small piece of the plastic and smell the vapour produced. *CARE*: Do not inhale excessively as some of the vapours are harmful or toxic in large amounts.

(*a*) A smell of phenol indicates a phenolic resin such as Bakelite.

(*b*) A smell of fish or methanal (formaldehyde) from white or coloured resins indicates either urea or melamine methanal (formaldehyde) resins.

3. Identification of thermoplastic resins:

(*a*) Drop the plastic on a hard surface. If it makes a loud

metallic noise it is most likely *polyphenylethene* (*polystyrene*). If the noise is dull apply the following test:

(*b*) Place the plastic in soapy water and observe whether it floats or sinks.

Plastic floats	Plastic sinks
Attempt to scratch the plastic with the fingernails: 1. *Polyethene* (*polythene*) will scratch fairly easily* 2. *Polypropene* (*polypropylene*) does not scratch	Set a piece of the plastic alight and note the colour of the flame: 1. Clear flame when extinguished gives a vapour smelling like *ethanol* (*methylated spirits*), it comes from *methyl-methylpropanoate* (*methyl-methacrylate*) or Acrylics. A smell resembling burning paper and ethanoic acid is produced by *cellulose acetate* 2. A flame with a greenish tinge is produced from *polychloroethene* (*polyvinyl-chloride*) (P.V.C.) 3. A yellow flame when extinguished producing a vapour smelling of burning hair is formed by *Nylon 66*

*Low density or conventional polythene floats, whilst high density rigid polythene sinks.

Action of solvents, acids, and alkalis on resins

Place samples of different plastics in test tubes containing small amounts of acetone, carbon tetrachloride, 10 per cent sodium hydroxide, dilute hydrochloric acid, and water. Set aside for a week and observe any changes that occur.

PLASTICS IN FOOD PACKAGING

Apart from paper, glass, and metal used in food packaging, increasing amounts of plastic *film* find use in displacing traditional materials.

Low density polyethene (*polythene*) is used for shrink wrapping of many foods. It has a fairly low permeability to water vapour, but shows some permeability to oxygen and carbon dioxide. It has wide use for polythene bags and for rigid snap-on containers for refrigerated ice-cream.

Polychloroethene (*polyvinyl chloride*) *and polypropene* (*polypropylene*) are used for wrapping cheese, sliced meat, and bacon which are inert gas sealed or vacuum sealed. These plastic films show a very low permeability to oxygen, carbon dioxide and water vapour.

Polypropene (polypropylene) finds extensive use for bottles as wine and fruit juice containers.

Polyvinylidene chloride is frequently a copolymer with polyvinylchloride and acrylic plastics to produce films which are gasproof, and waterproof, making them suitable for packaging dry crispy food such as biscuits, and potato crips which are inert gas packed or vacuum packed.

Polymethylpentene or TPX is a hard plastic suitable for packaging foods which are to be reheated in the pack and can stand temperatures up to 220°C, which other plastics such as polythene, and polypropylene are unable to tolerate without melting.

Polymerized hexamethylene hexanamide, Nylon-6-(*polyamide*) is a fairly gasproof film, but shows a high permeability to water vapour.

Cellulose films show a high permeability to water vapour.

Laminate plastic films are composed from more than one layer of different plastics in order to benefit from strength, clarity, or such a property as gas permeability.

Sterilizable pouches are food containers made from aluminium foil with an outer polyester plastic coat (see page 150) and inner polyethylene lining, which can be sterilized in an autoclave at a high temperature.

PAINTING MATERIALS

Painting or surface-coating materials can be sub-divided into:

(*a*) *obliterating* surface coatings including water, oil, enamel, gloss, emulsion paints, and distemper;

(*b*) *transparent* surface coatings such as polishes, varnishes, and lacquers.

Composition of obliterating surface coatings

Water, oil, enamel, gloss, emulsion, primer, and undercoat paints have three main components:

(*a*) *Pigments* providing colour, bulk, and the means of obliteration.

(*b*) *Vehicle*, the liquid portion in which the pigment is dispersed; it is composed of (i) the binder or non-volatile portion, and (ii) thinners, the volatile portion.

(*c*) *Driers*, being the agents which speed the drying process. *Pigments* are the solid particles in a paint and are present either as an *emulsion* as in emulsion water-thinned paints or as a *suspension* as in oil paints. The table indicates the range of substances used as paint pigments.

PAINT PIGMENTS

Pigment	Surface coating preparation
Powdered calcium carbonate ($CaCO_3$)	Water paints, distempers, and cheap oil paints
Red iron(III) oxides	Water and oil paints
Insoluble coal tar dyes	Water and oil paints
Red lead (Pb_3O_4) dilead(II) lead(IV) oxide	Red lead primer paint
China clay	Distempers and cheap oil paint
Powdered metals: aluminium, bronze, lead or zinc	Metal primers and decorative paints
Plastics: polyvinyl acetate, butadiene or polyphenylethene (polystyrene)	Emulsion paints

Vehicle or liquid portion of paints. The *binder* is mainly such an oil as linseed, tung or a fish oil which is non-volatile and oxidizes in air to form oxidized oils or *oxyns*.

$$\text{Oil} + \text{oxygen} = \text{oxyns}$$

The oxyns then *polymerize* to form oil polymers which bind the pigment particles together and form a hard skin:

$$\text{Oxyn} + \text{oxyn} = \text{polymerized oil}$$

Distempers and water paints usually have glue size, gelatine or gums as binder. Many paints have as binders such synthetic plastic resins as polyurethane, carbamide (urea), phenolic, melamine, polyphenylethene (polystyrene), and vinyl resins.

Solvents, or thinners, form the volatile component and also alter the body or viscosity of the paint. Water is the solvent for emulsion paints, while turpentine, white spirit or mineral oils, and methyl butyl ethanoate (amyl acetate) or methyl propyl ethanoate (butyl acetate) are used for oil and cellulose paints respectively.

Driers are salts of lead, manganese, or cobalt used in oil paints to speed up the oxidation of the oil binder.

Oil paint drying is basically a three-stage process, involving:

(*a*) *The evaporation* of the volatile solvent or thinners:

(*b*) *Oxidation* of the non-volatile binder oil, for example converting linseed to oxyns; and

(*c*) *Polymerization* of the oxyns to produce the skin. Beneath the apparently dry skin is a layer of liquid paint slowly hardening by the polymerization process.

Effect of environment on paints

Paints are liable to be affected by a number of environmental conditions, the main factors affecting surface coatings being summarized in the table.

ENVIRONMENTAL EFFECTS ON PAINTS

Factor	Effects
Alkalis such as strong sodium hydroxide and sodium carbonate	Can form soaps with the oil binder causing the paint to blister and wash away. A dilute solution cleans paint, while a more concentrated solution strips it
Acids present in industrial and town air such as carbonic H_2CO_3 and sulphurous H_2SO_3	Main cause of disintegration of exterior painted surfaces
Hydrogen sulphide (H_2S) gas produced by cooking	Causes darkening and discoloration of lead paints. Lead paints are poisonous
Humidity and rain	Painting on damp surfaces produces blistering. Rain weathers paint surfaces
Temperature changes	Heat causes the paint film to expand; cold induces contraction and cracking. High temperatures discolour a paint and cause blistering. An aluminium paint is best for metal surfaces subject to heat
Pinewood resins or knots in wood	Knots in pinewood produce turpentine which dissolves oil paint. Knots should be sealed with aluminium paint or lacquer prior to painting
Moulds	Moulds will grow in damp, humid, warm conditions causing discoloration of paints and emulsions

Lead in paints

Lead paints can cause poisoning if foods are contaminated or if the paint is ingested by children from toys and furniture. The use of such paints in the home or kitchen is to be discouraged.

COMPOSITION OF TRANSPARENT SURFACE COATINGS

French polishes, lacquers, and varnishes consist of (a) resins, and (b) suitable solvents.

(a) *Resins*. Copals and shellac are the main natural resins used for French polish and varnish manufacture. Synthetic resins or plastics are used for clear lacquer finishes for wood on floors, table tops, and furniture. The chief ingredients are epoxy and polyurethane resins intended to polymerize by the addition of a reagent called an *activator*. These coatings are extremely hard, being suitable for floors. Cellulose ethanoate (acetate) is an important resin for producing cellulose paints and lacquers.

(b) *Solvent*. The solvent normally used for French polish and varnish is ethanol (methylated spirits), methyl propyl ethanoate (butyl acetate) or methyl butyl ethanoate (amyl acetates) and propanone (acetone) are employed for clear lacquers and cellulose paints. The drying process for varnish, polish, and lacquer is essentially a rapid evaporation of the solvent and deposition of the resin surface coating. Good ventilation is advisable; naked lights should be avoided since the solvents are flammable.

Experiment

To show the effect of different reagents on painted surfaces:

Obtain samples of materials painted with oil paint, emulsion paint, varnish and cellulose paint. Immerse them in 10 per cent sodium hydroxide, 10 per cent sodium carbonate, trichloroethene, propanone (acetone), methyl butyl ethanoate (amyl acetate), ethanol (methylated spirits), and turpentine. Note the effect of each reagent, recording results in tabular form.

Painting new untreated surfaces

For coating wood, metal, or absorbent plaster surfaces it is essential to apply a primer surface which clings strongly. Adhesion is by chemical and physical means.

Iron and steel surfaces should be treated with primer paints containing red lead or zinc chromate. Wood is best primed with paints containing white lead, while resinous pinewood should be sealed with aluminium paint. Absorbent plaster brick should be treated with a dilute emulsion paint. Oil paints will form soaps if applied to plaster surfaces containing plentiful alkali. The primer is followed by an undercoat which obliterates and adheres to it, forming a foundation for the gloss enamel paint.

SUGGESTIONS FOR PRACTICAL WORK

See *Experimental Science for Catering and Homecraft Students*, Practical work 80, 81, 82, 84, 85 and 86.

QUESTIONS ON CHAPTER 20

1. Name three metals found in the kitchen or home. Describe how each is protected from corrosion. State what substances would corrode them.

2. Give a list of the metals used in the production of cooking utensils. Describe the effect of three of the metals on cooked food.

3. Describe experiments you have performed to show the effects of ethanoic acid (vinegar), sodium carbonate, and water on copper, tin, aluminium, and zinc.

4. Give a short account of the chemical composition and uses of: (a) metal polish; (b) furniture polish; and (c) French polish.

5. Give two examples of thermoplastic and thermosetting resins and give applications of their use in the home.

6. Write short notes on the composition and use of these resins: (a) polyethene; (b) phenol methanal (formaldehyde); (c) polymethyl methyl propanoate; (d) polychloroethene and (e) polytetrafluoroethene.

7. Name four synthetic resins and state what household reagents and conditions will affect them.

8. What household substances affect oil paints? Give an account of methods used for cleansing paintwork and lacquered articles.

9. What substances can remove or damage: (a) oil paint; (b) shellac varnish; and (c) cellulose ethanoate (acetate) paint?

10. State the effect of the following spilt liquids on the named surfaces: (a) perfume on French polished wood; (b) nail varnish on a cellulose sprayed table top; (c) whisky on a varnished table top; (d) spilt nail varnish on vinyl floor tiles; and (e) sodium carbonate solution on painted wood.

11. Give a brief account of the use of plastics in food packaging.

MULTIPLE CHOICE QUESTIONS ON CHAPTER 20

1. Plated steel is usually coated with:
   (a) lead   (c) aluminium
   (b) copper   (d) tin
2. One of the following is plated with silver:
   (a) chromium   (c) aluminium
   (b) zinc   (d) nickel
3. The component of air mainly responsible for rusting of iron is:
   (a) carbon dioxide   (c) oxygen
   (b) nitrogen   (d) helium
4. One of the following can give iron a non-stick coating:
   (a) polythene   (c) polyvinyl chloride
   (b) polytetrafluorethane (d) vitreous enamel
5. Plastics or synthetic resins are composed of large molecules called:
   (a) polymers   (c) isomers
   (b) monomers   (d) polyhedrons
6. Which of the following resins is synthetic?
   (a) acrylic   (c) rubber
   (b) shellac   (d) amber

7. Which is a thermoplastic resin?
   (a) phenol-formaldehyde (methanal);
   (b) melamine-formaldehyde
   (c) polypropylene
   (d) urea (carbamide)-formaldehyde

8. Emulsion paints can be thinned with:
   (a) turpentine   (c) linseed oil
   (b) water   (d) white spirit

9. The pigment in an oil based paint is present as the:
   (a) suspension   (c) solution
   (b) emulsion   (d) foam

10. When a gloss paint dries the thinners component will:
    (a) crystallize   (c) evaporate
    (b) gel   (d) sublimate

21 Textiles, wood, and ceramics

TEXTILES

Clothing, bedding, carpets and soft furnishings are made from either *natural*, *regenerated* or *man-made* fibres.

A fibre is a solid material with a length much greater than its width, and may also show varying degrees of fineness. Most fibres are flexible and elastic, being able to recover their original shape provided they are not overstretched.

Types of fibres

Natural fibres include those from plants and animals, and to a lesser extent from minerals, e.g. asbestos and glass.

Man-made fibres include those which are *regenerated* from either plant or animal materials, or those made from synthetic plastics or synthetic resins. In both cases the fibres are *spun* by special spinning processes.

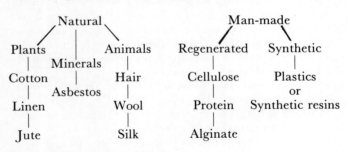

Chemical structure of fibres

Most textile fibres are chemically composed of very large *molecules*, made up of repeating units joined together in *polymers*, these have already been described with reference to polysaccharides (page 107), proteins (page 122), and plastics (page 139). The unit forming the polymer is called a *monomer*, and are made to join together by the chemical change called *polymerization*.

$$\text{Monomers} \xrightarrow{\text{polymerization}} \text{Polymers}$$

The molecules of polymers resemble long chains which in many cases are coiled like a spring to provide certain elastic properties to the fibre. Textile fibres may be classified according to their chemical composition and method of manufacture into three main groups, *protein*, *cellulosic*, and *plastics* or synthetic resins.

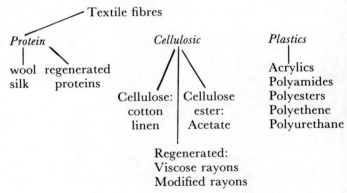

IMPORTANT PROPERTIES OF FIBRES

Different textile fibres show different *physical* properties which give them individual advantages for their use in clothing, bedding, carpets and furnishing. Frequently different fibres are *blended* together in order to gain more than one advantage from the fibres.

Strength of fibres is considered as the force required to break or snap a fibre, it also includes its *resilience* to stretching and bending, and its resistance to wear or *abrasion*. Many fibres lose strength when wet, calling for care in washing.

Water absorbency, some natural and regenerated fibres show considerable ability in absorbing water or are very hygroscopic (see page 43). The water enters the *interior* of the fibre, this water absorption must not be confused with *capillarity* when water rises *between* fibres as in paper tissues, or towels. Many man-made fibres of plastics are almost nonhygroscopic and are unable to absorb water, these will exhibit rapid drying ability after the wash.

Bulk is the result of wavy or crimped fibres which interlock air in the spaces between the fibres, giving a feeling of softness, lightness, and warmth. Many man-made fibres are crimped in the manufacture process. *Heat* in washing, drying and ironing, can affect the fibre by causing it to melt, or form creases, this calls for care when ironing the material and attention to ironing temperatures.

Chemicals present in washing powders, soaps, bleaches, and dry cleaning solvents have variable effects on the different fibres. Similarly chemical dyes may be taken up with difficulty or ease by different textile fibres, also they may remain attached to the fibre with varying degrees of fastness.

SUMMARY OF THE CLASSIFICATION OF TEXTILE FIBRES

Fibre	Chemical name and brand name
Protein	Keratin; wool, hair, angora, alpaca, cashmere Fibroin; silk
Regenerated protein	Soya protein glycinin; textured protein Milk casein; *Fibrolane*
Cellulose	Cotton, linen, kapok, jute, and sisal
Regenerated cellulose	Viscose and modified *rayons*
Acrylic	Polymers of acrylo nitrile – *Acrilan, Orlon, Courtelle*
Chlorofibre	Polymers of chloroethene (vinyl chloride) – *Saran, Cleryl* or vinylidene chloride
Glass	*Fibreglass*
Metallic	Aluminium metal coated with plastics – *Lurex* and *Rexor*
Modacrylic	Modified form acrylic treated with chloroethene (vinyl chloride) – *Dynel, Teklan*
Polyamides	Polymers of amides such as hexamethylene hexanamide (adipamide), or caprolactam – *Celon, Brinylon, Enkalon, Blue C, Perlon*
Polyester	Polymers of ethylene glycol terephthalate ester – *Dacron, Terylene*
Polypropylene	Polymers of propene (propylene) – *Ulstron, Meraklon*
Polythene	Polymers of ethene (ethylene) – *Courlene*
Polyurethene	Polymers of compounds similar to ethyl carbamate-urethane – Elastomeric or highly elastic – *Lycra, Spanzelle*

Moths and moulds are most likely to damage those fibres providing a source of food such as cellulose or protein, in contrast to the inedible synthetic resins which are mainly resistant to moth and moulds.

Fibre spinning

Plants produce fibres mainly in their stems as in linen, or in the fruit after flowering as in cotton; animals produce fibres as outgrowths of the skin in wool and hair. Silk is produced by forcing liquid protein silk through two tiny holes in the silk gland *spinneret* which forms a *continuous* filament of a compound silk thread. Man-made and regenerated fibres are produced in ways resembling the silk glands of spiders and silkworms.

Melt spinning involves the forcing of melted polymer material through spinnerets composed of many tiny holes in a nozzle; the fibre filaments solidify on emerging after cooling.

Wet spinning requires the fibre material to be dissolved in a solvent and the solution passed through the spinnerets into a warm atmosphere which evaporates the solvent forming the solid fibre filament. Alternatively the raw material is dissolved in *alkali* and spun into an *acid* bath.

Fibre length may vary from *continuous* filaments of immense length, such as fine nylon filament in fishing reels, or as *staple* fibres which are short and vary between 1 and 20 cm, such as found in cotton, wool, and hair. Man-made fibres can be produced as continuous filament or staple filament of lengths depending on the final purpose of the fibre.

Yarns

Yarns are fibres or filaments spun together by pulling and twisting them into threads for making fabrics.

(a) Continuous filament yarns are made as a *single* monofilament or as a continuous *multifilament* yarn twisting several fine filaments together in the production process. Natural silk is an example of a continuous filament yarn. This type of yarn finds use in making satin and taffeta fabrics.

(b) Spun or Staple Yarn are produced by *combing* man-made or natural staple fibres arranging them so they point in the same direction. The combed fibres are of similar length and are then drawn and spun into continuous lengths of spun or staple yarn. The staple length affects the yarn quality, for example *short* staple wool is spun into a yarn which is fluffy and hairy, loose and bulky, in contrast to the longer staple wool which spins into a *worsted* wool yarn with a finer, smoother appearance.

Man-made Nylons, and Rayon may be spun into either continuous filament yarns or staple yarns.

Two or more yarns can be twisted together producing 2, 3, and 4 ply or *multiple* yarns used mainly in knitted fabrics.

Textured yarns are either *bulked* or *stretch* yarns. Bulked yarns are made from most man-made fibres to produce a yarn suitable for making into soft, warm fabrics.

Stretch yarns made from man-made fibres produce fabrics which are both stretchable and also soft and warm.

Fabrics

Fabrics are produced from the yarns by either *knitting* or *weaving*. Woven fibres having a *weft* of crosswise threads, and a *warp* of lengthwise threads.

Fabrics can be made from one component fibre or from blends of mixed fibres. Certain fibres can be used in the warp of a fabric whilst another fibre is used in the weft, for example a fabric can be woven with rayon in the warp and cotton in the weft.

PROTEIN FIBRES

Wool

Sheep wool, soft human hair, mohair, camel, cashmere and rabbit fibres have a closely similar fibre structure as they are outgrowths from the skin hair follicle, and are usually coated with a greasy water repelling substance, called *lanolin* in sheep wool.

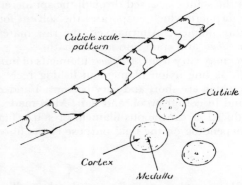

Figure 21.1. Wool fibre – longitudinal view and cross section

Fibre structure

Wool fibres vary in length up to 30 cm, depending on the breed of sheep. The fibre is cylindrical with a scaly surface *cuticle*, with the scales overlapping each other like the tiles on a roof. Felting of wool is partly due to the interlocking of adjacent fibres by means of the cuticle scales. Beneath the cuticle is the *cortex* layer of cells which have a spindle shape, inside these cells the natural colour pigment or the dyes are locked in. Coarse wool fibres of black face mountain sheep have a central *medulla* and are used for carpet manufacture. Softer and finer knitting wools are without this central medulla and such nonmedullated wool fibres are from Suffolk and Merino sheep.

Composition and properties

Wool and most other animal fibres are composed of the protein *keratin*. This is a large polymer molecule of amino acid units, arranged in the form of a closely coiled spring accounting for the elasticity of the wool fibre and its ability to stretch up to one third of its original length.

Strength of wool is not equal to that of one of the strongest fibres, cotton, with which the strength of most fibres can be simply compared.

Water absorbency of wool and keratin fibres is very high in being able to absorb up to one third of their dry weight in water which enters the cortex of the fibre. Wet wool loses its strength and stretches easily to almost twice its length, consequently care is needed in washing woollen fabrics.

Heat causes wool to char and scorch, whilst at higher temperatures it smoulders and burns producing a smell similar to burnt feathers and leaving an ash residue resembling a blackened ball.

Moist heat is used in pressing woollen woven fabrics, permanent set pleats are introduced by steam pressing. Chemicals can be used to permanently pleat wool woven fabrics in a similar way to permanently waving hair with *ammonium thiolethanoate* (*thioglycollate*).

Silk

Silk is spun as the continuous compound thread of approximately 1 200 m long, through the spinnerets of the cultivated silkworm. The cocoon is unwound in a hot solution of soap which dissolves the *sericin* gum layer.

Fibre structure

Silk fibres have a fairly smooth surface and appear triangular in cross section.

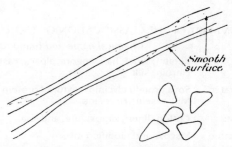

Figure 21.2. Silk fibre – longitudinal view and cross section

Composition and properties

Silk is mainly composed of the protein *fibroin*. This is a very strong, inelastic fibre whose strength is equal to that of cotton.

Water absorbency of silk is good as shown by its ability to take up 10 per cent of its dry weight of water. Heat causes the scorching and charring of silk. It burns with a smell resembling that of burning feathers, the remaining ash from pure silk resembles a black ball, whilst 'weighted' silk leaves a white ash skeleton of the fibre or fabric.

Regenerated protein

Details of the production of textured regenerated *food* protein have already been given on page 125. The regenerated *textile* of importance is produced by dissolving *casein* protein from milk in alkali and spinning the fibre into an acid bath through spinnerets. The regenerated fibre is hardened by treatment with methanal (formaldehyde). The brand name for this fibre is *Fibrolane* which is similar to wool in being a soft, resilient, warm fibre often blended with wool or cotton in lower priced carpets.

CELLULOSIC FIBRES

Cotton

Cotton is produced from the seed hairs found in the fruit or 'boll' of a cotton plant. The cotton fibres are separated from the seed by a process called 'ginning' to produce cotton lint with a fibre length between 1 and 3 cm which are carded, and spun into cotton staple yarn.

Fibre structure

A cotton fibre resembles a twisted ribbon similar to a twisted barley sugar stick. The fibres have a tubular structure with a hollow interior lumen; as the fibre dries out it develops the twisted structure.

Short cotton fibres or 'fuzz' unsuitable for spinning into cotton yarn are used for rayon manufacture as cotton *linters*.

Composition and properties

Cotton is a giant polysaccharide molecule composed of over 2 000 glucose monomer units joined end to end in long chains. Cotton shows remarkable strength and is known for its tough wearing quality, apart from the delicate cotton lace materials.

Water readily enters the cotton fibre which acquires a greater strength due to the swelling of the fibre lumen, than the strength shown by the dry fibre.

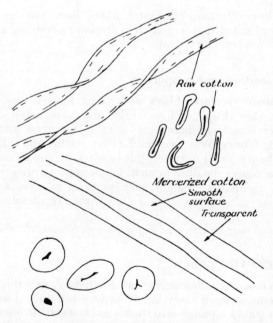

Figure 21.3. Raw and mercerized cottons – longitudinal and sectional views

Heat causes the cotton fibres to lose water at 160°C and become scorched at 250°C. They then burn with a yellowish white flame producing a soft grey ash and a smell similar to that produced by burning paper.

Cotton withstands boiling and can be ironed with a hot iron, whilst chemicals present in most washing powders have no harmful effect on the fibre.

Mercerized cotton has an attractive silky appearance produced by immersing cotton yarn in 10 per cent sodium hydroxide solution, which causes the swelling of the cotton fibre.

LINEN

Linen fibres are produced from the *stems* of flax plants and originate from the part of the stem consisting of fibre cells which protect the soft cells of the *bast* in the vascular bundle (see Figure 21.10). These fibre cells are removed from the stem by a process of softening the flax stems in water, called *retting*, the retted fibres are then *scutched* to separate the line fibres into three grades (*a*) finest or line with very long strands; (*b*) short or variable strands called machine *tow*; (*c*) low grade coarse or short strands. Each of these three grades of fibres are spun into linen yarn.

Fibre structure

A linen fibre shows a resemblance to bamboo canes with *nodes* at intervals along the fibre length which can be up to 3 cm. Each fibre shows an angular cross sectional appearance.

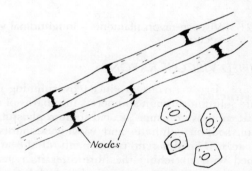

Figure 21.4. Linen fibres – longitudinal view and cross section

Composition and properties

Linen is mainly composed of cellulose, and other components, hemi-cellulose, pectin, and wooded fibre lignin. The tensile strength of linen is greater than that of cotton which partly explains the longlasting qualities of linen fabrics.

Linen shows closely similar properties to cotton in water absorbency, effect of heat, and chemicals in washing.

VISCOSE RAYON

Cellulose present in cotton linters, or in wood pulp, is prepared in a soluble form and then regenerated as insoluble cellulose rayon by spinning through spinnerets into an acid bath. The wood pulp is treated with sodium hydroxide and carbon disulphide forming soluble cellulose xanthate, this is spun into a bath of sulphuric acid to regenerate the filament of viscose rayon.

Fibre structure

Viscose rayon fibres appear as cylindrical fibres with longitudinal stripes. In cross section the fibre appears rectangular in shape with scalloped edges.

Composition and properties

Viscose rayon is pure cellulose.

It has a high water absorbency almost twice that shown by cotton and shows a strength equal to that of cotton.

Heat at high temperatures produces scorching and burning with a smell resembling burning paper, to leave a fine grey ash.

Brand names include *Fibro* and *Courtauld's Viscose Rayon*.

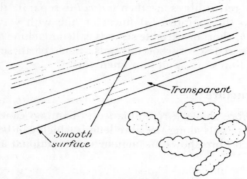

Figure 21.5. Viscose rayon filaments – longitudinal view and section

MODIFIED VISCOSE RAYON

These are viscose rayons produced by spinning cellulose xanthate solution through spinnerets into baths of different chemical composition such as acid sodium phosphate, zinc sulphate, sodium sulphate, and varying amounts of sulphuric acid. The different components of the acid bath combined with stretching the fibre after its regeneration produces the modified rayons typical of the following brand names:

Durafil, a very tough rayon used in blends for fabrics subject to very hard wear in upholstery, uniforms, or pocket linings.

Evlan, a hardwearing resilient rayon specially crimped for use in upholstery and carpets.

Sarille, a crimped rayon used for blankets, bedding, and clothing because of its soft, warm properties.

Vincel and Zaryl, very strong, shrink resistant used alone or in blends with cotton, wool, and man-made fibres for clothing fabrics.

CELLULOSE ESTERS

Cellulose of wood or cotton linters is made to combine with ethanoic (acetic) acid to form cellulose ethanoate (acetate) and cellulose triethanoate (triacetate), both of which are esters.

CELLULOSE ETHANOATE (ACETATE)

Also called ethanoate (acetate) is made by dissolving cellulose in ethanoic (acetic) acid and ethanoic (acetic) anhydride and converting the cellulose to cellulose ethanoate (acetate) by a process of ethanoylation (*acetylation*). The cellulose ethanoate (acetate) is dissolved in the solvent propanone (acetone) and the solution dry spun into hot air causing the propanone (acetone) to evaporate forming continuous filaments of cellulose ethanoate (acetate). The ethanoate (acetate) staple is made by cutting the thick spun rope into short staple lengths which are spun into cellulose ethanoate (acetate) staple yarn.

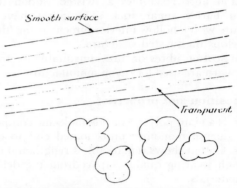

Figure 21.6. Cellulose acetate – longitudinal view and section

Fibre structure

Cellulose ethanoate (acetate) fibres have one to three longitudinal stripes with a cross section resembling a three or more lobed clover leaf.

Composition and properties

Ethanoate (acetate) fibres and yarns have a rich silky lustre, they drape well in fabrics and have a fair crease recovery, making them very suitable for dress and furnishing fabrics. Water enters the fibre readily and it has an absorbency equal to cotton but is not as strong as cotton.

Heat causes the fibre to melt, followed by burning with a smell resembling ethanoic acid (vinegar) to leave a black beadlike ash. Propanone (acetone) readily dissolves the fibre.

Brand names: *Albene, Celafibre, Dicel, Rhodia, Rhodiaceta*.

TRIACETATE

Also known as cellulose triethanoate (triacetate), this is the *fully* ethanoylated (acetylated) form of cellulose compared to the *partly* ethanoylated (acetylated) form in ethanoate (acetate), cellulose ethanoate (acetate).

Fibre structure resembles the ethanoate (acetate) fibre.

Composition and properties

Cellulose triethanoate (triacetate) has a lower water absorbency than acetate, which it closely resembles in its strength, attractive lustre, and crease resistance. It is a quick drying fabric.

Heat causes the fibre to melt, and advantage is taken of this in forming durable pleats in dress and suit materials.

Solvents such as tricholoroethene should not be used for dry cleaning the fabric.

Brand names: *Arnel*, *Rhonel*, and *Tricel*.

ACRYLIC

Acrylic fibres are polymers made from acrylonitrile which polymerizes into a giant long chain molecule, the polymer is dissolved in a solvent and spun through spinnerets into hot air to form a continuous *tow* of acrylic filament, which is cut up into short staple fibres.

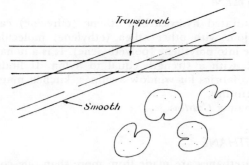

Figure 21.7. Acryclic fibre – longitudinal view and section

Fibre structure

The acrylic fibre *Acrilan* has a longitudinal stripe and appears kidney shaped in cross section. The acrylic fibre *Orlon* also has a longitudinal stripe but shows a dumbbell shape in cross section.

Properties

Acrylic fibres show little if any water absorbency and are consequently quick drying. The fibre has a very high wet and dry strength almost the same as cotton.

Heat causes the melting of this *thermoplastic* fibre and allows for permanent pleats to be heat set in the fabric. It is a warm, soft, and light fibre suitable for knitwear, either alone or with wool which it closely resembles, or with cotton in various clothing fabrics, and in carpets.

Brand names: *Acrilan*, *Courtelle*, and *Orlon*.

MODACRYLIC FIBRES

These are chemically modified acrylic fibres which contain at least 85 per cent acrylonitrile, and include other *copolymers* such as polyvinylidene chloride.

Properties

Similar in many respects to acrylic fibres but differing in

being a thermoplastic fibre which does not flare up and is consequently used in *flameproof* fabrics for clothing, upholstery, and curtains.

Brand names: *Dynel, Kanekalon, Acrilan,* and *Teklan*.

CHLOROFIBRE

This is made by the polymerization of chloroethene (vinyl chloride) to form the polychloroethane (polyvinyl chloride or PVC). Vinylidene chloride may also be polymerized to produce a similar chlorofibre.

Properties

This fibre is *nonabsorbent* and shows strength equal to cotton. It has a flameproof property similar to modacrylic fibres.

It is used in fabrics for upholstery, curtains, and can be made into blend with wool for rainwear.

Brand names: *Cleryl, Movyl* and *Saran*. Saran transparent film is used for shrink wrapping in food packaging.

GLASS

Glass is melted and spun into filaments of glass fibre.

Properties

Glass fibres are *nonabsorbent*, are very brittle and are liable to break readily on frequent abrasion. It is an excellent flame resistant fabric for curtains and for insulated attic roof spaces as a loose matted blanket. The harmful fibres readily penetrate the skin and a mask should be worn when handling the fibre glass blanket to prevent inhalation of tiny fibres.

Brand names: *Duraglass*, and *Fibreglass*.

POLYAMIDES

These are synthetic man-made fibres also called nylons. Nylon 6·6 is made from an alkaline chemical compound called hexamwthylene and an acid hexanedioc (adipic) acid, they combine together forming hexamethylene hexanamide (adipamide), this is polymerized into long chain molecules of Nylon 6·6.

Nylon 6 is a polymer of caprolactam, and is made from cyclohexanone and hydroxylamine.

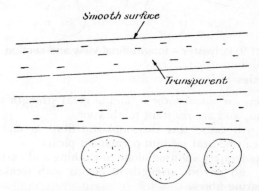

Figure 21.8. Polyamide fibres – longitudinal view and section

The molten nylon polymers is spun through spinnerets into a continuous filament or cut up into short staple filaments.

Fibre structure

Nylon fibres show a smooth cylindrical structure with a circular cross section.

Properties

Nylon fibres have a very *slight* water absorbing property which gives them a quick drying ability. The fibres of nylon are very strong, much stronger than cotton, and also have elastic properties. The fibres are hard wearing and resistant to abrasion. Both nylons have the ability to attact soil and dirt by electrostatic attraction (see page 46).

Heat will cause these thermoplastic resins to melt, and this is used in the heat setting of permanent pleats in nylon fabrics. Higher temperatures cause nylon fibres to melt, forming a hard round bead, the fibre does not burn readily.

Nylons are used alone or in blends with other fibres, for clothing, bedding, and carpets.

Brand names: Nylon 6·6 *Blue*, *Bri-nylon*; Nylon 6 *Celon*, *Enkalon*.

POLYESTER

Esters are made by reacting alcohols with acids, ethane-diol (ethylene glycol) is made to *esterify* with terephthalic acid, to form ethylene glycol terephthalate, this ester is then polymerized into the polyester material. Spinning of the polyester fibre is by the spinneret.

Fibre structure

Polyester fibres are transparent, cylindrical in shape with elongated surface pits.

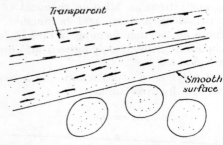

Figure 21.9. Polyester – longitudinal view and section

Properties

Polyesters are nonabsorbent, and of great strength similar to nylons, and are resistant to abrasion.

Heat will cause this thermoplastic fibre to melt, and fabrics can be heat set into permanent pleats.

The polyesters are used alone in clothing and curtaining fabrics, and provide strength to blends with weaker less hardwearing fibres.

Brand names: *Dacron*, *Terlenka*, *Terylene*, *Trevira*.

POLYPROPYLENE

The unsaturated hydrocarbon propene (propylene) is made to polymerize forming the polymer with other propene (propylene) molecules. The molten polymer is then spun into continuous filaments or cut up into short staple fibres.

Properties

Polypropene fibres are nonabsorbent and of much greater strength than nylon, and very resistant to abrasion. It finds application for kitchen floor covering, and woven material for garden furniture.

The low heat conductivity of the fibre make it warm to touch, and the soft spun fibre is used for knitted and woven blankets, and also in carpets.

Brand names: *Meraklon*, *Ulstron*.

POLYETHYLENE

The unsaturated hydrocarbon ethene (ethylene) can be made to join with other ethen (ethylene) molecules to polymerize into polythene (polyethylene). It is a nonabsorbent fibre, with a strength equal to nylon. It finds use woven into fabrics for window awnings, kitchen mats and garden furniture.

Brand name: *Courlene*.

POLYURETHANE

The polyurethanes are made from more than one component, and may include isocyanates and an alcohol compound that can be polymerized into these polymers with high elastic properties which gives them the name of *elastomeric* fibres.

Properties

Their remarkable elastic property exceeds that of wool and nylons, makes them components of surgical stockings, stretch swimwear, and foundation garments. The fibres are not affected by perspiration as natural rubber is, that tends to absorb perspiration products.

Brand names: *Lycra*, *Spanzelle*, and *Vyrene*.

FLAMMABILITY OF FABRICS

The following summarizes the effect of bringing a naked flame into close contact with different fabrics;

Not flammable	Wool and modacrylics
Flammable	Acrylics and cotton
Flame-resistant finish	*Darelle* – viscose rayon
Melt but do not catch fire	Nylons and polyesters

Flame-proofing of various fabrics can be achieved by treating the fabric with various chemicals such as ammonium chloride which will slow down the rate of burning of normally flammable fabrics.

FABRIC CONDITIONERS

When textile fibres rub against each other during wear or laundry, it causes them to acquire a negative charge of static electricity, this in turn attracts dust and dirt, as seen on collars and cuffs subjected to frequent rubbing.

The accumulation of the negative charge of electricity is more rapid in *dry* fabrics, and is rapidly lost when they are wetted. Consequently many man-made synthetic fibres with a low water absorbency, such as acrylics, nylons, and polyesters, will retain their acquired charges much longer than cotton, wool, and rayon.

Fabric conditioners provide a positively charged chemical compound which neutralizes the acquired charge and in addition serves to *lubricate* the individual fibres allowing them to move freely across each other in the fabric, without gaining electric charges.

Oily substances such as castor oil, olive oil, and soya bean oil have been used for this purpose, these have now been superseded by quaternary ammonium compounds (see pages 130 and 204) which, apart from neutralizing the acquired charge, also give the fibre a soft feeling or handle.

CARPETS

Carpets are amongst the more expensive textile products purchased for catering establishments and the home. The following account deals with the fibres used in carpets and the manufacture of carpets:

Fibres used in carpets

Acrylic, Acrilan, Courtelle, Orlon, are fibres which are fairly expensive, and have good wearing property in being resilient and in resisting flattening by traffic and heavy furniture. It is soft and warm like wool, but being nonabsorbent is easier to clean and shampoo and to mop up spilt liquids.

Modacrylic, Teklan is a nonflammable fibre suited to carpet making instead of acrylics, a point of consideration in fire precautions.

Polyamides include the nylons, *Bri-nylon, Celon, Enkalon,* and *Blue C.* They are expensive, but have hard wearing property due to their resistance to abrasion. They are resilient fibres and overcome furniture marks. They acquire dirt and soil easily, due to the electrostatic charge which accumulates in low humidity conditions.

The fibres melt but do not catch fire, whilst the very low water absorbency makes them easy to clean and mop up spilt liquids.

Polyester, Dacron and *Terylene* are also fairly expensive fibres, but are hardwearing, and resilient. They also share the dirt collecting property of most man-made fibres, but are easy to clean due to their low water absorbency.

Viscose Rayons, Fibro are modestly priced, but lack resilience, flatten easily, and are not hardwearing. Also they have a high water absorbency, will soak up spilt liquids, and are difficult to wash or clean. They are used in blends with wool to reduce the price of otherwise expensive yarns.

Modified Rayons, Darelle are faily good in wear, but have a high water absorbency. The important property is the flame resistant nature of *Darelle*.

Cotton is a cheap fibre which lacks resilience and flattens easily, but has a fairly good wearing property. Its high water absorbence causes it to soak up spilt liquids which are added to it in cleaning, unless they are small rugs which can be machinewashed.

Wool is amongst the expensive fibres, and is hard wearing, very resilient in resisting flattening, and soft and warm to touch. The water absorbing property, apart from helping to control the humidity of a room, makes it difficult to clean and will also tend to mop up spilt liquids.

Unfortunately wool carpets must be made mothproof.

Wool carpets are not flammable and burns are easily brushed away.

Fibre blends in carpets

Blending of two or more fibres in yarns results in obtaining certain beneficial physical properties that may result in a cheaper carpet.

Nylons are frequently blended with wool, as 80 per cent wool and 20 per cent nylons, other blends include 85 per cent modified viscose rayon with 15 per cent nylons; 42·5 per cent acrylics, 42·5 per cent modified viscose rayons, 15 per cent nylons; 50 per cent wool, 50 per cent acrylic; 85 per cent viscose rayon and 15 per cent nylons; 80 per cent polyesters and 20 per cent nylons.

Carpet construction

Carpets are made up of two main parts; the backing, and the pile. The backing is woven and composed of a warp usually of cotton, and a weft, of jute or man-made fibre.

Carpet pile, or its surface, is fixed into the backings as either *cut* or *loop*, this fixing may be done either in the *weaving* process or *stitched* in as tufts, or the tufts may be stuck in with an adhesive.

The *density* of the carpet pile is the number of tufts or loops in a square centimetre, the greater the pile density the better its wearing quality. The length of the pile in the tufts is another quality which adds to the wearing property.

Types of carpet

Broadly there are four main types of carpet; *Axminster* are those carpets in which the cut pile tufts enter the backing in the weaving process. Many colours can be used and the design is seen through into the backing.

Wilton carpets are also woven carpets in which the dense cut pile is fixed to the backing during weaving. They are generally plain carpets with up to five different colours in them.

Tufted carpets are made by stitching pile tufts into a previously made backing, and leaving the tufts as loops or cutting them. The pile may be fixed with a further backing and adhesive, and may have a polyurethane foam backing.

Cord carpets are similar to Wiltons except that the pile is uncut and remains as a loop pile tightly fixed into the backing.

WOOD

Soft stems of herbs and herbaceous plants have *vascular bundles* made up of *xylem* or wood cells, and *phloem* or bast cells (see pages 168 and 169) arranged in a circular manner amongst the soft cells of the *cortex* and *medulla*. The soft, thin-walled cells of the cortex and medulla are permeated with air spaces between the cells. These cells are called *parenchyma* cells and form the major part of leaves, stems and roots which are used as vegetable foods.

Cells which are thickened with *cellulose*, and which are strengthening tissues in stems, leaves and leaf stalks are called *collenchyma* cells. In the flax plant stems, the soft cells of the bast or phloem are prevented from being crushed by the *fibres* which are the main component of linen fibres (see also page 168).

Trees commence life as soft stemmed plants in their first year of growth resembling the stems of herbs. In subsequent years the stem becomes thickened and increases in girth. The increasing girth of a tree is due to the formation of rings of new xylem or wood cells, called *secondary xylem*. Similar growth of secondary phloem occurs, whilst the outer epidermis is replaced by the *bark* consisting mainly of *cork* cells.

Each year's growth of the tree is seen as an *annual ring* of secondary xylem, with radiating lines of *medullary rays*, contributing to the grain of the wood. The outer rings of secondary xylem carry sap, and are called the *sapwood*. The central *heartwood* of an old tree develops an attractive coloured appearance which makes it suitable for veneers such as figured walnut.

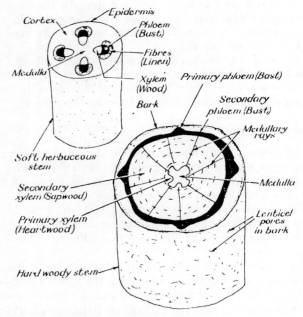

Figure 21.10. Structure of plant stems

Cork for bottles and floor coverings is the product of the bark of a tree called the Turkey Oak.

Knots seen in sawn wood are the side *branches* of the tree and are seen to occur at regular intervals in pine and similar resinous woods.

Softwood and hardwood

The major chemical component of wood is the complex substance called *lignin*.

Softwoods are produced by cone bearing trees, which have narrow needlelike leaves, and also a resinous wood (see page 117). This kind of wood is easier to saw and shape with tools. Examples of this wood include; Pine, Red Cedar, Douglas fir, Parana pine, and Western hemlock, all of which possess an attractive resinous smell produced from the resin glands. This resin is often seen exuding out of woods which have not been *sealed* before painting with shellac varnish applied to the knots.

Softwoods are mainly used in house building for wooden frames of roofs, windows and doors, also for floorboards and joists. (See Figure 3.1, page 17.)

Hardwoods are obtained from trees which have broad leaves, such as Oak, Walnut, Ash, Beech, Mahogany, Elm, and certain imported timbers such as African Afromosia, Iroko, Mahogany, Obeche, Sapele, and Teak.

These timbers have attractive colours and grain, and are mainly used in furniture, or as thin veneers on softwood, blockboard, or chipboard. As the name suggests, they are harder to cut and shape with tools, and are more hardwearing and suited for wood block and parquet floors. There are certain hardwoods which are softer than most softwoods to work.

Wood preservation

After felling, the trees are sawn and the timber dried in air and kilns to produce a timber with a water content of less than 16 per cent; higher concentration of water will lead to dry and wet rotting and attack by insects and beetles. Certain untreated woods contain natural preservatives mostly found in the heartwood. Sapwood below the bark attracts wood pests which feed on the foods present in the bast.

The following timbers have a high durability in very wet conditions; Western Red Cedar, Afromosia, Iroko, Obeche, and Teak. Most other timbers require some form of preservative using an *insecticide* or *fungicide*, varnish, or paint. This treatment is needed to prevent wet and dry rot, and attack by woodworm.

WOOD-BORING INSECTS

The most common cause of damage to timber by wood-boring insects is by the common furniture beetle – *Anobium punctatum*.

Life cycle

Flying furniture beetles land on the *softwood* timber surface and lay their *eggs* in cracks and crevices. The eggs take a month to hatch out into *larvae* or grubs which tunnel into the softwood, feeding on the poly-saccharides and making extensive tunnels throughout the wood for a period of up to three years.

The larva then enters a resting stage called the *pupa* and remains pupated for up to 2 months after which it changes into the winged insect or *imago* that leaves the wood by flying out of a tiny circular hole, called the *flight holes* which indicate that damage has *been* done to the wood and the insect has flown away. This emergence of the flying woodworm beetle occurs in May to August when it may be seen as a tiny brownish insect 3 to 6 mm long.

Infested wood will show the flight holes and piles of gritty powdery dust outside

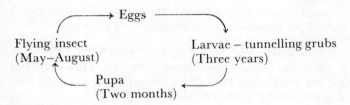

Methods of infestation

Woodworm beetles can fly into a house from sources outside, otherwise, infested wood and furniture may be brought into the house. Roof spaces may become infested by birds building nests with infested nesting material, or by storing infested furniture in the attic space.

Location of infestation

Woodworm flourish where they are least disturbed in roof space timbers, beneath floorboards, behind furniture, and in locations which may be damp near to sinks, washbasins, baths, lavatory pans, and window frames. They are also seen in wood which has the remains of bark clinging to it indicating the sapwood.

Treatment and prevention

Timbers should be kept dry, and sprayed with preservative or insecticide which poisons the feeding larvae or grub, such insecticides include *Cuprinol*, *Rentokil*, *Solignum*, and *Wykamol*.

Seriously infected timbers may need to be cut out and replaced with treated wood.

Other wood beetles

Powder post – *Lyctus* beetle attacks hardwood sapwood. Death watch beetle – *Xestobium* attacks fungus infested rotting hardwoods in very old buildings.

The House Longhorn beetle is found mainly in parts of Surrey.

DRY ROT

This is a serious infestation of wood by a fungus mould, called *Merulius lacrymans*.

Life cycle

Moulds develop from tiny *spores* easily carried by air currents, the spore germinates into a tiny threadlike *hypha*, that branches repeatedly to form a dense mat or *mycelium*. The hyphae of the mycelium penetrate into the wood by *rhizoids* which secrete enzymes and digest the wood cellulose.

Infected wood appears dry or parched and brittle, the fungus mycelium appear as a greyish white growth and produce a mushroomlike smell. The mycelium of dry rot can spread rapidly along wood, and behind plaster carrying its water supply along the hyphae.

Fruiting bodies which produce the spores, are produced periodically as either small brown coloured mushroom buttons, or fairly large pancakes with a white edge and rusty red centre.

Spores are then liberated and carried as a fine light dust to infect new wood. Poor ventilation will encourage the rapid spread of dry rot by the accumulation of damp, therefore spaces below floors should be well ventilated through wall ventilator bricks. (See Figure 3.1.)

Treatment

Prevention by keeping timber dry and air spaces well ventilated. Infected timber requires extensive special treatment, including the removal of infected wood and plaster, sterilization of exposed brickwork with gas torches, and the use of fungicide applied to new wood. In addition all causes of damp must be removed.

WET ROT

This is the infection of wet wood by a fungus mould called *Coniphora cerebella*.

Life cycle

The life cycle resembles that of dry rot in that a *spore* germinates into a *hypha* thread which rapidly branches into an extensive *mycelium*. Later the spore producing organs are formed which shed new spores.

Infected timber is covered with the greyish coloured threadlike growth which thrives on wet wood with at least 50 per cent water in it. The wood darkens and cracks, finally to crumble. The wood is continually wet on floors, and frames of doors and windows. (See Figure 3.1.)

Treatment

Essentially the removal of the cause of damp, followed by the removal of infected wood and replacement with fungicide treated new wood. The sterilization of the surrounding area with heat is not required. Advice should be obtained to identify the type of wood rot.

CONCRETE AND BRICKS

Portland cement is a substance made by baking a mixture of calcium carbonate (limestone), clay which is a complex mixture of aluminium oxides and silicates, and coal dust in cement furnaces. The product is ground up into a fine powder and acts chemically as a mixture of *calcium silicate* and *calcium aluminate*. When cement is mixed with water it forms a colloidal gel, of a liquid in a solid, this slowly loses water over a very long period of years and produces the very hard mass of set cement.

Concrete is a mixture of *cement*, water, and *aggregate*. This latter is a mixture of sand, stone, or gravel. The sand used in concrete is called sharp sand and is a more coarse form than that found on the seashore. Stone chippings or stone from 5 to 20 mm in size are used and washed to make them free from dirt.

Concrete mixtures

Two main kinds of concrete mixtures are used;
  (*a*) one with a high proportion of sand and gravel;

  cement 1;   sand $2\frac{1}{2}$;   gravel 4.

This is used for foundations to houses, bases of garages, and driveways.
  (*b*) This mixture has a greater proportion of cement;

  cement 1;   sand 2;   gravel 3.

This is a very strong concrete used for footpaths and for layers less than 7 cm thick (see Figure 3.1).

Bricks and blocks

These are the regular shaped stone or other solid material for building walls.

Bricks measure 337·5 mm long, 225 mm wide, and 112·5 mm high, they are made from either baked clay, concrete, or calcium silicate.

Clay bricks are a reddish colour and are used for general building work. Stronger, blue coloured bricks called engineering bricks are used to lay house foundations and to support damp proof courses because of their nonabsorbency of water, compared to the highly absorbent red brick.

Calcium silicate bricks are made from sand, calcium hydroxide, lime, and water, are available in different colours. Different kinds can be used for foundations, internal and external walls.

Concrete bricks are moulded from suitable concrete mixtures and are much less commonly found than the other types.

Blocks are made from various mixtures of concrete and usually made in a size which is three bricks high, and two bricks long. Blocks can be of dense concrete and are very strong and heavy, suitable for foundations. Less dense blocks which may incorporate air bubbles or use low density *clinker* aggregate, will provide blocks with good heat insulating properties.

Mortar

Bricks, blocks, and stone are fixed together by means of *mortar*. Three main kinds are available:

Lime mortar composed of calcium oxide or hydroxide, clean fine sand and water. This is an old type of mortar seldom used today.

Cement mortar composed of portland cement, fine sand and water, together with a plasticizer, allows air bubbles to be mixed into the mixture. This is most often used.

Cement and lime mortar are made from portland cement, lime or calcium oxide and hydroxide, sand and water.

GLASS

Silicon (Si) is a chemical element, found mainly as chemical compounds consisting of silicon dioxide SiO_2 found as sand, and quartz. Other chemical compounds of silicon are the *silicates* or salts of the *acidic* silicon dioxide found in clay and cement.

Acidic silicon dioxide SiO_2 will combine with alkalis such as sodium hydroxide to form *silicates*, for example

sodium hydroxide + silicon dioxide = sodium silicate + water.

Sand and clay are therefore very important raw materials for the production of building materials, bricks, concrete, cement, earthenware, porcelain and *glass*.

Glass is a mixture of various silicates in many different kinds of glass. Glass is made by heating mixtures of pure sand, silicon dioxide, sodium carbonate, and calcium oxide with scrap glass to help in the melting process in glass furnaces. The following are some of the main kinds of glass.

Window glass also called soda glass or soft glass, since it is easily marked with a glass cutter or diamond cutter, and melts easier than other glass, is made from sodium carbonate, sand, calcium oxide. Sheetglass may be either polished thick *plate* glass, or unpolished flawless *float* glass, used for sliding patio windows.

Hard glass or Bohemian glass is more difficult to melt and is used for cheap glassware and made using *potassium* carbonate instead of sodium carbonate.

Crystal glass or flint glass is the glass used for cut-glassware and is made from similar ingredients to window and hard glass but oxides of lead are added. This glass has the characteristic bell-like ring it produces when tapped.

Heat resistant glass. Pyrex glass is rich in *borates* or boron, to form boro-silicate glass, it can withstand sudden changes of temperature and is used for oven table ware.

Glass is considered to be a super-cooled liquid or a liquid that has not crystallized.

Water-glass is a viscous solution of sodium silicate, the chemical component of most glass, which is used in sealing the pores of egg shells in egg preservation.

CERAMICS

Pottery and porcelain used for tableware, cooking utensils, and sanitary ware such as water closets, bidets, kitchen sinks and wash basins, are materials closely resembling cement, bricks, and glass being chemically composed of *silicates*.

The raw materials for making pottery and porcelain include, *clay*, consisting of aluminium and silicon dioxide;

quartz which is mainly silicon dioxide, and *feldspar* sodium and potassium aluminium silicates.

Earthenware pottery is made from washed blue clay, which is a purer form of clay than that used in making bricks. The clay is baked in kilns when it loses water to form a hard, porous, and opaque solid mass. This type of clay is used for making the cheaper earthenware tableware and sanitary ware.

Stoneware is made from china clay kaolin, blue clay, chinastone, and powdered flint, this produces a nonporous, opaque stoneware used for cheaper tableware.

True porcelain is made by firing or baking a hard paste of 50 per cent china clay or kaolin, with 20 per cent quartz, and 30 per cent feldspar, after firing it produces a translucent, very hard, nonporous *biscuit* or unglazed porcelain.

English Bone China is made from a hybrid paste consisting of a similar mixture to true porcelain, but includes 30 to 50 per cent of calcium phosphate or bone ash, it is translucent, and nonporous.

Glazing is the important process of giving earthenware, porcelain and bone china a surface of *glass*. Lead salts are used to glaze fine earthenware used for tableware, whilst sodium chloride is used to salt glaze cheaper earthenware goods. Porcelain is dipped in a mixture of substances before baking on the glaze. During this heating process the glass forms on the earthenware or porcelain surface. Prior to glazing the pottery or porcelain may be *painted* with oxides of different metals which form different coloured glasses on with the glaze.

SUGGESTIONS FOR PRACTICAL WORK

See *Experimental Science for Catering and Homecraft Students*, Practical work 55 to 65 and 70 to 79.

QUESTIONS ON CHAPTER 21

1. Sketch the structure of a plant fibre and an animal fibre. Give two tests that would distinguish one from another.

2. Give an outline classification of textile fibres. Describe the production of one natural fibre and one man-made fibre.

3. Compare the water absorbency of natural fibres with that of man-made synthetic fibres.

4. Which physical properties are looked for in selecting a fibre for warm winter clothing?

5. What are the most suitable textile fibres for making (*a*) towels; (*b*) tea towels; (*c*) blankets; (*d*) bed sheets; and (*e*) tablecloths.

6. Write brief notes concerning the composition, physical properties and use of (*a*) acrylics; (*b*) polyamides; (*c*) viscose rayons.

7. State the main properties of (*a*) modacrylics; (*b*) modified rayons.

8. Give a brief summary of the most suitable fibres used in heavy domestic carpet manufacture.

9. Distinguish between cement, concrete, and mortar.

10. Describe the structure of a plant stem, indicate the origin of linen fibres and describe how wool is formed.

11. Distinguish between a softwood and hardwood. What methods of preservation are used for timbers?

12. Name some pests that can attack house timbers and describe the ways in which they cause damage.

13. Silicon is an element providing many materials in the home, give a brief account of the silicon compounds manufactured for use in the home and in its construction.

14. Briefly describe each of the following; (*a*) keratin; (*b*) elastomers; (*c*) fibreglass; (*d*) crystal glass; (*e*) water glass.

15. Give a brief account of pottery and porcelain used in tableware. What advantage has glazed pottery over unglazed pottery?

MULTIPLE CHOICE QUESTIONS ON CHAPTER 21

Figure 21.11 shows a cross-section of a woody stem.

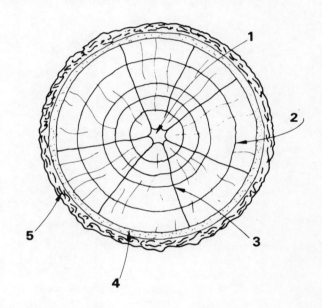

Figure 21.11.

1. Which part of Figure 21.11 is called the sapwood?
   (*a*) 1   (*c*) 3
   (*b*) 2   (*d*) 4

2. Which part of Figure 21.11 is called the heartwood?
   (*a*) 1   (*c*) 3
   (*b*) 2   (*d*) 4

3. Which of the following partly form the grain of a wood?
   (*a*) bark   (*c*) knots
   (*b*) sapwood   (*d*) medullary rays

4. Cork will be found in part:
   (*a*) 2   (*c*) 4
   (*b*) 3   (*d*) 5

5. Dry rot in timber is caused by a:
   (a) moth
   (b) beetle
   (c) fungus
   (d) rodent

6. Which of the following textile fibres is attacked by a moth?
   (a) wool
   (b) acrylic
   (c) polypropylene
   (d) polyamides

7. Which of the following textile fibres shows the least hygroscopic property?
   (a) wool
   (b) cotton
   (c) nylons
   (d) linen

8. Which one of the following is an example of a continuous filament yarn?
   (a) wool
   (b) silk
   (c) linen
   (d) cotton

9. The edible man-made protein which is spun into long filaments and used as a meat substitute or extender is produced from:
   (a) cotton waste
   (b) wood pulp
   (c) soya bean
   (d) cattle skin and ligaments

10. Cut glassware is recognised by the bell-like sound it produces when tapped and is also called:
   (a) boro-silicate glass
   (b) soda glass
   (c) flint glass
   (d) water glass

22 Components of foods, natural and additional

Natural foods can be considered as made up of six naturally occurring components: carbohydrates, lipids, proteins, minerals, vitamins, and water. Processed and manufactured foods, however, have a seventh component, *additives*.

Macronutrients include carbohydrates, lipids and proteins needed in relatively large amounts to provide energy and to produce and maintain tissues.

Micronutrients are nutrients needed in small amounts to maintain health; they include vitamins and trace mineral elements.

$$\text{Natural food composition} = \begin{cases} \text{Carbohydrates} \\ \text{Lipids (or oils and fats)} \\ \text{Proteins} \\ \text{Minerals} \\ \text{Vitamins} \\ \text{Water} \end{cases} + \text{additives} = \begin{array}{c} \text{processed or} \\ \text{manufactured} \\ \text{food} \end{array}$$

Food additives are materials which alter the flavour, colour, and keeping qualities or increase the nutritional value of food with additional minerals or vitamins.

Vitamins, although naturally occurring substances, are dealt with here because of their affinities with additives.

VITAMINS

Vitamins are substances required by the human body for growth and protection against disease in very small amounts. They were discovered by feeding rats and mice with such chemically pure foods as refined fats, sugars, proteins, and minerals. The animals fed in this way did not thrive as did those fed on unrefined foods. Evidently refining removed some *essential* substances. Chemical examination of natural foods led to the isolation of vitamins which are present in the very small amounts of about a few parts per million, or mg or μg per 100 g of food (see Appendix B).

Diets poor in vitamins lead to *deficiency diseases* such as night blindness, skin disorders, anaemia, neuritis, and defects of teeth and bones; *excessive* intakes of vitamins A retinol and D cholecalciferol can, however, be harmful; this is called *hypervitaminosis*.

CHEMICAL COMPOSITION OF VITAMINS

Vitamins are complex organic compounds, some being alcohols, acids, and amines containing carbon, hydrogen, oxygen, nitrogen, and occasionally sulphur and chlorine. Before the exact chemical composition of the vitamins was known, they were labelled A, B, C, etc.; later chemical names were created but the alphabetical system remains. As chemical research progressed it was found that a vitamin previously regarded as a single substance, such as vitamin B, was a *mixture* of several. Hence arose the terms vitamin B *group* or *complex*, and such distinctions as B_1, B_2, B_6, and B_{12}.

SOLUBILITY OF VITAMINS

Vitamins are soluble in either water or lipids. *Water-soluble* vitamins include all members of the vitamin B complex and vitamin C. Lipid-soluble are vitamins A, D, E, and K. The solubility of vitamins is important when cooking food since boiling and steaming will remove the water-soluble vitamins B and C to a certain extent. This explains why vegetable cooking water is best used for soups, stocks, and gravy.

Lipid-soluble vitamins can be stored in the body fat and

drawn upon as required. The water-soluble ones are easily lost from the body and cannot be stored to any great extent. A daily supply is thus needed.

VITAMIN A, RETINOL

This is *retinol* and can be produced synthetically. Its molecule consists of a hydrocarbon chain with a functional —OH group of alcohols.

Natural sources

Vitamin A retinol is closely linked with the orange/yellow pigments or *carotenes* in yellow-coloured vegetable foods such as carrots and unripe tomatoes, present also in cabbages and other green vegetables though masked by the green chlorophyll. Carotenes are *hydrocarbons* converted to vitamin A retinol within the liver and intestine:

$$\text{Carotenes} \longrightarrow \text{vitamin A}$$
$$\text{(provitamin)} \qquad \text{retinol}$$

Fresh green vegetables, carrots, and yellow tomatoes are therefore good sources of the *provitamins* or carotenes.

Being soluble in fats and oils vitamin A is present in cream, milk, butter, egg yolk, liver, and fish oils. Margarine usually contains added vitamin A, which in view of its animal origin is replaced by carotene provitamin in *vegetarian* margarine. The use of natural carotene as a colouring agent for margarine is our first example of a food additive to improve colour and nutritional value in a processed food. Fresh cream and milk owe their natural colour to carotenes.

Function

1. It is necessary for healthy skin.
2. The linings of the gut and lungs, i.e. the *mucous membranes*, are kept moist and healthy by it.
3. It is needed for good vision at night as a component of the eye *retina*.
4. It helps develop strong teeth and bones (but excessive intake causes painful swelling of bones).

Deficiency

Lack of the vitamin A causes the following deficiency diseases:
1. Poor resistance to skin disease, coughs and colds, and lowered resistance to infection.
2. Night blindness, of serious consequences to night drivers of aeroplanes, cars, ships, and trains.
3. Retarded growth in children.
4. *Xerophthalmia* and *keratomalcia* include dryness and ulceration of the eye surface leading to blindness.

Daily requirements (see Appendix C)

The human liver stores sufficient vitamin A for several months. The unit for measuring vitamin A is the *microgram* (µg) retinol equivalent. One retinol equivalent equals one microgram (one-millionth of a gram) of pure retinol.

Children under 12 years of age require 450 to 575 µg retinol equivalents vitamin A, whilst adults and children over 12 years need 725–750 µg retinol equivalents daily. This is provided by 8 g of liver, 16 g of carrots, or a few drops of halibut liver oil. Additional amounts help those on low-fat diets.

Six parts by weight *carotenes* = one part by weight *retinol*.

Effect of cooking

Carotenes in vegetables are not affected by the boiling process. Oxidation of carotenes by air causes deterioration and grated vegetables lose their carotene content on long exposure.

Vitamin A retinol is oxidized by air and dehydrated foods exposed to air will suffer loss. Vitamin A and carotenes are not affected by cooking and being insoluble in water are not removed by moist cooking processes. Sunlight ultraviolet radiation destroys the vitamin; hence the need to wrap and store butter and margarine away from the strong sunlight.

Liquid paraffin, a *hydrocarbon oil*, has a solvent effect on vitamin A. Vitamin A deficiency can therefore occur in people who consume liquid paraffin for medicinal purposes or as a substitute for cooking oil and fat, the oil removing vitamin A from the food in the gut.

VITAMIN B GROUP OR COMPLEX

Vitamin B is a group divided into two: vitamin B_1, which is decomposed by heat, and the remaining *heat-resistant* B vitamins. Most of the B group vitamins can be formed by micro-organisms living in the human intestine.

VITAMIN B_1 OR THIAMIN

This can be manufactured or synthesized. It is an organic *base* similar to pyrimidine (see page 95).

Natural sources

Vitamin B_1 or thiamin is found in many foods but not in large amounts. Whole cereals, wheat germ, liver, pork, and yeast extract are important sources.

Function

All body cells require thiamin as a coenzyme in carbohydrate usage.
1. It improves appetite and digestion.
2. It promotes healthy nerves.
3. It promotes healthy growth in children.

Deficiency

1. A deficiency may cause poor appetite and fatigue, the 'run-down' condition.
2. It leads to digestive upsets.
3. It causes neuritis.
4. It lowers resistance to disease.
5. *Oriental beriberi* among rice-eating people in the East is

caused by a deficiency of thiamin in a diet in which the cereal germ containing the vitamin has been removed from polished or processed rice. Symptoms include loss of appetite, weakness and tiredness affecting the legs, and heart failure.

Alcoholics may also suffer nervous disorders due mainly to a shortage of B group vitamins arising from defective diets.

Daily requirements (see Appendix C)

Since it is not stored in the body the daily intake for adults is about one *milligram* (1·0 mg), which is contained in about 150 g of cooked pork, 60 g of cod roe or 30 g of yeast extract. Excessive intakes are excreted in the urine.

Effect of cooking

1. Vitamin B_1 is destroyed by alkaline solutions, sodium hydrogen carbonate and sulphur dioxide.
2. High temperatures, as used in roasting, will destroy 30 to 50 per cent of the vitamin while temperatures obtained in boiling and canning produce losses of 50 to 75 per cent.
3. Water will dissolve large amounts of the vitamin causing considerable loss. This can only be compensated by using the water for stock and gravies.

Shortage of this vitamin is of national importance compelling the British and American governments to advise the use of vitamin B_1 thiamin as an additive for enriched flour to fortify white bread. Approximately 500 g of bread will provide the daily requirement of thiamin. Intestinal bacteria can form small amounts of thiamin.

VITAMIN B_2, RIBOFLAVIN

This is a yellowish-green organic substance.

Natural sources

It is found in wheat germ, yeast, liver, kidney, milk, fish, meat and yeast extracts, and eggs.

Function

1. It is essential for a healthy skin and nervous system.
2. It promotes growth in children.

Deficiency

This causes:
1. A soreness of the mouth, tongue and lips.
2. The onset of skin dermatitis.
3. A susceptibility to nervous disorders.
4. It checks growth in children.

Daily requirements (see Appendix C)

The daily intake for adults is about 1·5 mg which is contained in about 60 g of liver or 40 g of brewer's yeast. Vitamin B_2 is also formed by bacterial action in the intestine of man.

Effect of cooking

Sunlight will destroy this vitamin and so milk should not be exposed to direct sunlight. Roasting causes destruction of some vitamin B_2 riboflavin in meat, but boiling has little effect. A small amount of vitamin B_2 dissolves in hot water.

NICOTINIC ACID [NIACIN]

It is a member of the vitamin B group, which is not numbered. It is manufactured as a sour-tasting water soluble white powder. In the human body it is synthesized from the essential amino-acid *tryptophan*, intestinal bacteria can also make this vitamin in the form of *nicotinamide*.

Natural source

It is found in liver, meat, yeast, cereals, pulses and wheat germ. The vitamin occurs in many cereals as *niacytin*, which cannot be absorbed in the gut. When treated with *alkali* the nicotinic acid is released from cereals

$$\text{NIACYTIN} \xrightarrow{\text{ALKALI}} \text{NICOTINIC ACID}$$

Daily requirements (see Appendix C)

Approximately 18 *milligrams* daily, as provided by 15 g meat extract or 160 g liver alone, is recommended for the adult male, 15 mg adult female, and 5 to 16 mg for children.

Sixty parts by weight of tryptophan=*one* part by weight nicotinic acid.

Effect of cooking

Boiling dissolves the vitamin from meat and vegetables. Heating has a negligible effect on nicotinic acid. A powder of nicotinic acid and vitamin C has been used as a meat-reddening mixture.

FOLIC ACID

Folic acid is a name from the Latin word *folium* or 'leaf'. Most leafy vegetables are rich sources, also yeast, liver and kidneys. It is required for the formation of new blood cells and its deficiency causes a form of anaemia. It is made in large amounts by intestinal bacteria.

VITAMIN B_{12}, CYANOCOBALAMIN

This is found in yeast, meat extracts, and liver. It is essential for the formation of red blood cells and the healthy functioning of nerves and digestive system. The complex molecule contains the element *cobalt*. Vitamin B_{12} is a complex of four different cobalamins of which cyanocobalamin is the main one.

Deficiency of the vitamin causes pernicious anaemia, digestive disorders, and degeneration of the nerves causing paralysis. Treatment formerly consisted of eating raw liver, but is now by injections of synthetic cyanocobalamin.

Both folic acid and vitamin B_{12} cyanocobalamin are produced by bacteria within the digestive tract, the bacteria being to some extent destroyed by antibiotics such as penicillin.

Vegan diets will be deficient in vitamin B_{12}.

OTHER MEMBERS OF THE VITAMIN B GROUP

These include vitamin B_6 or *pyridoxine*, pantothenic acid, choline, inositol, vitamin H or biotin, and para-amino-benzoic acid. These are widely distributed and unlikely to cause deficiency diseases.

VITAMIN C, ASCORBIC ACID

Vitamin C or *ascorbic acid* can be produced synthetically in the form of a white crystalline water soluble solid with an acid taste. It is chemically a form of *hexose* sugar. Another form *erythorbic acid* is an anti-oxidant without a biological function.

Natural sources

Ascorbic acid is found mainly in fresh fruits and vegetables. Blackcurrants, strawberries, oranges, and grapefruit are particularly rich in the vitamin, while cauliflowers, sprouts, and cabbage are good vegetable sources. Small amounts are found in *fresh* meat, liver, and milk. It is also added to flour as a maturing agent. Loss of the vitamin occurs on deep-freezing fruits and vegetables.

Function

1. Vitamin C is concerned with the formation of teeth and bones.
2. It heals wounds and aids the process of cementing new cells together, i.e. formation of collagen.
3. It strengthens blood vessels.

Deficiency

A gross deficiency causes *scurvy*. This disease, once prominent amongst seafarers fed on diets lacking in fresh fruit and vegetables, showed itself as pains in the joints, swollen and bleeding gums, loose teeth, and general weakness with small haemorrhages beneath the skin. Scurvy can occur in infants, elderly people, and alcoholics.

Daily requirements (see Appendix C)

For a healthy adult 30 mg of vitamin C ascorbic acid are adequate. Children require 15 to 30 mg, and expectant and nursing mothers 60 mg daily provided by blackcurrants, raw orange juice or *raw* cabbage.

Effect of cooking

Cabbage when boiled loses two-thirds of its vitamin C content, resulting from destruction by heat and to the leaching effect of water on the soluble vitamin. Boiled milk loses 20 per cent of the vitamin.

Oxidation can cause the breakdown of the vitamin in fruits and vegetables cut up and exposed to the air. Shredded raw vegetables for salads should be served as soon as possible after preparation. Raw cabbage loses as much as 20 per cent of its vitamin content on shredding. Dried fruits and vegetables including dehydrated foods do not contain vitamin C, since the drying process destroys it.

Bottle-fed babies should receive a supplement of vitamin C as orange juice, since the dried or pasteurized milk will be deficient in the vitamin as against natural human milk. 250 cm^3 of human milk supplies a baby's daily requirement of 15 mg vitamin C.

VITAMIN D

The provitamin of vitamin D is a compound called *7-dehydrocholesterol*, found only in animals including man, changed by sunlight or ultra-violet rays into vitamin D_3:

VITAMIN D_3, CHOLECALCIFEROL

$$7\text{-dehydrocholesterol provitamin} \xrightarrow{\text{Sunlight}} \text{Vitamin } D_3$$

Natural sources

The provitamin of vitamin D_3, 7-dehydrocholesterol, is found in the greasy secretion of human skin. On exposure to sunlight, it becomes vitamin D_3. The body is therefore able to produce its own requirements, granted an outdoor life with plenty of sunshine. Polluted atmospheres prevent the sun's ultra-violet rays reaching the skin leading to deficiency in the vitamin among city children. Another provitamin is called *ergosterol*, which is changed by sunlight into vitamin D_2 or *ergocalciferol*. Fish-liver oils, margarine, butter, and egg yolk are rich in vitamin D which are fat-soluble. Vegetable liquids, with the exception of *red palm oil* are devoid of vitamins A and D. (See page 116 for ergosteral.)

Function

It is concerned with the absorption of calcium from the diet and consequently it is important to the hardening and growth of teeth and bones. The greatest intake will be required during childhood.

Deficiency

Lack of vitamin D causes the disease of children called *rickets* which shows itself as a softening of the bone, the development of bow legs, the tendency to chest disorders and to tooth decay. Its cure lies in the provision of vitamin D and exposure to sunlight or artificial sun-ray treatment. Excessive intake of the vitamin can be harmful.

Osteomalacia is a form of bone softening occurring in *adults* due to vitamin D deficiency.

Osteoporosis is the liability of bones to break in elderly people due to protein shortage; it does not respond to vitamin D treatment.

Daily requirements (see Appendix C)

Vitamin D is measured in *micrograms* (μg) of cholecalciferol. Children under 5 years need 10 μg daily, while adults and children over 5 years need 2·5 µg daily. Nursing mothers require 10 µg daily. Foods rich in the vitamin which will provide the daily requirement for adults are: 1 g cod-liver oil, 25 g egg, or 30 g margarine. Most of the vitamin is formed by the effect of sunlight on the skin.

Effect of cooking

Vitamin D is unaffected by cooking, the main cooked food rich in vitamin D being cooked liver. The use of butter and margarine in cooking will increase the food's vitamin D content.

VITAMIN E, TOCOPHEROLS

There are seven forms of this vitamin, the main ones being called α alpha, β beta, and γ gamma tocopherols, found in wheat germ oil, soya, cotton-seed and corn oils. Lettuce, liver, eggs, peas, and wheat germ are useful dietary sources.

Function

1. Vitamin E (tocopherols) is a natural *anti-oxidant* which prevents rancidity in oils and fats. Its presence in vegetable oils improves their keeping qualities as compared to animal oils.

2. It appears to be concerned with muscular activity. It is not yet clear whether it is essential in the human diet and no daily requirement values have been suggested. No deficiency diseases have been attributed to lack of the vitamin, and the vitamin does not appear to be synthesized in the intestine.

VITAMIN F OR THE ESSENTIAL FATTY ACID

Vitamin F corresponds to the fatty acid *linoleic*, which appears to be essential to the condition of human skin. So far it has not been accepted as a true vitamin. Vitamin F or the essential fatty acid is found mainly in vegetable oils. It is similar to vitamin A in its functions in maintaining healthy skin. Margarine contains 35 per cent essential fatty acid, whilst butter contains 2 per cent. Corn, soyabean, sunflower and safflower oils all contained over 50 per cent.

VITAMIN K (MENAQUINONES)

This is found chiefly in cabbage, spinach, brussel sprouts and green vegetables. A form of vitamin K can be produced by bacteria within the human digestive tract, as can folic acid and cyanocobalamin of the vitamin B group.

Vitamin K is necessary for the clotting of *blood*. This closely identifies it with the B group vitamins folic acid and cyanocobalamin, vitamin B_{12}.

FOOD ADDITIVES (see Appendix A)

Substances deliberately added to foods are called *food additives*. *Food contaminants* include *pesticides*, and metals such as copper and mercury.

The use of food additives is controlled by laws, such as the Food & Drug Act, and by bodies such as the Food Standards Committee, the Food Additives and Contaminants Committee, the Food Safety Research Committee, the Ministry of Agriculture, Fisheries & Food (MAFF) in the United Kingdom and by food directives from the European Economic Community (EEC).

The chemical substances added to foods divide into (*a*) colourings; (*b*) flavours; (*c*) physical conditioning agents; (*d*) preservatives; and (*e*) nutritive additives. The permitted substances being tested rigorously for harmful effects on laboratory animals over long periods, sometimes extending over several generations. Extremely small quantities are used, for example: only 0·01 per cent anti-oxidant is added to cooking fat, i.e. 10 mg of chemical to each 100 g of fat.

FOOD COLOURS (Appendix A – E100:199)

Colour is an important factor in making food appetizing. Food colours can be either natural or synthetic. The colour of food can be measured by instruments called *colorimeters* and *spectrophotometers*. Appendix A lists the permitted food colours.

NATURAL FOOD COLOURS

1. White foods such as potato, onion, and cauliflower have no natural colours.

2. Green foods such as peas, beans, cabbage, and lettuce contain the plant pigment *chlorophyll*, present in the chloroplasts of the cells.

3. Yellow and orange foods such as tomatoes, carrots, peaches, lobsters, crabs, and prawns contain the *carotene* pigments or provitamin of vitamin A, which gives milk, cream, eggs, and beef fat their yellow colour.

4. Red and blue to violet coloured fruits such as cherry, strawberry, bilberry, blackberry, grape, and the colours of red and blue flowers are due to the pigments called *anthocyanins*. Pickled red cabbage is red when the anthocyanins are in the presence of vinegar. If it is boiled in water containing a pinch of sodium hydrogen carbonate it turns blue, and finally green, thus showing the indicator properties of the anthocyanin similar to litmus.

5. Brown colours of tea, cocoa, coffee, beer, and wines such as sherry are due to pigments called *tannins*.

6. Fresh meat is red because of *myoglobin*, a combination of the red pigment *haem* and the muscle protein *globin*. Myoglobin has the important property of combining with oxygen to form a bright red *oxymyoglobin*. This can be seen on cutting fresh meat and observing how the dark red meat (myoglobin) becomes bright red on exposure to air (oxymyoglobin). The pale pink of bacon and ham is a further example of oxidation of the myoglobin by means of the curing agent, potassium nitrate(V).

When meat is cooked the attractive brown is produced by denaturation of the protein in the haemoglobin and also myoglobin, the denatured proteins containing the brown pigment *haemin*.

7. Browning of foods can be of three kinds:

(*a*) *Enzymatic* browning of sliced apples, potatoes, and other fruits and vegetables. This is due to the reaction of the cell contents with one another in the presence of oxygen from the air and cell. It is prevented by leaving the fruits and vegetables under water or by adding sulphur dioxide or sodium sulphate(IV) (sulphite) to the water as with potato whiteners. Fruits for freezing are usually blanched by immersing them briefly in very hot water; the scalding destroys the vital *enzymes* which cause this enzymatic browning.

(*b*) *Maillard* browning is produced in toasted bread, cereals, and fried chipped potatoes. It results from the chemical reaction between protein amino-acids and carbohydrate monosaccharides.

(*c*) *Caramelization* is the browning produced by the action of heat on sucrose, important in toffee-making, the use of *caramel* for gravy browning, and as a colouring for vinegar.

IMPORTANT NATURAL COLOURING MATERIALS FOR FOODS

Annatto is a yellow dye from the pulp surrounding the seeds of a Brazilian shrub, the pigment being due to *bixin* and *orellin*. Annatto is used for butter, cheese, and chocolate.

Alkanet is red dye from the alkanet plant, a fairly common weed in Britain. The red alkanet changes to blue in the presence of alkalis and baking soda. It is used for colouring essences.

Carotene and chlorophyll, as alcoholic extracts, are used as food colours.

Cochineal is a well-known red dye from a cactus plant insect. The dried bodies are crushed and the dye dissolved in water or alcohol. *Cocoa* is also an important natural colouring. *Carbon black* is a colouring for liquorice.

Saffron is a yellow dye extracted from the female parts or stigma of the saffron crocus plant of the Mediterranean. It is very soluble in water and has an oriental flavour, and is a useful food spice (see page 170).

Turmeric is a bright yellow powder extracted from the roots of a plant grown in India. Its use is mainly in curries and piccalilli.

Paprika is used for soups, snacks, and French dressings. Together with Annatto and Saffron it is classed as *carotenoid* in having a yellow orange shade.

Lycopene is red pigment of tomato.

Betanin is red pigment of beetroot; it may cause urine to turn red.

SYNTHETIC FOOD COLOURS

The use of certain synthetic chemical coal tar dyes is permitted by British government food regulations. Their discovery showed several advantages over natural dyes – economic price, permanent quality, brilliant colours, and resistance to heat, light, and to acids and most alkalis. Alkalis alter the colours of most vegetable dyes. But some are toxic and harmful in *large* quantities; they may cause cancer. The properties of most have been examined and the dyes grouped according to their toxic and non-toxic effects and suitability.

Group A

Colours that available evidence suggests are suitable for use in food are: Amaranth which is a red dye, and Green S which is green.

Group B

Colours which are provisionally acceptable but about which further information is necessary are: Carmoisine, Ponceau 4R, Erythrosine BS, Ponceau MX, Fast Red E, Sunset Yellow FCF, Tartrazine, Black P.N., Indigo-carmine, and Black 7984. Tartrazine and Sunset Yellow FCF are *allergens* in certain people.

Other groups of colours are listed in the Ministry of Agriculture, Fisheries and Food report on colouring matter of the Food Standards Committee, 1964. Synthetic colours are used in the colouring of soft drinks, confectionery, ice-cream, custards, jellies, biscuits, cakes, and jam manufacture.

BLEACHING AGENTS IN FOODS

Flour is at once bleached and improved by oxidizing agents. *Chlorine dioxide* and *dibenzene carbonoyl peroxide* (*benzoyl peroxide*) a highly flammable and explosive substance, are the main agents for flour. Others such as *potassium bromate* and ammonium peroxodisulphate (persulphate) mature or improve a flour but do not bleach it.

Peeled potatoes in large kitchens and canteens are kept in water containing potato whiteners, a bleaching agent such as sodium sulphate(IV) (sulphite); the latter attacks the thiamine vitamin B_1 content.

FOOD FLAVOURINGS

The flavour of food is due to the combined effect of the odour and taste. Measurement of flavour is by human tasting panels. Flavour in contrast to food colour and texture cannot be measured by instruments. Food flavours arise from:

1. *Natural* food flavours from the volatile ingredients such as essential oils of oranges and tangerines, and the products of thermal decomposition of proteins as in cooked meat.

2. *Sodium chloride* (*salt*) is one of the basic natural food flavours and an important aid to digestion.

3. *Acids*, such as hydroxypropane tricarboxylic (citric) and ethanoic (acetic) as food components control alkalinity.

4. *Alkalis* and salts serve to control the acidity of foods and are important in baking powders.

5. *Synthetic flavours* and essences are compounds prepared from vegetable extracts such as vanilla, or from mixtures of such chemical compounds as alkanals (aldehydes), esters, and alkanones (ketones) as in many synthetic essences.

6. *Sweetening agents* other than sugar and honey are synthetic compounds of low or no nutritional value, such as hexahydroxyhexanes (*sorbitol*, *mannitol*), and *saccharine*. Sodium cyclamate has been banned for use in food.

7. *Flavour intensifiers* such as *sodium glutamate* (sodium-2-amino-pentane-5-oate-1-oic acid) an important ingredient of Japanese soy sauce, concentrates the flavour of meats and

meat preparations, such as soups. Sodium quanylate and also inosinate are used to enhance flavour in meat dishes. It is a *non-essential* amino acid.

8. *Herbs and spices* provide a variety of food flavours, and were the earliest food additives in use. (See page 118.)

PHYSICAL CONDITIONING AGENTS

These are listed in Appendix A as E400–499. They are the food additives that alter or maintain the physical condition of the food forming emulsions or creams, or thickening the food. In this group are emulsifiers, stabilizers, thickeners, and humectants.

1. *Emulsifiers* are substances that assist in the dispersion of oil in water forming an emulsion. They include such natural agents as gelatine, gums, and lecithin, from eggs or soya beans. The synthetic emulsifying agents are propanediol octadecanoate (glyceryl monostearate (G.M.S.)), and methyl ethyl cellulose (see page 133).

2. *Stabilizers and thickeners* are substances which prevent the emulsion of oil in water separating, and also thicken the food. Natural stabilizers and thickeners include lecithin, gums, pectin, starches, and soya bean oil. The synthetic materials used are propanediol (propylene glycol), sodium alginate, sodium carboxy methly cellulose, and methyl cellulose.

3. *Anti-spattering agents* are added to cooking fats to prevent spattering of the fat by water. The substances used are similar to stabilizers preventing the water droplets coming together to form the large drops which cause the fat to bubble. The main substances used for this purpose are lecithin, and certain *sugar ester* detergents.

4. *Humectants* are substances added to foods to keep them moist and to prevent them becoming stale. Preserved fruits, cherries, and desiccated coconut may be treated with either propanetriol (glycerine) or hexahydroxyhexane (sorbitol).

PRESERVATIVES

These are listed in Appendix A as E200–299, and are substances added to foods to prevent their decomposition or attack by moulds and bacteria. Their maximum concentrations range from 70 to 3 000 parts per million, depending on the food and specific preservative.

1. *Natural preservatives* include the use of sodium chloride, sugar, propanetriol (glycerine), ethanoic acid, ethanol, olive oil, and essential oils from herbs and spices. All are used in traditional preservation methods.

Potassium nitrate(V) (saltpetre) has for long been a preservative for bacon and ham. Hops contain a natural preservative which also contributes to the flavour of beer.

2. *Chemical preservatives* permitted in Britain are *sulphur dioxide* (SO_2) mainly for fruit preservation before jam making and *benzene carboxylic (benzoic) acid* (C_6H_5COOH) for coffee extract and soft drinks manufacture.

Sorbic acid is a preservative used in flour confectionery, margarine, and marzipan; quantities are very small, between 0·02 and 0·1 per cent. Sodium propanoate (propionate) and propanoic (propionic) acid are used as preservatives in white bread.

Nisin is an *antibiotic* capable of destroying bacteria, and is a permitted preservative for cheese and certain canned milk products and vegetables in the UK.

The presence of antibiotics such as penicillin in milk is troublesome being harmful to those sensitive to the antibiotic. Penicillin enters the milk from antibiotic ointments used to treat mastitis or inflammation of the udder.

3. *Anti-oxidants* are substances added to fats and foods containing fats to prevent rancidity caused by oxidation. Natural anti-oxidants include hydroxypropane tricarboxylic (citric), dihydroxybutanedioic (tartaric), and ascorbic acids, vitamin C, some spices, and tocopherols, or vitamin E (see Appendix A).

Synthetic anti-oxidants are *phenolic* compounds (page 106), propyl gallate, octyl gallate, dodecanyl gallate, and methyl propyl hydroxy methoxybenzene (butylated hydroxy anisole (B.H.A.)). The quantity used is extremely small, between 0·01 and 0·1 per cent. Synthetic anti-oxidants are permitted in cooking oils, fats, margarine, shredded suet, vitamin oils, and essential oils only; the food packet must be labelled accordingly. Lard containing B.H.A. can have a storage life of up to two years. Methyl propyl hydroxy methyl benzene (butylated hydroxytoluene (B.H.T.) is also a permitted anti-oxidant used in potato powder.

Nitrosamines are compounds known to cause cancer in animals. They form by reaction of *nitrites* with *amines* (see page 95) in foods. *Nitrates* can be reduced to nitrites, and both salts are being carefully tested for further evidence concerning their safe use in foods.

Nitrosamines are found in small amounts in mushrooms, and smoked and pickled foods containing nitrate and nitrites.

NUTRITIONAL SUPPLEMENTS

The main nutritional additives are vitamins and minerals. Vitamins A and D are used to fortify margarine and calcium carbonate has been used to fortify flour during the war years of 1939–45 in National Flour. Vitamin C is frequently added to soft drinks containing fruit juice to restore the ascorbic acid content to the amount normally present in the fruit ingredients. *Infant milk* preparations are fortified with vitamins A, D and C, together with iron.

Usually there is little reason for the use of nutritional additives except in margarine and bread, since a balanced diet will provide the body with sufficient vitamins and minerals.

FOOD LABELLING

The Food Standards Committee and the European Economic Community issue regulations concerning food labelling.

The labels must show the following information:

1. *Food name*: this is either the customary name (such as fish fingers) or the *descriptive* name, giving the true nature of the food.

2. *Ingredients* must be listed in descending order of weight. The food additives are shown by their category preservative, colour, etc., followed by the chemical name or EEC serial number, E100, E200, E300 or E400.

3. *Net quantity*: this is shown in metric grammes or imperial ounce measure.

4. *Datemark* is now compulsory for most foods, such as 'Best before –', 'Best before end –' or 'Sell by –'.

5. *Storage conditions* are shown in order to support the datemark.

6. *Instructions for use* are shown when necessary.

7. *Place of origin* is shown when necessary.

8. *Manufacturer*, packer or seller's name is shown in order to give information about the food or in the event of complaint.

Certain foods are exempt from general food labelling regulations, such as sugar, cocoa, chocolate, milk and honey products, hen's eggs, coffee, and wines.

SUGGESTIONS FOR PRACTICAL WORK

1. Collect labels from processed food packets or containers and record the names of the additives they contain.

2. See *Experimental Science for Catering and Homecraft Students*, Practical work 2.6, 7, 10.1, 10.3, 13.4, 22.2, 22.3, 33.5, 34.4, 36 to 36.3, 38.1 and 52.

QUESTIONS ON CHAPTER 22

1. Write an essay entitled 'Food colour'.

2. State the effect on the vitamin content of cooking: (*a*) meat; (*b*) eggs; and (*c*) potatoes.

3. Give a brief account of the use of food preservatives.

4. Write brief notes on: (*a*) vitamin A retinol; (*b*) vitamin D cholecalciferol; (*c*) anti-oxidants; and (*d*) the use of sodium hydrogen carbonate in cookery.

5. Describe the occurrence and function of vitamin C ascorbic acid. What effects have cooking processes on the vitamin C ascorbic acid content of foods? Describe how any vitamin loss in cooking can be overcome or prevented.

6. What vitamins are added to margarine and why? Give an account of food additives present in cooking fats and oils.

7. What materials contribute to the flavour of food?

8. Give an account of the main sources, function, and effect of cooking on: (*a*) vitamin A thiamin; (*b*) vitamin B_1 thiamin; (*c*) vitamin C ascorbic acid; and (*d*) vitamin D cholecalciferol.

9. Write brief notes on: (*a*) hydroxy propane tricarboxylic (citric) acid; (*b*) ascorbic acid; (*c*) nicotinic acid; (*d*) folic acid; (*e*) benzenecarboxylic (benzoic) acid; and (*f*) dihydroxybutanedioic (tartaric) acid.

10. Give an account of the browning processes which can occur in foods.

MULTIPLE CHOICE QUESTIONS ON CHAPTER 22

1. The daily requirements of the vitamin A – retinol, and vitamin D – cholecalciferol are measured in:
(*a*) gram
(*b*) microgram
(*c*) milligram
(*d*) kilogram

2. The vitamins least affected by the cooking process are:
(*a*) vitamin A – retinol, vitamin D – cholecaliferol
(*b*) vitamin C – ascorbic acid, vitamin E – tocopherols
(*c*) vitamin B1 – thiamin, B2 – cyanocobalamin
(*d*) vitamin B2 – riboflavin, and nicotinic acid

3. Which two of the following vitamins enter the cooking water from the meat and vegetables of a cooked stew?
(i)   vitamin A
(ii)   vitamin B group
(iii) vitamin C
(iv)   vitamin D
(v)   vitamin E
(vi)   vitamin K

(*a*) i and ii
(*b*) ii and iii
(*c*) iv and v
(*d*) v and vi

4. The use of alkaline sodium hydrogen carbonate in the cooking water can be the means of destruction of the following vitamins in foods:
(i)   vitamin A
(ii)   vitamin B1
(iii) vitamin B2
(iv)   vitamin C
(v)   vitamin D
(vi)   vitamin E

(*a*) i and iii
(*b*) ii and iv
(*c*) iii and v
(*d*) v and vi

5. Which of the following vitamins is destroyed by sunlight?
(*a*) vitamin A – retinol
(*b*) vitamin B2 – riboflavin
(*c*) vitamin D – cholecalciferol
(*d*) vitamin E – tocopherols

6. One of the following is a natural food colouring material:
(*a*) tartrazine
(*b*) carmoisine
(*c*) indigo-carmine
(*d*) carotene

7. Sugar and sodium chloride are preservative materials which act through:
(*a*) being disinfectants and destroying bacteria
(*b*) fermentation in producing ethanol as a preservative
(*c*) withdrawing water from the food cells and microbes
(*d*) forming a crust which excludes air and microbes from food

8. The two vitamins added to fortify margarine are:
(i)   vitamin A – retinol
(ii)   vitamin B1 – thiamin
(iii) vitamin B2 – riboflavin
(iv)   vitamin B12 – cobalamin
(v)   vitamin C – ascorbic acid
(vi)   vitamin D – tocopherols

(*a*) i, vi
(*b*) iii, iv
(*c*) ii, v
(*d*) iv, vi

9. Antioxidants serve to protect one of the following components of a food from chemical changes in store:
(*a*) carbohydrates
(*b*) lipids
(*c*) minerals
(*d*) proteins

10. Two of the following are useful antioxidants in foods:
(i)   vitamin A – retinol
(ii)   vitamin C – ascorbic acid
(iii) vitamin E – tocopherols
(iv)   propanetriol (glycerine)
(v)   olive oil
(vi)   nisin

(*a*) i, iv
(*b*) ii, iii
(*c*) iv, v
(*d*) v, vi

PART III

Biological Aspects

INTRODUCTION – BIOLOGICAL ASPECTS

In this part the relationship between *living* things is considered, particularly the relationship between human beings and plants and animals as *food* sources, food *pests*, and the cause of *disease*. The healthy functioning of the human body and food needs form the study of human *nutrition*.

23 Plant products and man

The science of life and living things is *biology*, subdivided into *botany*, the science of plants, and *zoology*, the science of animals. Since the health, food, and clothing of man are closely concerned with plants and animals biology is relevant in its applications to catering and health.

CELL STRUCTURE

Cells. All living things are built up from small units called *cells*. Very simple forms of life are one-celled or *uni-cellular* as are yeast and certain micro-organisms. Man and all other plants and animals, are built up of many cells or are *multi-cellular*.

Experiment

Cut an onion in half and remove one of the fleshy scales. Peel away the lining from the inside of the scale. Put it on a microscope slide, cover it with a drop of water and place a cover glass over it. Observe its multi-cellular structure through a low-power microscope lens (Figure 23.1).

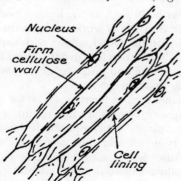

Figure 23.1. Structure of onion-scale cells

CELL STRUCTURE OF PLANTS

The onion cell has an appearance typical of living plant cells, a rigid *cell wall* of *cellulose* surrounding the cell substance or *cytoplasm* and a central structure, the *nucleus*. The cellulose wall provides the *dietary fibre* of vegetable foods while the *cytoplasm* with its carbohydrates, oils, and proteins, present in a *colloidal* form within the cell sap, gives the plant its nutritional value. The *nucleus* controls life within a cell and protein manufacture and cell division or growth; life soon ceases in a cell without a nucleus.

Cells are cemented together by a material rich in *pectin* and *calcium pectate*, valuable for giving jams their setting properties (see page 109).

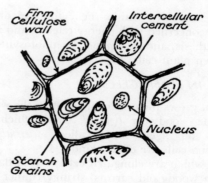

Figure 23.2. Structure of cells in a potato tuber

Potatoes sliced thinly produce sections with a structure like that in Figure 23.2. The cells have a cellulose wall surrounding many prominent starch granules amongst which is the solitary nucleus. Starch granules are the potato's method of storing carbohydrate; the granules have a structure of layers of starch around a centre. Rice, maize, and wheat starch granules have a different appearance to potato granules.

Cells such as the potato and onion described above having thin walls with air spaces between the cells, are called *parenchyma cells*. Somewhat similar cells are found in the middle of leaves and stems (see also page 152).

CELL STRUCTURE OF ANIMALS

Experiment

Using the handle of a spoon, scrape the inside of the cheek and transfer the specimen to a drop of water on a slide. Cover it with a glass slip and observe the cell structure under a microscope (Figure 23.3).

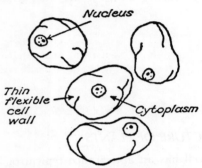

Figure 23.3. Cells from the lining of the mouth

Animal cells have a *nucleus* surrounded by cytoplasm and a cell membrane or *plasmalemma*. The cell membrane, however, does not have a rigid structure, but is flexible or elastic. The flexible nature of animal cells can be shown in the way the human skin can be pulled. Cell membranes are composed of *lipo-proteins*, which are digestible in contrast to the cellulose of plant cell walls which is indigestible and forms the bulk of *dietary fibre*.

CYTOPLASM ORGANELLES

These are structures within the cytoplasm and include; *mitochondria* concerned with energy release, and *ribosomes* for protein synthesis, and *chloroplasts*, for photosynthesis found only in green plant cells.

CHANGES IN PLANT CELLS

As the plant grows the cells change; often the walls thicken and become woody or *lignified*. Cells which have this thickening of *lignin* are called *sclerenchyma* cells. Sclerenchyma cells are of two kinds:

(*a*) *fibres* which are elongated cells seen in flax, see page 152, and in woody old carrots, stringy runner beans, and woody asparagus spears. These fibres serve to strengthen and support old stems and roots. Lignin is the material which gives soft and hard woods their typical properties.

(*b*) *Stone* cells which are oval shaped cells thickened with *lignin* and are responsible for the gritty texture of certain pears, nuts and plant seed coats.

Unlike *collenchyma* cells (see page 152) which are thickened with cellulose, the lignified fibre and stone cells cannot be softened by cooking processes.

Cells of mosses and seaweeds become slimy or *mucilaginous* as with carrageen moss and slippery elm. Similarly *gums* form in certain plants by the breakdown of the cell structure. Fruits produce a large amount of pectin and inter-cellular cementing substances which tends to disappear on overripening (see page 110).

ACTIVITIES OF LIVING CELLS

Most fruits, vegetables, and flowers, when freshly picked or cut remain *alive* for a considerable time. Fresh fruits, vegetables, and flowers are *living things* to be treated with care in order to preserve their vital nature. Meat from slaughtered animals is not composed of living cells and rapidly decomposes in contrast to fruit and vegetables, which can be stored for long periods with special treatments (see *gas storage*, page 103).

All *living* cells are active because of chemical changes within them which is called *metabolism*. The following are some of the main metabolic activities occurring in living cells. Some are concerned with breaking down chemical substances, that is liberating *energy* from stored food. Such processes are called *katabolic*. Others such as forming new cell walls are building or *anabolic* processes.

1. *Nutrition* is the process of feeding the cell or body.
2. *Respiration* is the katabolic process of liberating energy from food.
3. *Growth* is the process of increasing the size of the cell or body.
4. *Excretion* is the process of getting rid of the waste products of metabolism.
5. *Movement* is evident in animals, but takes place also in the buds and flowers of plants.
6. *Sensitivity* is the response of the plant or animal to its surroundings.
7. *Reproduction* is the vital process which distinguishes all living things from non-living materials.

TISSUES, ORGANS, AND SYSTEMS

In a multi-cellular body such as the human body there is a need for the specialization of work amongst the cells, some being concerned with the blood, others with supporting the body, etc. The cells are therefore grouped into *tissues* which have the same structure and purpose; nerve tissues, muscle tissue, and lining tissue are examples.

Frequently tissues join to form an *organ*; for example the stomach is composed of muscle, nerve, lining, and blood tissues. Similarly, plants are composed of different tissues: those which carry water and salts or organic foods, those which manufacture foods, and glandular tissues which make sweet smelling essential oils. Different plant tissues form the main plant organs such as leaves, stems, roots, and flowers (see page 152).

PHOTOSYNTHESIS

This is the process whereby *green* plants manufacture sugars from such simple raw materials as carbon dioxide and water. The carbon dioxide is drawn into the leaves from the air through pores called *stomata*. Water with the dissolved salts is absorbed from the dampened soil by way of the *root hairs*.

Water and the dissolved salts are carried from the roots via the stem to the leaves through the tubular conducting tissue or wooden *xylem* cells of the vasular bundles (*see* Figures 21.10 and 23.4.). There the water and carbon dioxide combine by means of energy supplied by sunlight, the whole process being influenced by the *chlorophyll* in the chloroplasts of the cells. Glucose is first produced but soon changes to large granules of starch for storage purposes.

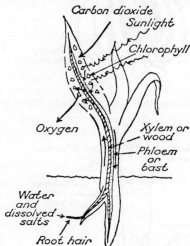

Figure 23.4. General structure of a plant to show the food-manufacturing and storage organs

All surplus foods are transported through the *phloem* or bast to be stored by the plant, mainly in the *roots* and occasionally the *stems* in the form of insoluble granules of starch. This food is utilized for rapid growth in the early spring.

The transportation of raw materials and manufactured foods is achieved by means of the *vascular tissue*. This consists of: (*a*) *Xylem* or wood which carries the water and salts from the roots to the leaves. It becomes the main component of wood; and (*b*) *Phloem* a comparatively soft tissue transporting food from the leaves to the storage organs. Flax fibres are produced from the phloem tissues of flax stems, the fibres serving to strengthen the bast (see Figure 21.10).

Proteins and *lipids* are manufactured in plants from carbohydrates, by combination with compounds of nitrogen from the soil or by removal of hydrogen and oxygen to form carbon-rich lipids.

Oxygen is an important by-product of photosynthesis and serves to enrich the atmosphere for the purposes of respiration and combustion:

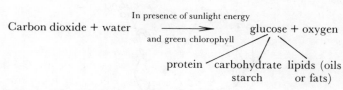

the chemical changes can be shown as:

$$\underset{\text{carbon dioxide}}{6CO_2} + \underset{\text{water}}{6H_2O} \underset{\text{sunlight energy}}{\overset{\text{Chlorophyll and}}{=}} \underset{\text{glucose}}{C_6H_{12}O_6} + \underset{\text{oxygen}}{6O_2}$$

This chemical equation is important since, in reverse, it occurs under the study of *respiration*.

OUTLINES OF PLANT STRUCTURE

A flowering plant consists essentially of: (*a*) the *vegetative* parts – root, stem, and leaves, concerned with food manufacture, storage, or transport; and (*b*) the *reproductive* parts – flowers, fruit, and seeds, concerned with propagation.

VEGETATIVE PARTS OF A FLOWERING PLANT

1. *Stems* are easily recognized since they have *buds* closely associated *with leaves*. If the leaves are not present they are evident as *leaf scars* or *scale* leaves (see Figure 23.5).

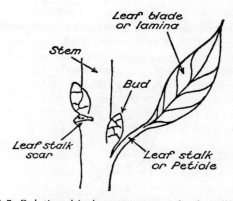

Figure 23.5. Relationship between stem, bud and leaf

Tubers are swollen underground food storage organs which can be roots or stems (Figure 23.6), found in potato, sweet potato, taro, yam and cassava.

Kohlrabi is an unusual vegetable consisting of a swollen overground stem covered with scale leaf scars and leaves. Swede, beets, celeriac, and turnip are of an intermediate structure being composed of swollen stems and roots (see Figure 23.7). Jerusalem artichokes are swollen underground stems or *rhizomes*, as evident in the scale leaves which cover the rhizome (Figure 23.8). Asparagus is a stem vegetable though the stem is leafless.

2. *Leaf*. Leaves consist of a broad leaf blade or *lamina* and leaf stalk or *petiole*. Vegetables derived from the plant leaves are well known, in the form of cabbage, lettuce, spinach, and parsley. Rhubarb and celery are essentially the *leaf stalk*

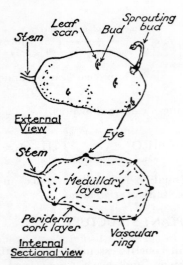

Figure 23.6. Structure of a potato stem tuber

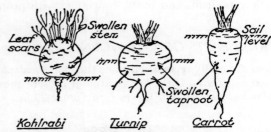

Figure 23.7. Kohlrabi swollen stem compared to swollen stem and root of turnip and carrot

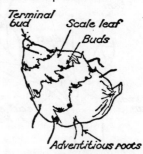

Figure 23.8. Stem rhizome of Jerusalem artichoke

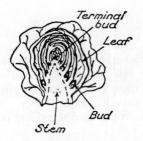

Figure 23.9. Structure of brussels sprout

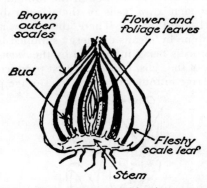

Figure 23.10. Swollen underground bud structure of onion

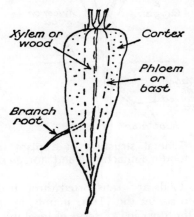

Figure 23.11. Swollen taproot of carrot

or petiole; the rhubarb leaf is poisonous due to its ethanedioic (oxalic) acid content.

3. *Buds.* Buds can be regarded as a closed telescoped form of a stem with its attached leaves. The brussels sprout is an *overground bud* with short stem surrounded by closely-packed, overlapping leaves (Figure 23.9). Bulbs of onions, garlic, and shallots are swollen *underground* buds where the leaves have become white and fleshy. The food reserves surround a central bud (see Figure 23.10).

4. *Roots.* Roots lack leaves and buds. Carrots and horseradish are *swollen taproots* consisting of a soft bast with a central xylem which becomes hard and woody in mature carrots or horseradish (see Figure 23.11). Chicory, witloof, or French endive are also swollen roots used raw or cooked.

REPRODUCTIVE PARTS OF A FLOWERING PLANT

Cauliflower and broccoli are vegetables formed from the flowers of the plant. The flower consists of four parts:

(*a*) *sepals* which protect the flower in bud and frequently remain in such ripe fruit as tomatoes;

(*b*) the coloured and scented *petals* which attract insects to aid pollination;

(*c*) *stamens* or male parts which produce the pollen and are responsible for allergies such as hay fever; and

(*d*) *pistil*, the female part, receives the pollen and fertilizes the eggs which now become seeds surrounded by the fruit wall (see Figure 23.12). The remains of the pistil are often seen in a ripe fruit.

All these are attached to the floral axis or *receptacle* which forms the basis of such fruits as the strawberry.

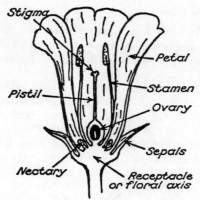

Figure 23.12. Diagrammatic structure of a flower

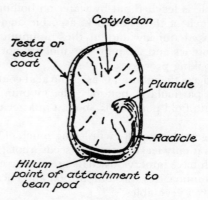

Figure 23.14. Structure of broad-bean seed

FRUITS

Flowering plants produce fruits in order to protect and feed the developing seeds. The fruit wall is sometimes fleshy and succulent as in ripe berries and plums, but can become hard and dry when ripe as in the case of nuts.

The botanical definition of a fruit is a matured ovary including seeds with the remains of stigma, style, stamens, petals, and sepals attached. The culinary definition covers plant parts which are sweet and succulent and *excludes* peas, beans, tomatoes, marrows, and cucumbers which are botanically fruits.

Fruits are classified as *true* fruits in which the wall is formed from the ovary, and *false* fruits in which the fruit derives from some part of the flower other than the ovary. Apples, pears, and strawberries are formed from swollen receptacles or floral axes (see Figure 23.13).

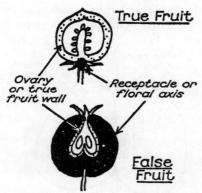

Figure 23.13. True and false fruit formation

SEEDS

These are the products of pollination and fertilization and are miniature plants made up of leaves, stems, and roots, called *cotyledon*, *plumule*, and *radicle*, respectively. They contain a supply of food for early growth (Figure 23.14). The miniature plant is called the *embryo* and sometimes the *germ*, particularly in wheat and other cereals.

Food reserves exist either within the cotyledons as in peas and beans, or around the embryo as in the *endosperm* of cereals. Cereal grains have closely-connected fruit wall and seed coats forming the *husk* which must be removed by milling. *Pulses* are the dry seeds of peas, beans, lentils and soya beans.

COMPOSITION OF VEGETABLES (see Appendix B)

Vegetables have a very high water content, particularly in vegetables marrows, cucumbers, and tomatoes and to a lesser extent in tubers and seeds. The energy value is therefore low, between 30 and 100 kilojoules per 100 g for most vegetables except potatoes and pulses – 300 kJ/100 g.

Carbohydrates and proteins form the main nutrient present in vegetables but are not abundant except in potatoes and peas. Vegetable marrows, cucumbers, and similar fruits have very low nutrient value. Lipids are completely absent from vegetables. Most vegetables are good sources of *dietary fibre*.

Vitamin C ascorbic acid is present in most vegetables, while vitamin A, as carotenes, is abundant in carrots and sweet potatoes but *absent* from other underground roots, tubers, bulbs, and the blanched stems of celery. Green *leafy* vegetables are a rich source of *folic acid*.

Calcium is the commonest mineral in vegetables forming the inter-cellular cementing substances of cell walls. Iron occurs in the green vegetables particularly spinach; phosphorus is found in peas, potatoes, and cauliflowers.

EFFECT OF COOKING AND STORAGE

1. The cellulose walls of the cell, swell, soften, and finally break down, making the food tender. The *parenchyma* cells of *young* leaves, stems, and roots break down readily on cooking. *Collenchyma* cells present in most stems, roots, and leaves will break down on increasing the cooking time in the presence of an acid pH through added vinegar or lemon juice.

Tough, old vegetables will have considerable *sclerenchyma* fibres that are unaffected by any cooking process.

2. Starch granules also swell and form gels.

3. The vitamin C ascorbic acid and B_1 thiamin content of

the vegetable is leached out by water on boiling. The heat destroys much of the vitamin C ascorbic acid unless the food is cooked quickly and in the minimum amount of water. Carotenes and vitamin A retinol are not affected by common cooking processes.

Storage affects the vitamin C ascorbic acid content of most vegetables, particularly potatoes; the vitamin C ascorbic acid content of old potatoes is about a quarter that of fresh ones.

Leafy vegetables rapidly wilt losing much of their water. This makes it only feasible to store seeds, roots, tubers, and bulbs which have impervious coats preventing evaporation. The table summarizes the composition and energy value of raw or cooked vegetables:

AVERAGE PERCENTAGE COMPOSITION OF VEGETABLES

Vegetable	Energy value kJ/100 g	Water	Carbohydrate	Protein
Type: Example				
Leafy: cabbage	100	92	6	1·5
Stem: celery	190	88	1·5	0·9
Flower: cauliflower	100	92	5	1·9
Root: carrot (cooked)	120	92	6	0·5
Fruits: marrow	30	98	1·5	0·5
Tubers: potato	360	78	20	2
Seeds: peas (cooked)	300	82	13	3·5
Bulbs: onions	170	89	9	0·9

FRUITS

Fruits are those parts of the flowering plant containing *seeds*. The botanical definition includes such vegetable fruits as marrow and tomato, together with the fruits within the culinary meaning, apples, oranges, etc.

CLASSIFICATION OF FRUITS

The botanical classification of fruits is into either *true* or *false*:

(*a*) *True fruits* are subdivided into fleshy and dry:

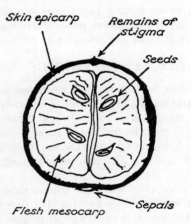

Figure 23.15. Structure of a berry – the orange

(i) *Fleshy fruits* include:

Berries are fruits such as oranges, currants, blueberries, and gooseberries with seeds within a succulent flesh (*mesocarp*), the fruit surrounded by a skin (*epicarp*) or peel (see Figure 23.15).

Drupes are the fruits of plums, peaches, cherries, and avocado pears. They consist of a single seed surrounded by a fruit wall in three layers, the stone (*endocarp*), flesh (*mesocarp*), and outer skin (*epicarp*) (see Figure 23.16). A modification is the *drupel*, a cluster of miniature drupes around a central flora axis, as in the raspberry, blackberry, and loganberry.

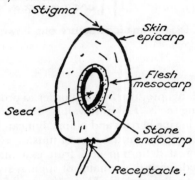

Figure 23.16. Structure of a drupe – the plum

(ii) *Dry fruits* include the *pods* of peas and beans which become dry when *fully* ripe, and the nuts, such as hazel.

(*b*) *False fruits* include apples, strawberries, figs, and pineapples. The fleshy parts are formed from the floral axis, or receptable, and can be a modified flower as in the pineapple.

Pomes. Apples and pears have fleshy parts formed from a swollen floral axis, the true fruit with its hard wall surrounding the seeds to form the *core* with its *pips*. The remains of the sepals are in the end of the pome opposite the stalk (see Figure 23.17).

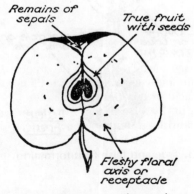

Figure 23.17. Structure of a pome – the apple

Strawberries have false fruits in which the succulent portion is an enlarged floral axis with sepals at the base. The true fruits are the pips covering the surface.

Figs are cup-shaped, succulent receptacles with the true fruits within (see Figure 23.18).

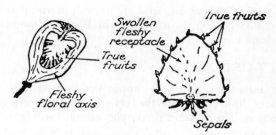

Figure 23.18. False fruits of strawberry and fig

COMPOSITION OF FRUITS (see Appendix B)

Fruits, particularly water melons have a very high water content (92 per cent). This reduces their energy value to 60–200 kJ/100 g. Dried fruits with a water content between 15 and 25 per cent have much higher energy values of 600–1 000 kJ/100 g. Skins, stones, seeds, or pips are indigestible waste. Seeds are *resistant* to attack by digestive juices.

Carbohydrates are the main nutrient of fruits, the content being 5–20 per cent in fresh fruits and 40–65 per cent in dried fruits. *Sucrose* is the main sugar in apricots and peaches, *fructose* predominates in apples and pears. Fruits supply 10 per cent of carbohydrate in our diet.

Dietary fibre is present in all fruits as indigestible *cellulose*, and *pectin* is associated with the inter-cellular cementing substances abundant in such *under-ripe* fruits as citrus fruits, plums, apples, and pears, though less plentiful in strawberries and cherries.

Lipids are completely absent from fruits except avocado pears (25 per cent) and olives (13 per cent) where the amounts are unexpectedly high and of important nutritional value.

Proteins occur in very small amounts in dried fruits such as prunes, apricots, and figs; the quantity present in fresh fruit is negligible.

Vitamins

Vitamin C ascorbic acid is particularly abundant in blackberries, strawberries, and citrus fruits. Dried fruits lack vitamin C ascorbic acid which is decomposed by the drying process. Fruit and vegetables provide 35 per cent of vitamin C ascorbic acid in the UK diet.

Vitamin A in the form of the provitamin *carotenes* is found in useful quantities in tomatoes, peaches, apricots, cherries, and prunes.

Nicotinic acid is present in most dried fruits.

Minerals

Calcium is present in all fruits as calcium pectate, the inter-cellular cementing substance, and is particularly abundant in fresh blackcurrants and dried figs.

Iron is found in dried fruits, and *potassium* occurs in large amounts in all fruits.

The following table summarizes the percentage composition and energy value per 100 g of some common fresh and dried fruits

AVERAGE PERCENTAGE COMPOSITION AND ENERGY VALUE OF FRUITS

Fruit	Energy value kJ/100 g	Water	Carbohydrate	Protein
Berries				
Orange	190	87	11	0·8
Tomato	100	93	4	0·9
Blackcurrant	117	87	6	0·9
Grape	290	82	15	0·6
Melon	115	92	7	0·5
Drupes				
Olive	550	86 [Lipid-13]	4	1·5
Plum	210	84	13	0·6
Peach	200	86	12	0·6
Avocado pear	1 030	65 [Lipid-26]	5	1·7
False fruits				
Apple (eating)	240	84	5	0·3
Strawberry	155	89	8	0·6
Pineapple	200	87	12	0·5
Dried fruits				
Currant	1 090	22	63	1·7
Raisin	1 130	23	71	2·3
Prune	1 130	23	71	2·4
Apricot	1 030	24	67	4·8
Fig	1 130	22	73	3·1

EFFECT OF COOKING

Three-quarters of vitamin C ascorbic acid is destroyed by cooking, the acid present in the fruit preventing the complete decomposition. The boiling of fruits as in jam making softens the cellulose releasing the inter-cellular pectin and gums vital for setting. The *skins* of fruits are mainly composed of waxy, fatty and cork materials, which resist softening in cooking or in digestion. The parenchyma in *unripe* fruits is intact, whilst in *ripe* fruits the parenchyman disintegrates, consequently cooking softens unripe fruits. The *core* of fruits is mainly collenchyma, whilst the stones of fruits and pips consist of sclerenchyma.

Enzymatic browning occurs in cut apples, pears and bananas, this can be overcome by *blanching* at 90°C to destroy enzymes.

EFFECT OF STORAGE

The vitamin C ascorbic acid content of fruits decreases with storage, but less than with green vegetables; fruits contain acids which protect the vitamin from decomposition. Bruised and cut fruit rapidly lose their vitamin C ascorbic acid content owing to oxidation; *undamaged* fruits only should be stored. Carbon dioxide gas slows the ripening process of fruit in *gas storage* (see page 103).

NUTS

Nuts are dry fruits with very hard fruit walls. Botanically nuts can be divided into the *true* nuts and the *nut-like* fruits.

True nuts include hazel, cob, filberts, and Barcelona nuts,

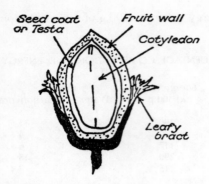

Figure 23.19. Structure of a hazel nut

which have a hard, woody fruit wall, surrounding the seed or *kernel* (see Figure 23.19). The mature fruit has a leafy bract. Sweet or Spanish chestnuts are surrounded by a prickly bract.

Nut-like fruits include almonds, coconut, walnut, peanut, Brazil, and cashew nut. Almonds are the stones of the plant drupes, just as the coconut is the stone of the coconut fruit surrounded by the outer fibrous copar. Walnuts are also the stones of the drupe-like fruits frequently pickled in their green form.

Brazil nuts are found as twelve to twenty seeds within a pot-shaped fruit. Cashew nuts are attached as seeds in pear-like fruits or pomes on the Brazilian cashew tree. Ground or peanuts are seeds found in underground pods.

COMPOSITION OF NUTS

The following table indicates that nuts are very rich sources of proteins and lipids, the latter consisting of over 80% *unsaturated* fatty acids.

Carbohydrates are found in amounts, between 10 and 20 per cent in all nuts; chestnuts contain about 45 per cent with very small amounts of fat and protein.

Nuts are of a very high energy value, between 1·250–2·500 *megajoules*/100 g. One hundred grams of roasted peanuts provide 2·5 MJ, and are equal in energy value to 100 g of fried bacon.

AVERAGE COMPOSITION (%) AND ENERGY VALUE OF NUTS

Nuts	Energy value kJ/100 g	Water	Carbohydrate	Lipid	Protein
Almond	2 500	5	20	53	20
Barcelona	2 800	6	18	60	12
Brazil	2 580	5	11	65	13
Chestnut*	900	48	45	2	4
Coconut	1 470	48	12	36	4
Peanut (roasted)	2 480	5	18	49	28
Walnut	2 760	3	15	64	12

*Note the high carbohydrate content.

Vitamins appear to be absent from nuts with the exception of small amounts of the vitamin B complex group. *Red palm oil* from the oil palm nut skins is rich in *carotenes*, the vitamin A provitamin.

Minerals. Calcium and iron are present in useful amounts in all nuts and fairly abundant in Brazil, almonds, and Barcelona nuts.

EFFECT OF COOKING

Most nuts appear to be improved by roasting which liberates lipid oil from the cells and is a stage in oil extraction. The vitamin B complex content will be reduced by heating.

EFFECT OF STORAGE

Nuts are stored in cool, dark dry conditions. Their high lipid content is liable to oxidation in the light and they become rancid. Stored nuts are attacked by moulds and insect mites.

CEREALS

Cereals are one of the main food sources for the world. The cereal grain is the *fruit* of plants of the grasses or *graminae*, whose flowers are reduced to the essential stamens and pistil. Rice, wheat, maize, ordinary and waxy varieties, oat, barley, sugar, and bamboo canes are all important in this family.

STRUCTURE OF THE CEREAL GRAIN OR CARYOPSIS

Cereal grains are botanically dry fruits, called a *caryopsis*, in which the fruit wall and seed coats are joined to form a singe *husk* or *bran*.

The cereal fruit grain within the fused fruit wall and seed coat or husk (12%) consists of:

(*a*) the embryo or *germ* (3%) consisting of a cotyledon (seed leaf), plumule (future shoot), and radicle (future shoot), in effect a miniature plant;

(*b*) the food reserve in the form of an *endosperm* (85%) consisting mainly of starch and an *aleurone* layer, of protein surrounding the endosperm. Figure 23.20 shows the structure of the cereal grains of wheat, rice, maize or corn.

WHEAT

There are two distinct botanical groups of wheat:

(*a*) *Triticum vulgare*, or common wheat used for making flour for bread, cakes, and biscuits.

(*b*) *Triticum durum*, or durum wheat, used for making semolina or flour for spaghetti, pasta, or macaroni.

The process of separating the indigestible bran or husk from the endosperm and germ is called *milling*. The processes for wheat *and* durum flour production are:

(*a*) *Wheat cleaning and grain conditioning*. Impurities are sieved away and air is blown over the sieved wheat to remove dust. Magnets remove metal particles and the grain is washed and centrifuged. Finally the damp wheat is dried to a certain moisture content and stored in bins until ready for milling.

(*b*) *Breaking the wheat*. Rollers break open the conditioned

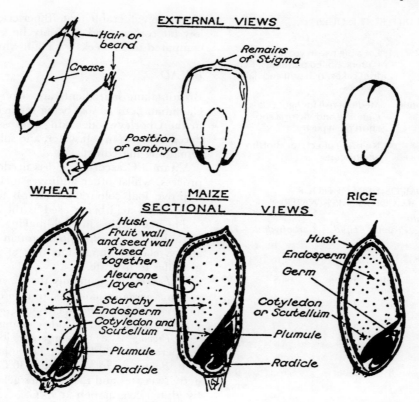

EXTERNAL VIEWS

Hair or beard

Crease

Remains of Stigma

Position of embryo

WHEAT   MAIZE   RICE

SECTIONAL VIEWS

Husk
Fruit wall and seed wall fused together
Aleurone layer
Starchy Endosperm
Cotyledon and Scutellum
Plumule
Radicle

Husk
Endosperm
Germ
Cotyledon or Scutellum
Plumule
Radicle

Figure 23.20. Structure of wheat, rice, and maize grains

grains and cut away the endosperm from which flour or semolina is made.

(*c*) *Bran sifting*. Bran is sifted from the broken wheat. Different grades, middlings and toppings, result depending on the amount of endosperm clinging to the husk. Bran is an important source of *dietary fibre*.

(*d*) *Reducing the purified endosperm to required size*. Purified endosperm passes through reduction rolls and is sieved to produce wheat flour or semolina of different particle sizes.

Coarse semolina is used mainly for puddings, etc., while *fine* semolina is the raw material for macaroni, spaghetti, and pasta.

Wheat flour is made by regrinding and resifting, up to thirty times, the endosperm to produce flour of different grades of fineness. Finally dibenzenecarbonyl peroxide (benzoyl peroxide) or chlorine dioxide bleach and mature the flour. Semolina flours are never bleached.

EXTRACTION RATE OF WHEATEN FLOURS

The extraction rate is a percentage figure of the flour obtained from the wheat after milling. Obviously if the flour is carefully purified and separated from the bran, a low extraction flour will be obtained.

Wholemeal flour or wholewheat flour of 100 per cent contains all the grain, 90 per cent brown flour 90 per cent. White enriched flour has an extraction rate of 70 per cent of the grain, 30 per cent having been removed as bran, germ and husk, and consist mainly of endosperm.

COMPOSITION OF WHEATEN FLOUR (see Appendix B)

The table, page 176, shows the composition of wheaten flours. Wheat flour is rich in carbohydrates; mainly *starch* 65–80 per cent, protein (glutenin/gliadin) 8–12 per cent, and fat 1–2 per cent. The endosperm provides most of the starch, the percentage of which increases as the extraction rate decreases. Protein from the aleurone layer close to the husk *decreases* as the extraction rate decreases; the fat, vitamins, and minerals yield decrease as the wheat germ is removed.

The quantity of protein in a flour determines whether it is a strong or bread flour, or a soft cake flour. Strong flours derive from Canadian wheat and have a protein gluten content of 10–12 per cent. Soft flours come from English wheat grown in a damp climate and have a protein content of 8–10 per cent.

Wholemeal flour contains *three times* more dietary fibre than white flours.

VITAMINS

Wholewheat is a valuable source of thiamin, riboflavin, and nicotinic acid. These vitamins of the B group are found mainly in the *wheat germ* and therefore the vitamin content

USES OF DIFFERENT FLOURS

Flour	Use
Strong Canadian flours 10–12% protein	For a big rise in yeast goods, batters, boiled puddings, rich fruit cakes, rich puff and flaky pastries
Soft English flours 8–10% protein	Medium rise for light cakes, Genoese and Victoria sponges, short crust pastry
Very soft English flours, low protein content with added rice or cornflour starch	No rising effect, for shortbread and biscuits

AVERAGE COMPOSITION OF FLOURS
(PERCENTAGE, ALL CONTAIN 15% WATER)

Flour	Energy value kJ/100 g	Protein	Lipid	Carbohydrate	Fibre
100% Canadian wholewheat	1 400	12	2·5	67	2
90% Canadian brown flour	1 425	11·8	1·9	68·5	1·09
80% Canadian extraction flour	1 430	11·5	1·4	70·1	0·16
White Canadian, enriched 70% flour	1 455	11·1	1·2	72·3	0·12
English wholewheat 100% flour	1 360	9	2·2	67	2·0
English 70% extraction flour	1 460	8	1·0	76	0·15

of wholemeal and wholewheat flours is much higher than that of 70 per cent extraction flour. Vitamin C ascorbic acid is added to the flour, yeast, and water mixture in the rapid Chorleywood breadmaking process. Enriched white flour has added thiamine and nicotinic acid. Vitamins D and C are absent from wholewheat flour.

MINERALS

Wholemeal flour is a poor source of minerals. Calcium is usually added to all flours except wholemeal in the form of 400 g of calcium carbonate to each 130-kg sack. Flour contains *inositols* or *phytic acid* which combines with calcium to yield *calcium phytate*, a form which cannot be used by the body. Therefore sufficient calcium carbonate is added to provide an excess for nutritional purposes.

EFFECT OF COOKING

The protein gluten is of importance in baked flour products. The elastic gluten forms the skeleton or framework of the baked product, its elasticity allowing expansion or rising. Starch is trapped within the framework with the leavening agent giving the food its lightness. The vitamin B group complex content is not greatly affected by baking temperatures.

EFFECT OF STORAGE

Flour can turn rancid because the lipid content oxidizes, and should be stored in a cool, dark place, in sealed containers. Wholemeal flours with a higher lipid content are more vulnerable that 70 per cent extraction flours with low fat content and can only be kept for about 8 weeks, compared to 25 weeks for plain white flour.

BREAD

Breadmaking ingredients are strong or weak flour; strong Canadian flour is now being replaced by soft English flour in the Chorleywood baking process. Hard water is considered better than soft water, and solid fats and yeast are the remaining ingredients.

Vitamin C ascorbic acid is needed for the Chorleywood process, whilst other additives include soya bean flour to improve loaf colour and crumb texture, with propanoic (propionic) acid being used as the antistaling agent.

The main stages in breadmaking are summarized briefly;

1. *Mixing*. To allow flour protein to hydrate and form the sticky, elastic, gluten mixture, and also allow the starch granules to hydrate.

2. *Fermentation* is mainly the enzyme activity in which the enzyme *amylase* changes starch into dextrins, glucose, and maltose, whilst the yeast enzyme *zymase* changes glucose into ethanol and carbon dioxide causing the dough to rise.

3. *Proving* is a resting stage for the cut dough at a temperature of 30°C and relative humidity of 85 per cent.

4. *Baking* is in ovens at 230°C. At 70°C all enzyme activity ceases and the starches gelatinize at 65°C, followed by gluten coagulation at 75°C.

During the baking in infra red ovens the crust forms dextrins, and they may caramelize, and browning of the crust occurs with the Maillard reaction between amino acids and monosaccharides. Browning does not occur in steam oven baking.

Breads are produced in great variety of shapes and types from many different mixtures and recipes. The following shows the average composition of some types of bread:

AVERAGE PERCENTAGE COMPOSITION AND
ENERGY VALUE OF BREADS

Bread	Energy value kJ/100 g	Carbohydrate	Protein	Lipid
Wholemeal (100% extraction flour)	1 000	47	9·5	3
Brown (90–80% extraction flour)	990	50	9·2	1·8
White (70% extraction flour)	1 060	55	8·3	1·7
Starch reduced	980	48	10·5	1·5
Malt bread	1 050	49	8·3	3·3

Bread, flour and cereals provide 35 per cent of the UK daily carbohydrate intake, 35 per cent of the daily protein, and 10 per cent of the daily lipid requirements (see page 219).

OTHER CEREALS

Maize, oats, rice, barley, and rye are cereal grains with the caryopsis structure similar to wheat.

The table summarizes the composition and energy value per 100 g of important cereals.

The *milled* cereals, such as polished rice, are deficient in vitamins of the B group, and vitamin E.

AVERAGE PERCENTAGE COMPOSITION AND ENERGY VALUE OF CEREALS

Cereal or flour	Energy value kJ/100 g	Carbohydrate	Protein	Lipid
Barley (pearl)	1 470	76	9	1·4
Oats, oatmeal	1 700	72	12	9
Rye, 100% rye flour	1 470	75	8	2
Polished rice, or ordinary white rice	1 510	86	6	1
Maize flour	1 525	72	9	4

USES OF IMPORTANT CEREALS

Cereal	Culinary use	Manufactured food
Wheat (*Triticum vulgare*)	Flour for bread, cakes, and biscuits	Flaked, puffed grain, shredded cooked wheat, and granules for breakfast cereals
Durum wheat (*Triticum durum*)	Macaroni, puddings, soups. Spaghetti for entrées. Semolina	Pasta for various processed foods
Rice	Polished rice for puddings and curries	Breakfast cereals
Maize	Cooked sweetcorn: Cornflour for custard and sauce. Maize oil for cooking oil	Custard, blancmange powders. Flaked and puffed grain breakfast cereals
Oats	Oatcakes	Porridge, Breakfast cereals
Barley	Pearl barley for soups. Malt from germinated or sprouted barley	Beer, malt, and malt extracts
Rye	Rye bread and pumpernickel	Crispbread

AVERAGE PERCENTAGE COMPOSITION AND ENERGY VALUE OF COOKED OR PROCESSED CEREALS

Cereal	Energy value kJ/100 g	Carbohydrate	Lipid	Protein
Pasta: macaroni and spaghetti (cooked)	620	30	0·5	5
Noodles (cooked)	525	23	1·5	4
Corn flakes	1 495	80	0·8	8
Rice crispies	1 481	86	0·8	6
Rye bread	1 021	52	1·1	9

Most breakfast cereals are fortified with useful amounts of B group vitamins and *iron*.

FARINACEOUS NON-CEREALS

Arrowroot, sago, tapioca, and soya bean flour are those flours associated with cereals, but having their origins from roots, stems, or bean seeds are not true cereals.

The table summarizes the nutritive value of the farinaceous non-cereals flours.

AVERAGE FOOD VALUES OF NON-CEREAL FLOURS (%)

Flour	Energy value kJ/100 g	Carbohydrate	Lipid	Protein
Arrowroot	1 530	94	0·1	0·4
Sago	1 470	86	0·2	0·4
Soya flour	1 750	13	23·0	40·0
Tapioca	1 490	88	0·1	0·4

Soya bean flour is a useful food containing both fat, protein and carbohydrate. Soya bean flour is considered suitable as a food in regions where the diet is low in protein and fat, or as a famine relief food. It is the raw material for manufacture of textured protein (see page 125).

Sago, tapioca, and arrowroot with a high starch content are not suitable staple foods since vitamins and proteins is negligible or completely absent.

SOURCE AND USES OF OTHER CEREALS

Cereal	Source and use
Sago	From centre of the sago palm tree trunk Puddings
Tapioca	From root of the cassava plant Puddings
Arrowroot	From the tubers of the maranta plant Invalid diet
Soya bean	Seed of pods from the soya plant Diabetic foods, ice-cream, and cakes

FLOUR CONFECTIONERY

(*a*) *Batters* for coating foods and pancakes are made from 50 per cent flour, and 50 per cent liquid ingredients.

(*b*) *Soft doughs* for buns and scones are made from 65 per cent flour and 35 per cent other components and liquids.

(*c*) *Stiff pastes* for biscuits are made from a mixture of 80 per cent flour with 20 per cent of other components and liquids.

The use of varying amounts of eggs, fats, sugar, and fruits produces the great range of cake and flour confectionery.

AVERAGE PERCENTAGE COMPOSITION AND ENERGY VALUE OF FLOUR CONFECTIONERY

Item	Energy value kJ/100 g	Carbohydrate	Protein	Lipid
Pancake	920	26	7	9
Plain bun	1 350	54	8	8
Water biscuit	1 850	73	9	12

SUGAR CONFECTIONERY (see Appendix B)

These are preparations made from sucrose sugar which provide the high carbohydrate content (40·80 per cent) of sweets, jams, jellies, and chocolates. Jams are the traditional methods of preserving fruits.

Invert sugar is a component of most boiled sweets, toffees, and jams (see page 111).

Useful amounts of *iron* and *calcium* are present in liquorice, fruit gums and chocolate.

AVERAGE PERCENTAGE COMPOSITION AND ENERGY VALUE OF SUGAR PRODUCTS

Product	Energy value kJ/100 g	Carbohydrate	Protein	Lipid
Jam	1 170	70	0·3	0·5
Jelly	1 050	65	–	0·3
Milk chocolate	2 280	54	34	6
Plain chocolate	2 000	62	30	2
Toffees	1 820	70	17	2

BEVERAGE PLANTS

Tea, coffee, and cocoa are important plant products used as beverages.

Tea consists of the dried leaves found towards the *tip* of the stem together with the leaf buds.

Coffee is the seed of the fruit from the coffee shrub. The drupe or cherry contains two seeds called the coffee beans; these are dried, roasted, and ground ready for use.

Cocoa is produced from the seeds of the cocoa tree fruit, which is a pod containing a sweet pulp and beans. Dried and crushed they produce cocoa powder and cocoa butter.

Cola beans are used for cola soft drinks and contain caffeine.

COMPOSITION OF BEVERAGES

Tea and coffee infusions have very little food value apart from that provided by the added milk and sugar. Tea and coffee infusions provide stimulation and refreshment deriving from the alkaloid *caffeine* which is a nerve stimulant and diuretic. An infusion of coffee contains four times as much caffeine as does one of tea. *Tannin* is an ingredient of the beverages, their flavour being partly due to tannin in its colloidal form. Essential oils provide the aromas and predominant flavours. Tea contains fluoride as much as fluoridated water.

Cocoa is a valuable drink in view of its food value, and its stimulant property due to its small *caffeine* and *theobromine* content. Cocoa powder contains 20 per cent protein, 25 per cent fat, and 35 per cent carbohydrate making cocoa beverage and chocolate foods of high calorific value.

Cocoa contains useful quantities of calcium and iron and an unusually large amount of *copper*. Traces of such vitamins as carotenes are found in cocoa, and small amounts of vitamins B_1 thiamin, B_2 riboflavin, and nicotinic acid occur in all three drinks. Tea as a drink is the more useful source of the vitamin, five cups with added milk providing 27 per cent of an adult's daily requirement of vitamin B_2 riboflavin.

AVERAGE PERCENTAGE COMPOSITION OF BEVERAGES

Beverage	Energy value kJ/100 g	Protein	Lipid	Carbohydrate
Tea leaves	235	14	0	0
In infusion	4	0·1	0	0
Coffee beans	1 260	12	15	28
In infusion	12	0·2	–	0.3
Cocoa	1 870	20	25	35

SUGGESTIONS FOR PRACTICAL WORK

1. Examine and draw a selection of vegetables, fruits, and nuts, indicating the important botanical features of the specimen.

2. Examine prepared slides showing longitudinal sections of maize and wheat grains. Draw the structure of the grain as seen under a low-power microscope.

3. Obtain ripe ears of wheat, oats, barley, and rye and draw the botanical features of these cereals.

4. Place some maize grains and a little butter in a pan with a tight-fitting lid, heat and observe the puffed appearance of the grain – of popcorn.

5. Heat dry grains of rice, wheat, maize, barley, and oats separately in a boiling tube to observe the bursting of the grain.

6. Obtain a strong and a weak flour. (a) Squeeze samples in your hand proving that the weak flour can be moulded while the strong flour falls apart. (b) Knead the flours into dough samples and compare their stretching powers.

7. Take a known weight of flour and knead it into a stiff dough. Place the dough in a muslin bag and wash away the starch. Bake the remaining gluten in a hot oven then weigh the gluten residue. Compare the weights of gluten remaining from similar weights of different flours to determine their relative strengths. Wholemeal, brown, and self-raising flours can be compared in this manner.

8. Determine the water-absorbing power of different flours using the following method. Take 100 g of flour and fill a 50 cm^3 measuring cylinder with water. Mix the flour with water from the cylinder, adding the minimum needed to obtain a firm dough. Repeat the experiment with different flours observing the amount of water needed.

9. See *Experimental Science for Catering and Homecraft Students*, Practical work 9 to 16 and 40.

QUESTIONS ON CHAPTER 23

1. Outline the process of photosynthesis and discuss its importance in relationship to the food supplies of man.

2. Draw and describe, giving named examples of vegetables derived from plants: (a) stems; (b) tubers; (c) roots; (d) buds; and (e) flowers.

3. Give an account of the following and their use as fruits and vegetables: (a) drupes; (b) berries; and (c) buds.

4. Draw and describe the structure of wheat and maize grains. Outline the process of milling to produce wheat flour.

5. Write short notes on: (a) rice; (b) durum wheat; (c) soya bean flour; (d) sago; and (e) cornflour.

6. Compare the approximate composition of the following vegetables: (a) potatoes; (b) cabbage; and (c) cauliflower. What is the effect of long storage on vegetables?

7. Compare the composition and nutritive value of: (a) potato; (b) soya bean flour; (c) Brazil nuts; and (d) apples.

8. Give two named examples and draw diagrams to show the structure of the following types of fruits: (a) drupe; (b) berry; (c) false fruit; and (d) pod.

9. Compare the nutritive value of tea with that of cocoa. Explain the following: (*a*) boiled coffee tastes differently from infused coffee; (*b*) boiled tea tastes differently from infused tea; (*c*) tea containing milk loses its bitter taste; and (*d*) tea made from previously infused leaves by adding fresh hot water is less stimulating.

10. Outline the importance of fresh fruit in a healthy diet.

11. Give an account of the minerals present in: (*a*) tap water; (*b*) vegetables; (*c*) nuts; and (*d*) fruits.

MULTIPLE CHOICE QUESTIONS ON CHAPTER 23

Questions 1 and 2 refer to Figure 23.21 which shows a sectional view of a wheat grain.

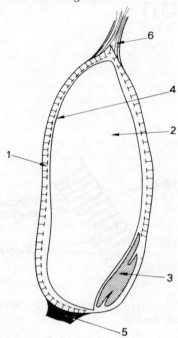

Figure 23.21.

1. Wholemeal wheat flour consists of the parts labelled:
(*a*) 1, 2   (*c*) 1, 2, 3, 4
(*b*) 1, 2, 3   (*d*) 2, 4, 5, 6

2. Wheat bran is derived mainly from parts labelled:
(*a*) 1, 2   (*c*) 2, 3
(*b*) 1, 4   (*d*) 2, 4

3. The composition of a wholewheat flour is shown as follows:

	% water	% protein	% lipid	% carbohydrate
(*a*)	4	0·5	–	95
(*b*)	12	7	0·5	80
(*c*)	35	9	3	50
(*d*)	15	9	2	72

4. The cementing substance between the cells of unripe fruit is mainly:
(*a*) cellulose   (*c*) pectin
(*b*) lipid   (*d*) dextrin

5. Apples have a carbohydrate content of:
(*a*) 5%   (*c*) 25%
(*b*) 15%   (*d*) 35%

6. Which of the following has the highest lipid content?
(*a*) pears   (*c*) olives
(*b*) raspberries   (*d*) oranges

7. Which of the following indicates the composition of a raw potato?

	% water	% carbohydrate	% protein	% lipid
(*a*)	50	20	10	20
(*b*)	6	50	7	37
(*c*)	78	20	2	–
(*d*)	–	60	40	–

8. Plunging green vegetables into boiling water for a short time helps to break down:
(*a*) the green chlorophyll making them white
(*b*) the enzyme which destroys vitamin C – ascorbic acid
(*c*) the soluble sugars into brown caramel
(*d*) lipids which cause the rancid flavours

9. The browning seen on the exposed cut surfaces of fresh apples is due to:
(*a*) caramelization of sugars
(*b*) amino acid and sugar interaction
(*c*) enzyme activity
(*d*) iron in the fruit

10. The main carbohydrate present in a potato is:
(*a*) sucrose   (*c*) starch
(*b*) glucose   (*d*) glycogen

24 Body structure and function

The human body is a complex structure made up of millions of cells grouped into tissues and organs finally combining to form the following systems:

THE SKELETON

The skeleton consists of a soft substance called *cartilage* hardened with deposits of calcium and also by the effect of vitamins A retinol, D cholecalciferol and C ascorbic acid. An adult requires 500 mg of calcium per day, children and nursing mothers between 600 and 1 200 mg, the increased supply being for bone growth and teeth (see Appendix C).

The human skeleton divides into the *axial* portion including the skull and backbone, and the *appendicular* portion including the bones of the limbs. The skeleton bone forms 15% of the human body weight.

Function of the skeleton

1. It provides support for the muscles and gives shape to the body.

2. It protects the softer organs; the skull protects the brain and the rib cage the heart and lungs.

3. Movement of the body is effected through the joints of the skeleton.

4. Blood cell formation in the *red* bone marrow.

THE MUSCLES

The *contraction* and *relaxation* of the muscles account for the movement of our bodies. There are three kinds of muscle, voluntary, involuntary, and heart or cardiac muscle; these form 45% of the human body weight.

1. *Voluntary muscle* (Figure 24.1) is also known as striped

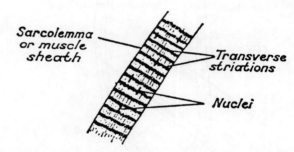

Figure 24.1. Voluntary-muscle fibres as seen under the microscope

or striated muscle. It is attached to the bones through *tendons* and can be moved by command of the brain. It forms the main part of lean meat which consists of long cylindrical cells or *muscle fibres*, each with a nucleus and many cross stripes surrounded by an *endomysium*. The individual muscle fibres form bundles by means of connective tissue, called the *perimysium*. These bundles give a grainy appearance to meat (*see* Figure 25.2).

The body can vary its movements according to the type of joint associated with the muscle. Figures 24.2 and 24.3 show the *synovial* joint of the knee and elbow and the *plane* joint of the backbone. The important features of joints are: (*a*) the tough *ligaments* joining the bones and (*b*) the cartilage bones at the extremities which allow smooth movement of the bone surfaces over each other.

Experiment

Examine typical meat joints for the tough yellow ligaments and smooth, ivory-like cartilage surfaces. Note the white tendons connecting the meat to the bone.

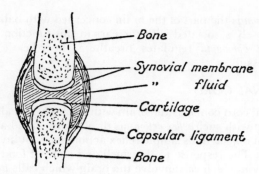

Figure 24.2. Synovial joint

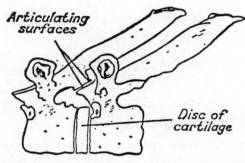

Figure 24.3. Two vertebrae, illustrating plane joint

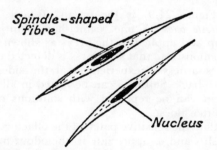

Figure 24.4. Involuntary muscle fibres as seen under the microscope

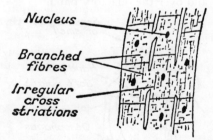

Figure 24.5. Cardiac muscle as seen under the microscope

2. *Involuntary muscle* or unstriped and smooth muscle (Figure 24.4) is found in the walls of the stomach, intestine, blood vessels, and reproductive organs and cannot be controlled at will. This muscle is important in driving food along the alimentary canal by *peristalsis* (see page 184).

3. *Cardiac or heart muscle* (Figure 24.5) is the muscle of the heart and causes its automatic rhythmic contraction throughout a person's life. Cardiac muscle has an appearance intermediate between that of voluntary and involuntary muscle.

Red and white meat

Raw meat colour is due to blood pigment *haemoglobin*, and muscle pigment *myoglobin*. The proteins of lean meat are *myosin* and *actin*. The heart, leg, and rib muscles require more oxygen and contain more myoglobin than the white muscle in chicken, turkey, and duck breast. White meat occurs in muscle not often used such as the breast meat of the flightless hen, turkey, and duck; by contrast the pheasant's is red (see page 188).

CONNECTIVE TISSUE

This is an important tissue associated with bone and muscle. Ligaments tendons, cartilage, and fat are connective tissues associated with meat. The tissue serves to *enswathe*, *support* or *bind*.

(*a*) *Ligaments* link bones and are formed of yellow elastic tissue mainly composed of a protein called *elastin*. They are unaffected by cooking and account for the toughness of certain meats.

(*b*) *Tendons* join muscles to bones and consist of white, inelastic fibres composed of the protein *collagen*, which is softened by boiling or moist heat by conversion into gelatine (Figure 24.6) (see also page 124).

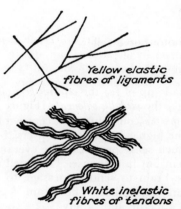

Figure 24.6. Connective tissue composed of yellow and white fibres as seen under the microscope

(*c*) *Cartilage* is found in joints forming much of the bones of young animals such as calves and chickens.

(*d*) *Lipid*, or *adipose* tissue, is a connective tissue producing the marbling effect valued in prime-quality meat (see Figure 6.1), and found in the fat depots beneath the skin and around the kidneys.

Connective tissue proteins

The main protein of connective tissue is *collagen* which binds cells together and forms tendons, skin and bone. *Reticulin*, found also between cells as a surrounding network, is found in meat muscle, kidney, liver and nerves. It is similar to collagen in forming gelatin. *Elastin* is the yellow elastic fibres found in lungs and artery walls. It does not yield gelatin as it is unaffected by cooking.

THE NERVOUS SYSTEM

The nervous system co-ordinates the work of different parts of the body and makes a person aware through the sense organs of changes in his surroundings.

The nervous system is composed of nerve cells which basically consist of a *cell body* with its nucleus and dendrites, and the *axon*, or nerve fibre, surrounded by a nerve sheath. Nerve cells (Figure 24.7) are found in the brain and spinal cord, or *central nervous system*, while nerve fibres resembling cotton are found in the arms and legs, or in the peripheral nervous system. Some nerve fibres can be over 50 cm long.

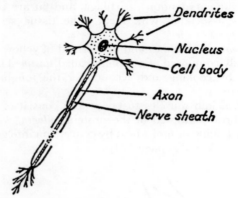

Figure 24.7. A motor-nerve cell

THE BRAIN

The brain is made up of (*a*) the *cerebral hemispheres*, (*b*) the *cerebellum*, and (*c*) the *medulla oblongata* (Figure 24.8).

Cerebral hemispheres constitute the centre of reasoning, memory, and the higher intellectual powers. Messages are received from such sense organs as the eye and nose, and messages are sent out in response. The smell and sight of food causes the brain to send a message to prepare the digestive system for action. The brain *hypothalamus* is concerned with appetite and satiety.

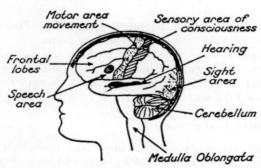

Figure 24.8. The main parts of the brain

Cerebellum is the part of the brain concerned with balance and is closely associated with the ears in this function.

Medulla oblongata regulates breathing, heartbeat, and blood pressure.

THE SPINAL CORD

The spinal cord connects the brain with the body and also is concerned with such *reflex actions* as drawing the hand away from a hot object. This simple reflex action does not involve the brain. The response to the smell and sight of food is a reflex action which *does* involve the brain which calls many organs including the salivary glands, the stomach, and intestines into action.

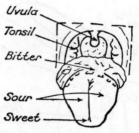

Figure 24.9. The different taste regions of the tongue

TASTE AND SMELL

The tongue (Figure 24.9) is the organ of taste, being covered with *taste buds*. A fine, camel-hair paint brush dipped in syrup and applied to the areas as shown in the diagram will demonstrate that sweetness is detected only at the tip, while sourness is experienced at the sides, and bitterness at the back. Saltiness can be tasted in all areas. This experiment can be repeated with solutions of salt, vinegar, and bitter aloes.

Smells stimulate the sensitive patch of the olfactory nerve (see Figure 24.10) and to appreciate it, the odour must be sniffed quickly over the patch. Severe head colds cause nasal obstruction preventing the entry of smell sensations into the nose and over the olfactory patch.

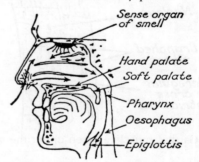

Figure 24.10. Structure of the nose, mouth, and larynx

Taste and smell are intimately linked in the process of savouring food. In the absence of sense of smell only sweet, sour, salt, and bitter tastes can be distinguished. Tangerines will taste sweet but lack the flavour caused by the essential oils which cannot stimulate the olfactory patch.

DIGESTIVE OR ALIMENTARY SYSTEM (GUT)

The digestive system consists of: (*a*) the alimentary canal, and (*b*) the accessory digestive glands.

ALIMENTARY CANAL

The alimentary canal is basically a tubular structure approximately 9 to 10 m in length and accordingly coiled inside the abdomen. The alimentary canal consists of six parts (see Figure 24.11): (*a*) mouth, (*b*) pharynx, (*c*) oesophagus, (*d*) stomach, (*e*) small intestine, and (*f*) large intestine ending in the rectum and anus.

DIGESTIVE GLANDS

Glands produce *digestive* juices which are poured on to the food in the alimentary canal. This converts it into a simple form capable of passing through the alimentary canal into the blood. There are five digestive glands: (*a*) salivary glands in the mouth, (*b*) gastric glands in the stomach, (*c*) pancreas or stomach sweetbread, (*d*) liver, and (*e*) intestinal glands found in the small intestine.

It takes food approximately 18–24 hours to travel from mouth to anus and be eliminated as *faeces*, after the digestion and absorption of the simple food components.

The mouth

The teeth, jaws, and tongue masticate food and mix it with saliva produced from the salivary glands at the sight and smell of food. Sudden shock or fright stops the secretion of saliva.

The teeth appear as two sets during the lifetime of a person, the temporary milk teeth, and the permanent set. The adult has three types of teeth:

1. Incisors, or sharp cutting teeth.
2. Canines, pointed for piercing and tearing flesh.
3. Pre-molars and molars, for crushing and grinding, have broad crowns (see Figure 24.12).

A tooth consists of a very hard enamel surrounding a bone-like *dentine* in the centre of which is the *pulp* cavity supplied with nerves and blood vessels. The tooth is fixed into sockets of the jaw by means of the dental cement and the gum.

Tooth decay is caused by bacteria changing sucrose into *acids*, which attack tooth enamel.

DIGESTION

This is the process by which complex food materials are converted into *simple soluble* substances by the action of *enzymes*. Carbohydrates are converted into monosaccharides, such as glucose and fructose. Lipids are converted into fatty acids and propanetriol (glycerol). Proteins are converted into amino-acids.

ENZYMES

Enzymes are the active components of the digestive juices,

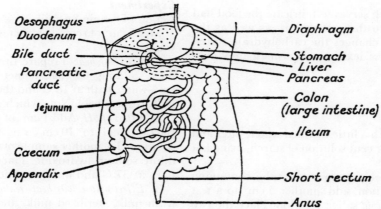

Figure 24.11. The human alimentary canal

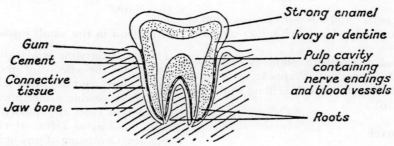

Figure 24.12. Longitudinal section of a tooth with two roots

being responsible for the chemical changes within the living cells of plants and animals, their important properties and activity factors being:

1. *Heat* and high temperatures prevent enzyme action; milk at a temperature *above* blood temperature 36·8°C will not clot and produce junket with rennet enzyme extract.

2. *Specific* changes are brought about by individual enzymes. Lipids can be changed only by a lipid-splitting enzyme, *lipases* and proteins by *proteases*, the *proteolytic* protein-splitting enzymes and carbohydrates by *glycosidase* enzymes. Nucleic acids are changed by *nucleases*.

3. *Catalysts* promote chemical changes though remaining unchanged themselves. Enzymes are called biological catalysts.

4. *Hydrolysis*, the process of reacting a chemical compound with water, is the main type of change brought about by enzymes. Most digestive processes involve the addition of water to a chemical compound.

5. *pH* affects the activity of enzymes. The enzymes in saliva function only in the alkaline condition of the mouth, while stomach enzymes require an acid pH as in the gastric juice.

6. *Vitamins of the B group* play an important part in enzyme activity and are called *coenzymes*.

Enzymes are important in the chemical changes forming the basis of respiration, fermentation, in the process of excretion, and are responsible for enzymatic browning of foods (see page 162).

Digestion in the mouth

Saliva contains *mucin* which serves to lubricate the food ball or bolus as it travels down the oesophagus, as well as the enzyme α-amylase which changes the carbohydrate starch into the disaccharide *maltose* dextrins and a small amount of *glucose*.

Experiment

Enzyme action of saliva:

Rinse out the mouth with a little distilled water, filter and set it aside. Prepare a 1 per cent solution of starch, using hot water and allow it to cool.

Add 5 cm³ of starch solution to a test tube containing 5 cm³ of *boiled* saliva solution, add another 5 cm³ to a test tube containing 5 cm³ of *cold* saliva solution. Place the two labelled test tubes in a water bath at 37°C for 30 minutes. Test the contents of the tubes as instructed:

Tube containing boiled saliva. Add a few drops to a drop of iodine on a white tile. A blue–black coloration indicates unchanged starch.

Tube containing fresh saliva. Test with iodine as above and note that the blue–black colour does not appear, evidence of changed starch. Test the remainder with Fehling's solution, or Clinistix reagent strip.

Digestion in the stomach

Food is passed from the mouth to the stomach by waves of muscular contraction known as *peristalsis*. Gastric juice containing 0·4 per cent of hydrochloric acid is secreted by the lining of the stomach. The acid is a food disinfectant and halts the action of the saliva amylase; it also commences the digestion of some proteins and curdles the milk.

Gastric juice contains the enzyme *pepsin* which changes proteins into simpler *peptones*. Rennin is another enzyme which clots or curdles milk and is active only in the gastric juice of babies in forming *casein* curds.

The secretion of gastric juice increases at the sight and smell of food, of meat extracts and soups in particular. This explains the effectiveness of soup as an *appetizer*.

Lipids are not digested in the stomach except in young children. Large amounts cause the food to remain longer in the stomach by slowing the production of gastric juice. This gives a feeling of fullness or satiation.

After 2–4 hours the food is well churned by stomach movements into cream and is passed into the small intestine via the duodenum.

Experiment

Action of gastric enzyme pepsin:

Prepare a 1 per cent solution of pepsin enzyme from pepsin powder. To test tubes containing respectively 5 cm³ distilled water and 5 cm³ 0·2 per cent hydrochloric acid, add pieces of freshly boiled egg white and 5 cm³ of 1 per cent pepsin solution. Place the two test tubes in a water bath at 37°C and observe the egg white dissolving in the pepsin/acid mixture.

Experiment

Action of rennin on milk:

Mix 5 cm³ of rennet extract with 100 cm³ of cold, distilled water.

1. *Effect of heat.* Prepare three test tubes of 10 cm³ raw milk, adding 0·5 cm³ rennet solution. Place one in a cold-water bath at 18°C and the others in baths at 35°C and 55°C respectively. Note which milk sample coagulates first.

2. *Effect of pH.* Add 1 cm³ of 1 per cent hydroxypropanoic (lactic) acid to 10 cm³ raw milk and 5 cm³ of rennet solution. To another sample of milk and rennet add 2 cm³ of dilute sodium hydroxide. Place both test tubes in a water bath at 37°C and observe which milk sample clots.

3. *Effect of previous heat-treatment of milk.* Take samples of fresh milk, sterilized milk, and long-life U.H.T. milk. To 10 cm³ samples add 0·5 cm³ of rennet extract, place in a water bath at 37°C, and obsereve which milk sample coagulates.

Digestion in the small intestine

The small intestine is a region of great digestive activity owing to the effects of the liver, pancreas, 'stomach sweetbread', and intestinal juice.

1. *Liver* produces bile juice which collects in the gall bladder to enter the duodenum. Bile juice contains bile salts, emulsifying agents which convert lipid oils into a fine *emulsion*. Consisting of tiny lipid drops the emulsion offers a large surface subjected to rapid enzyme action.

2. *Pancreas* produces the *hormone* insulin (see page 189) which is concerned with blood sugar control, and the important digestive enzymes *trypsinogen, amylase, nuclease,* and *lipase.*

Trypsin converts peptones into amino-acids. This enzyme is so powerful that when first formed it is in the *inactive* form *trypsinogen* becoming *active* trypsin in the small intestine by the action of *enterokinase* made by the juice of the small intestine:

$$\text{Peptone proteins} \xrightarrow{\text{Trypsin}} \text{amino-acids}$$

Amylase changes starch and glycogen into maltose, also small amounts of dextrins and glucose:

$$\text{Starch and glycogen} \xrightarrow{\text{Amylase}} \text{maltose, dextrins and glucose}$$

Lipase is the important lipid-splitting enzyme which changes lipid oils and fats into fatty acids and propanetriol (glycerine):

$$\text{Lipids} \xrightarrow{\text{Lipase}} \text{fatty acids + propanetriol (glycerine)}$$

Nucleases break down nucleic acids into organic bases, phosphates, and pentose sugars.

$$\text{Nucleic acids} \xrightarrow{\text{nucleases}} \text{organic bases + phosphates + Pentose sugars}$$

3. *Small intestine* produces intestinal juice enzymes which change remaining *disacchorides* into *glucose, fructose* and *galactose.* Some lipase and nuclease are also formed.

No digestion occurs in the large intestine.

ABSORPTION OF DIGESTED FOOD

The simple substances produced by the digestive process pass through the wall of the alimentary system into the blood and circulatory system. *Diffusion* partly explains the absorption of digested food through the cells of the intestine lining. The regions of the alimentary canal concerned with absorption of digested and easily assimilable foods are the mouth, stomach, and small and large intestine.

The small intestine is the main region of absorption. The lining of the small intestine consists of millions of tiny projections called *villi* (Figure 24.13). Each is supplied with an artery and vein and a *lacteal* vessel. Glucose, maltose, and sucrose and amino-acids pass through the wall of the villi straight into the circulatory bloodstream.

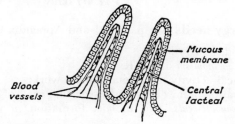

Figure 24.13. Villi (longitudinal section)

Fatty acids and propanetriol (glycerine) enter the lacteal vessel and some finely emulsified lipid enters the bloodstream without undergoing enzymatic fat-splitting. Water, minerals, and vitamins are absorbed within the small intestine.

The mouth lining has powers of absorption limited to water.

The stomach absorbs very small amounts of glucose directly into the bloodstream. Ethanol in alcoholic beverages is rapidly absorbed into the blood via the stomach wall, the more easily on an empty stomach.

The large intestine, together with the rectum, is concerned with the absorption of water and minerals from the indigestible remains of the food which become consolidated and form the *faeces.* These are removed by the process of *defaecation,* some 18–24 hours after food ingestion.

Coeliac disease in young children is due to a sensitivity to flour gluten, and the small intestine lining becomes defective. A *gluten-free* diet overcomes this disability.

THE LIVER

The liver functions primarily for the secretion of bile and storage of food, especially the carbohydrate glycogen. Its functions are:

1. Storage of glycogen made from surplus glucose and amino acids.

2. Conversion of surplus amino-acids into glycogen and carbamide (*urea*) which is excreted through the kidneys;

3. Lipids are converted into a form ready for providing energy.

3. Iron and vitamins A, D and B_{12} are stored.

5. Heat is generated in the liver which becomes the warmest part of the body.

Much of the surplus lipids in the bloodstream is stored around the kidneys, further deposits being produced beneath the skin or within the muscles.

RESPIRATION

Respiration is a process for *liberating energy* from foods. It takes place either with the use of oxygen in *aerobic* respiration as is usual in animals and plants, or without oxygen, a

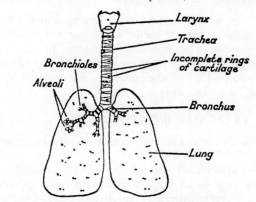

Figure 24.14. The respiratory organs

less efficient process called *anaerobic* respiration, as in yeast and certain micro-organisms during fermentation. (See page 214.)

A. AEROBIC RESPIRATION

Aerobic respiration takes place in the mitochondria of living cells (see page 168). The lungs bring oxygen from the air into intimate contact with the bloodstream. Air enters the lungs through the trachea, bronchi, bronchioles (Figure 24.14) and finally the alveoli which are in close contact with the network of blood capillaries (Figure 24.15). The area for exchange of gases in the lung is about 60–100 square metres.

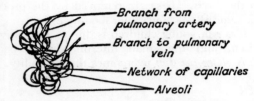

Figure 24.15. Alveoli and associated blood capillaries

Oxygen combines with the haemoglobin of the blood cell and then is carried to every living cell as bright red *oxyhaemoglobin*. The liberated oxygen release energy from the glucose food in the cell mitochondria with the aid of certain respiratory *enzymes*. This produces carbon dioxide, water, and energy, the last providing heat for cell maintenance and the life of the body. The chemistry of liberating energy from food is:

Glucose + oxygen = carbon dioxide + water energy
$$C_6H_{12}O_6 + 6O_2 = 6CO_2 + 6H_2O + energy$$

The energy released from glucose passes to an energy store substance called *adenosine triphosphate* or ATP, found in muscle cells and causes muscle contraction.

The waste products of respiration, carbon dioxide and water, are now excreted. They dissolve in the blood and return to the lung where they enter the alveoli and are exhaled.

B. ANAEROBIC RESPIRATION

Anaerobic respiration *without* oxygen can occur for a short time in skeletal muscle cells following very strenuous physical exercise. The blood sugar glucose produces *lactic* (2-hydroxypropanoic) acid, plus a *small* amount of energy, which is only 5% of the amount formed by aerobic respiration (see page 214).

PRODUCTS OF AEROBIC RESPIRATION

1. *Carbon dioxide* is expelled from the body in 'breathing out'.

2. *Water*, also called *metabolic water*, can be used by the living cells, and is an important source when people are deprived of water; otherwise small amounts of water are expelled in breathing out.

100 g lipids produces 107 g metabolic water
100 g carbohydrate produces 55g metabolic water
100 g protein produces 42 g metabolic water

3. *Energy*: almost 50% of this is in the form of *heat energy*, providing warmth and a suitable temperature for all the body's chemical changes (*metabolism*). The other 50% is energy by way of ATP (Adenosine triphosphate) for all body *work* inside the cells, and for moving the body externally.

Food energy values

The energy conversion factors of the different nutrients are 17 kJ/g for protein and carbohydrate, 37 kJ/g for lipid, and 29 kJ/g for ethanol. These are *net values*, and are *less* than the *chemical combustion* values obtained by calorimetry (see page 26). The losses occur in the body when some of the nutrients enter the *faeces* undigested, or when 30% of protein energy is lost in the urine as *urea* (carbamide).

Human body energy reserves

An adult man has about 500 MJ of energy stored mainly in the *lipids* in the skin, around the kidneys and, in a small amount, in muscle. Other long-term reserves are the *proteins* of skin and muscle. The *daily* energy supply is mainly in blood *glucose* and *glycogen* of the muscles and liver.

A *starving* man, providing he has a water supply, can survive for up to one or two months, using these various body energy reserves.

BASAL METABOLIC RATE (BMR)

An adult human body *resting*, in a moderate room temperature of 20°C, some 12 hours *after* a meal, uses energy at the *basal* or lowest rate, just to maintain the heart beat, breathing and to keep the body warm or maintain *basal metabolism*, which keeps the body alive. It excludes *any active* physical movement, such as sitting, standing or walking, or working (see page 54).

Calculation of BMR

$$\frac{\text{Daily BMR}}{\text{of an adult}} = \frac{\text{Body weight}}{\text{in kg}} \times 24 \text{ hours} \times 4{\cdot}25$$

(e.g., for a 70 kg adult man)

Daily BMR requirement = 70 × 24 × 4·25
= 7 140 kJ per day
= *7·14 MJ* daily

Daily energy needs (see page 221 and Appendix C)

Food provides *energy* for:
1. *Basal metabolism* or BMR;
2. Physical activity or skeletal muscle work;
3. Formation of new cells and tissues in *growth* of babies, children, *convalescents*, and in *milk* formation in nursing mothers.

Physical activity, milk and new tissue formation require

between 75% and 50% *more* energy than the daily basal metabolic rate.

Daily energy needs = $\underset{(25–50\%)}{\text{BMR}}$ + $\underset{\text{activity}}{\text{physical}}$ + $\underset{\underset{(50–75\%)}{\smile}}{\underset{\text{tissue formation}}{\text{milk and new}}}$

The following affect the daily energy needs:

1. *Physical activity*, work or occupation: sitting, standing and walking need one-half, double and four times the energy used for lying down at the BMR.

Different *occupations* have differing energy needs. *Light* occupations include those of office and shop workers, teachers, the unemployed and professional workers. *Moderately active* jobs include those of students, farm workers, housewives and factory workers. *Very active* jobs include those of soldiers, mineworkers, dancers and athletes. *Exceptionally heavy* jobs include those of lumberjacks, blacksmiths, construction workers and rickshaw pullers.

2. *Body size and sex*: the body size or framework means *more* cells in larger bodies and fewer cells in smaller bodies. Females, who have more body fat than males, require less energy than males.

3. *Age*: the basal metabolic rate and physical activity *decline* above the age of 40.

4. *Climate*: people are less active and tend to eat less food in hot climates.

5. *Thyroid* gland disorders cause an increase in BMR if the gland is overactive, and a decrease if it is under-active.

6. *Children and adolescents*: BMR is at its highest rate in infants, and increases again in adolescence, when *growth* rates are highest.

7. *Pregnancy and lactation*: during pregnancy extra energy is needed for *growth* of the baby. Nursing mothers who are breast-feeding need extra energy for *milk production*; the daily amount of breast milk is 850 ml, requiring 3 MJ of energy, obtained in the mother's daily food intake.

The table below, prepared by the Food and Agriculture Organization of the United Nations shows recommended daily amounts (RDA) of nutrients (see also Appendix C), detailing the basic energy needs for different ages of people in all countries of the world. Individual countries, including the United Kingdom and the United States, also issue RDA tables, although these recommend slightly different energy intake values (see Chapter 28).

EXCRETORY SYSTEM

Excretion is the process of eliminating the waste products of metabolism or of eliminating chemical waste. The main excretory products are some 2 litres of water, carbamide

(urea), sodium chloride, and carbon dioxide. They are removed from the body by: (*a*) kidneys (*b*) skin, (*c*) lungs, and (*d*) large intestine.

KIDNEYS

Blood containing waste products reaches the kidneys which act as filters by withdrawing *urine* from the blood. The kidneys then pass it down the ureters into the bladder. Periodically the bladder is emptied by the process of *micturition* (see Figure 24.16).

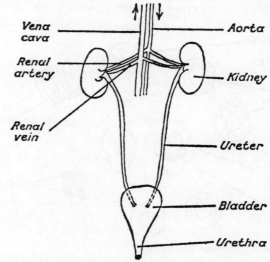

Figure 24.16. The excretory system of the kidneys

The kidneys control the amount of water in the blood; an increase in fluid intake results in more urine being produced. In addition to sodium chloride and carbamide (urea), sugar is produced in the urine after increased muscular activity and in sugar diabetes. The daily output of water from the kidneys is 0·5–1·5 litres.

SKIN

Water and sodium chloride are eliminated through the sweat glands, the evaporation producing a cooling effect. Since the skin is an excretory organ it should be kept thoroughly clean.

LUNGS

During the process of respiration the lungs excrete carbon dioxide and water. The skin and lungs together give out about 0·7 litres of water daily.

RECOMMENDED DAILY ENERGY NEEDS
(Food and Agricultural Organization/World Health Organization, 1974)

Age Sex	Below 1	1–3	4–6	7–9	10–12 boys	10–12 girls	13–15 boys	13–15 girls	16–19 boys	16–19 girls	Adults men (mod. active)	Adults women (mod. active)	Pregnancy last 6 months	Lactation first 6 months
Body weight	7·3	13·4	20·2	28·1	36·9	38·0	51·3	49·9	62·9	54·4	65·0	55·0	–	–
Energy (MJ)	3·4	5·7	7·6	9·2	10·9	9·8	12·1	10·4	12·8	9·7	12·6	9·2	plus 1·5	plus 2·3

THE LARGE INTESTINE

This can be regarded as an organ of excretion since it absorbs water from the faeces. This is transported by the blood to the kidneys which disposes of the bulk.

THE CIRCULATORY SYSTEM

The blood is an important *connective tissue* consisting of red and white blood cells suspended in a liquid *plasma* (see Figure 24.17). In addition to the red and white cells there are tiny *platelets* concerned with the clotting of blood.

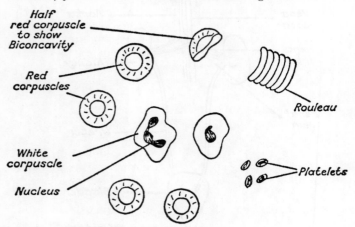

Figure 24.17. Human blood cells

Red blood cells, or *erythrocytes*, contain *haemoglobin* and serve to carry oxygen and also give meat part of its red colour. White blood cells, or *leucocytes*, cleans the blood keeping it free of foreign bodies and micro-organisms. They are very active when a wound becomes infected.

Plasma is the straw-coloured fluid which transports glucose, amino-acids, fatty acid, propanetriol (glycerine), sodium chloride, carbamide (urea), and hormones through the body. Similarly carbon dioxide is carried in the plasma for elimination from the lungs.

Functions of the blood

1. It aids respiration in carrying oxygen and carbon dioxide.
2. It transports absorbed food from the small intestine.
3. It takes excretory products to the skin and kidneys.
4. It is a defence against micro-organisms through the white blood cells.
5. It distributes heat through the body from the liver and muscles.
6. It carries hormones.

Tissue fluid from the blood surrounds and bathes all the body's living cells. It contains the essential *nutrients* (see page 157) in addition to oxygen: water, glucose, amino and fatty acids, mineral ions kept at a steady concentration, at a temperature of 38°C and pH 7·3, by an automatic control process called *homeostasis*, aided by insulin, the liver, kidneys and skin.

HEART

The heart (Figure 24.18) pumps oxygen-rich blood through the body by way of the *arteries*; these supply individual cells and tissues through a capillary network. Impure blood is returned by way of the *veins*.

The heart is made up of cardiac muscle and is divided into four chambers, two thin-walled *auricles* and two thick, muscular *ventricles*. Between the auricles and ventricles on the left and right sides of the heart are *valves* which prevent the backflow of blood.

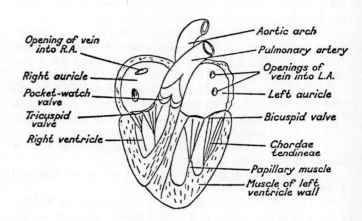

Figure 24.18. Internal structure of the heart

BLOOD CIRCUIT

There are 5·7 litres of blood in the body in constant circulation round all the cells of the adult body. Periodically new blood cells are added from the *marrow* tissue of bones, while worn-out blood cells are destroyed in the liver and *spleen*.

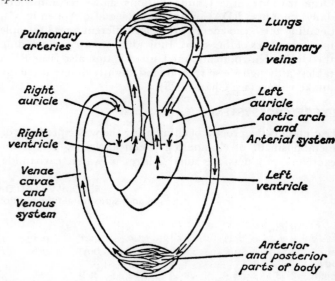

Figure 24.19. Diagrammatic representation of the double circuit of the blood

The blood circulates in a *double circuit* (see Figure 24.19) completely separating pure oxygen-containing blood and impure blood.

Heart disease

Cholesterol (see page 116) is produced in the human body, and is present in eggs, bacon, milk products (including butter), liver and shellfish. High levels of cholesterol can collect in the blood and can be deposited on the inside walls of the arteries. This blockage can cause the heart to pump much harder than it normally does, resulting in a *high blood pressure*.

A *heart attack* may occur when the heart's own arteries become blocked by a blood clot. A *stroke*, resulting in paralysis, is caused by blockage of a brain artery, or bleeding from the artery.

High blood pressure can also affect the *kidneys* and can cause *eye* damage.

High blood pressure can be avoided by eating less hard saturated *animal lipids* and less *salt*, by weight reduction where there is obesity, and by giving up *smoking* and avoiding worry or *stress* (see also page 222).

ENDOCRINE GLANDS

Two distinct type of glands are found in the body. The first, *ducted glands*, produce secretions which travel directly through the body via tubes or ducts; for example the bile duct of the liver and the salivary duct of the salivary glands. The second type is without a duct being called *ductless* or *endocrine glands*. They discharge their secretions, called *hormones*, directly into the bloodstream which rapidly distributes it throughout the body. Figure 24.20 shows the situation of the more important ductless or endocrine glands in the human body.

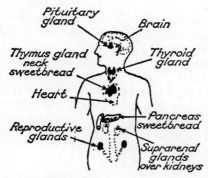

Figure 24.20. Distribution of the endocrine glands in the human body

Pancreas produces a hormone *insulin* by means of cells called the *islets*. Insulin aids the utilization of sugar by the body. The amount of sugar in the blood is 0·08–0·18 per cent in a healthy person; if it falls below this level the person may die and if excessive it is eliminated in the urine. Insulin stimulates the entry of glucose into body cells; if insufficient, sugar will collect in the blood causing sugar diabetes.

The *thyroid* gland situated in the neck near the windpipe produces the hormone *thyroxine* containing iodine. This gland controls the rate of metabolishm. Excessive secretion of thyroxine increases the speed of metabolic processes, while undersecretion slows them down. A normal BMR would be 7·15 megajoules MJ. If the thyroid gland is overactive the BMR will be *above* 7·15 MJ/day; if under active it will be less than 7·15 MJ/day. Over-active thyroid glands increase the heartbeat making the individual over-excitable, and under-active thyroid glands make one slow, apathetic, and listless (see page 187).

Thymus gland, also called the neck sweetbread found between the lungs and the heart, is considered to be associated with the development of the sex organs.

Pituitary gland is not much bigger than a pea and is situated at the base of the brain. It is important in controlling other endocrine glands and in controlling bone growth.

Adrenal glands, found above each kidney, produce *cortisone* and *adrenaline*. The latter serves to prepare the body for action, releasing sugar from the liver to the muscles while increasing the heartbeat and rate of breathing.

Parathyroid glands produce parathormones, are situated close to the thyroid glands, are concerned with the quantity of *calcium* in the body. An over-active gland causes calcium to be removed from the bones making them brittle and easily fractured

SUGGESTIONS FOR PRACTICAL WORK

1. The general dissection of a small mammal such as a rat or rabbit should be performed in order to observe the arrangement of the main organs of digestion, respiration, excretion, and blood circulation.

2. Examine the following, either as abbatoir or butcher's offal: Sheep's pluck, kidneys, liver, heart, bladder, tripe, and intestines. Compare the appearance of neck and gut sweetbreads.

3. See *Experimental Science for Catering and Homecraft Students*, Practical work 6.1, 20.1, 21.6, 22.1, 24.2, 28.3, 30.1, 30.2, 35.1, 37, 38 and 39.

QUESTIONS ON CHAPTER 24

1. Write short notes on: (*a*) the function of the skeleton; (*b*) the structure of a tooth; and (*c*) the endocrine glands.

2. Draw a labelled diagram of the alimentary system, showing where the digestion of protein and carbohydrates takes place.

3. Define the terms: (*a*) excretion; (*b*) respiration; (*c*) defaecation; and (*d*) digestion.

4. Give an account of the processes of digestion, absorption and utilization of lipids.

5. Describe the process of respiration in animals.

6. Outline the process of digestion of a sugar cube from the time it enters the mouth until its absorption into the blood.

7. State the composition of potato. Describe the process of digestion of the components of a potato.

8. Give a short account of muscle and connective tissues.

9. Write short notes on: (a) red and white meat; (b) ligaments; (c) tendons; and (d) cartilage.

10. Give an account of the structure and care of the teeth.

11. State how the energy requirements of a person can be measured. What is the basal metabolic rate?

12. What are the energy requirements of a moderately active man and woman? What factors affect the individual's energy requirements?

13. Briefly outline the daily energy requirements of: (a) young children under 10; (b) nursing mothers; (c) teenagers; (d) sedentary female workers; and (e) quarrymen.

MULTIPLE CHOICE QUESTIONS ON CHAPTER 24

The following questions refer to Figure 24.21.

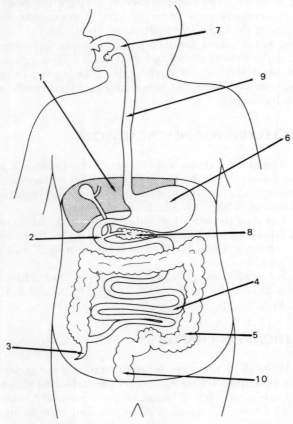

Figure 24.21. The digestive system

1. Which of the following labelled parts of Figure 24.21 is unable to produce digestive juices of any kind?

(i) 3   (iv) 6
(ii) 4   (v) 7
(iii) 5   (vi) 8

(a) i, iii   (c) iv, vi
(b) ii, v   (d) v, vi

2. The parts of the digestive system concerned with absorbing digested foods are:

(a) 1   (c) 4
(b) 3   (d) 5

3. In which part of the digestive tract are vitamins manufactured for the use of the body:

(a) 2   (c) 7
(b) 5   (d) 8

4. Vitamins A – retinol and vitamin D – cholecalciferol together with the mineral iron are found in large amounts in the part labelled:

(a) 1   (c) 6
(b) 3   (d) 8

5. The part labelled 5 in Figure 24.21 serves to absorb one of the following:

(a) bile pigment   (c) mucus
(b) water   (d) cellulose

6. The process of breaking down complex foodstuffs by digestion within the body is basically a chemical process called:

(a) neutralization (c) hydrolysis
(b) condensation   (d) dissociation

7. Carbohydrates are digested by one of the following agents:

(a) proteases   (c) lipases
(b) nucleases   (d) glycosidases

8. Which of the components of bile juice functions to emulsify lipids?

(a) mucin   (c) bilirubin
(b) cholic acid   (d) cholesterol

9. One of the following is a product of trypsin enzyme activity:

(a) glucose   (c) amino acids
(b) fatty acids   (d) propanetriol

10. Which of the following parts of the digestive system is unable to produce a carbohydrate digesting enzyme?

(a) pancreas   (c) stomach
(b) small intestine (d) mouth

25 Foods from animals

Foods of *plant origin* form about 75% of the world's food supply and are important sources of carbohydrate, vitamin C and folic acid and *unsaturated lipids*. They are the sole sources of *dietary fibre*, vitamin K and phytic acid.

Foods of animal origin form about 25% of the world's food supply and are important sources of protein, with most of the essential amino acids and *saturated* lipids (with the exception of marine fish oils). They are the sole sources of vitamins D and B$_{12}$, and of cholesterol. *Iron* from foods of animal origin is better absorbed than iron from foods of plant origin.

MEAT, MEAT PRODUCTS, POULTRY, AND GAME

Edible meat consists of skeletal or *striped muscle* in cattle, sheep, pigs, poultry, and game, and of involuntary and cardiac muscle in such *offal* as intestines, and heart.

STRUCTURE OF MEAT OR MUSCLE MEAT

Muscle meat is made of 55 per cent *myosin*, 25 per cent *actin*, 20 per cent other proteins, forming the individual *muscle fibres* surrounded by an *endomysium* sheath. These are grouped into bundles wrapped around with a *perimysium*. The tendon binding the muscle to a bone is continuous with the perimysium. The ultimate meat muscle consists of many muscle fibres surrounded by an *epimysium* (see Figure 25.1):

Myson (55%) + actin (25%) + 20% other protein + endomysium = muscle fibre

Many muscle fibres + perimysium = bundle of muscle fibres
Many bundles of muscle fibres + epimysium = meat muscle

Connective tissue forms an important part of meat muscle structure. Two proteins, *collagen* and *elastin*, form the main components of this tissue:

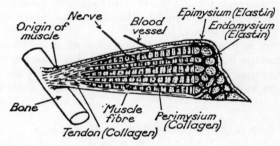

Figure 25.1. Structure of meat

Collagen forms tendon, the perimysium of muscle fibre bundles, cartilage, and bone.

Elastin forms most of the elastic ligaments, a small amount occurs around muscle, a larger amount forms the walls of arteries.

Reticulin is mostly found in muscle endomysium, and surrounding cells of kidney, liver, and nerves. Tough stringy meat 'gristle' consists mainly of elastin and reticulin.

A fine deposit of lipid fat around the muscle fibres is responsible for 'marbling' in meat.

The tenderness of meat depends on the amount of connective tissue and in particular the amount of elastin in the meat muscle. Young, inactive animals produce tender meat with little elastin; old, active animals develop considerable elastin causing toughness of the meat. Muscles which are seldom used such as loin and rib, yield tender meat in comparison to the tougher meat from muscles of the legs, such as shin which are in frequent use.

COMPOSITION OF MEAT (see Appendix B)

Meat muscle fibres consist of 65–75 per cent water, proteins, lipids, vitamins, and minerals. Meat contains 10–25 per cent protein, composed of all the essential amino-acids necessary for body building. Such offal as heart and sweetbreads contain 20–25 per cent protein.

The amount of lipid in meat varies according to the age, type of muscle, feeding, breed and species of animal. Veal and lamb contain very little, 3–10 per cent, and fat pork and mutton chops 45–50 per cent. Meat lipids are composed of over 50% *saturated* fatty acids.

Carbohydrates are not abundant in meat. *Glycogen* or animal starch is normally found in *live* muscle (1 per cent), but in dead meat the glycogen is changed to hydroxypropanoic (*lactic*) acid. Liver has some 5 per cent of carbohydrate in the form of glycogen.

Vitamins, except the vitamin B group, thiamin, riboflavin, and nicotinic acid are poorly represented in meat. A little vitamin E, tocopherols, occurs in pork, bacon, and beef. Liver offers plentiful vitamin A retinol, some D cholecalciferol, C ascorbic acid, and members of the B group; kidney supplies small amounts of the same vitamins. Meat extracts contain useful amounts of vitamin B, nicotinic acid and riboflavin.

Meat such as pork, heart, and sweetbreads, is rich in *phosophorus*. *Iron* is present in liver and kidney to the extent of 15 mg in 100 g offal, equal to the daily iron intake of an adult. (See Appendix C.)

Calcium is not abundant except in venison and sweetbreads; tripe is unusually rich, much being added during cleansing and dressing. The table summarizes the percentage composition and energy value per 100 g of meat and offal.

AVERAGE PERCENTAGE COMPOSITION AND ENERGY VALUE OF MEATS

Meat	Energy value kJ/100 g	Protein	Lipid	Carbohydrates	Water
Beef, steak (cooked)	1 590	21	32	0	46
Veal (cooked)	1 000	32	11	0	58
Lamb (cooked)	1 150	24	19	0	56
Pork (cooked)	1 400	23	26	0	50
Offal					
Liver (raw)	570	20	4	5 (Glycogen)	70
Kidney (raw)	587	15	8	1	75
Heart (raw)	455	17	6	0	75
Tripe (cooked)	415	19	2	0	79

Cholesterol is present in liver, brain and kidney.

Effect of cooking

Since meat consists of the proteins myosin and actin, the main effect of the heat is to *denature* and *coagulate* the protein (see pages 123 and 197).

The connective tissues are then subject to the effects of heat. *Collagen* and *reticulin* is attacked by moist heat and converted into soluble *gelatine* (see Figure 25.2). *Elastin* forming the surrounding endomysium envelope of the muscle fibres contracts on heating, causing the meat to shrink. The combined effect of the coagulation of the protein and the *shrinkage* of the muscle fibre endomysium, is that some juices are squeezed out.

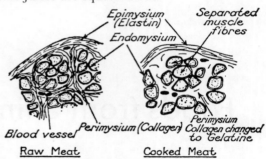

Figure 25.2. Comparison of fine structure of cooked and uncooked meat

Tender meat with little connective tissue is cooked by dry heat – roasting, grilling, and baking. The muscle fibres separate due to the combined effect of the so called dry heat, the moisture present in the meat attacking the collagen of the connective tissue. Moist heat – boiling, stewing, and steaming – is suitable for *tough meat* with large amounts of connective tissue.

In cooking, muscle proteins denature at 40°–50°C, and shrinkage of the meat occurs at 65°C. Well-cooked meat will reach an internal temperature of 80°C whilst 'rare' cooked meat reaches an internal temperature of 65°C.

The colour of meat is due to the pigments of the muscle fibre and to the blood; the muscle fibre colour derives from *myoglobin* and the blood colour from *haemoglobin*. Freshly cut meat exposes myoglobin to oxygen forming *oxymyoglobin* which gives a bright red colour, slowly darkening. Young animal meat is lighter in colour than that of older animals; muscles frequently used are darker in colour than those seldom used.

On cooking, the red haemoglobin and myoglobin pigments are denatured to *globin haemochrome* of brown colour, also *Maillard browning* by reaction of amino acid with sugars occurs; under-done meat retains some of its original pigments (see page 162).

Vitamins of the B group, particularly thiamine, are affected by cooking, and much water-soluble B group vitamins are leached out by boiling, stewing, or braising. Fat *dripping* from roasting meat contains cholesterol, and vitamins A, D and E.

Effect of storing

Meat which is freshly slaughtered is not suitable for immediate cooking, meat which has been stored is more tender.

All animals are *rested* before slaughter to allow glycogen accumulation in the muscle. On hanging freshly killed meat the glycogen changes into hydroxypropanoic (*lactic*) acid, which improves the tenderness, keeping quality, and flavour. Most meats are hung 7–10 days before sale. Animals exhausted by exercise or struggling before slaughter give poor-quality meat with very little hydroxypropanoic (lactic) acid and of poor keeping quality.

TENDERIZING OF MEAT

A number of methods are used for tenderizing meat.

1. *Mechanical* damage causing separation of the muscle fibres can be achieved by hammering, beating and dicing. Mincing and scoring the meat allows tougher meats to be cooked by dry heat.

2. *Enzyme action* takes place when meat is stored or hung since certain protein-splitting enzymes called *cathepsins* attack the connective tissues, thus separating the muscle fibres, by the process of *autolysis*.

Prolonged storage until meat becomes high, because of the activity of micro-organisms, achieves greater tenderness through the action of the micro-organisms attacking the tissues.

3. *Tenderizers*, as solutions or powders, are sprinkled on to the meat before cooking. They contain plant enzymes such as *papain* from the juice of the papaya plant, *bromelin* from pineapple juice, and *ficin* from figs. Cattle are also injected with sterile papain solution a short time before slaughter.

POULTRY AND GAME

The meat from poultry and game birds have a similar composition and undergo identical changes on cooking and storage as meat from cattle. The table shows the approximate percentage composition and energy value per 100 g of different cooked poultry. Chicken has the *lowest* energy value in contrast to the fatty meat of duck and goose, and also has the *highest* content of *unsaturated* fatty acids.

AVERAGE PERCENTAGE COMPOSITION AND ENERGY VALUE OF COOKED POULTRY MEATS

Poultry	Energy value kJ/100 g	Protein	Lipid	Water
Chicken	775	20	11	68
Duck	1 345	16	28	54
Goose	1 470	16	32	51
Turkey	1 125	20	20	58

Cholesterol is present in poultry and large amounts of goose liver.

FISH

Fish fall into two groups, from the nutritional aspect: *white fish* and *oily fish*. This classification depends on the amount of lipids in the fresh fish, irrespective of whether it is freshwater or sea fish.

Fish flesh (*see* Figure 25.3) is made up of muscle blocks or *myomeres* with connective tissue or *myocommas*. Myocommas are made entirely of collagen. When cooked the connective tissue is readily converted into gelatine and the myomeres

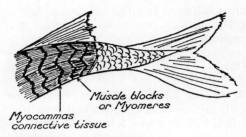

Figure 25.3. Structure of fish flesh

separate into flakes. The breakdown of myocommas in uncooked fish is called 'gaping', seen in haddock.

Fish bones are of two types, *cartilage* or soft bones found in ray, skate, and dogfish. They are not hardened with calcium salts and on cooking are softened by conversion of their collagen into gelatine, making them quite edible. The majority of fish have bones hardened or ossified with calcium salts, providing useful nutrient mineral from sardines, sprats, and pilchards.

COMPOSITION OF FISH (see Appendix B)

Of oily and white fish, the former have 10–25 per cent lipid in the fresh flesh whilst the white fish have 1–5 per cent lipid.

Fish contain a higher proportion of water than most meats and more discarded waste in the form of bones, fins, scales, guts and head and tail amounting to 35–45 per cent.

Fish provides high biological value protein containing all the essential amino-acids needed for body building. Protein content is 14–20 per cent. Oily fish contain 10–12 per cent of lipid composed of *polyunsaturated* fatty acids PUFA (see page 110). Carbohydrates are not present. Vitamins A retinol, and D cholecalciferol are abundant in oily fish with useful quantities of the vitamin B group, especially in the liver and roes. Fish provides calcium and phosphorus but contains little available iron. Sea fish are the main source of *iodine* apart from drinking water and table salt.

AVERAGE PERCENTAGE COMPOSITION AND ENERGY VALUE OF FISH

Fish	Energy value kJ/100 g	Protein	Lipid	Water
White fish				
Cod (raw	295	17	1	82
Haddock (raw)	310	17	1	77
Oily fish				
Herring (raw)	580	19	12	73
Salmon (canned)	855	22	12	65
Sardine (canned)	875	25	11	57

Cholesterol is present in fish roes and cod liver oil.

Fish are unfortunately very perishable. Fish struggle when caught resulting in exhaustion of their glycogen which prevents the formation of hydroxypropanoic (*lactic*) acid, which would improve keeping quality. In addition the flesh contains a nitrogenous compound, *trimethylamine*, causing the familiar odour of bad fish on staling. Long storage in deep freeze causes the protein to *denature* and the oil in fatty fish to *rancidify*.

SHELLFISH

Shellfish include the crustaceans and molluscs, each biologically distinct from the other and from fish. *Crustaceans* used as food include crabs, lobsters, shrimps, and prawns, while the main *molluscs* are oysters, mussels, winkles and cockles.

Molluscs have a large amount (60 per cent) of waste in the form of shells, the crustaceans a lesser amount in the hardy, outer *exoskeleton*.

Both are rich in protein (10–18 per cent) and contain very little lipids, between 1 and 5 per cent. Carbohydrates as *glycogen* are present in molluscs. Vitamin A as carotenes is found in shrimps and oysters together with small amounts of the B group vitamins. Certain oysters can contain considerable amounts of vitamin C ascorbic acid. Shellfish are particularly rich in minerals. Cockles contain certain amounts of *iron* equal to that in ox liver, while all shellfish provide substantial calcium and phosphorus, iodine and zinc.

The energy value per 100 g for molluscs is less than half that of crustaceans as shown in the table:

AVERAGE PERCENTAGE COMPOSITION AND ENERGY VALUE OF SHELLFISH

Shellfish	Energy value kJ/100 g	Protein	Lipid	Carbohydrate [Glycogen]	Water
Crab (cooked)	450	17	3	1·3	74
Lobster (cooked)	360	18	1	0·1	77
Mussel	260	11	2	3	78
Oyster	210	6	1	3	87
Winkles	313	15	2	2	72

Cholesterol is present in all shellfish.

EGGS

Edible eggs are produced by hens, geese, ducks, plovers, and gulls; this account is concerned with the hen's egg only. In the ten-months laying period a bird will lay up to 190 eggs. The egg is primarily a means of reproduction and so contains sufficient food for the developing chick for its twenty days in the shell. The fully formed egg consists of shell, white, and yolk (see Figure 25.4).

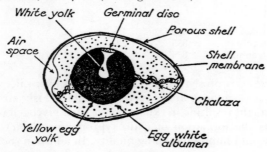

Figure 25.4. Structure of a hen's egg

(i) *Shell*. The shell is *porous* with millions of tiny holes, essential to allow air to enter for the developing chick to breathe. The shell is made of calcium carbonate (chalk) which can be dissolved by dilute acid to reveal a skin or egg membrane surrounding the egg. At the broad end of the egg is the *air-space* between shell and membrane. This increases in size as the egg gets older because of evaporation through the porous shell. Eggs are examined or *candled* for freshness by holding them up to a strong light to observe the size of the air-space.

The shell being porous lets gases and odours penetrate it causing off flavours. Eggs should therefore be stored away from odorous substances.

(ii) *Egg white*. The egg white forms 65 per cent of the egg. It serves to protect the developing chick and has little food value. Egg white in a fresh egg has a thick consistency which slowly thins on ageing, the white and yolk ultimately running together. A fresh egg broken on to a plate has a whole dome-shaped yolk supported by a thick, firm white (see Figure 25.5).

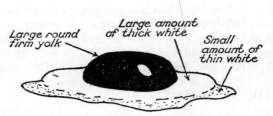

Figure 25.5. Appearance of a fresh egg with firm thick white and domed yoke

(iii) *Egg yolk* (35 per cent). The yellow colour is due to *carotenes* present in the hen food, yellow corn. Pale yellow eggs indicate vitamin A present in such foods as seed cake pellets, by-products from vegetable-oil production.

The yolk consists of the *germinal disc* where the young chick develops; it is connected to the yolk sac which supplies food directly into the alimentary system of the chick. The *chalaza* cord prevents the rotation of the chick with the egg.

COMPOSITION OF THE EGG

Eggs resemble meat in having a high protein content (12 per cent) and correspondingly high lipid content (12 per cent). Very small amounts (1·0 per cent) of carbohydrates are present. Water accounts for 74 per cent and calcium, phosphorus, and iron form 1 per cent of total weight.

AVERAGE COMPOSITION (%) AND ENERGY VALUE OF EGG

One hen's egg = 55 g

Portion of egg	Energy value kJ/100 g	Protein	Lipid	Carbohydrate	Water
Yolk	1 500	16	32	1	48
White	195	12	0·2	0·7	86

Vitamins A retinol, D cholecalciferol, E tocopherols, K and B group and folic acid are all present in fresh, whole eggs.

The table shows the distribution of nutrients between egg white and yolk, which has an energy value *eight* times that of the white.

Egg fat is present as an emulsion in the yolk being stabilized and emusified by *lecithin*. Thus egg yolks only are used in mayonnaise and salad-cream emulsions.

Egg protein provides high biological value protein containing all essential amino-acids. The protein of egg white is 63 per cent *ovalbumin* and 37 per cent other proteins; the egg yolk consists chiefly of liproteins – *lipovitellin* and *lipovitellenin* amounting to 32 per cent, other yolk proteins include *livetin*, a phosphoprotein.

Cholesterol is present in considerable amounts 1·6 g/100 g of egg yolk.

Effect of cooking

Heat coagulates the egg protein; egg white coagulates at approximately 60°C and egg yolk at 68°C. If beaten together coagulation occurs at 63°–65°C.

Vitamin B_1 thiamin is destroyed in cooked eggs the remaining vitamins being unaffected. A *green* colour develops around the yolk in hard-boiled eggs possibly due to iron(II) sulphide compounds formed by the combination of iron and sulphur present in the egg.

Effect of storing

Eggs having porous shells lose water readily by evaporation. As storage time proceeds the white becomes *alkaline* and thin, causing the water to enter the yolk. Bacteria penetrate the shell and decay begins, producing offensive smelling hydrogen sulphide gas (H_2S) as a by-product. As eggs are laid they are coated with *mucin* which prevents the entry of bacteria. This natural seal is removed by washing, and water and bacteria can enter. Eggs should therefore be *wiped* with a cloth, and stored with the blunt end uppermost away from odours and high-flavoured foods. Waterglass, sodium silicate, preserves eggs by blocking the pores of the shell. Storage of eggs at −1°C in air containing 2·5 per cent carbon dioxide is employed for commercial gas storage.

Egg freshness index

This is a measure or *ratio* of the yolk height divided by its diameter. High yolk indexes indicate freshness.

Food poisoning from eggs

Birds like all animals are liable to disease. Harmful microbes can enter the egg before the shell is formed. Ducks, which have unhygienic feeding habits, are susceptible to infection by a microbe *Salmonella*, and duck eggs should be well cooked in order to destroy the microbe. The hen's egg is not often subject to *Salmonella* infection (see pages 208 and 210).

MILK AND MILK PRODUCTS

Milk is the secretion of the mammary glands of the mammal. It can be used untreated or be processed to provide such important foods as butter, cream, cheese, and processed milk. The most common in use is cow's milk; other sources are goat's and to a lesser extent sheep, buffalo, and mare's. This account deals with cow's milk only.

AVERAGE COMPOSITION OF MILK (see Appendix B)

Milk is primarily a food in itself and is therefore to some extent a completely balanced nutrient for feeding the young suckling animal. The table indicates the *average* composition of cow's milk:

COMPOSITION AND USE OF COW'S MILK

Component	Percentage	Purpose
Water	87·54	Body building
Lipid	3·71	Energy
Protein	3·29	Body building
Milk sugar (lactose)	4·70	Energy
Minerals (calcium and phosphorus)		
Vitamins A retinol, the B group, C ascorbic acid, D cholecalciferol, and E tocopherols,	0·76	Protection and body building

Energy value = 274 kJ)100 g

Milk provides many of the nutrients essential for energy, protection, and body building.

Milk protein consists mainly of *casein* and to a lesser extent as *lactalbumin* and *lactoglobulin*. All contain the essential amino-acids of high biological value protein. Lactose or milk sugar is a disaccharide which gives milk its pleasant, sweet flavour.

Milk lipids are dispersed through the liquid as an emulsion stabilized by the casein. On long standing the oil droplets come together and form the cream line. The lipid content consists of about 60% *saturated* fatty acids, and 7% *polyunsaturated* fatty acids PUFA. Milk is rich in the calcium and phosphorus essential for building new bones and teeth.

Vitamins A retinol, D cholecalciferol, and E tocopherols are present in milk; the quantity of vitamin A retinol and D cholecalciferol varies being greater in summer milk than in winter milk. Vitamin B_2, riboflavin, nicotinic acid, and B_1 thiamin, together with vitamin C ascorbic acid are found in *untreated* milk, but are reduced severely in quantity by processing and storage.

Cholesterol is present in small amounts.

Energy value of milk

One litre of milk provides 2·8 megajoules MJ (670 Cal) or one-quarter of the daily requirement of a sedentary adult. A child under 1 year would need 1·07 litres daily to provide its needs of 3·3 megajoules MJ/day.

Effect of storing

Milk exposed to sunlight in glass bottles rapidly loses its vitamin C ascorbic acid and B_2 riboflavin; cardboard or similarly opaque containers prevent this loss. Untreated, raw milk is attacked by microbes and can cause milk-borne disease through infected cows or milk handlers.

Souring is brought about by the bacteria in raw milk which produce hydroxypropanoic (lactic) acid. The process is rapid in warm weather, but slow or inhibited entirely in cold weather. Raw milk should therefore be stored in a cold, dark place.

MILK PROCESSING

The consumer has available the following treated and untreated milks.

Tuberculin tested or T.T. milk. The cows have been tested for tuberculosis and the hygiene of the farm and dairy workers approved. The milk can be sold as either *untreated*, tuberculin tested milk; or it can be pasteurized to become *pasteurized*, tuberculin tested milk.

Pasteurized milk. Raw milk is heated to 72°C for 15 seconds by the high temperature, short-time method, which destroys most of the harmful bacteria and reduces the vitamin C ascorbic acid and B_1 thiamin content. The milk is then sealed in sterile bottles.

Sterilized milk. The raw milk is heated in the bottle at 107°C for 30 minutes, a space being left above the milk to allow for expansion. The process is carried out in autoclaves.

Sterilized milk will keep unopened for at least a week; its vitamin C, ascorbic acid, and B_1 thiamin content is less than that of pasteurized milk.

Long life milk. Raw milk is heated to 132°C for less than a second; it is called ultra heat treated (U.H.T.) milk. Unopened aluminium-foil packs will keep from 2 to 3 weeks.

Homogenized milk. This is milk in which the fat globules have been broken up and dispersed making the fat easily digestible. Tuberculin tested and pasteurized milk can be homogenized.

Evaporated milk. Milk is evaporated under *reduced* pressure to three-fifths of its original bulk and is then homogenized and canned.

Condensed milk. Raw milk is preheated, filtered, and separated. The last process produces condensed *skim* milk with a minimum of 26 per cent milk solids. Otherwise *full cream* condensed milk is made with a minimum of 31 per cent total milk solids including 9 per cent milk lipids.

Sugar is added as a *preservative* to the extent of 41–45 per cent. Vacuum evaporation proceeds until 60 per cent of water is removed, the condensed, sweetened full cream or skim milk then being canned.

Dried milk. Dried milk is produced either from whole, half cream or skimmed separated milk. The milk is dried by: (*a*) roller-drying, by which milk evaporates from a hot rotating roller the dried milk being scraped off; or (*b*) spray-drying, in which milk is sprayed down a tower up which travels a blast of hot air, the milk powder falling to the bottom.

Fresh skim milk, with its extremely low lipid content (0·1%), is an increasingly popular fresh whole-milk *substitute* for *adults*. It is *not* suitable for infants, due to its low vitamin A and D content. Otherwise, it is nutritionally similar to whole milk, having *half* its energy content, and very little cholesterol.

MILK PRODUCTS

CREAM

Experiment

Place some fresh milk in a centrifuge tube attached to the hand centrifuge apparatus. On rotating observe how the cream separates into a distinct layer above the skim milk. Cream is produced from milk by separation in a *centrifugal* cream separating machine.

Cream contains all the fat and cholesterol of the milk with the vitamins A retinol and D cholecalciferol. The yellow colour of cream and milk comes from carotenes, the vitamin A provitamin. Three types are available: single cream, double cream, and clotted cream.

(1) Single cream contains 18 per cent lipid, 3 per cent carbohydrate and 2·4 per cent protein and is produced by separating fresh milk.

(2) Double cream is made by again separating single cream and contains 48 per cent lipid, 2 per cent carbohydrate, and 1 per cent protein.

(3) Clotted cream is made by skimming cream from fresh milk and reducing the water content by slow evaporation. It contains 55 per cent lipid and has a similar composition to double cream.

Whipped cream. The minimum content of fat for a cream to whip is between 30 and 32 per cent. Below this cream will stiffen only. The temperature should be below 4°C during whipping. The protein of the cream is *denatured* to form a framework supporting the air in water foam. *Half cream* contains 12 per cent lipid, and *sterilized* cream has 23 per cent lipid.

ICE CREAM

Dairy ice-cream is prepared from milk, cream, sugar, flavouring, and added gelatine. Non-dairy ice-cream consists of an oil-in-water emulsion into which air is incorporated; margarine and non-milk solids are used mainly. Dairy ice-cream contains not less than 5 per cent milk lipid with not less than 7·5 per cent non-lipid milk solids or dried skim milk.

AVERAGE PERCENTAGE COMPOSITION AND
ENERGY VALUE OF ICE-CREAM

Protein	Lipid	Carbohydrate	Water	Energy value kJ/100 g
4	10	25	60	840

Cholesterol is present in dairy ice-cream and absent from non-dairy ice-cream.

BUTTER

Butter is produced by separating cream from milk (see page 116). *Ripened cream* or sour butter is prepared by allowing the cream to sour. It is exposed to the air or a souring agent in the form of a culture of micro-organisms is added. The sour cream is then churned as a sweet cream butter. English butter is a sweet cream butter, Danish butter being a sour cream.

AVERAGE COMPOSITION OF BUTTER AND MARGARINE

Component	Butter	Margarine
Water (%)	12·0	13·0
Protein (%)	1·0	0·2
Lipid (%)	83·0	82·0
Minerals		
Ca (per 100 g)	15 mg	4·1 mg
P (per 100 g)	24 mg	12 mg
Vitamins (per 100 g)		
Vitamin A	1 050 μg retinol equivalents	890 μg retinol equivalents
Vitamin D	1·75 μg cholecalciferol	8·2 μg cholecalciferol
Vitamin E	1·75 mg/100 g	52 mg/100 g
Energy value	3·34 MJ/100 g	3·34 MJ/100 g

Butter is a concentrated source of lipid with a very high energy value per 100 gram. It is rich in Vitamin A retinol, but does not provide as much vitamin D cholecalciferol and E tocopherols as margarine.

The polyunsaturated fatty acid PUFA content of butter is much greater than most margarines.

Cholesterol is present in butter and absent from margarine.

CHEESE

The process of cheese-making in outline:

1. The milk is *pasteurized* and cooled to destroy undesirable micro-organisms.

2. Milk-*souring* bacteria are added as a starter and rapidly sour the warmed milk.

3. *Rennet* is added to the sour milk when it has reached the correct acidity to produce a curd.

4. The curd is left to harden and is then *cut* with cheese knives into 1/cm cubes and the greenish-yellow whey drained off.

5. The curd is heated or *scalded* to harden the curd, that is coagulate the protein, and facilitate draining of the whey. Sodium chloride is added.

6. After draining the curd is pressed in moulds to squeeze out any remaining whey.

7. Finally the pressed curd is allowed to mature. Moulds and micro-organisms attack the butter fat and convert it into the cheesy-smelling *butanoic (butyric) acid* and other products which provide the characteristic flavour.

The presence of moulds give a cheese a coloured veining evident in Stilton and Roquefort. Depending on consistency cheeses are (a) hard or pressed cheese such as Cheddar and Cheshire, (b) soft cheese as Camembert and Brie, and (c) cream cheese made from double or single creams.

Composition of cheese

The table shows the composition of hard and soft cheeses:

AVERAGE PERCENTAGE COMPOSITION AND ENERGY VALUE OF CHEESE

	Energy value kJ/100 g	Protein	Lipid	Water
Cheddar	1 700	27	33	34
Camembert	1 300	20	25	51
Cream cheese	1 550	7	36	55
Roquefort	1 640	21	33	37

Cheese is an excellent source of high biological value protein and lipid. Calcium is abundant making it a valuable body-building food; 150 g Cheddar cheese provides the daily intake of calcium (1 200 mg) for a nursing mother, and useful amounts of vitamins A, D, B_2, B_{12} and folic acid.

Cholesterol is present in all cheeses.

SUMMARY OF THE EFFECT OF HEAT ON FOODS

1. The reasons for cooking food

(a) To render it more digestible by softening. Close and tough textured foods cannot be masticated without cooking and digestive juices cannot penetrate them.

(b) To render it more palatable since cooking enhances flavours, odours, and colours.

(c) To achieve partial sterilization and improve its keeping qualities.

(d) To improve appearance.

(e) To facilitate variety by combining foods, flavours, and colours.

(f) To improve food value, e.g. adding fat to fish when frying.

2. The effects of cooking meat

All methods of cooking meat cause:

(a) The denaturation and coagulation of protein.

(b) The shrinkage of elastin in the walls of muscle fibre.

(c) The conversion of collagen to gelatine causing fibres to become tender and separated. Where collagen is prevalent conversion to gelatine is only achieved satisfactorily in moist heat at below 100°C.

(d) The red colour caused by myoglobin and haemoglobin turns to brown.

(e) Solid lipids melt and liquefy. In dry heat it becomes brown.

(f) Moist heat causes soluble meat proteins, mineral salts, extractives, and vitamin B group to be dissolved out. Vitamin B_1 thiamin is the only vitamin to be lost provided the meat gravy is used.

3. The effects of cooking fish

The effects are similar to those on meat but less marked.

(a) Proteins denature and coagulate but fish shrinks to a lesser extent.

(b) Long, slow methods of tenderizing are not necessary since the fibres are more delicate, and the connective tissues less coarse and prevalent.

4. The effects of cooking milk

(a) Cooking denatures and coagulates protein causing a skin to form.

(b) It caramelizes lactose in slow cooking.

(c) It precipitates calcium salts.

(d) It softens milk fat making warm milk easier to digest.

(e) It destroys pathogenic bacteria by pasteurization.

There is some loss of vitamin C ascorbic acid and to a lesser extent vitamin B group. Flavour is not affected, though it is by sterilization.

5. The effect of cooking eggs

(*a*) It denatures and coagulates protein, the white being affected at a lower temperature than the yolk.

(*b*) The yolk becomes powdery on prolonged cooking

(*c*) The white is easier to digest when lightly cooked than when raw.

(*d*) Oven cooking causes shrinkage of proteins. If the eggs are mixed with liquids this shrinkage produces curdling.

(*e*) There is slight loss of vitamin B group.

(*f*) Dry heat at fairly high temperatures causes carbonization. Eggs are therefore useful for glazing.

6. The effects of cooking on cheese

(*a*) The solid lipids melt

(*b*) The proteins denature, coagulate and shrink. Long cooking causes roughening and stringing.

(*c*) Dry heat causes carbonization, cheese being therefore useful to top savoury dishes.

(*d*) There is no loss of nutritive value, although over-hardening of the protein makes it less digestible.

7. The effects of cooking on lipids

(*a*) Solid lipids liquefy.

(*b*) At high temperature lipids decompose into propanal (acrolein) and fatty acids; the colour darkens.

(*c*) Lipids decompose at different temperatures, butter at relatively low temperatures compared to vegetable oils.

(*d*) Water is driven off from hot lipid oils or foods fried in lipid oils.

(*e*) Vitamins A retinol and D cholecalciferol are unaffected.

8. The effect of cooking cereals

(*a*) Cooking is necessary for digestion.

(*b*) Starch grains burst and gelatinize absorbing any liquid.

(*c*) Dry heat causes dextrinization and carbonization.

(*d*) There is some loss of vitamin B_1 thiamin.

9. The effect of cooking vegetables

(*a*) The parenchyma and collenchyma cellulose walls are softened by moist heat, but will also soften by dry heat in vegetables containing large amounts of water such as potatoes.

(*b*) Starch in potatoes will gelatinize and become powdery.

(*c*) Colour is intensified.

(*d*) The starch is easier to digest.

(*e*) Soluble mineral salts and vitamins are leached out in moist cooking. Vitamin C ascorbic acid is vulnerable to oxidation and decomposition by heat. Conservative methods of cooking should be used carefully in all vegetable cookery.

10. Effects of cooking on fruit

(*a*) The parenchyma cellulose walls are softened by moist heat.

(*b*) The vitamin C ascorbic acid is partially destroyed. Pasteurization of fruit juices conserves large amounts of vitamin C ascorbic acid.

(*c*) Mineral salts, fructose, and carotenes are leached into the water. These can be retained if syrup is served with fruit.

11. Effects of cooking on sugar (see page 111)

(*a*) The solubility of sugar increases with temperature.

(*b*) If all water is boiled away from a syrup the sugar will caramelize. Caramel reaches varying degrees of hardness at different temperatures.

(*c*) Crystallization occurs if syrup is frequently stirred or moved during the boiling process.

(*d*) In jam making the presence of added or natural fruit acids causes inversion of the sucrose.

12. Effects of cooking on bread

(*a*) The dough rises rapidly following expansion of the carbon dioxide.

(*b*) As the temperature rises the activity of the yeast increases.

(*c*) At a loaf temperature of 55°C yeast is killed.

(*d*) As the temperature continues to rise the starch grains swell and gelatinize.

(*e*) At 70°C the gluten coagulates.

(*f*) In spite of high temperatures in the oven the interior of the loaf never exceeds 100°C.

(*g*) Water and carbon dioxide are driven off during baking.

(*h*) Starch dextrinizes and the sugars caramelize.

The Chorleywood rapid breadmaking process uses vitamin C ascorbic acid as a flour improver, which is added to the flour, and double the normal yeast quantity. A very intensive mechanical mixing process is employed. Breadmaking time by this process is reduced from 5 hours to $1\frac{3}{4}$ hours.

FOOD COMPOSITION

The composition of foods *varies*, because most foods are *mixtures* of nutrients. Differences in composition can be due to the season, method of feeding or cultivation, or from the *cut* of meat or fish. Appendix B lists the *general* composition of some selected foods with respect to those nutrients essential to a healthful diet.

SUGGESTIONS FOR PRACTICAL WORK

1. Determine the amount of water in meat. (See method in Chapter 19.)

2. Determine the percentage ash in the dried meat by carefully heating dried meat in the evaporating basin over a

Bunsen burner flame until a white ash remains. Weigh the dish when cool and calculate the percentage present in the original *moist* meat.

3. Observe the effect of heating a portion of Cheddar cheese, first heating gently and then more strongly.

4. Determine the temperature of coagulation of egg white and egg yolk by placing samples in test tubes and immersing them in water which is gently heated.

5. See *Experimental Science for Catering and Homecraft Students*, Practical work 21.1, 26 to 34.

QUESTIONS ON CHAPTER 25

1. State the components of a glass of milk and describe the process of their digestion.

2. Describe the changes occurring when the following foods are cooked: (*a*) meat; (*b*) eggs; and (*c*) fish.

3. Give an account of the composition of meat and its digestion.

4. Describe the structure of lean meat. What changes take place in tough and tender meat when they are cooked with moist heat?

5. Give an account of the composition of fish. What is the most suitable method for cooking fish? Give reasons for your choice.

6. Describe the structure of a hen's egg, outlining the composition of its three main parts. State why eggs do not shrink on cooking.

7. What ingredients of eggs are responsible for emulsification, thickening, and foaming.

8. Give an account of the food value of milk. What types of processed milk are available to the consumer?

9. What diseases are transmitted by impure milk? Describe how milk is made safe and the effect of these processes on the nutritive value.

10. Write short notes on: (*a*) meat tenderizers; (*b*) tough meat; (*c*) tender meat; and (*d*) meat shrinkage in cooking.

MULTIPLE CHOICE QUESTIONS ON CHAPTER 25

Questions 1, 2 and 3 refer to Figure 25.6, a lamb chop.

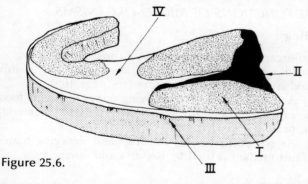

Figure 25.6.

1. Which part of Figure 25.6 indicates the location of myosin?
(*a*) I
(*b*) II
(*c*) III
(*d*) IV

2. The adipose tissue in the meat chop is indicated by:
(*a*) I
(*b*) II
(*c*) III
(*d*) IV

3. The part labelled I is mainly composed of:
(*a*) muscle fibres
(*b*) tendons
(*c*) ligaments
(*d*) bone

4. Gelatin is produced from one of the following during moist heat cooking:
(*a*) elastin
(*b*) collagen
(*c*) glycogen
(*d*) myosin

5. Glycogen found in small amounts in live meat muscle, is changed into one of the following after slaughter of the animal:
(*a*) glucose
(*b*) hydroxypropanoic (lactic) acid
(*c*) octadecanoic (stearic) acid
(*d*) ascorbic acid

6. Which of the following indicates the composition of a herring?

	% proteins	% lipids
(*a*)	15	0·5
(*b*)	16	1
(*c*)	17	0·5
(*d*)	20	10

7. Milk sugar is digested in the alimentary tract to produce the following products:
(*a*) lactose and sucrose
(*b*) glucose and fructose
(*c*) glucose and galactose
(*d*) galactose and fructose

8. Which of the following would indicate the composition of evaporated skim milk?

	% water	lipid	% protein	% carbohydrate
(*a*)	87·6	3·8	3·3	4·7
(*b*)	80·0	0·2	7·4	10·7
(*c*)	68·5	9·2	8·4	12·0
(*d*)	25	9·2	8·4	55·4

9. Which three of the following are components of milk but are almost absent from butter?
(i) lactose
(ii) carotene
(iii) vitamin C – ascorbic acid
(iv) vitamin D – cholecalciferol
(v) vitamin B1 – thiamine
(vi) water
(*a*) i, iii, v
(*b*) ii, iv, vi
(*c*) iii, iv, v
(*d*) iv, v, vi

10. Fresh whole egg contains little if any of two of the following nutrients:
(i) protein
(ii) lipid
(iii) carbohydrate
(iv) vitamin A – retinol
(v) vitamins of the B group
(vi) vitamin C – ascorbic acid
(*a*) i, ii
(*b*) iii, vi
(*c*) iv, v
(*d*) iv, v

26 Microbiology and food poisoning

Good health and its maintenance is everyone's desire; any departure from the state of normal health is called a disorder or a *disease*. Diseases are of four main kinds:

(*a*) *Deficiency* diseases are chiefly caused by shortage of certain foods or nutrients. For example scurvy results from vitamin C ascorbic acid deficiency and thyroid disorders from iodine deficiency. (See Chapter 22.)

(*b*) *Organic* diseases owing to faulty organs of the body. A faulty pancreas causes diabetes.

(*c*) *Infectious diseases* are those passed from person to person by direct or indirect contact. Tuberculosis, influenza, and food poisoning are instances.

(*d*) *Parasitic diseases* are caused by various simple animals which are parasistes called 'worms'. Pork and beef *tapeworms* grow to a length of 3 and 10 metres respectively in the human gut. Fish *tapeworms* grow to 10 metres in the human gut following a meal of uncooked, infected fish. Pork worm, *trichinella*, embeds itself in human skeletal muscles after infected pork has been eaten. Roundworm, *ascaris*, found 25 cm long in human gut, comes from unwashed vegetables and salads contaminated with manure. Threadworms, tiny worms 5 mm long, are common in children.

MICRO-ORGANISMS

All matter found in, on, and around the earth is either *living* or *non-living*. Animals and plants constitute the group of living things, while chemical compounds, rocks, and minerals compose non-living substances.

All life and living things evolved from non-living substances. Simple chemical elements such as carbon, hydrogen, oxygen, sulphur, nitrogen, and phosphorus combined together to form compounds, which later changed into very complex compounds with a composition resembling *proteins*. An extremely complex form of protein was evolved which developed an ability to feed, reproduce, and grow; these are the vital characteristics of living things. The *viruses* are considered to be the most primitive form of living things and are closely related to *protein compounds*. They are only 4–10 times the size of the protein molecule egg *ovalbumin*.

Micro-organisms are very small living things which can only be seen with an ordinary light microscope magnifying up to 2 000 times or with the electron microscope magnifying 500 000 times. The study of these organisms is called *micro-biology*.

There are five groups of micro-organisms, (*a*) viruses, (*b*) bacteria, (*c*) fungi, (*d*) algae, and (*e*) protozoa; each group will be considered individually.

VITAL FUNCTIONS OF MICRO-ORGANISMS

Feeding

Micro-organisms can feed by any of three methods:

(*a*) Like plants using the method of *photosynthesis*; this method is used by the green algae (see page 169).

(*b*) As *parasites* by feeding on living things obtaining food at the expense of the host; this method is used by bacteria, fungi, protozoa, and viruses.

(*c*) As *saprophytes* feeding on dead and decaying materials; this method is used by bacteria and fungi.

Respiration

The micro-organisms obtain their energy either with or without oxygen (see page 185):

(*a*) *Aerobic* respiration uses oxygen to release energy from food; it is the method used by algae, protozoa, and some bacteria.

(*b*) *Anaerobic* respiration is a less efficient method of respiration *without* oxygen; it is used by many bacteria, fungi, and viruses.

Micro-organisms and disease

Micro-organisms, particularly parasites, bacteria, fungi, protozoa, and viruses, produce waste products by their metabolic processes, which are poisonous or *toxic* to a living cell. These *toxins* cause the symptoms of the disease such as headache, pain, a temperature, and vomiting.

Micro-organisms which cause disease are described as *pathogenic* microbes; the harmless microbes are said to be *non-pathogenic*.

BACTERIA

Bacteria are found in and on soil, water, air, animals, plants, man, and his food. All bacteria are very small, between 1/60 000 and 1/6 0000 cm, but can be seen through a high-powered microscope.

Experiment

Obtain prepared microscope slides of typhoid or *Anthrax bacillus* examining them with low- and high-powered object

lenses. A greater magnification is obtained with an oil immersion, 2-mm object lens. Magnifications of between 800 and 1 200 times can be achieved with the oil immersion lens.

Bacteria feed either as parasites or saprophytes though some obtain their energy from chemical changes. Some bacteria live in the large intestine of man and produce valuable B group vitamins. These are called *symbionts*, *symbiosis* being a beneficial association of two living things. In this case bacteria is given food and shelter by the human host, offering valuable different vitamins of the B group in return.

SHAPE AND CLASSIFICATION OF BACTERIA

The variations in the size and shape of bacteria cells are used for identifying them (see Figure 26.1).

(*a*) *Spherical bacteria* are called *cocci* and consist of small balls linked in chains of *streptococci*. These cause scarlet fever and tonsillitis; grouped in pairs as *diplococci* they cause pneumonia.

Staphylococci are clusters of spherical bacteria responsible for food poisoning, boils, pimples, and septic wounds.

(*b*) *Rod-shaped bacteria* are called *bacilli* and *clostridia*. Some may have tiny hairs or *cilia* which enable them to swim in fluids. The bacilli cause diphtheria, tuberculosis,

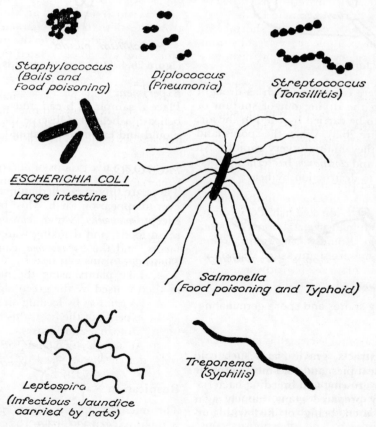

Figure 26.1. Shape and classification of bacteria

typhoid, and food poisoning, and the clostridia another type of food poisoning. Certain *coliform* bacilli are normal inhabitants of the intestine of man.

(*c*) *Spiral-form bacteria* are called *spirilla, spirochaet, vibrios,* and *treponema*. They account for such diseases as syphilis and forms of cholera.

Names of bacteria are written in Latin or Greek and are in two parts, the first the *generic* name and the second the *species* name. For example, for the bacterium *Clostridium welchii*, the first part of the name, *Clostridium*, is for the genus, while the second part of the name, *welchii* – after the Doctor, Dr Welch, who discovered it – is the specific name.

Reproduction

Bacteria can reproduce by dividing themselves into two by binary fission (Figure 26.2). This proceeds rapidly in favourable conditions of plentiful food, warmth, no sunlight, and preferably no oxygen. A single bacterium can produce 16 million descendants in 12 hours. Such large numbers together become visible to the naked eye as a *colony*.

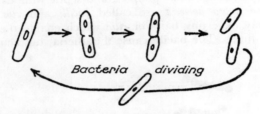

Figure 26.2. Division of a bacteria cell

If bacteria encounter severe conditions such as drought and dry conditions causing the drying out of sputum or faeces, *spores* are produced to be carried by wind in the air, in dust, and dry foods (Figure 26.3). When the spores land on a suitable food supply they multiply very rapidly. An important feature of *bacillus* and *clostridium* bacteria spores is their considerable *resistance* to destruction by heat.

Figure 26.3. Bacteria forming spores and spore germinating

Cultivation of bacteria

Broths containing meat extracts, gravies, and such cold foods as jellies, custards, meat pies, and cold meats provide an excellent *culture media* for growing and breeding bacteria. In the laboratory specially prepared gums, namely agar gained from seaweed, are used, being fortified with nutrients.

Anaerobic bacteria include *Clostridium welchii* and *Clostridium*

botulinum. These are cultivated in media *without* air or oxygen.

Facultative bacteria, *Salmonella* and *Staphylococcus aureus*, can be cultivated either in the presence or in the absence of air or oxygen.

Most other bacteria are *aerobic*, requiring air or oxygen.

FUNGI

This group of plants includes the very small microorganisms, *moulds* and *yeasts* as well as mushrooms and toadstools. Fungi are mainly parasites and saprophytes. Ringworm is the mould parasitic on the skin and hair, whereas moulds are saprophytes found on bread, jam, timber, etc. Reproduction is achieved by tiny *spores* (Figure 26.4) being carried by the air and deposited on any suitable material. Yeast is described on page 213.

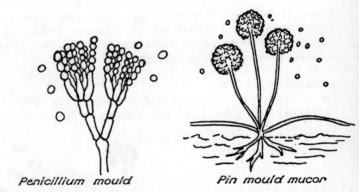

Penicillium mould   Pin mould mucor

Figure 26.4. Structure of moulds showing spore formation

Experiment

Place a sample of bread and a sample of cheese in a dish beneath a bell-jar. Observe the appearance and growth of mould and examine the mould with a hand lens.

PROTOZOA

These are tiny one-celled animals considered to be the first ever to appear on earth. Most protozoa are non-pathogenic except *entamoeba*, which causes *amoebic dysentery* through salad foods, and drinking water contaminated by infected faeces, and the *trypanosoma*, causing sleeping sickness (see Figure 26.5).

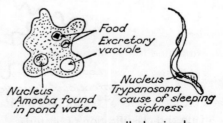

Figure 26.5. Protozoa or one-celled animals

ALGAE

These are mainly minute, one-celled green plants but can also include the gigantic seaweeds (Figure 26.6). The *uni-cellular* algae are found in fresh water and sea water, and are important in water purification and sewage treatment. They form the *plankton* food of such sea fish as herrings.

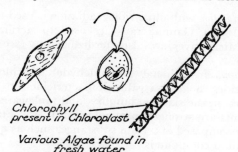

Various Algae found in fresh water

Figure 26.6. Algae or one-celled plants

Algae are non-pathogenic with the exception of *Gonyaulaux catenella*. This is found in sea water plankton and renders molluscs, mainly cockles, mussels, and oysters, poisonous, though fortunately it is very rarely found in shellfish in Britain.

VIRUSES

Viruses appear to be the micro-organisms which bridge the gap between *inanimate* proteins and *living* micro-organisms.

Virus diseases

Poliomyelitis and *infectious hepatitis* are viral diseases transmitted by faecal contaminated foods, raw milk, drinking water and shellfish. Other viral infections are *herpes*, shingles, cold sores, mumps, warts and some tumours or cancers.

Shape

Viruses can only be seen with a powerful *electron* microscope. They appear as rods, spheres, and icosahedrons, a figure with 20 triangular faces. Others appear as coils surrounded by a jacket (see Figure 26.7).

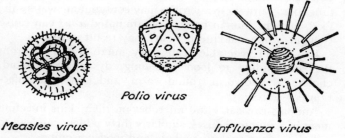

Measles virus   Polio virus   Influenza virus

Figure 26.7. Simplified forms of common viruses

Nutrition

Viruses feed on *living* cells of plants and animals and are pathogenic, causing various diseases. Many enter a living cell and destroy it, as in polio virus which destroys nerve cells to cause paralysis. Viruses have the unique capacity of becoming inanimate, resting for long periods in a crystalline form.

CONDITIONS NECESSARY FOR GROWTH OF MICRO-ORGANISMS

The important conditions required for the growth of micro-organisms are:

1. *Food* in such a soluble form as broths, jellies, and cold meats.

2. *Oxygen* is required by aerobic bacteria. Certain anaerobic micro-organisms such as yeast and tuberculosis bacteria do not need it. Certain pathogens will flourish in poorly ventilated conditions.

3. *Water* or moist conditions encourage the growth of bacteria, algae, fungi, and moulds. Humidity in kitchens should be offset by ventilation. Foods are best stored in dry, airy, and cool stores.

4. *Heat* at a temperature equal to the body's (37°C) will *incubate* microbes. Temperatures above 70°C will destroy microbes and heating at 150°C for 1 hour kills all bacteria. Low temperatures slow down the rate of growth of microbes but do not destroy them, and contaminated foods taken from the refrigerator produce microbe growth. Most micro-organisms, including pathogens found in perishable foods, will grow between temperatures of 10° and 45°C.

5. *Sunlight or ultra-violet rays* will destroy most microbes but darkness encourages their growth (see page 74).

6. *pH* which microbes prefer is a neutral or slightly alkaline medium which at 7·4 prevails in human blood. Therefore *warm, moist, dark, airless, slightly alkaline* conditions with plenty of rich *soluble food* will promote the multiplication of micro-organisms.

PREVENTION OF MICRO-ORGANISM GROWTH IN CATERING PRACTICE

1. *Cooked food* cooled to blood heat provides an excellent medium for microbe growth. Food should be served quickly or cooled to below blood heat, and kept in refrigerators.

2. *Working surfaces* should be hard and non-absorbent, of stainless steel or plastics. Soft, absorbent, wooden surfaces provide moist conditions suitable for microbe growth.

3. *Towels, handkerchiefs, and cleaning cloths* absorb water and collect food debris and are readily seeded with microbes from hands and dirty surfaces. Disposable paper towels are more hygienic.

4. *Cuts, wounds, and abrasions* expose the blood, an excellent nutrient medium for the growth of microbes. Cover cuts and boils with *waterproof* dressings.

5. *Human skin, nose, and mouth* are suitable for microbe growth, particularly the conditions within the mouth and nose.

6. *Ventilation* overcomes humidity and dampness and also supplies oxygen. Food stores and dwelling places should be bright and airy, with good circulation of air between working spaces, beds, and storage racks.

bright and airy, with good circulation of air between working spaces, beds, and storage racks.

7. *Sunlight* or ultra-violet ray apparatus sterilizes the air.

8. *Dishwashing* is a vitally important process aimed at providing heat to destroy microbes, and a detergent to dislodge food debris. The removal of food debris from between the prongs of forks prevents microbe growth and infection.

9. *Refrigerators and cold storage* halts the growth of microbes but does *not* destroy them.

DISINFECTION AND STERILIZATION

Disinfection is the process of destroying *harmful* micro-organisms, leaving less harmful ones. *Spores* of bacteria are not usually destroyed.

Sterilization is the process of complete destruction of *all* forms of micro-organisms.

Bactericides are substances which kill all bacteria and *bacteriostats* slow or stop the growth of bacteria.

Disinfection and sterilization are achieved by:

1. *Heat* is more important in disinfection and sterilization and the following processes involve heat:

(a) *Moist heat*, rinsing with hot water at 75°C, disinfects crockery and cutlery after washing in detergent at 60°C. The items are *not* sterile but most harmful microbes will be removed. Boiling soiled laundry items, contaminated crockery, cutlery, and babies' feeding utensils will disinfect safely.

(b) *Steaming* laundry items, pillows, linen, and blankets, at 100°–120°C is a useful method of *disinfecting* textiles.

USES OF IMPORTANT DISINFECTANTS

Chemical	Use
Soap and soapless detergent	Skin, laundry, and dishwashing
Iodine and certain dyes	Skin cuts and abrasions
Ethanol (alcohol)	Skin
Methanal (formaldehyde)	Disinfectant for bedding, brushes, and air purifier
Phenols and methylphenols (cresols)	General disinfectants, cleansing floors, surfaces, drains and toilets, and timber preservation
Chlorine	Sterilizing water supplies
Sulphur dioxide	Sterilizing fruit juices and preserving fruits
Potassium manganate(VII) (permanganate), Condys fluid	Cleaning drains
Hydrogen peroxide	Cuts, wounds, and mouth wash
Quaternary ammonium compounds	Bactericides used in dishwashing and skin ointments
Ethanediol (ethylene glycol)	Antiseptic air sprays or purifiers

(c) *Autoclaving*, or the use of water boiling under pressure, as in pressure cookers at a temperature of 120°C and 100 kN/m^2 pressure for 20 minutes will produce completely sterile articles. It is used for canning, bottling, and for sterilizing babies' feeding utensils and milk.

(d) *Pasteurization* or the heating of milk, wine, and fruit juices at 50°–60°C for 2 minutes effectively removes most bacteria.

(e) *Dry heat*, or heating articles in an oven at a minimum temperature of 160°C for 1 hour, is useful for articles not affected by this temperature. Baked or roast foods are sterilized in this manner, bacteria being completely destroyed.

2. *Irradiation* with ultra-violet radiation is used to sterilize food surfaces. Gamma rays are used to sterilize certain foods. Microwaves are also sterilizing rays (see pages 70 and 73).

3. *Chemicals* methanal (formaldehyde) and chlorhexidine bactericides. Soap is a valuable bactericide for destroying microbes on the skin, on laundry, and tableware. Soapless detergents are stronger, particularly if they contain or are entirely composed of certain substances such as quaternary ammonium compounds.

Many disinfectants such as phenol, iodine, and silver salts destroy bacteria by coagulating the proteins. Other oxygen-rich disinfectants, e.g. hydrogen peroxide, potassium manganate(VII) (permanganate), (Condys fluid), sodium chlorate(I) (hypochlorite) destroy *anaerobic* microbes by means of their oxygen.

ANTIBIOTICS AND CHEMOTHERAPY

Many chemical substances or drugs are used to destroy bacteria and protozoa which cause disease. The most important are the sulphonamides compounds, and the antibiotics *penicillin* and *streptomycin* produced by moulds and bacteria.

Penicillin is occasionally found in milk from cows treated with penicillin ointment. It prevents the milk-souring process caused by the micro-organisms, rendering it unsuitable for cheese-making.

DISTRIBUTION OF MICRO-ORGANISMS

Micro-organisms are widespread and ultimately affect the health of man.

SOIL MICRO-ORGANISMS

Soil can contain up to 2 500 million bacteria and 700 000 fungi per gram; these microbes may contaminate water, air, food, and the human body. Contaminated *water* can cause typhoid, while soil entering cuts may result in *tetanus*.

Unwashed vegetables can carry micro-organisms from the soil leading to food poisoning, dysentery, typhoid, cholera, threadworm, round-worm, and tapeworm infection.

Animals can carry soil microbes on their skins infecting meat in slaughter houses; similarly dirty udders can lead to milk infections such as typhoid and food poisoning.

Dry soil blown in the air may contain harmful microbes which settle on food.

Footwear can pick up contaminated soil and carry it into food-preparing areas. Separate footwear for use exclusively in food-preparing areas is advisable.

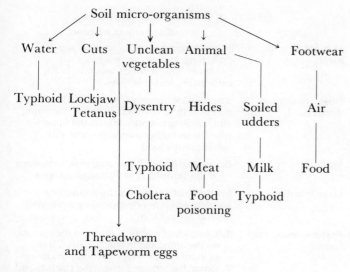

MICRO-ORGANISMS IN THE AIR

Fresh outdoor air contains appreciably fewer micro-organisms than air inside buildings. Indoor air is contaminated with spores of bacteria, moulds, viruses, and algae, together with *dust*. This dust is mainly a mixture of fine particles of soil, textile fibres, skin scales, pollen grains, and large numbers of bacteria and mould spores. Dust alone can cause allergic respiratory diseases in man.

Microbes found in air include:

(*a*) Viruses causing influenza, colds, pneumonia, measles, chickenpox, polio, and smallpox.

(*b*) Bacteria causing tuberculosis, diphtheria and the souring of milk.

(*c*) Fungi causing dry rot and wet rot (see page 153).

(*d*) Eggs of threadworms.

PREVENTION OF AIR CONTAMINATION AND INFECTION

1. Reduce the number of people in small working areas. Over-crowding causes cross-infection through sneezing, coughing, and talking.

2. Reduce dust by careful sweeping methods, using oiled or disinfected sweeping compounds or vacuum cleaners.

3. Air entering the building should be filtered and disinfected by ultra-violet radiation, or by aerosol disinfectants.

4. Ventilation should be adequate and air-conditioning effective.

5. Masks, gowns, overalls, and head covers should be worn.

6. Room temperatures and humidity should be carefully controlled to prevent moist, warm conditions suitable for microbe multiplication.

7. *Water seals* or traps prevent entry of odours from drains (see Figure 26.8).

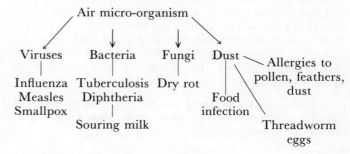

MICRO-ORGANISMS IN WATER

Rain becomes contaminated with microbes. Further microbes are added as the water flows over plants, animals,

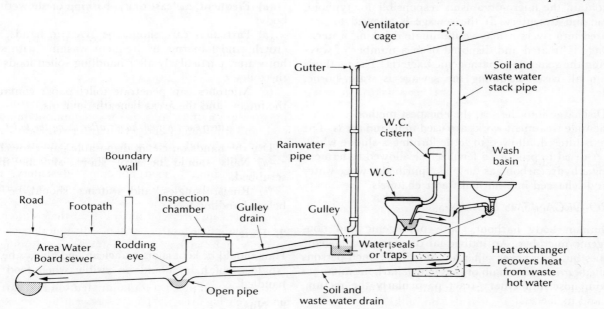

Figure 26.8. Drainage system

and buildings; finally it drains through soil, picking up yet more micro-organisms eventually collecting in rivers and lakes as more or less contaminated water.

Drainage systems are water carriage systems carrying micro-organism contaminated faeces, urine and waste water (see Figure 26.8).

Drinking water

Impure water can contain the bacteria responsible for *typhoid* and *cholera*. These bacteria can enter the water through contamination with sewage or faeces. The bacteria *Escherichia coli* are usually present in faeces.

All drinking water supplied for domestic and general use is purified on a large scale:

1. *Storage* of the water for about four weeks in large reservoirs enables sediment to settle and the sun, air, fish, and tiny algae to begin purification.

2. *Filtration* of the water is achieved by:

(*a*) the slow sand filter in which the water slowly passes over sand grains covered in a slime of algae and bacteria, a biological filter, which purifies the water;

(*b*) rapid sand filtration which involves adding aluminium(III), ammonium sulphate(VI) to water. This coagulates and precipitates the impurities to be filtered off through plain sand.

3. *Sterilization* of the stored and filtered water by means of chlorine destroys all the pathogenic micro-organisms, leaving the water pure.

Sewage

Sewage is the discharge from water-closets, baths, washbasins, urinals, rainwater from gutters, and the fluid waste products from factories. Sewage contains faecal waste and may contain the micro-organisms responsible for typhoid, cholera, and dysentery. If the sewage is allowed to flow untreated into rivers it may contaminate drinking water.

Sewage is treated and disposed of in a number of ways involving the removal of pathogenic bacteria. The methods used, in all cases assuming the sewage is water-borne, include:

1. Discharge into the sea, the cheapest method.
2. Sewage treatment works are used in inland areas. The sewage is filtered, allowed to settle forming a sludge which is either dried to produce a fertilizer or allowed to ferment yielding a hydrocarbon gas fuel. The purified sewage water is then discharged into normal water channels.

MICRO-ORGANISMS IN MAN

The human body harbours both pathogenic and non-pathogenic microbes. An individual can carry pathogenic microbes but may never suffer any ill effects. Such persons are called *carriers*. The main organs which harbour microbes are skin, nose, alimentary tract particularly the rectum, anus, and its faeces.

The table summarizes the organs associated with bacteria and their effects, beneficial or harmful.

EFFECTS OF BACTERIA ON THE BODY

Organ	Bacteria and its effect
Skin of face and hands	*Staphylococcus aureus*, causes food poisoning through an *enterotoxin* it produces. It also infects wounds, boils, carbuncles, and abscesses
Nose, mouth and throat	*Staphylococcus aureus* as above. Greater numbers in nose which filters air. Touching and handling the nose infects the fingers which infect other part of the face and subsequently food
Stomach	Because of hydrochloric acid which sterilizes food the stomach is fairly free of bacteria
Large intestine	Synthesis of vitamins of the B group by bacteria which are destroyed by antibiotics such as *terramycin*
Rectum, anus, and faeces	1. *Clostridum welchii* is found in the rectum, on the anus, and in faecal matter. It is responsible for a type of food poisoning 2. Colon bacteria or *Escherichia coli* is found in the intestine; it is mainly non-pathogenic but it can infect wounds 3. Bacteria constitute 8% of dry faeces
Carriers and infected people	Carry the pathogenic bacteria responsible for typhoid, dysentery, cholera, and salmonella food poisoning. These are harboured in the large intestine, faeces, and urine. The microbes can be carried in the body for many years before detection

PERSONAL HYGIENE OR CLEANLINESS

Cleanliness of the body involves particular attention to care of the skin, hair, nose, mouth, teeth, clothing and the care of cuts, wounds, and abrasions.

1. Skin

(*a*) Frequent, at least daily, bathing or showering of the body.

(*b*) Particular care should be given to hands, armpits, crotch, and forearms by frequent washing with soap and hot water, particularly after handling soiled foods or using the toilet.

(*c*) Microbes can penetrate toilet paper contaminating the fingers and the areas beneath the nails.

Always wash your hands after using the toilet

Dry the hands on clean, disposable paper towels.

(*d*) Nails should be kept short, and be frequently scrubbed.

(*e*) Rings, bangles, and watches should be removed before handling food.

2. Hair

Hair should be kept short and clean and always be covered. No locks of hair should be visible when food is being handled.

3. Nose

Touching the nose contaminates the fingers. Sneeze and

cough into a paper handkerchief away from food; *never shake the handkerchief*. People with severe head colds and discharging noses should not handle food.

4. Mouth

Touching the lips as in cigarette smoking contaminates the fingers. Smoking and the use of snuff is forbidden when handling and preparing food. A face mask should be worn.

5. Teeth

Teeth should be cleaned and inspected frequently. Infected teeth and gums contaminate fingers and the breath.

6. Clothing

Overalls should be changed frequently. Separate overalls should be worn for vegetable preparation and handling soiled foods. Underclothing absorbs sweat and should be changed daily. Outdoor wear should be replaced by protective clothing in suitable changing rooms.

7. Cuts, wounds, and abrasions

Wounds are ideal media for bacteria growth and should therefore be covered with blue-coloured waterproof dressings.

FOOD POISONING

Food poisoning is a disease with the symptoms of severe diarrhoea, vomiting, pain in the abdomen, and sometimes dizziness. It can be caused by chemicals contaminating the food, bacterial infection of the food, or by natural poisons present in the food.

Chemical poisoning

Chemical poisoning is caused by metals or chemical compounds entering the food from its container or perhaps mistakenly being added to the food. Signs of chemical poisoning of food occur *very rapidly*, within a few minutes or at most 2 hours of eating the food

ORIGINS AND SYMPTOMS OF FOOD POISONING

Chemical	Origin	Symptoms
Zinc	Stewing or keeping fruit in galvanized iron containers	Abdominal pain and diarrhoea
Lead	Beer pump pipes, white lead paint in toys	Abdominal pain, vomiting, and diarrhoea
Antimony	Acid foods in cheap grey enamelware	Vomiting
Cyanide	Silver polish on cleaned silverware	Diarrhoea and vomiting
Sodium fluoride, ant killer	Mistaken for baking powder	Vomiting, abdominal pain, and partial paralysis
D.D.T., fly killer	Mistaken for baking powder	Vomiting and partial paralysis
Trimethylphenol phosphate	Mistaken for cooking oil	Diarrhoea and abdominal pain

Natural food poisons

Certain plant and animal foods contain poisonous components. Rhubarb leaves cause severe cramp pains and even death, while the death cap mushroom causes abdominal pain, vomiting, diarrhoea, and can also be fatal.

SYMPTOMS OF POISONING

Poisonous food	Symptoms
Mushroom poisoning from the olive green death cap mushroom *Amanita*	Abdominal pain, vomiting, and severe diarrhoea
Rhubarb poisoning from eating the leaves	Cramp pains
Rye meal or bread infected with a fungus *Ergot*	Headache, dizziness, pain in limbs and convulsions
Cockles, oysters, and mussels. Can contain a parasite, *Gonyaulux*, which is toxic. Rare in Britain	Difficulty with breathing, loss of muscle power in limbs and neck, and vomiting

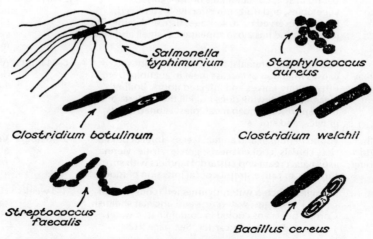

Figure 26.9. Appearance of some bacteria responsible for food poisoning

Bacterial food poisoning

This is the disease caused by pathogenic bacteria (see Figure 26.9), present in food. Bacterial food poisoning is of two main types:

1. *Infectious food poisoning* caused by bacteria called *Salmonella* which enter the human body in contaminated food and then *multiply* within the alimentary canal causing abdominal pain, diarrhoea, vomiting, and fever.

2. *Food poisoning due to the poisonous products or toxins of bacteria.* When certain bacteria grow on such foods as meat, cream, milk, and custard they produce *toxins* which cause the symptoms of the disease. The disease is not caused by the bacteria multiplying within the body. *Staphylococcal*, *Welchii*, and *Botulism* are examples.

3. *Diseases caused by food-borne infection.* Typhoid, paratyphoid, and epidemic dysentery are diseases caused by bacteria and produce symptoms similar to those of food poisoning. They differ in being slower to develop (1–3 weeks) and last much longer (1–2 months). Food poisoning develops very rapidly, between 2 hours and 3 days, and the illness is of short duration.

Campylobacter is a recently recognized cause of *campylobacteriosis*, a form of micro-organism-caused food poisoning. It is transmitted from cows, pigs, poultry, cats and dogs to contaminate water and *raw* milk. The time of onset is 2 to 5 hours with symptoms of abdominal pain, watery diarrhoea, some fever or general illness, and sometimes vomiting.

The table below summarizes the most common causes of bacterial food poisoning and food-borne diseases.

FOOD ALLERGY

Certain people may show a *sensitivity* towards certain *protein* components of foods called *allergens*, present in milk, eggs, cheese, wheat, shellfish, certain fruits and nuts. Certain food additives – e.g., *tartrazine* and Sunset Yellow FCF, yellow food dyes – and preservatives, sodium benzoate or sulphur dioxide, are causes of allergy, which may be seen as skin rashes, asthma or gut disorders, vomiting and diarrhoea.

SUGGESTIONS FOR PRACTICAL WORK

See *Experimental Science for Catering and Homecraft Students*, Practical work 42 to 54.

QUESTIONS ON CHAPTER 26

1. Given an account of food poisoning due to *Clostridium perfringens (welchii)* stating the type of foods infected.

CAUSES OF FOOD POISONING AND FOOD-BORNE DISEASES

Cause of food poisoning or disease	Method of infection and foods involved	Time of onset	Symptoms and duration of illness
Salmonella food poisoning mainly by *Salmonella typhimurium*. Salmonellosis is an infective food poisoning, the bacteria multiplying inside the body. Cause of 70% food poisoning cases	Infected faeces and carriers. Cat, dog, rat, mouse, and duck faeces. Infected flour, salads, milk, cream ice-cream, sliced cooked meat, brawn, sausage, or pies. Duck eggs and imported dried eggs. Foods should be cooked *thoroughly* to destroy the bacteria	12–48 hours	Headache, vomiting, abdominal pain diarrhoea, and fever. Lasts 7 days and can be fatal. Patients become carriers
Staphylococcal food poisoning by *Staphylococcus aureus*. Food poisoning due to preformed toxins. Cause of 10% food poisoning cases	Skin, nose, mouth, cuts, septic wounds, and boils. Septic cow udders. Non-pasteurized milk, cream, custards, cooked meat, brawn, pies, gravy, and ice-cream. Cooking or reheating kills the bacteria but *not* the toxin	1–6 hours	Violent vomiting, diarrhoea, and exhaustion. Recovery in 1–6 days
Botulism cause by *Clostridium botulinum*. Food poisoning due to the *exotoxin* produced by the bacteria	Found in soil, contaminates home-canned vegetables, and fruits not effectively sterilized. Home-preserved ham, sausage, fish, and game. The infected food has a *bad* appearance, smell and taste	12–36 hours	Double vision, difficulty with talking, swallowing, and breathing. Fatal in 60% of cases or very slow recovery over many months
Welchii, caused by *Clostridium perfringens (welchii)*. Poisoning may be due to toxin *and* to multiplication of bacteria within the gut. Cause of 20% food poisoning cases	Found in soil, animals, hides, and intestines. It causes infection of carcass meat in abattoirs from dirty cutting knives and infected floors. Boiling, steaming or stewing does not kill the bacteria or their spores. Found in meat, pies, canned meats, gravies, and stocks	8–24 hours	Abdominal pain, headache and diarrhoea. Recovery is *rapid* in 1–2 days
Non-specific bacterial causes. Other bacteria *Streptococcus faecalis* and *Bacillus cereus* cause food poisoning by multiplying inside the body	Found in human and animal faeces. Infect cooked rice, cereals, cooked meats, gravies, trifle, vienna sausages, cream and custard. Handlers with sore throats can cause streptococcal infection of foods	2–18 hours	Vomiting, diarrhoea and abdominal pains. Recovery is *rapid* in 1–3 days
Typhoid and paratyphoid fever. Caused by *Salmonella typhi* and *Salmonella paratyphi*	Sewage, infected water, fly-infected foods, cream cakes, dried eggs, watercress and unclean shellfish. Corned beef cans cooled in contaminated water. Faeces and urine of a carrier. See page 212	1–3 weeks	Headache, tiredness, high fever, rash and haemorrhage. Recovery is slow in 1–2 months
Epidemic dysentery caused by *Shigella*	From infected faeces following overcrowding and poor sanitation. It is transmitted by flies		Diarrhoea and fever

2. What kinds of foods are most likely to be associated with food poisoning?

3. Name three types of bacteria associated with food poisoning and describe the symptoms they produce in the human body.

4. Write short notes on: (*a*) Staphylococcal food poisoning; (*b*) Botulism; and (*c*) Salmonellosis.

5. Compare the diseases caused by: (*a*) *Salmonella typhimurium*; and (*b*) *Salmonella typhi*.

6. Describe the conditions favourable to the growth of bacteria and state how these conditions can be provided in food preparation.

7. Write short notes on the following as agents responsible for disease: (*a*) viruses; (*b*) bacteria; (*c*) fungi; and (*d*) protozoa.

8. What measures can be taken in catering practice to prevent the growth and multiplication of bacteria?

9. What is meant by disinfection, sterilization, and antisepsis? Describe methods which involve heat, radiation, and chemicals.

10. What microbes are associated with air, soil, and water?

11. Describe what measures are taken for the supply of pure water to the home.

12. Outline methods of disposal for sewage and kitchen waste.

13. 'Man and animals are reservoirs of bacterial infection.' Discuss this statement, outlining the main parts of the animal body which function as bacterial reservoirs.

14. How does the body defend itself against food poisoning? Should meat and eggs be eaten raw?

15. Give an account of how the cleanliness and care of the following contributes to personal hygiene: (*a*) hands, forearms, and nails; (*b*) hair; (*c*) mouth, teeth, and nose; (*d*) clothing; and (*e*) cuts.

16. List ten simple rules of hygiene for food handlers and preparers.

17. Describe the conditions of people who should *not* be allowed to handle or prepare food.

18. Give an account of food poisoning caused by chemicals and natural toxic components of food.

19. Write short notes on the following unhygienic practices: (*a*) smoking; (*b*) fingering the nose; (*c*) snuff taking; (*d*) dirty cotton bandages on septic cuts; (*e*) long finger nails; (*f*) licking fingers and tasting food with fingers; (*g*) shaking a dirty handkerchief; (*h*) stroking the kitchen cat; and (*i*) uncovered hair.

MULTIPLE CHOICE QUESTIONS ON CHAPTER 26

1. Which of the following micro-organisms manufactures its own food by photosynthesis?
   (*a*) fungal moulds   (*c*) unicellular yeasts
   (*b*) unicellular algae   (*d*) protozoa

2. Which of the following bacteria form spores?
   (*a*) *Clostridium*   (*c*) *Salmonella*
   (*b*) *Escherichia*   (*d*) *Staphylococcus*

3. Which of the following are not easily destroyed by moist heat within the temperature range 55–80°C?
   (*a*) yeasts   (*c*) moulds
   (*b*) bacteria vegetative cells   (*d*) bacteria spores

4. The majority of food poisoning incidents in the UK are caused by:
   (*a*) *Clostridium perfringens*   (*c*) *Salmonellae* species
   (*b*) *Staphylococcus aureus*   (*d*) *Shigella* species

5. Eggs, particularly duck eggs are foods susceptible to support growth and be a vehicle of human infection from:
   (*a*) *Staphylococci*
   (*b*) *Clostridium welchii* (perfringens)
   (*c*) *Salmonellae*
   (*d*) *Gonyaulax* toxin

6. Most micro-organisms multiply within the following temperature ranges:
   (*a*) −40° to −20°C   (*c*) −10° to 4°C
   (*b*) 10° to 60°C   (*d*) 80° to 100°C

7. Which of the following water treatment processes sterilizes the water:
   (*a*) fluoridation   (*c*) aeration
   (*b*) chlorination   (*d*) sedimentation

8. Antibiotics are produced by two of the following organisms:
   (i)   unicellular algae   (iv) viruses
   (ii) protozoa   (v) bacteria
   (iii) moulds

   (*a*) i and ii   (*c*) iii and iv
   (*b*) ii and iv   (*d*) iii and v

9. Which of the following chemicals is used as a disinfectant of bacterial culture dishes?
   (*a*) ethanol   (*c*) iodine
   (*b*) methanal   (*d*) hydrogen peroxide?

10. Food containers can only be sterilized by:
    (*a*) a hot water rinse at 75°C
    (*b*) autoclaving at 120°C
    (*c*) exposure to ultra-violet radiation
    (*d*) rinsing in ethanol

27 Food spoilage and preservation. Yeast

FOOD SPOILAGE AND PRESERVATION

Spoilt food *looks* harmful and unfit to eat, having an unattractive smell, taste and appearance. *Contaminated* food, which may contain chemicals or bacteria, may *not look* harmful or have an unattractive smell, taste or appearance.

Foods can be spoilt or made unfit for eating in a number of ways:

(*a*) *Chemical changes* such as the development of rancidity in fats and fatty foods through *oxidation*.

(*b*) *Micro-organism infection* causing *decay*.

(*c*) *Pest* spoilage of food by insects, rats, and mice.

(*d*) *Enzyme action* (see pages 161 and 193) or *autolysis*, the

CONTAMINATION AND SPOILAGE OF FOOD

Food	Contamination or spoilage
Vegetables	1. Soil main contaminant; also handling 2. Watercress and lettuce contaminated with infected sewage can cause typhoid 3. Lettuce grown with animal manure can be infected with threadworm, roundworm, and tapeworm eggs 4. Bruising and cutting by insects and rodents causes rapid spoilage All vegetables particularly if to be eaten raw, should be thoroughly washed
Fruits	1. Soil contamination and handling 2. Damage by insects and rodents 3. Need for washing of fruit to be consumed raw
Meat	
1. Fresh butcher's meat	Meat can be contaminated by (*a*) natural disease of the animal or (*b*) be externally contaminated during dressing and handling: 1. *Diseased meat* inspected by local authority for tuberculosis, anthrax, swine fever, enteritis, etc., and for infection by worms and tapeworms 2. *Contaminated meat.* Slaughtered meat can be contaminated from soil, water, dust, faeces, flies, dirty knives, and by handling. Chopped sliced, and minced meats are more susceptible to spoilage. *Clostridum welchii* is one of the main pathogenic microbes of fresh meat

CONTAMINATION AND SPOILAGE OF FOOD

Food	Contamination or spoilage
2. Cooked meats	*Contaminated* by handling and by cutting with knives contaminated from raw, infected meat, or flies, and dirty surfaces and utensils
Fish	1. *Contamination from gutting.* The intestinal microbes which infect gutted fish are easily transferred to fillets by dirty knives, hands, and water 2. Salmon are affected by *furunculosis* disease and carp by *tuberculosis*. Both are unfit for consumption
Shellfish	1. Oysters and mussels can become infected with typhoid from sewage-polluted water near sewage outlets 2. All molluscs for consumption are cleansed in the UK using sterile sea water in specially constructed cleansing tanks.
Milk	1. Raw, untreated milk may cause tuberculosis, typhoid, salmonella food poisoning, sore throat, diphtheria, cholera, and dysentery 2. Contamination externally is due to soil, faeces, udder disease, dust, dirty hands, milking equipment, bottles or containers
Eggs	1. *Natural infection. Eggs can be infected by Salmonella typhimurium* causing food poisoning. Duck eggs are most susceptible. Hen's eggs because of hygienic rearing methods are not liable to infection 2. *External infection* particularly of *imported* dried egg owing to unhygienic processing or natural infection of egg
Canned and bottled foods	1. Ineffective sterilization can produce Salmonellosis, Botulism, and Staphylococcal food poisoning 2. Blown cans bulging with gas produced by anaerobic bacteria. Contents unfit for consumption 3. Canned corned beef infected by cooling cans in typhoid-infected water which penetrated through pin holes
Bread	Bread can be contaminated by heat-resisting bacteria which causes the loaf to become soft, sticky, and dark in colour with an unpleasant smell. This condition is known as *rope*. Bread can develop blue and green moulds in storage

process of self-digestion which occurs in most foods by the effect of various enzymes. *Blanching* fruits and vegetables in hot water at 92°C destroys the enzymes. *Refrigeration* halts their activity in all other foods.

(*e*) *Physical damage* in harvesting, transport, causing bruising, discoloration, cracking (eggs), crushing (fruits, etc.).

PERISHABLE FOODS

Foods most liable to spoil or perish are those containing *large amounts of water*, together with cold processed or cooked foods.

Least likely to spoilage are dry foods with a *low moisture content*, due to *salt*, or acid as well as those containing plentiful sugar such as biscuits, bread, baked confectionery, sweets, jams, pickles, dried fruit and dehydrated foods.

The table summarizes the methods of contamination and spoilage of important foods:

PESTS

Food in storage or otherwise always attracts *pests* as well as *pets*; all by their unhygienic habits constitute a menace to health. The table summarizes the main pests which spoil food and indicates their occurrence, the diseases they transmit, and preventive measures.

COMMON PESTS AND THEIR EFFECTS

Pest	Occurrence	Disease or harmful effect	Preventive measure
Insects			
Cockroaches of three types: 1. Black cockroach 2. Steamfly 3. Brown American cockroach	Warm places in kitchens, canteens, bakeries and food factories. Have a characteristic smell. Feed at night and hide by day	Contamination and tainting of food by droppings causing salmonellosis	1. Prevent accumulation of food debris with good hygiene 2. Insecticide, dusts, sprays, or lacquers painted on floors
Mites 1. Flour mite 2. Dried fruit mite	Dark, poorly ventilated food stores	Contamination of food with droppings	1. Fumigation 2. Insecticides; dust, sprays, and lacquers 3. Good hygiene with frequent examination of stored goods
Larder beetle	In bacon, ham or cheese	Maggots contaminate food	1. Cool, clean stores 2. Frequent inspection of stock 3. Fumigation of store
Warehouse moth	Chocolate, cereals, dried fruit, spice, and nuts attacked by grubs	Contamination by faeces	1. Stock inspection 2. Fumigation 3. Insecticides, sprays, and powders
Biscuit beetles	Packed biscuits, flour, cereals and spices	Contamination by faeces	1. Stock inspection 2. Fumigation 3. Insecticides, sprays, and powders
Common housefly and blowfly	Eggs laid in warm, moist refuse decaying matter, or faecal matter. Feed on any food containing sugar, or filth, excreta, decaying matter. Hairy bodies pick up micro-organisms	1. Regurgitates on food, then sucks up soluble food 2. Contact of body and method (1) infects human food 3. Causes food poisoning, typhoid, and dysentery	1. Good hygiene, i.e. clean bins, no food debris, covering food, and clean utensils 2. Fly sprays and swatting 3. Insecticidal paints on walls and ceilings 4. Spraying or destruction of breeding sites 5. Fly screens on windows and ventilators
Rodents			
Rats are of two types: 1. Common rat or brown rat is large with a short tail	Brown rats found in drains, sewers or refuse tips. It stays at ground level. Sausage shaped faeces.	1. Gnawing habits cause destruction of wood, pipes, cables, boxes, and fabrics 2. Fouling of food and water causes salmonellosis, typhoid and dysentery 3. Rat fleas cause plague 4. Rat bites cause rat bite fever	1. Good hygiene with avoidance of food debris 2. Good storage and protection of food 3. Traps 4. Rodenticide (Warfarin) 5. Sewer treatment
2. Ship's rat or black rat is small with a long tail	Black rats are climbers and are found in warehouses and private houses. Spiral shaped faeces.		
The common house mouse	Mice are found everywhere in Britain. Each colony restricts itself to a small area. Leaflike faeces.	1. Gnawing habits cause destruction of wood, pipes, cables, boxes and fabrics 2. Fouling of food and water causes salmonellosis, typhoid and dysentery	1. Good hygiene with avoidance of food debris 2. Good storage and protection of food 3. Traps 4. Rodenticide (Warfarin)
Birds			
Sparrows and pigeons	Warehouses, shops, shopping centres and markets	Faces contaminate exposed food, causing salmonellosis	1. Traps 2. Repellent strips 3. Netting on open windows and ventilators

SUMMARY OF MAIN METHODS OF FOOD CONTAMINATION

Food contamination results from:

1. Soil and dust
2. Water contaminated with sewage
3. Faeces
4. Insect, bird and rodent pests
5. Pets
6. Human carriers
7. Unclean handling of food
8. Unclean food containers, and
9. Hand, nose, and throat microbes transmitted to foods.

FOOD PRESERVATION

Food which is surplus or is to be stored can be preserved by a number of methods, all being based on the principle of retarding autolysis and the growth of micro-organisms. Preservation involves the exact *opposite* of conditions required for micro-organism growth, namely dry conditions, or no moisture, low temperatures or high temperature, acid pH, the use of chemicals or preservatives and the destruction of microbes by rays. The table summarizes the main methods of food preservation (see page 203).

METHODS OF PRESERVING FOOD

Preservation method	Application
Heat [See pages 196 and 204]	
1. Pasteurization	Milk and fruit juices if held at 70°C for 15 seconds are sterilized from most harmful, pathogenic micro-organisms
2. Boiling	During cooking of foods and for producing sterilized milk. Temperatures of 100°C are not high enough to destroy all microbes for long storage. Stewed meat can be contaminated with *Clostridium welchii*. Spores are not destroyed during boiling
3. Cooking by roasting, grilling, and cooking	Temperatures of 115°C destroy food poisoning and spoiling bacteria. Cooking should be *thorough* to allow full penetration. *Reheating* should be thorough
4. Canning and bottling	Canning and bottling involves heating the food to 115°–125°C in an oven or pressure cooker destroying the harmful botulism bacteria. Foods containing *acids* such as fruit do not require heating above 100°C since the acid prevents the growth of the bacteria. The foods are sealed in containers entirely free of air (or one in which the air is replaced by nitrogen) which discourages aerobic bacteria
Refrigeration	
1. Ordinary refrigerators	Low temperature slows down the rate of growth of micro-organisms but they are *not* killed. The temperature in the household refrigerator is 0°–5°C and perishable foods can be preserved no longer than 2 weeks. See star rating, page 41
2. Deep freezing and quick freezing	Foods are frozen by temperatures below −30°C allowing preservation for many months at −20°C
Dehydration [See pages 40 and 134]	
Foods are dried by (*a*) spray, or (*b*) vacuum drying methods	The presence of moisture is essential for the growth of micro-organisms so removal ensures preservation. Dried fruit, coffee extract, milk, soups, potatoes, eggs, fish, and meat are preserved in this way

Preservation method	Application
Preservatives [See Appendix A and page 153]	These are mainly chemical substances which prevent the growth or kill the micro-organisms like disinfectants and bactericides
1. Chemical preservatives [E200–299]	Sulphur dioxide is used for preserving fruits and fruit juices. Benzene carboxylic (benzoic) acid is allowed in artificial creams. Propanoic (propinonic) acid and propanoates are flour preservatives
2. Sugar	Sugar syrups are used to preserve fruits
3. Salt	Sodium chloride used in salting vegetables, fish, and bacon. Brine is injected into bacon by pumping
4. Vinegar or ethanoic acids	The acid pH preserves pickles, sauces and certain acid fruit juices
5. Carbon dioxide [See page 103]	Apples, bananas and other fruits are stored in large, gas storage warehouses, in an atmosphere containing 2% carbon dioxide at a temperature of 2°C. These conditions slow the ripening of the fruits
6. Smoking	Smoking of fish and ham over smouldering oak chips produces a smoke containing certain volatile preservative chemicals such as methanal (formaldehyde), phenols, and methanol (methyl alcohol), which also flavour the food
Irradiation [See pages 74 and 204]	
1. Ultra-violet rays	Will surface sterilize baked bread and other baked foods.
2. Ionising irradiation or Gamma rays	Exposure destroys all micro-organisms. It has produced undesirable colours, flavours, and physical conditions in food; nevertheless a promising method
Accelerated freeze-drying [See page 41]	Food is quickly frozen, the frozen water being rapidly removed by *sublimation* under a high vacuum with gentle heat. Freeze-dried foods have a sponge-like texture and an unchanged volume. Reconstitution is effected by adding water. Fruit juice, shrimps, crab, peas, pork, beef, and mushrooms have been preserved by this method
Preservation by micro-organisms	Butter and cheese are foods preserved by the action of milk-souring micro-organisms which produce the antibiotic *nisin*.
Antibiotics [See page 204]	Antibiotics such as tetracycline in ice have been used effectively in preserving fish. Nisin is used in the U.K. to preserve *canned* fruits, vegetables and fish.

YEAST

Yeast is living matter and a member of a group of plants called the fungi. Large quantities of yeast are specially

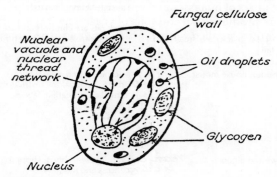

Figure 27.1. The yeast cell

grown for use in baking as well as for use as a food in its own right.

STRUCTURE OF YEAST

The yeast plant is a tiny, uni-cellular fungus about 1/75 000 cm in diameter and can be seen through an ordinary microscope (see Figure 27.1).

Experiment

Mix a little dried yeast with water and transfer a drop of the mixture on to a microscope slide covering the specimen with a glass cover slip. Observe its appearance through a low-powered object lens.

The cell is surrounded by a cell wall made of *fungal cellulose*. The cell contents consist of a *nucleus*, together with a vacuole, with lipid oil droplets and grains of *glycogen* scattered through the cell material. Yeast is a useful food material since it contains proteins, carbohydrates as glycogen, lipids, and valuable amounts of vitamins of the B group. Brewer's yeast contains 15 times more vitamin B_1 thiamin than baker's yeast and twice as much B_2 riboflavin and nicotinic acid.

Composition of dried brewer's yeast:

Energy value kJ/100 g	Protein	Lipid	Carbohydrate
1 180	38%	1%	38%

TYPES OF YEAST

Baker's and brewer's yeast is botanically *Saccharomyces cerevisiae*; yeasts used in making wine are *Saccharomyces ellipsoideus*. Their structure and appearance are similar but they differ in their fermenting action and the materials they affect.

Production of baker's yeast

Saccharomyces cerevisiae is produced on a large scale commencing with a single healthy cell of a vigorous growing strain. This cell is placed in a nutrient culture containing molasses and nutrient salts, ammonium chloride and calcium sulphate. There it multiplies itself by budding into many daughter cells (see Figure 27.2).

The growing yeast is transferred to large, stainless steel culture tanks of molasses and nutrient salts. It multiplies for 12 hours producing several tons of yeast which is separated by filtration, washed with pure water, and dried under a

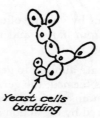

Figure 27.2. The yeast plant budding

vacuum. During the process of growth pure *air* is bubbled through it to provide necessary oxygen for *aerobic* respiration.

Yeasts can also be produced by feeding them on oil *alkane* hydrocarbons instead of molasses, mainly for animal feed, and TVP textured vegetable protein production.

Forms of baker's yeast

1. *Compressed yeast* is in the form of blocks used for fermenting dough.

2. *Dried baker's yeast* is made by dehydrating moist, compressed yeast to produce a form which will keep for months in cool conditions since the yeast cells are in a resting stage. When the yeast is required for *domestic baking* it is mixed with a little warm water and becomes active and ready for the fermenting process. Dried yeast is convenient for domestic baking.

3. *Dried flake yeast.* This is an inactive form not used for leavening. It is intended solely as food for man either as such or in the form of yeast extract. This yeast is called *Torula utilis.*

FERMENTATION

Experiment

Dissolve 5 g of glucose in 100 cm^3 of water in a 1-litre flask. Add 2 g of compressed or dried yeast and stir gently. Set up the apparatus shown in Figure 27.3 and place the flask in a warm room or near to a radiator.

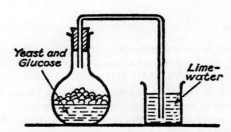

Figure 27.3. Fermentation of glucose by means of yeast

The mixture soon beings to froth owing to the formation of carbon dioxide which turns calcium hydroxide (lime water) cloudy. Leave the mixture for a week and then filter. Note the alcoholic smell of the liquid. This smell of *ethanol* (ethyl alcohol) is also evident in freshly baked, yeast-leavened bread.

Yeast produces a number of enzymes collectively called *zymase*, including the *invertase* which can change sucrose into invert sugar, glucose, and fructose. When sucrose is used in baking the yeast changes the sucrose into invert sugar before any fermentation can commence. Most flours contain 1 per cent maltose, sufficient for the needs of the yeast. Starch present in the flour is converted to *maltose* sugar by *amylase* enzyme in the yeast (see page 184).

Zymase of yeast attacks the glucose sugar, changing it into ethanol (ethyl alcohol) and carbon dioxide. Ethanol is the active component of fermented wines, while the carbon dioxide is the essential leavening agent for baking, being also responsible for the sparkle or froth in alcoholic beverages. The fermentation process of *anaerobic respiration* can be summarized as (see page 186):

$$\text{Sucrose cane sugar} \xrightarrow[\text{yeast}]{\text{Invertase}} \text{glucose} + \text{fructose}$$

$$C_{12}H_{22}O_{11} \xrightarrow[+ H_2O]{\text{Enzyme}} C_6H_{12}O_6 + C_6H_{12}O_6$$

$$\text{Glucose or fructose} \xrightarrow[\text{of yeast}]{\text{Zymase}} \text{ethanol (ethyl alcohol)} + \text{carbon dioxide}$$

$$C_6H_{12}O_6 \xrightarrow[\text{Respiration}]{\text{Anaerobic}} 2C_2H_5OH + 2CO_2$$

YEAST IN BAKING

The usefulness of yeast in leavening dough depends on its ability to produce carbon dioxide from glucose. This gas is then made to expand during baking. Expansion of the flour dough is effected by the elastic gluten which finally coagulates at high baking temperatures 70°C to form the firm skeletal framework of the baked food.

The fermenting property of yeast is affected vitally by temperature. A temperature between 21° and 27°C is most suitable for yeast action. Low temperatures slow its action and temperatures above 55°C destroy the *enzymes* making it ineffective.

Experiment

1. *To show how the activity of yeast is affected by temperature*:
Stir 7 g of dried baker's yeast into 120 cm³ of water warmed to about 45°C. Mix 100 g of strong flour and 5 g of glucose with a yeast suspension to form a smooth cream. Pour the cream into a 1-litre measuring cylinder ensuring that none touches the sides (see Figure 27.4). Note the volume of the mixture, taking further readings every 3 minutes until there is no further increase.

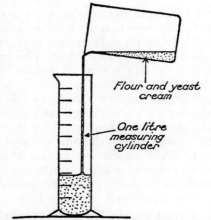

Figure 27.4. Pouring the yeast cream into the measuring cylinder

Repeat the experiment using water at the following temperatures: 0°, 18°, 26·8°, and 60°C. Construct a graph of volume increase against time as in Figure 27.5. This shows that at first the graph is fairly level corresponding to the time during which the flour starch is changed to maltose and glucose. The curve then rises as carbon dioxide is produced by the action of zymase of yeast upon the glucose.

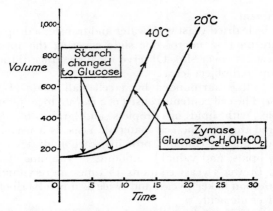

Figure 27.5. Graph showing effect of temperature on yeast activity

Experiment

2. *To compare the fermenting power of equal weights of dried and compressed baker's yeast*:
Repeat the previous experiment with the same weight of dried yeast. Compare the time it takes to start producing carbon dioxide in comparison with compressed yeast.
Note. In order to maintain fairly constant temperatures for the fermentation process the measuring cylinder and its contents can be immersed in a large bucket of water maintained at the temperature of the experiment by adding small amounts of warm or cold water.

ALCOHOLIC BEVERAGES

Ethanol (ethyl alcohol) is formed by the fermentation with yeast of any material containing carbohydrate. The process is one of *anaerobic respiration*. Alcoholic beverages are classified into beers, wines, spirits, and liqueurs. The energy value of pure ethanol (ethyl alcohol) is 29 kilojoules per gram, a value greater than equivalent amounts of carbohydrate and protein (see pages 26 and 221).

Beers

Contain 4–6 per cent by volume of ethanol (ethyl alcohol) and are produced from barley and the yeast *Saccharomyces cerevisiae*. In brewing:

(i) Barley grains are allowed to germinate or sprout and an enzyme *diastase* is formed; the germinated barley is now called malt and contains the sugar *maltose*.

Maltose is produced by the action of the enzyme diastase on the *starch* of the barley endosperm:

Starch   Diastase maltose
barley endosperm ———⟶ of malt

(ii) The malt is now heated and the malted barley dried. If dried at *low* temperatures a pale beer will be produced, while *high*-temperature drying yields dark colours evident in stouts. After drying the malt barley is mixed with hot water and the wort boiled with hops to give the beer a bitter flavour.

(iii) A pure yeast strain is then added to the cool, sterile malt wort and the fermentation process allowed to proceed to a certain stage. It is then stopped and the beer removed and casked or bottled after a maturing process. Bottled and canned beers are pasteurised at 68°C for a few seconds.

Malt extract is a vacuum evaporated preparation consisting mainly of maltose and enzyme diastase. With added vitamins A and D it is a valuable food preparation.

Wine

Wines are produced by the fermentation of grape juice by the yeast *Saccharomyces ellipsoideus*. This is found on the skins or is *added* as a specially grown culture. The grapes are crushed and the juice and the yeast allowed to ferment in vats for 1–2 months.

As the fermentation proceeds the amount of ethanol (ethyl alcohol) increases to 16 per cent by volume. The fermentation now stops because the yeast has been poisoned by the ethanol (ethyl alcohol) it has produced. Wines, other than *fortified* wines, contain no more than 16 per cent of ethanol (ethyl alcohol).

Sweet wines contain a proportion of unfermented grape sugar while *dry* wines contain very little. Sauternes wine contains 6 per cent sugar and 10 per cent ethanol; Chianti wine contains 0·2 per cent sugar and 9 per cent ethanol.

Sherry and port wines are *heavy* or fortified natural wines to which brandy has been *added* to give an ethanol content of 16–20 per cent by volume.

Spirits

Brandy, gin, rum, and whisky are drinks of high ethanol (ethyl alcohol) content between 30 and 40 per cent by volume. They are produced by distilling various alcoholic liquors:

Brandy is produced by distilling wine.
Rum is the product of distilling fermented molasses.
Whisky is the product of distilling fermented malt or rye grains.
Gin is the product of distilling silent spirit from cereal grains with juniper berries, coriander seeds, and other herbs or roots. These produce essential oils which give gin its characteristic flavour (see page 117).

Liqueurs

Silent spirit produced by the distillation of fermented cereal grains is treated with a variety of herbs or essences and sweetened with sugar. Liqueurs hold 30–55 per cent by volume of ethanol and 20 per cent by volume of sucrose.

Methylated or denatured spirits

Ethanol (ethyl alcohol) is required for a number of industrial manufacturing processes and finds many domestic uses as a solvent and fuel. To render the ethanol unfit for human consumption a number of *denaturants* are added such as methanol (methyl alcohol), naphtha, a mixture of hydrocarbons, and pyridine together with distinctive dyes.

Proof spirits

The unit of measuring drinkable spirits is the proof gallon. Proof spirit is a mixture of 57·1 per cent of ethanol (ethyl alcohol) and 42·9 per cent of water by volume and is described as 100 per cent *proof*.

Gin is 30 per cent *under* proof or 70 per cent proof. This means that it contains 70 per cent of 57·1 per cent ethanol, that is 40 per cent ethanol and 60 per cent water. Similarly a spirit which is 70 per cent *over* proof, or 170 per cent proof, contains 170 per cent of 57·1 per cent ethanol, that is 97 per cent ethanol and 3 per cent water, by volume. Beer is 51 per cent *below* proof.

AVERAGE PERCENTAGE COMPOSITION AND ENERGY VALUE OF ALCOHOLIC BEVERAGES

Product	Energy value kJ/100 g	Ethanol	Carbohydrate	Protein
Beer	200	4	4	Trace
Wine dry	160	5	1	–
Port wine	650	15	14	–
Brandy	1 000	40	–	–
Whisky	1 200	42	–	–
Rum	1 250	44	–	–

Vinegar

Vinegar or sour wine is made by allowing wine, cider or beer containing a *little* vinegar to trickle down a tower packed with beechwood shavings. As the wine passes over the wood shavings it meets a current of air which oxidizes the ethanol (ethyl alcohol) to ethanoic (acetic) acid by means of certain bacteria called *Acetobacter* found on the beechwood surface (see pages 88 and 94).

Malt vinegar or double fermented vinegar is made from malt which is allowed to ferment and produce an alcoholic liquor. This is refermented to produce 5% ethanoic (acetic) acid by the *Acetobacter*. Frequently malt vinegar contains tiny nematode worms harmless to man called vinegar worms.

Spirit vinegar is produced by fermenting ethanol produced from potatoes or cereals.

White vinegars are produced by fermenting white wine or by distilling malt vinegar.

Artificial non-brewed vinegar is a 5% solution of ethanoic (acetic) acid and caramel.

Alcoholism

The ethanol content of alcoholic beverages, together with any carbohydrate content, is a source of body energy (28 kJ/100 g ethanol). It is *not* an *essential* nutrient or component for a *normal* healthful diet.

Alcoholic intoxication is an excessive intake when the blood alcohol level reaches 0·1%, and *death* occurs when it reaches 0·5%.

Alcoholism is an addiction involving a *regular* high intake over a long period resulting in *physical* and *psychological* dependence with compulsive craving. Withdrawal of alcohol causes *delirium tremens*, shakiness, convulsions, sweating and hallucinations.

Heavy regular drinking is *associated* with liver damage, high blood pressure, obesity, vitamin deficiency, stomach disorders, brain damage and certain forms of cancer.

The few benefits associated with small intakes – an enhanced sense of well-being – do not compare with the risks arising from over-indulgence.

SUGGESTIONS FOR PRACTICAL WORK

See *Experimental Science for Catering and Homecraft Students*, Practical work 16.2, 16.3 and 16.4.

QUESTIONS ON CHAPTER 27

1. Describe why good ventilation and lighting is important in kitchen hygiene.

2. Describe how the housefly endangers health. What methods can be used to control this pest?

3. Describe three insect pests in the home and methods for controlling them.

4. List some bad food-handling methods which could cause the spread of microbes.

5. What foods are least likely to suffer spoilage in store and what foods are most likely to spoilage?

6. Briefly outline how the following foods can become contaminated: (*a*) vegetables; (*b*) meat; and (*c*) fish.

7. What are the main methods by which foods can become contaminated.

8. Compare the methods of food preservation by ordinary domestic refrigeration, deep freezing, and vacuum freeze drying.

9. What substances are used as food preservatives?

10. Describe the yeast plant and the production of baker's yeast. What temperatures are suitable for yeast activity?

11. Describe two processes of fermentation.

12. Give a brief account of the production of alcoholic beverages. What is proof spirit?

13. Name the animal pests associated with food contamination and their method of control.

14. Give an account of pests which attack furniture, clothing, and house timber and describe their control.

MULTIPLE CHOICE QUESTIONS ON CHAPTER 27

1. The cause of food spoilage by autolysis are:
   (*a*) enzymes   (*c*) micro-organisms
   (*b*) pests   (*d*) physical damage

2. The greenish blue growth seen on spoilt fruit and bread is due to:
   (*a*) unicellular algae   (*c*) yeasts
   (*b*) moulds   (*d*) bacteria

3. Bacteria are unable to multiply on biscuits, egg, milk, and custard powder or macaroni and noodles because of a lack of:
   (*a*) oxygen   (*c*) warmth
   (*b*) water   (*d*) suitable pH

4. Smoking of fish or ham is a means of preservation in which one of the following act from the smoke as preservatives:
   (*a*) methanal   (*c*) sulphur dioxide
   (*b*) carbon dioxide   (*d*) methane

5. Ethanol is a product of anaerobic respiration of:
   (*a*) unicellular algae   (*c*) yeasts
   (*b*) bacteria   (*d*) viruses

6. The oxidation of ethanol by air and certain bacteria produces:
   (*a*) methanal   (*c*) citric acid
   (*b*) ethanoic acid   (*d*) benzoic acid

7. The energy value of one gram of pure ethanol is:
   (*a*) 7 kJ   (*c*) 29 kJ
   (*b*) 17 kJ   (*d*) 37 kJ

8. The approximate ethanol content of port wine is:
   (*a*) 4%   (*c*) 50%
   (*b*) 15%   (*d*) 40%

9. Which of the following substances are liable to contaminate food with bacteria and moulds?
   (*a*) dried spice   (*c*) malt vinegar
   (*b*) granulated sugar (*d*) iodized salt

10. Blanching before canning vegetables serves three purposes one of the following is *not* a function of blanching:
   (*a*) sterilization   (*c*) tissue softening
   (*b*) enzyme inactivation (*d*) gas expulsion

28 Health and nutrition

HEALTH

Human beings have an *environment*, or live in conditions which either *promote health* or *cause disease*.

(*a*) *Health*-promoting conditions include: food, water, air, warmth, exercise, sleep, cleanliness, happiness, love and knowledge. A *deficiency* or *excess* of one or more of these factors can cause *ill-health* and *death*, through a disturbance of the *steady conditions* needed for a healthy life.

(*b*) *Diseases* affecting human health are caused by micro-organism *infections*, pest and parasite *infestations*, upsets or *trauma* to the body through physical *accidents*, poisonous *chemicals*, *drugs*, *alcohol*, smoking and *mental* or emotional disturbance (see page 200).

FOOD AND HEALTH

Food is one essential factor for health in human beings: and *excessive* intake or *defective* intake of one or more nutrients will cause *malnutrition*, or *over-nutrition* and *under-nutrition* with consequent *nutritional diseases* (such as scurvy) starvation or obesity.

A *healthful* or balanced diet is one in which the *diet*, or food intake throughout life, does not contain an excess or deficiency of any one nutrient. A *healthful diet* alone will not result in *good health*; the other factors of warmth, fresh air, clean water, exercise, sleep and happiness are also essential, together with freedom from infectious disease, accidents, drugs and mental disorders.

HUMAN BEINGS ARE DIFFERENT

Human beings, with the exception of *identical twins*, are different from one another in appearance, chemical com-position, height, weight, food likes and dislikes and so on. Similarly, plants and animals together with the foods obtained from them, are also different in their *composition*, as shown in Chapters 23, 24 and 25 (see also Appendix B).

GENES

Every living cell *nucleus* (see Figures 23.1 and 23.2) is composed of *genes*, each human being having a different *gene make-up*. Genes determine the production of *proteins* used in building the body *structure* (skin, muscle, bones) and the *functional* proteins, digestive enzymes and hormones. These are produced in *different* amounts, causing the *general differences* among individual human beings.

Hair, skin and eye *colour* and body *height* are characteristics controlled by genes, but body *weight* is *not* usually gene-controlled but mainly influenced by how *much* one eats. Human body height *cannot* be altered but human body weight *can*, consequently a *desirable* or *acceptable body weight* is related to different body heights; these body weights are those most suited to good health, and are between *under-weight* and *over-weight* as shown in Figure 28.1.

Check your height, without shoes, with what your *acceptable* or desirable weight, without clothes, should be from the graph shown in Figure 28.1.

HUMAN BODY CHEMICAL COMPOSITION

The chemical composition of the human body *varies* from person to person; men have *less* lipids and *more* protein, minerals and water than women. Similarly, chemical composition varies *within* the sexes; some *overweight* men and women have more lipids than other men and women. The

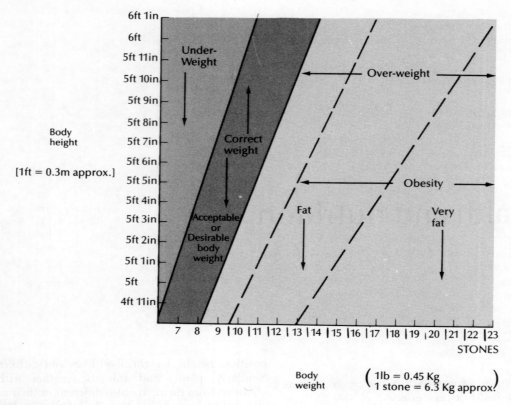

Figure 28.1. Body weight

chemical composition of children's bodies alters from birth through childhood (see table).

AVERAGE CHEMICAL COMPOSITION OF THE WHOLE HUMAN BODY

Chemical compound	Percentage composition		
	Men	Women	Children
Water	62	54	60–72
Protein	17	15	11–16
Lipids	14	25	14–26
Carbohydrate	1	1	1
Minerals	6	5	5–6

The table shows the importance of a diet of *mixed nutrients* to maintain the human body composition – in other words, 'we are what we eat'.

WHAT WE EAT

The earth produces a variety of foods, 75% from plant and 25% from animal sources, to be divided between about 4 000 million people. About 25% of the world population live in the wealthier, *'more developed'* countries such as the USA, UK, USSR, France, West Germany, Japan, Australia and New Zealand, and the remaining 75% of the world population live in the less wealthy, *'less developed'* countries.

The estimated *total diet* of the majority of people in the 'more developed' and 'less developed' countries is shown as follows:

	Countries	
Total dietary nutrients	'More developed' countries (%)	'Less developed' countries (%)
Protein	10	10
Lipid	40	10
Carbohydrate	50	80

'More developed' countries eat more lipids and proteins from *animal* source foods, while 'less developed countries' eat more carbohydrate and *dietary fibre* from mainly *plant* source foods, such as cereals.

Differences exist between what is eaten in various 'more developed' countries such as Japan, UK and USSR. This is shown as follows:

	Countries		
Total dietary nutrients	Japan (%)	USSR (%)	UK (%)
Protein	10	10	10
Lipid	10	30	40
Carbohydrate	80	60	50

The high carbohydrate intake of Japan is due to the traditional rice in the diet.

It is therefore evident that the *diet*, or what people eat, will *vary* from country to country, and will vary *within* the country, and again will vary from family to family, and also from person to person.

INDIVIDUAL DIETARY PATTERNS

The *individual* adult human being consumes about 500 kg of food a year in response to an inner sensory *drive* of hunger, an unpleasant sensation due to rhythmic muscle contraction of an empty stomach. *Appetite* is a pleasant sensation in response to sight, smell, thoughts and sounds associated with food.

Satiety is the feeling of fullness detected by a satiety centre in the brain hypothalamus region (page 182).

Other reasons for diet variation include the following:

(*a*) *Likes and dislikes* of certain foods, which are caused by the cell nucleus *genes* or *inborn controls*, are related to the amount of *enzymes* produced by the genes. This could possibly explain why 'Jack Sprat could eat no fat' because of lipase enzyme deficiency, and his 'wife could eat no lean', because of a protease deficiency. A certain minority of infants are unable to feed on milk, because they do not have the gene to produce the enzyme to change milk sugar *galactose* into glucose; this condition is inherited, and is called *galactosaemia*.

(*b*) *Ill-health* or *digestive disorders* will cause a lack of appetite.

(*c*) *Religious customs* may prohibit certain foods; Jewish and Muslim people are forbidden pork, and Hindus do not eat beef.

(*d*) *Social customs* in the form of fasts or feasts, parties, business entertaining and the provision of rewards are linked to food.

(*e*) *Psychological conditions* of loneliness, compulsive eating (*bulimia*) or starvation (as in *anorexia nervosa*).

(*f*) *Food cults*: vegetarians, consume foods of plant origin, with milk and or eggs; *vegans* consume *no* food of animal origin.

Knowledge of nutrition is important, because the consumer has information concerning food function and composition, and knows what to eat.

Food availability and income: few foods are *free*, consequently the food eaten depends on the money available to buy it.

OVER-NUTRITION AND UNDER-NUTRITION

The *individual* human being's consumption of food may be *excessive* or *defective* with respect to individual *nutrients* or *energy*.

Obesity is an excessive accumulation of body fat lipids, due to an excessive intake of *energy*-providing foods, carbohydrates, lipids and proteins, over a *long* period of time, *without* an equal energy output through lack of physical exercise (see Figure 28.1, also pages 186 and 221).

The table below lists the main conditions of under-nutrition and over-nutrition arising from dietary deficiency or excess.

CONDITIONS OF UNDER-NUTRITION AND OVER-NUTRITION ARISING FROM DIETARY DEFICIENCY OR EXCESS

Nutrient	Under-nutrition: dietary deficiency	Over-nutrition: dietary excess
Energy and protein	Starvation – all food and nutrients deficient. Marasmus – child starvation. Kwashiorkor – protein deficiency, adequate carbohydrate intake.	Obesity and overweight – energy intake exceeds energy output; due to overeating, and lack of exercise. Factor in heart disease, bowel disorders, sugar diabetes. Gout – joint disorders.

Vitamins – lipid soluble (see pages 158 and 160)

A	Night blindness and keratomalacia eye disorder.	Hypervitaminosis excess intake causes bone and muscle pains.
D	Rickets in children, osteomalacia in adults, bone softening and defective teeth.	

Vitamins – water soluble (see pages 159 and 160)

B₁	Beri-beri, affecting heart and nerves.	None – appetite stimulant
B₂	Pellagra, skin, nervous and digestive disorder.	
B₁₂	Pernicious anaemia, affecting certain red blood cells.	None – water soluble, therefore excess excreted in urine.
Folic acid	Type of anaemia.	
C	Scurvy – bleeding swollen gums and internal bleeding.	

Minerals (see page 83)

Calcium	Osteoporosis (bone softening)	Not harmful.
Iron	Nutritional anaemia, affecting red blood cells	Siderosis, iron collecting in liver and bone
Sodium	Dehydration and muscular cramps, mental apathy.	Harmful in babies. Cow's milk has more than human milk. Factor in heart disease.
Iodine	Goitre, thyroid gland enlargement.	Harmful and poisonous.
Fluoride	Tooth decay.	Fluorisis or enamel discoloration.

Dietary fibre (see page 111)

	Constipation, diseases linked include piles, bowel cancer, appendicitis, gall stones, heart disease.	Laxative, bowel toner. Phytic acid contents affects absorption of calcium, zinc and iron.

Water | Dehydration. | Water intoxication. |

ENOUGH ENERGY AND NUTRIENTS

The *right balance* between *under-nutrition* and *over-nutrition*, both of which cause *ill-health* or are *risk factors* as for example in heart disease, is difficult to achieve without a knowledge of nutrition or weight-watching.

A *healthful* or balanced diet, which promotes good health,

can be achieved by eating *recommended daily amounts* (RDA) of *essential* nutrients, which are found in tables produced by various countries and considered to provide sufficient nutrients for all healthy people in the population. The Food and Agriculture Organization of the United Nations has published RDA tables suited for those millions with an insufficiency of food in many less developed countries of the world. This important RDA table is given in Appendix C.

The following table summarizes how different countries and the F.A.O. recommend *different* dietary allowances for a *moderately active male*, age 20–30; the outstanding feature is the amount of protein recommended by the F.A.O. – namely, almost *half* that for the 'more developed' countries.

RECOMMENDEAD DIETARY *DAILY* ALLOWANCES FOR A MODERATELY ACTIVE 20–30-YEAR-OLD MALE

Dietary component	F.A.O.	UK	USA	Japan
Energy (MJ)	12·6	12·6	11·7	12·6
Protein (g)	37	75	65	70
Calcium (g)	0·45	0·5	0·8	0·6
Iron (mg)	7	10	10	10
Thiamin B$_1$ (mg)	1·2	1·2	1·4	1·5
Riboflavin B$_2$ (mg)	1·8	1·7	1·7	1·5
Nicotinic acid (mg)	19·8	18	18	15
Vitamin A (μg)	750	750	750	750
Vitamin C (mg)	30	30	60	65

HUMAN BODY ENERGY NEEDS

The energy requirements of the human body have been explained in Chapter 24, pages 26 and 186, and are listed in the RDA table in Appendix C.

The *energy-providing* nutrients – carbohydrates, lipids and proteins – are present in almost *every* food, and consequently in the more developed countries there is a danger of an excessive intake of sweetened foods with *sucrose* and fatty meats, dairy products with *lipids*. The surplus is *stored* in the body as fat, causing obesity and over-weight.

HUMAN BODY PROTEIN NEEDS

Protein is the main component of the body *structural* tissue skin, muscle and bones, and the *functional* enzymes and hormones. These are made from the 20 different *amino acids* under the influence of the cell nucleus *genes*.

Proteins in foods from plant sources have a different *biological value* from proteins in foods from animal sources (see page 123). Certain *essential amino acids* may only be present in small amounts in many proteins from plants. This can be overcome by *complementation*, or eating a varied and mixed diet – for example, cereals and legumes, fish and rice, or meat and potatoes, when the cereals, fish and meat compensate for any essential amino acid shortage in the legumes, rice and potato. Therefore it is important to obtain dietary protein from a *variety of foods*.

Protein forms about 10% of the *total diet*, when food is freely available. This quantity is used strictly for body *growth* and *repair*. Excessive protein intake is an *expensive* and *wasteful* source of energy, when a *cheaper* source of energy is available in carbohydrates and lipids. Excessive protein intakes are converted into fat, and 30% is lost as *urea* (carbamide) in the *urine*.

The daily protein requirements are greatest in babies, children and adolescents, whilst pregnant and nursing mothers need more than other adults, as shown in Figure 28.2.

MINERAL AND VITAMIN REQUIREMENTS

When food is freely available in quantity and variety to provide a *mixed diet*, sufficient minerals and vitamins will be available for the human body needs *without* the need of vitamin and mineral pills. The *special* needs of infants, children, adolescents and women during menstruation, pregnancy and lactation are important and any deficiencies guarded against. The table summarizes the vitamin and mineral needs of human beings throughout life.

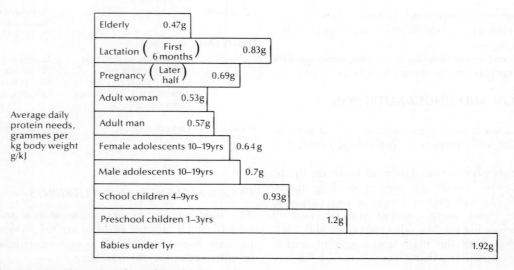

Average daily protein needs, grammes per kg body weight g/kJ

Elderly	0.47g
Lactation (First 6 months)	0.83g
Pregnancy (Later half)	0.69g
Adult woman	0.53g
Adult man	0.57g
Female adolescents 10–19yrs	0.64 g
Male adolescents 10–19yrs	0.7g
School children 4–9yrs	0.93g
Preschool children 1–3yrs	1.2g
Babies under 1yr	1.92g

Figure 28.2. Daily protein requirements throughout life

SUMMARY OF VITAMIN AND MINERAL NEEDS OF THE HUMAN BODY (per kg body weight)

Group of people	*Vitamins* A μg	D μg	B₁ mg	B₂ mg	Nicotinic acid mg	Folic acid μg	B₁₂ μg	C mg	*Minerals* Calcium mg	Iron mg
Babies under 1 year	40	1·37	0·04	0·07	0·74	8·2	0·04	2·73	75	1·03
Pre-school 1–3 years	18	0·74	0·037	0·06	0·67	7·4	0·067	1·50	34	0·56
School 4–9 years	14	0·25	0·033	0·05	0·55	4·2	0·062	0·82	19	0·31
Male adolescent 10–19 years	13	0·05	0·022	0·034	0·37	3·3	0·039	0·53	13	0·18
Female adolescent	14·5	0·05	0·020	0·030	0·33	3·5	0·042	0·56	13	0·33
Male adult	11·5	0·04	0·018	0·027	0·30	3·0	0·030	0·46	7	0·11
Female adult	13·5	0·04	0·016	0·024	0·26	3·6	0·036	0·55	8	0·38
Pregnancy	13·5	0·18	0·018	0·027	0·30	7·2	0·054	0·91	20	0·38
Lactation	22·0	0·18	0·020	0·031	0·33	5·4	0·045	0·91	20	0·38
Elderly men	12·0	0·04	0·013	0·027	0·28	3·0	0·03	0·48	7	0·12
Elderly women	14·0	0·04	0·014	0·025	0·28	3·0	0·03	0·57	8	0·33

A HEALTHFUL DIET FOR BRITAIN

A survey conducted in the UK in 1983 found that 39% of the men and 32% of the women were *over-weight*, and that 8% of the women and 6% of the men were *obese* (see Figure 28.1). These physical conditions are related to a high energy *intake* and a low energy *output* and insufficient physical exercise.

The following suggestions were made by the National Advisory Committee on Nutrition Education in 1983, in order to alter the dietary pattern in Britain, and help to overcome the diseases associated with obesity – namely, diabetes, arthritis, high blood pressure, stroke and heart attacks.

Energy intake is to remain as in RDA tables, but *more exercise* should be encouraged.

(*a*) *Sucrose* consumption should be *reduced*; between 43 and 38 kg is consumed annually by each person.

(*b*) *Hard fats* from animal source foods and their saturated fatty acids should be *reduced* and replaced by vegetable PUFA polyunsaturated oils.

(*c*) *Dietary fibre* from cereals, fruits and vegetables should be *increased*, which will at the same time replace the energy through sucrose reduction.

(*d*) *Protein* intake is to remain at its present level of 10–11%, with an *increase* in plant origin protein over animal origin protein with its associated hard saturated lipids.

(*e*) *Minerals*: the daily intake of *common salt* (sodium chloride) is 12 g (two teaspoonfuls), which is added at the table, in cooking, and in processed foods, should be reduced by about 10%. Experiments with laboratory animals show that it increases blood pressure when the intake is high.

(*f*) *Alcohol* is *not* an essential nutrient. It provides about 6% of the energy intake for those who consume alcohol. It is suggested the alcohol intake be reduced by 10%.

Summary for a healthful diet:
Eat more foods containing dietary fibre from plant sources.
Cut down on hard animal *fat, sugar, salt* and *alcohol*.

QUESTIONS ON CHAPTER 28

1. What are the main nutritional problems found in wealthy developed countries?
2. Give a nutritional and social reason for the occurrence of obesity.
3. Give an account of the factors which promote good health.
   What is the importance of: (*a*) protein and (*b*) dietary fibre in the diet?
4. Briefly outline what is meant by malnutrition; what are its causes?
5. Outline the dietary needs of a pregnant woman, a breast-feeding woman and an elderly woman.
6. Explain why protein is considered to be the most expensive nutrient.
7. Which foods have a high salt content?
8. What social factors influence the dietary pattern of (*a*) a housewife, (*b*) a college student, (*c*) a factory worker, (*d*) a business executive?

MULTIPLE CHOICE QUESTIONS ON CHAPTER 28

1. Protein forms which following approximate percentage of the total diet energy intake?
   (*a*) 10%   (*c*) 30%
   (*b*) 20%   (*d*) 40%
2. What is the daily energy requirement of an elderly person over the age of 75 years in good health?
   (*a*) 3 to 4 MJ   (*c*) 10 to 11 MJ
   (*b*) 8 to 9 MJ   (*d*) 14 to 15 MJ
3. Bottle or breast fed babies need 3·4 MJ of energy daily. The amount of pure protein in their daily milk intake should be:

(*a*) $\frac{3400}{17} = 200$ g   (*c*) $\frac{340}{17} = 20$ g

(*b*) $\frac{34000}{17} = 2\,000$ g   (*d*) $\frac{34}{17} = 2$ g

4. A person requires an intake of 10 MJ of energy daily. What weight of pure protein should he eat daily?

(a) 60 g   (c) 180 g
(b) 120 g   (d) 240 g

5. Beef contains 4 mg of iron per 100 g. What weight of meat provides the daily recommended intake of iron (10 mg)?

(a) $\dfrac{10 \times 100}{4} = 250$ g   (c) $\dfrac{10 \times 100}{40} = 25$ g

(b) $\dfrac{100 \times 100}{4} = 2\,500$ g   (d) $\dfrac{10 \times 100}{400} = 2 \cdot 5$ g

6. A pregnant woman must take in *double* the normal intake of one of the following nutrients between the sixth and ninth month of pregancy:

(a) protein
(b) vitamin B_1 – thiamin
(c) calcium
(d) vitamin B_2 – riboflavin

7. The vitamin which the expectant mother must increase from a normal intake of 2·5 microgrammes to 10 microgrammes between the sixth and ninth month of pregnancy is:

(a) vitamin A – retinol
(b) vitamin E – tocopherol
(c) vitamin D – cholecalciferol
(d) vitamin C – ascorbic acid

8. A further nutrient which is needed in *double* the normal amount by a mother between the sixth and ninth month of pregnancy is:

(a) sodium chloride   (c) iron
(b) vitamin C – ascorbic acid (d) glucose

9. Kwashiorkor is a disorder seen in young children at the weaning period, and is caused by a deficiency of:

(a) protein   (c) vitamin C – ascorbic acid
(b) carbohydrate   (d) vitamin A – retinol

10. People who are convalescent or are recovering from surgical operations or bone fractures require a diet high in the content of one of the following:

(a) protein   (c) sodium chloride
(b) carbohydrates   (d) lipids

Appendix A

Serial numbers which can be used on food
labels as alternatives to the specific names of
additives
(from the M.A.F.F. booklet
'Look at the Label', 1982)

Food colourings

E100	Curcumin	E160(c)	capsanthin or capsorubin
E101	Riboflavin or Lactoflavin	E160(d)	lycopene
E102	Tartrazine	E160(e)	beta-apo-8'-carotenal (C30)
E104	Quinoline Yellow	E160(f)	ethyl ester of beta-apo-8'-carotenoic acid (C30)
E110	Sunset Yellow FCF or Orange Yellow A	E161(a)	Flavoxanthin
E120	Cochineal or Carminic acid	E161(b)	Lutein
E122	Carmoisine or Azorubine	E161(c)	Cryptoxanthin
E123	Amaranth	E161(d)	Rubixanthin
E124	Ponceau 4R or Cochineal Red A	E161(e)	Violaxanthin
E127	Erythrosine BS	E161(f)	Rhodoxanthin
E131	Patent Blue V	E161(g)	Canthaxanthin
E132	Indigo Carmine or Indigotine	E162	Beetroot Red or Betanin
E140	Chlorophyll	E163	Anthocyanins
E141	Copper complexes of chlorophyll and chlorophyllins	E170	Calcium carbonate
E142	Green S or Acid Brilliant Green BS or Lissamine Green	E171	Titanium dioxide
E150	Caramel	E172	Iron oxide and hydroxides
E151	Black PN or Brilliant Black BN	E173	Aluminium
E153	Carbon Black or Vegetable Carbon	E174	Silver
E160(a)	alpha-carotene, beta-carotene, gamma-carotene	E175	Gold
E160(b)	annato, bixin, norbixin	E180	Pigment Rubine or Lithol Rubine BK

Food preservatives

E200	Sorbic acid	E231	2-Hydroxybiphenyl
E201	Sodium sorbate	E232	Sodium biphenyl-2-yl oxide
E202	Potassium sorbate	E233	2-(Thiazol-4-yl) benzimidazole
E203	Calcium sorbate	E236	Formic acid
E210	Benzoic acid	E237	Sodium formate
E211	Sodium benzoate	E238	Calcium formate
E212	Potassium benzoate	E239	Hexamine
E213	Calcium benzoate	E249	Potassium nitrite
E214	Ethyl-4-hydroxybenzoate	E250	Sodium nitrite
E215	Ethyl 4-hydroxybenzoate sodium salt	E251	Sodium nitrate
E216	Propyl 4-hydroxybenzoate	E252	Potassium nitrate
E217	Propyl 4-hydroxybenzoate sodium salt	E260	Acetic acid
E218	Methyl 4-hydroxybenzoate	E261	Potassium acetate
E219	Methyl 4-hydroxybenzoate sodium salt	E262	Sodium hydrogen diacetate
E220	Sulphur dioxide	E263	Calcium acetate
E221	Sodium sulphite	E270	Lactic acid

E222	Sodium hydrogen sulphite	E280	Propionic acid
E223	Sodium metabisulphite	E281	Sodium propionate
E224	Potassium metabisulphite	E282	Calcium propionate
E226	Calcium sulphite	E283	Potassium propionate
E227	Calcium hydrogen sulphite	E290	Carbon dioxide
E230	Biphenyl or Diphenyl		

Food antioxidants

E300	L-ascorbic acid	E332	Potassium dihydrogen citrate
E301	Sodium-L-ascorbate	E332	triPotassium citrate
E302	Calcium-L-ascorbate	E333	Calcium citrate
E304	6-*O*-Palmitoyl-L-ascorbic acid	E333	diCalcium citrate
E306	Extracts of natural origin rich in tocopherols	E333	triCalcium citrate
E307	Synthetic alpha-tocopherol	E334	Tartaric acid
E308	Synthetic gamma-tocopherol	E335	Sodium tartrate
E309	Synthetic delta-tocopherol	E336	Potassium tartrate
E310	Propyl gallate	E336	Potassium hydrogen tartrate
E311	Octyl gallate	E337	Potassium sodium tartrate
E312	Dodecyl gallate	E338	Orthophosphoric acid
E320	Butylated hydroxyanisole	E339(a)	Sodium dihydrogen orthophosphate
E321	Butylated hydroxytoluene	E339(b)	diSodium hydrogen orthophosphate
E322	Lecithins	E339(c)	triSodium orthophosphate
E325	Sodium lactate	E340(a)	Potassium dihydrogen orthophosphate
E326	Potassium lactate	E340(b)	diPotassium hydrogen orthophosphate
E327	Calcium lactate	E340(c)	triPotassium orthophosphate
E330	Citric acid	E341(a)	Calcium tetrahydrogen diorthophosphate
E331	Sodium dihydrogen citrate	E341(b)	Calcium hydrogen orthophosphate
E331	diSodium citrate	E341(c)	triCalcium diorthophosphate
E331	triSodium citrate		

Food emulsifiers and stabilizers

E400	Alginic acid	E450(b)	pentaPotassium triphosphate
E401	Sodium alginate	E450(c)	Sodium polyphosphates
E402	Potassium alginate	E450(c)	Potassium polyphosphates
E403	Ammonium alginate	E460(i)	Microcrystalline cellulose
E404	Calcium alginate	E460(ii)	Powdered cellulose
E405	Propane-1,2-diol alginate	E461	Methylcellulose
E406	Agar	E463	Hydroxypropylcellulose
E407	Carrageenan	E464	Hydroxypropylmethylcellulose
E410	Locust bean gum	E465	Ethylmethylcellulose
E412	Guar gum	E466	Carboxymethylcellulose, sodium salt
E413	Tragacanth	E470	Sodium, potassium and calcium salts of fatty acids
E414	Acacia or Gum Arabic	E471	Mono- and di-glycerides of fatty acids
E415	Xanthan Gum	E472(a)	Acetic acid esters of mono- and di-glycerides of fatty acids
E420(i)	Sorbitol	E472(b)	Lactic acid esters of mono- and di-glycerides of fatty acids
E420(ii)	Sorbitol syrup	E472(c)	Citric acid esters of mono- and di-glycerides of fatty acids
E421	Mannitol	E472(d)	Tartaric acid esters of mono- and di-glycerides of fatty acids
E422	Glycerol	E472(e)	Diacetyltartaric acid esters of mono- and di-glycerides of fatty acids
E440(a)	Pectin	E473	Sucrose esters of fatty acids
E440(b)	Pectin, amidated	E474	Sucroglycerides
E450(a)	diSodium dihydrogen diphosphate	E475	Polyglycerol esters of fatty acids
E450(a)	tetraSodium diphosphate	E477	Propane-1,2-diol esters of fatty acids
E450(a)	tetraPotassium diphosphate	E481	Sodium stearoyl-2-lactylate
E450(a)	triSodium diphosphate	E482	Calcium stearoyl-2-lactylate
E450(b)	pentaSodium triphosphate	E483	Stearyl tartrate

Appendix B

Composition of foods

Food 100 g edible portion raw uncooked unless stated otherwise	Water (g)	Kilojoule (jK)	Kilocalorie (kcal)	Protein (g)	Total lipid fat (g)	Total carbohydrate (g)	A retinol equivalents (μg)	D cholecalciferol (μg)	B_1 Thiamin (mg)	B_2 Riboflavin (mg)	Nicotinic acid equivalents (mg)	Free folic acid (μg)	B_{12} cyanocabalamin (μg)	C ascorbic acid (mg)	Ca calcium (mg)	Fe iron (mg)
			Energy					Fat-soluble vitamins				Water-soluble vitamins			Mineral elements	
Fruit																
Apples, sweet eating	84	240	58	0·3	0·6	15·0	9	0	0·04	0·02	0·1	3	0	5	7	0·3
Avocado pears	73·6	720	171	2·2	17·0	6·0	29	0	0·11	0·20	1·6	31	0	14	10	0·6
Bananas	75·7	360	85	1·1	0·2	22·2	19	0	0·05	0·06	0·6	12	0	10	8	0·7
Black currants, stewed with sugar	82	260	62	1·0	0·1	16·1	22	0	0·05	0·03	0·3	–	0	136	17	0·9
Lemons	90·1	110	27	1·1	0·3	8·2	2	0	0·04	0·02	0·1	7	0	80	26	0·6
Oranges	86·0	210	49	1·0	0·2	12·2	20	0	0·10	0·03	0·2	13	0	50	41	0·4
Prunes (dried plums)	28·0	1070	255	2·1	0·6	67·4	160	0	0·1	0·17	1·6	0·7	0	3	51	3·9
Raisins (dried grapes)	18·0	1210	289	2·5	0·2	77·4	2	0	0·1	0·08	0·5	4	0	1	62	3·5
Watermelon	92·6	110	26	0·5	0·2	6·4	59	0	0·03	0·03	0·2	2	0	7	7	0·5
Vegetables																
Broad beans, dry seeds	12·6	1420	339	24·0	2·2	58·2	3	0	0·53	0·30	2·5	–	0	6	77	6·3
Baked beans, canned	74·7	400	96	5·4	0·3	18·3	19	0	0·03	0·05	0·5	–	0	6	28	2·4
Brussels sprouts	84·8	200	47	4·7	0·4	8·7	55	0	0·10	0·16	0·9	45	0	90	32	1·5
Cabbage, savoy	90·0	130	31	3·0	0·4	5·6	20	0	0·05	0·06	0·3	60	0	45	47	0·9
Carrots	88·6	170	40	1·1	0·2	9·1	1100	0	0·06	0·12	0·6	15	0	8	37	0·7
Cassava (manioc) cooked	69·0	520	124	0·9	0·1	30·0	–	0	0·06	0·05	0·9	–	0	26	12	1·0
Lentils, dried	11·1	1420	340	24·7	1·1	60·1	6	0	0·25	0·49	2·0	25	0	0	79	8·6
Maize (sweet corn)	72·7	400	96	3·5	1·0	22·1	40	0	0·15	0·12	1·7	27	0	12	3	0·7
Onions	89·1	160	38	1·5	0·1	8·7	4	0	0·03	0·04	0·2	15	0	10	27	0·5
Peas, green, canned	82·3	280	67	3·4	0·4	12·7	45	0	0·11	0·06	0·9	8	0	9	25	1·6
Potatoes	79·8	320	76	2·1	0·1	17·7	trace	0	0·11	0·04	1·2	9	0	20	8	0·8
Spinach	90·7	110	26	3·2	0·3	4·3	810	0	0·10	0·20	0·6	176	0	51	106	3·1
Yams	69·0	500	119	1·9	0·2	27·8	trace	0	0·11	0·02	0·3	–	0	6	52	0·8

Food 100 g edible portion raw uncooked unless stated otherwise	Water (g)	Kilojoule (kJ)	Kilocalorie (kcal)	Protein (g)	Total lipid fat (g)	Total carbohydrate (g)	A retinol equivalents (μg)	D cholecalciferol (μg)	B₁ Thiamin (mg)	B₂ Riboflavin (mg)	Nicotinic acid equivalents (mg)	Free folic acid (μg)	B₁₂ cyanocabalamin (μg)	C ascorbic acid (mg)	Ca calcium (mg)	Fe iron (mg)
Cereals and grain products																
Maize, cornflakes	3·8	1610	385	7·9	0·4	85·3	0	0	0·43	0·1	2·1	14	0	0	3	1·4
Millet, peeled	11·8	1370	327	9·9	2·9	72·9	0	0	0·73	0·38	2·8	–	0	0	20	6·8
Oatmeal	10·3	1620	387	13·8	6·6	67·7	–	0	0·60	0·14	1·1	–	0	0	53	3·6
Pasta (macaroni, spaghetti)	10·4	1540	369	12·5	1·2	75·2	0	0	0·10	0·06	2·0	4	0	0	23	1·2
Rice (polished, cooked)	72·6	460	109	2·0	0·1	24·2	0	0	0·02	0·01	0·4	3	0	0	10	0·2
Wheat (whole or wholemeal flour)	12·6	1390	331	12·1	2·1	71·5	40	0	0·55	0·12	4·3	25	0	0	41	3·3
Wheat (bran)	8·0	850	202	14·0	5·5	71·0	0	0	0·90	0·40	30·0	130	0	0	110	13·0
Wheat (germ)	11·5	1520	363	26·6	10·9	46·7	65	0	2·0	0·68	4·2	257	0	0	72	9·4
Sugar and sweets																
Chocolate, plain sweet	0·9	2210	528	4·4	35·1	57·9	trace	0	0·02	0·14	0·3	–	0	0	63	1·4
Jams, various	29·0	1140	272	0·6	0·1	70·0	1	0	0·01	0·03	0·2	5	0	2	12	1·0
Nuts																
Peanuts, roasted	1·8	2440	582	26·2	48·7	20·6	36	0	0·33	0·13	17·1	28	0	0	74	2·2
Oils and fats																
Butter	17·4	3000	716	0·6	81·0	0·7	990	0·75	trace	0·01	0·1	0	trace	trace	16	0·2
Margarine, salted	19·7	2920	698	0·5	78·4	0·4	990	8·00	–	–	–	3	trace	–	13	0·05
Cod-liver oil	0	3770	901	0	99·9	0	25500	213	0	0	0	0	0	0	0	0
Fish and sea foods																
Fish: Cod	81·2	330	78	17·6	0·3	0	trace	trace	0·06	0·07	2·2	6	2	2	11	0·5
Herring	62·8	1020	243	17·3	18·8	0	40	23	0·06	0·24	4·3	3	10	0·5	57	1·1
Mackerel	67·2	800	191	19·0	12·2	0	135	18	0·15	0·35	7·7	–	10	0	5	1·0
Sardines, canned in oil	50·6	1300	311	50·6	24·4	0·6	55	7	0·02	0·16	4·4	6	23	0	354	3·5
Crustaceans: Crab, canned	77·2	420	110	17·4	2·5	1·1	trace	trace	0·08	0·08	2·5	3	trace	trace	45	0·8
Molluscs: Mussels	82·5	320	76	12·0	1·7	2·2	54	trace	0·16	0·22	1·6	–	–	trace	88	5·8
Meat, poultry and insects																
Meat: Bacon, medium fat	20·0	2620	625	9·1	65·0	trace	0	0	0·36	0·11	1·8	trace	trace	0	13	1·2
Beef, corned canned	59·3	900	216	25·3	12·0	0	0	trace	0·02	0·23	3·4	1	1·7	0	14	4·3
Ham, boiled	57·0	1130	269	19·5	20·6	0	trace	trace	0·54	0·26	4·2	1	0·3	0	10	2·5
Offal: Liver, average	70·7	570	136	20·1	4·3	3·88	9600	0·75	0·35	2·90	16·0	155	80	30	10	10·5
Tongue, average	70·0	770	184	16·8	12·0	0·6	trace	trace	0·15	0·28	10·0	2	5	trace	8	2·5
Poultry: Chicken (roasted fresh/skin)	67·0	1050	251	19·5	12·6	0	400	trace	0·08	0·12	7·4	–	–	–	11	1·5
Turkey, roasted	64·2	2180	910	20·1	15·0	0·4	trace	trace	0·13	0·14	7·9	2	–	–	8	1·5
Insects: Caterpillars (palm weevil larvae, smoked)	20·4	1400	333	62·3	4·6	6·5	0	–	0·10	0·12	4·2	–	–	0	513	7·0
Locusts, fried	48·0	900	215	30·0	10·0	–	–	–	–	–	–	–	–	–	150	5·0
Milk, milk products																
Cow's milk, pasteurized whole	88·5	270	64	3·2	3·7	4·6	42	0·15	0·04	0·15	0·07	5	0·3	1	116	0·04
Cow's milk, skimmed	90·9	140	34	3·5	0·07	4·8	trace	trace	0·04	0·17	0·1	4	0·3	2	123	0·1
Yoghurt	86·1	300	71	4·8	3·8	4·5	44	trace	0·04	0·02	0·18	1	0·2	2	150	0·2
Hard cheese (Cheddar)	37	1670	398	35·0	32·2	2·1	390	0·25	0·03	0·46	0·1	6	1·5	0	750	1·0
Soft cheese (Camembert)	51·3	1200	287	18·7	22·8	1·8	303	0·18	0·05	0·45	1·45	–	1·2	0	382	0·5

Food 100 g edible portion raw uncooked unless stated otherwise	Energy			Protein (g)	Total lipid fat (g)	Total carbohydrate (g)	Fat-soluble vitamins		B₁ Thiamin (mg)	B₂ Riboflavin (mg)	Water-soluble vitamins			C ascorbic acid (mg)	Mineral elements	
	Water (g)	Kilojoule (kJ)	Kilocalorie (kcal)				A retinol equivalents (μg)	D cholecalciferol (μg)			Nicotinic acid equivalents (mg)	Free folic acid (μg)	B₁₂ cyanocabalamin (μg)		Ca calcium (mg)	Fe iron (mg)
Miscellaneous																
Curry powder	–	840	200	10	25	–	–	–	–	–	–	–	–	–	650	75
Mayonnaise	15·1	3000	718	1·1	78·9	3·0	84	3	0·02	0·04	trace	14	0	0	18	0·5
Tomato ketchup	68·6	440	106	2·0	0·4	25·4	420	0	0·09	0·07	1·6	–	0	15	22	0·8

Source: Abstracted from and reproduced by permission of Ciba-Geigy from the *Geigy Scientific Tables*, vol. 1, 8th edn, 1981, and from the Food and Agriculture Organization of the United Nations, *Food Composition Tables for Use in Africa*, 1968.

Appendix C

Recommended Daily Amounts of Energy and Nutrients

Age	Body weight	Energy (1)		Protein (1, 2)	Vitamin A (3, 4)	Vitamin D (5, 6)	Thiamin (3)	Riboflavin (3)	Nicotinic acid (3)	Folic acid (5)	Vitamin B$_{12}$ (5)	Ascorbic acid (5)	Calcium (7)	Iron (5, 8)
	kg	MJ	kcal	g	μg	μg	mg	mg	mg	μg	μg	mg	g	mg
Children														
1	7·3	3·4	820	14	300	10·0	0·3	0·5	5·4	60	0·3	20	0·5–0·6	5–10
1–3	13·4	5·7	1 360	16	250	10·0	0·5	0·8	9·0	100	0·9	20	0·4–0·5	5–10
4·6	20·2	7·6	1 830	20	300	10·0	0·7	1·1	12·1	100	1·5	20	0·4–0·5	5–10
7–9	28·1	9·2	2 190	25	400	2·5	0·9	1·3	14·5	100	1·5	20	0·4–0·5	5–10
Male adolescents														
10–12	36·9	10·9	2 600	30	575	2·5	1·0	1·6	17·2	100	2·0	20	0·6–0·7	5–10
13–15	51·3	12·1	2 900	37	725	2·5	1·2	1·7	19·1	200	2·0	30	0·6–0·7	9–18
16–19	62·9	12·8	3 070	38	750	2·5	1·2	1·8	20·3	200	2·0	30	0·5–0·6	5–9
Female adolescents														
10–12	38·0	9·8	2 350	29	575	2·5	0·9	1·4	15·5	100	2·0	20	0·6–0·7	5–10
13–15	49·9	10·4	2 490	31	725	2·5	1·0	1·5	16·4	200	2·0	30	0·6–0·7	12–24
16–19	54·4	9·7	2 310	30	750	2·5	0·9	1·4	15·2	200	2·0	30	0·5–0·6	14–28
Adult man (moderately active)	65·0	12·6	3 000	37	750	2·5	1·2	1·8	19·8	200	2·0	30	0·4–0·5	5–9
Adult woman (moderately active)	55·0	9·2	2 200	29	750	2·5	0·9	1·3	14·5	200	2·0	30	0·4–0·5	14–28
Pregnancy (later half)	+1·5	+1·5	+350	38	750	10·0	+0·1	+0·2	+2·3	400	3·0	50	1·0–1·2	(9)
Lactation (first 6 months)		+2·3	+550	46	1 200	10·0	+0·2	+0·4	+3·7	300	2·5	50	1·0–1·2	(9)

Notes:
1. Energy and Protein Requirements. Report of a Joint FAO/WHO Expert Group, FAO, Rome, 1972.
2. As egg or milk protein (see page 123).
3. Requirements of Vitamin A, Thiamin, Riboflavin and Nicotinic acid. Report of a Joint FAO/WHO Expert Group, FAO, Rome, 1965.
4. As retinol.
5. Requirements of Ascorbic Acid, Vitamin D, Vitamin B$_{12}$, Folate and Iron. Report of a joint FAO/WHO Expert Group, FAO, Rome, 1970.
6. As cholecalciferol.
7. Calcium Requirements. Report of a FAO/WHO Expert Group, FAO, Rome, 1961.
8. On each line the lower value applies when over 25 per cent of calories in the diet come from animal foods, and the higher value when animal foods represent less than 10 per cent of calories.
9. For women whose iron intake throughout life has been at the level recommended in this table, the daily intake of iron during pregnancy and lactation should be the same as that recommended for non-pregnant, non-lactating women of childbearing age. For women whose iron status is not satisfactory at the beginning of pregnancy, the requirement is increased, and in the extreme situation of women with no iron stores, the requirement can probably not be met without supplementation.

Source: Reproduced from *The Handbook on Human Nutritional Requirements* with the permission of the Food and Agriculture Organization of the United Nations.

Bibliography

Bender, A. E. *Dictionary of Nutrition and Food Technology* (Butterworth).

Bingham, S. *Dictionary of Nutrition* (Barrie and Jenkins).

Ciba-Geigy, *Scientific Tables*, vol. 1 (Rome).

Finch, I. E. *Home Science Pamphlets* (67a Wallwood Road, London, E11 1AY).

Food and Agriculture Organization, *Handbook on Human Nutritional Requirements*.

Kilgour, O. F. G. *Mastering Nutrition* (Macmillan Press).

—— *Shopping Science* (Heinemann Educational Books).

—— *Multiple-choice Questions in Food and Nutrition* (Heinemann Educational Books).

—— *Multiple Choice Questions in the House and its Services* (Heinemann Educational Books).

—— and Aileen L'Amie. *Experimental Science for Catering and Homecraft Students* (Heinemann).

Ministry of Agriculture, Fisheries and Food. *Look at the Label* (H.M.S.O.).

Paul, A. A., and Southgate, D. A. T. *The Composition of Foods* (H.M.S.O.).

Paul, P. C., and Palmer, H. H. *Food Theory and Applications* (John Wiley).

Taylor, T. G. *Principles of Human Nutrition*, No. 94 (Edward Arnold).

—— *Nutrition and Health*, No. 141 (Edward Arnold).

Indexes

There are *three* indexes in this book. Carefully consider if the term or word you are looking for is *physical*, *chemical* or *biological*, then consult the appropriate index.

Et seq. means the main reference is on this page number and those that follow it.

PHYSICAL ASPECTS

CHEMICAL ASPECTS

BIOLOGICAL ASPECTS